Generations of Vicars in England

Nancy Marshall Family
Vol. I – Descendants of Richard Ormandy
Of England 1635

Compiled By
Michael Tieman
Oct 2020

Also By Michael Tieman
Behind The Paint - The First Chapter - National Parks
Behind The Paint - The First Chapter - New England
Behind The Paint - The First Chapter - My Sculptures
Our Mayflower Families - Fuller Vol. I
Our Mayflower Families - Tilley, Howland Vol. II
Ancestors & Descendants of Michael Tieman & Nancy Marshall
Vols. I, II, IV, V
Morrell Pioneers in America
We Started as Farmers in Prussia
Oregon Revolutionary War Memorial Muster Book
Behind The Paint - The First Chapter - France & Italy 2012
Behind The Paint - The First Chapter - Italy 2011
The Building of Courage

ISBN-13: 978-17354110-1-9

Design by Michael L. Tieman, Artists Gallerie, LLC   Printed in the United States

Printed in the United States of America
Published by Michael Tieman Publishing

15724 SW Flagstone Dr., Beaverton, OR 97007 United States www.artistsgallerie.com

But when you're gone, who remembers your
     name?
Who keeps your flame?
Who tells your story?
Who tells your story?
Your story?

          - Lin-Manuel Miranda

Prologue

I cannot take credit for writing this, I just researched the people, stories, places and histories and compiled them into this book. It has taken 35 years, finding the info and documenting all that I could according to Genealogy Standards.

Some of the stories are "family lore" which I could not prove or disprove but they are in here in hopes that someone after me will continue our story.

It has been passed down from generation to generation that the Ormandy family originally came from Normandy, now part of France. I have traced and documented the Ormandy family as far back as to Richard Ormandy b. 1635 to Broughton In Furness, Lancashire, England. Family lore that may very well be true places the Sir John Ormandy as the Vicar of the Old Church Holy Trinity in Millom, England before 1066. Which may mean that they might have come from present day France before then. Maybe.

Nancy, my wife and the daughter of Janet Ormandy Marshall did a DNA test through Ancestry and her results show that her ethnicity is 62% England, Wales & Northeastern Europe (which includes the Normandy area of France). Which means at some point her "family" were in that area. A good start, now to prove who and when.

Here then is the Ormandy Family History proven as far back as 1635 in England.

The surname Ormandy was first found in Suffolk where they held a family seat as Lords of the Manor. After the Battle of Hastings in 1066, William, Duke of Normandy granted most of Britain to his many victorious Barons.

In 1086 he commissioned a census of all of England, once and for all who held which land. The Doomesday Book, they would hold the land until the end of Time.

Ormandy is descended from the tenant* of lands at Bury. When Ormandy, son of Leuric was recorded in the Doomesday Book. They were believed to be of Ormanville in Normandy.

Spelling variations: Ormandy, Ormundy, Ormundie, Orman, Ormand, Ormond, Ormanville, Ormunderly, Normandy, Armand.

Now begins the search back in time to an Ormandy from Normandy, France.

*Tenants a term derived from the Latin tenere which means to hold. Denotes a person who help property but did not retain ownership, land was leased.

How it all started

The quest for Nancy and my history, or roots, began innocently enough, Christmas, 1982.

Nancy's maternal grandmother, Dede, gave us a book for Christmas titled "The History of Our Family." A book of empty pages with headings like: Our Children, Husband's Parents' Family and Where Our Ancestors Have Lived. As Nancy and I started to fill it out, we found that we knew almost nothing of our family from before our great-grandparents. My family when I asked them for information would tell me nothing as though our ancestors never existed.

I am an artist, and artists are a curious lot by nature, and we love knowledge. So, there it is, I was hooked.

First, my quest was "Who were my great-grandparents and where did they come from?" All I knew was that they came from Prussia in the early 1800's and that because they were of German descent living in the U.S. during two great wars; their past was never talked about. I then took it upon myself to try and fill in the blanks. First, I talked to my parents, and great-grand aunts, as no one else would tell me squat. I slowly began to fill in the names of our ancestors, with some questionable dates and stories. As time went on, I spent hundreds of hours in the archives and library of the Mormon Church. I was lucky that we lived in cities that had local libraries of the main church.

Back then, I had to search actual books and newspapers and hundreds of rolls of microfiche, searching out our ancestor's records of birth, censuses and parish records. It took a long time back then in the 80's, and money as I had to order the loan of papers records and history books from the Mormon Church archives in Salt Lake City, which I could only look at in their local church library. Anything I wanted copies of, I had to get their permission and pay them to copy. Their genealogical library is extensive, the largest in the world, and in the case of Prussia where my ancestors came from, they had the only info available as most of it was destroyed in the wars.

My list of ancestors started to become impressive, in the thousands. Then I asked, "Who were these people?" I started to collect stories from our relatives about our family. Oh, the stories I heard when the family finally decided to share. Some info turned out accurate as I researched, others, not so much. Like all families we were descended from kings and leading scholars and vice presidents and famous inventors. Or, so the stories went on that were handed down.

Then with the stories, I became interested in the towns, farms and countries our ancestors came from. What was Millom, England like in the 1600's when Nancy's ancestors lived there? Or "What was my Prussian ancestor's diet in the late 1700's?" So, I investigated the town histories, and when was Prussia a country, country histories, and maps of the periods when our ancestors lived. Plot maps where I found our family names.

Curious more, what did my ancestors wear and eat in the 18th century on their farms and what did they grow? What church did they attend and why were there no birth records in a period of the 1600's but there were baptism records instead? How did the family name change from Tiemann to Tieman? Was Nancy or my family in London during the Great London Plague in 1665/66 or in the original Black Death in Europe in the years 1346-53?

Because of *The History of Our Family* book and asking who was the great-grandfather I never knew, this project has now over 5400 people in our two families, over 1500 source documents dating back to the 1600's (some originals pre-19th century), and a collection of over 2000 original photos some dating back to the beginning of photography.

Our stories and memories will die with us if we do not pass it on to the future generations.

This is why I do it.

If I do not write down the stories of my ancestors, my children and their children will only remember us as someone they saw when they were very young, or as a photo in an album, and they will miss out on the real us.

I am selfish in that I want my grandchildren to remember me and know that I had the same ups and downs in life as they are going through and maybe my experiences will give them some guidance.

My hope is that this small document will grow over the decades and become volumes containing the stories of who we all were.

I hope you enjoy reading this project of mine, this labor of love. Are you in it, and your "Family Story"?

Contents

Gleaston Castle, Lancashire, England

The precise date of construction of Gleaston Castle is unknown. The first written record of the site dates from 1389 but a license to enclose a park there had been granted by Edward III in 1340 and John de Harrington is said to have died at Gleaston in 1369. Furthermore, Gleaston Castle seems to have undergone a period of (rapid) rebuilding and strengthening soon after construction and this is attributed to Robert the Bruce's 1316 raid into the Furness peninsula. On the balance of available evidence, it seems likely Gleaston Castle had probably been built by the late thirteenth century.

Thomas Ormandy, 1717-1776 was buried in the cemetery here on Dec 20, 1776.

Lineage Charts for Richard Ormandy

Justin Arthur SEBERS-ERWIN is the 10th great grandson of Richard Ormandy

Self

Richard Ormandy		**Elizabeth Atkinson**	
b:	1635	b:	30 Aug 1639
	Broughton In Furness, Lancashire, England		Lancaster, Lancashire, England
d:	06 Apr 1706	d:	10 Oct 1699
	Broughton In Furness, Lancashire, England		England

Son

William Ormandy	
b:	1680
	Broughton In Furness, Lancashire, England
d:	01 Jun 1766 (?1746)
	Aldingham, Lancashire, England

Grandson

Thomas Ormandy	
b:	Jun 1717
	Broughton In Furness, Lancashire, England
d:	Dec 1776
	Gleaston Castle, Lancashire, England

Great grandson

Thomas Ormandy	
b:	11 Jun 1749
	Broughton In Furness, Lancashire, England
d:	08 May 1827
	Aldingham, Lancashire, England

2nd great grandson

John Ormandy	
b:	05 Apr 1792
	Aldingham, Lancashire, England
d:	16 May 1846
	Thwaites Chapel In Millom, Cumberland, England

3rd great grandson

Thomas Ormandy	
b:	10 Aug 1823
	Twaites Chapel, Millom, Cumberland, England
d:	07 Mar 1864
	Cahaba, Alabama

4th great grandson

William Lewithwaite Ormandy	
b:	26 Oct 1847
	London, England
d:	01 Apr 1893
	Mt. Zion, Oregon

Justin Arthur SEBERS-ERWIN is the 10th great grandson of Richard Ormandy

5th great grandson

James Alma Ormandy
b: 12 Nov 1879
Pleasant Valley, Pawnee, Kansas, USA
d: 12 Sep 1958
Portland, Multnomah, Oregon, USA

6th great granddaughter

Janet Alma Ormandy
b: 20 Feb 1928
Portland, Multnomah, Oregon, USA
d: 07 Mar 2000
Portland, Multnomah, Oregon, USA

7th great granddaughter

Nancy Lee Marshall
b: 05 Mar 1952
Vancouver, British Columbia, Canada
d:

8th great granddaughter

Heather Anne Tieman
b: 17 May 1976
North Vancouver, British Columbia, Canada
d:

9th great grandson

Riley James Erwin
b: 27 Sep 1999
Portland, Multnomah, Oregon, USA
d:

10th great grandson

Justin Arthur SEBERS-ERWIN
b: 30 Aug 2020
Stanwood, Washington, USA
d:

Timeline for Richard Ormandy

Timeline: Descendants of Richard ORMANDY [3923]

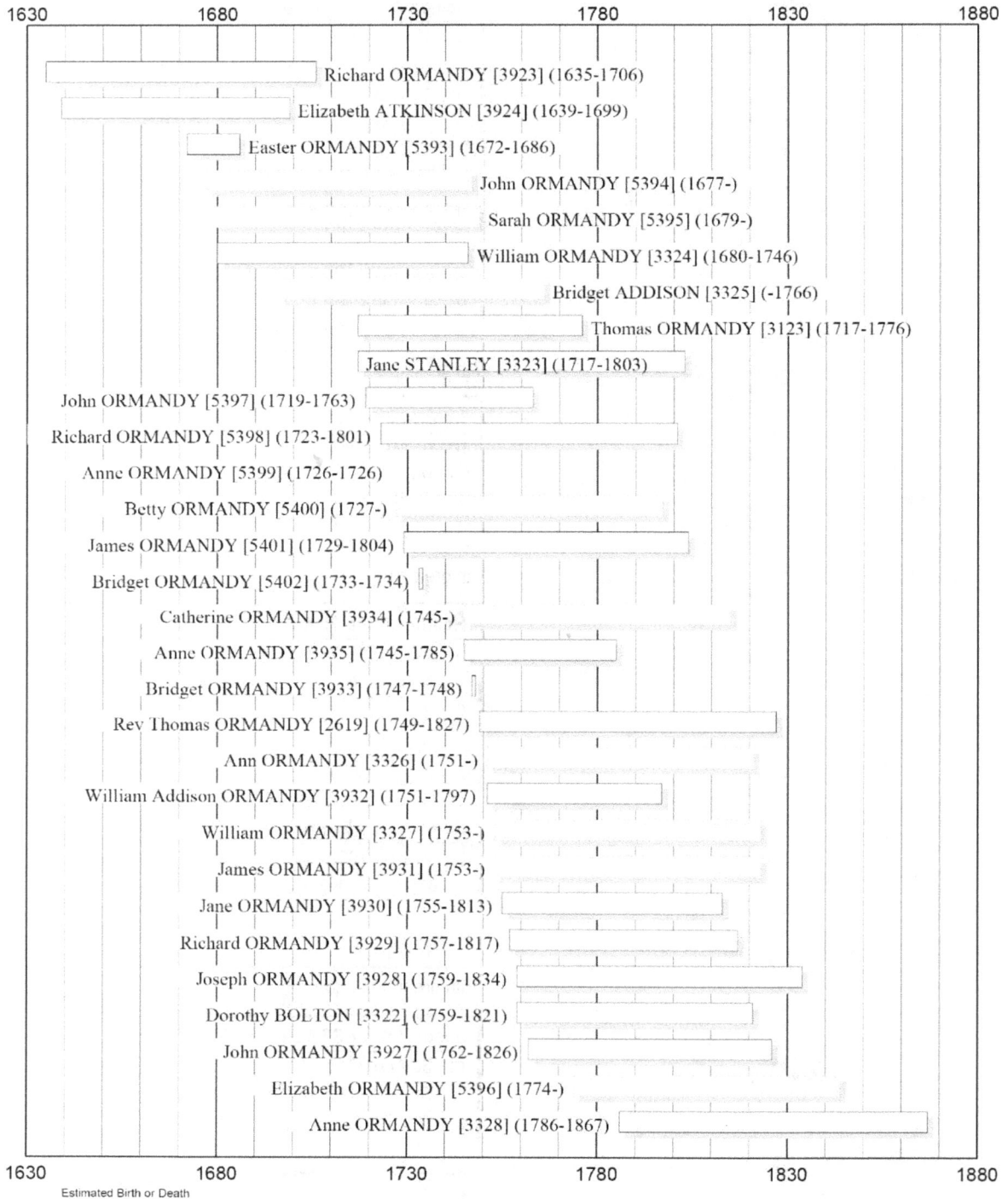

1630	1680	1730	1780	1830	1880

Richard ORMANDY [3923] (1635-1706)

Elizabeth ATKINSON [3924] (1639-1699)

Easter ORMANDY [5393] (1672-1686)

John ORMANDY [5394] (1677-)

Sarah ORMANDY [5395] (1679-)

William ORMANDY [3324] (1680-1746)

Bridget ADDISON [3325] (-1766)

Thomas ORMANDY [3123] (1717-1776)

Jane STANLEY [3323] (1717-1803)

John ORMANDY [5397] (1719-1763)

Richard ORMANDY [5398] (1723-1801)

Anne ORMANDY [5399] (1726-1726)

Betty ORMANDY [5400] (1727-)

James ORMANDY [5401] (1729-1804)

Bridget ORMANDY [5402] (1733-1734)

Catherine ORMANDY [3934] (1745-)

Anne ORMANDY [3935] (1745-1785)

Bridget ORMANDY [3933] (1747-1748)

Rev Thomas ORMANDY [2619] (1749-1827)

Ann ORMANDY [3326] (1751-)

William Addison ORMANDY [3932] (1751-1797)

William ORMANDY [3327] (1753-)

James ORMANDY [3931] (1753-)

Jane ORMANDY [3930] (1755-1813)

Richard ORMANDY [3929] (1757-1817)

Joseph ORMANDY [3928] (1759-1834)

Dorothy BOLTON [3322] (1759-1821)

John ORMANDY [3927] (1762-1826)

Elizabeth ORMANDY [5396] (1774-)

Anne ORMANDY [3328] (1786-1867)

1630	1680	1730	1780	1830	1880

Estimated Birth or Death

Timeline: Descendants of Richard ORMANDY

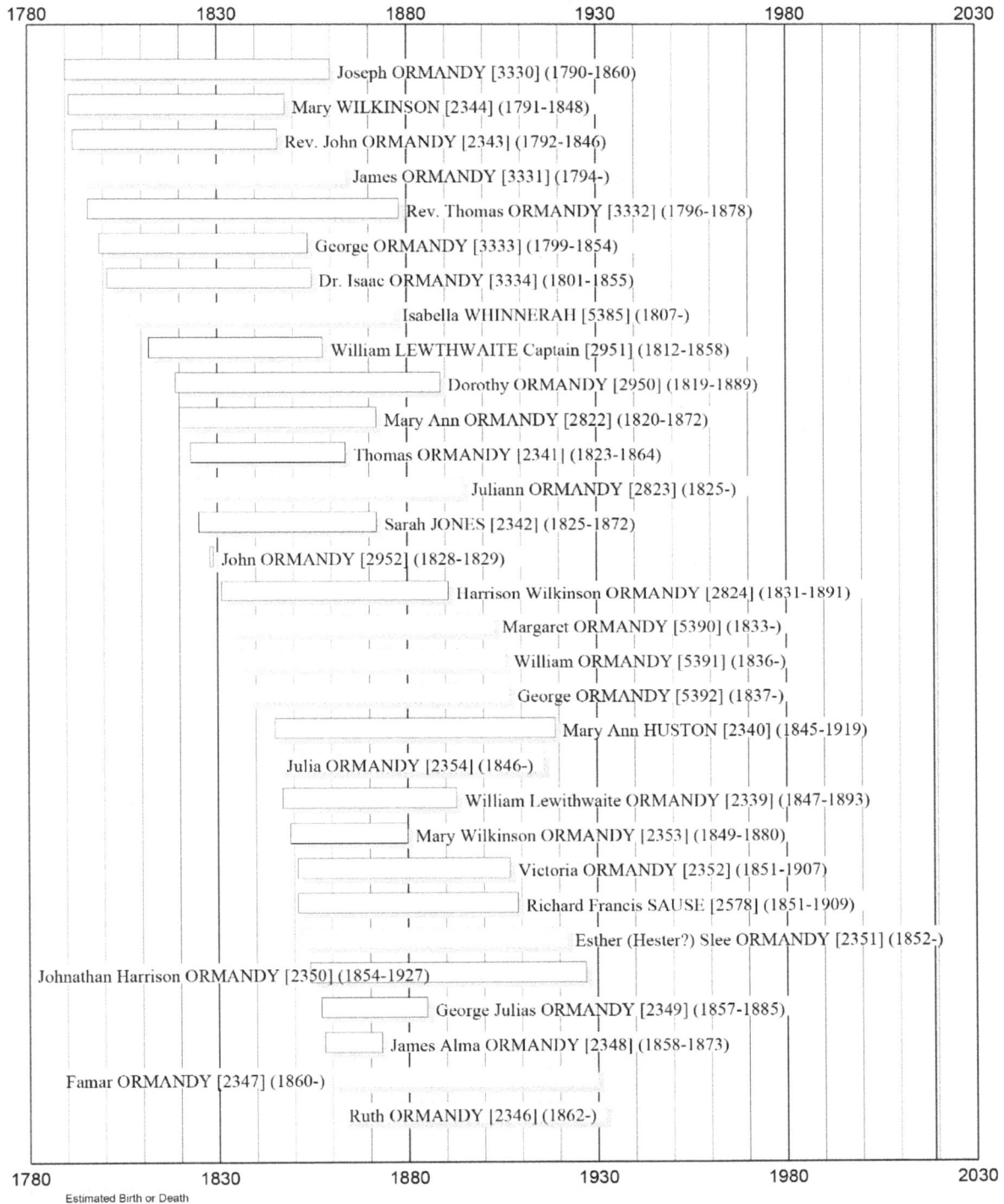

1780	1830	1880	1930	1980	2030

Joseph ORMANDY [3330] (1790-1860)

Mary WILKINSON [2344] (1791-1848)

Rev. John ORMANDY [2343] (1792-1846)

James ORMANDY [3331] (1794-)

Rev. Thomas ORMANDY [3332] (1796-1878)

George ORMANDY [3333] (1799-1854)

Dr. Isaac ORMANDY [3334] (1801-1855)

Isabella WHINNERAH [5385] (1807-)

William LEWTHWAITE Captain [2951] (1812-1858)

Dorothy ORMANDY [2950] (1819-1889)

Mary Ann ORMANDY [2822] (1820-1872)

Thomas ORMANDY [2341] (1823-1864)

Juliann ORMANDY [2823] (1825-)

Sarah JONES [2342] (1825-1872)

John ORMANDY [2952] (1828-1829)

Harrison Wilkinson ORMANDY [2824] (1831-1891)

Margaret ORMANDY [5390] (1833-)

William ORMANDY [5391] (1836-)

George ORMANDY [5392] (1837-)

Mary Ann HUSTON [2340] (1845-1919)

Julia ORMANDY [2354] (1846-)

William Lewithwaite ORMANDY [2339] (1847-1893)

Mary Wilkinson ORMANDY [2353] (1849-1880)

Victoria ORMANDY [2352] (1851-1907)

Richard Francis SAUSE [2578] (1851-1909)

Esther (Hester?) Slee ORMANDY [2351] (1852-)

Johnathan Harrison ORMANDY [2350] (1854-1927)

George Julias ORMANDY [2349] (1857-1885)

James Alma ORMANDY [2348] (1858-1873)

Famar ORMANDY [2347] (1860-)

Ruth ORMANDY [2346] (1862-)

1780	1830	1880	1930	1980	2030

Estimated Birth or Death

Produced by Legacy

Timeline: Descendants of Richard ORMANDY [3923]

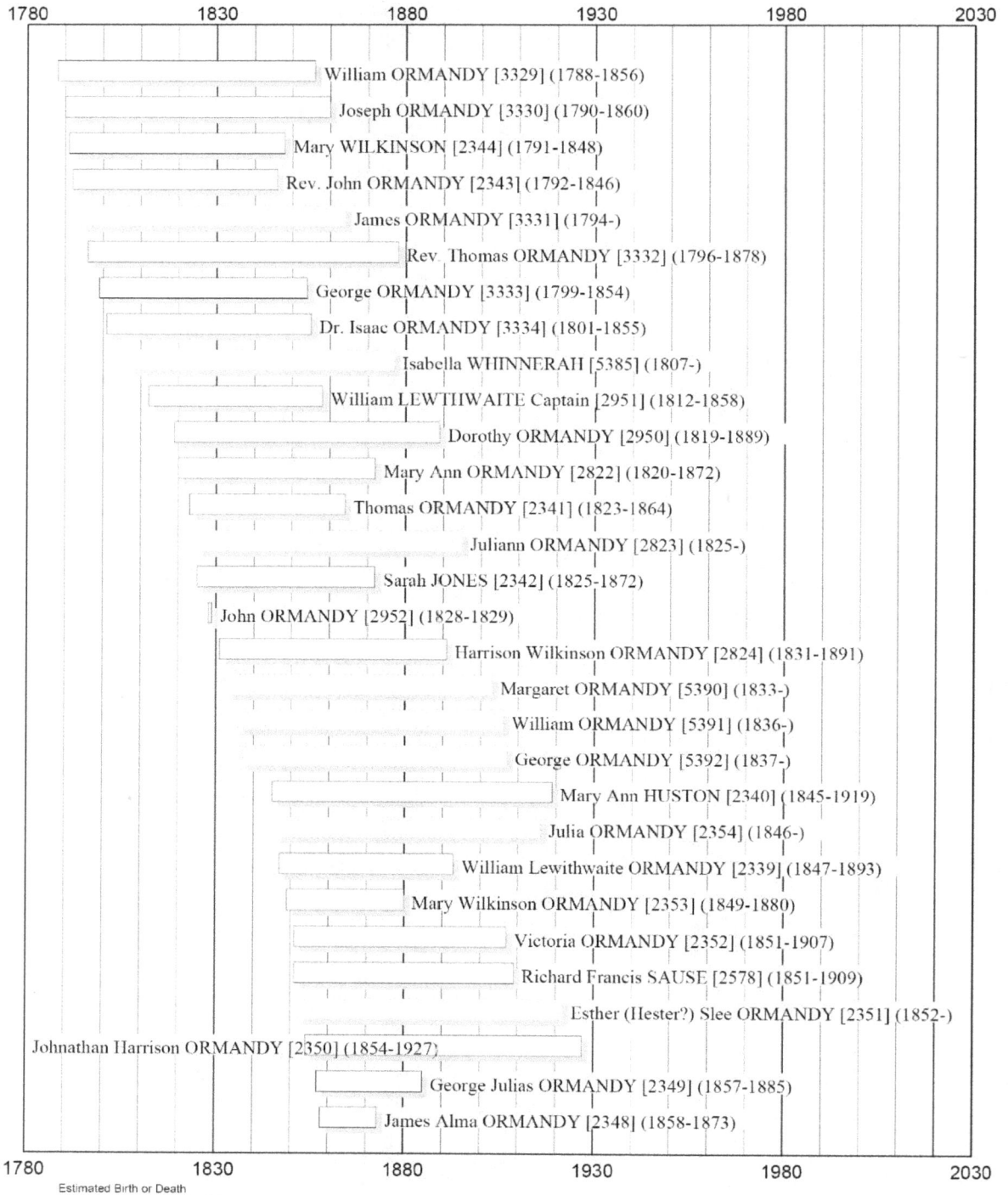

Page 2

1780	1830	1880	1930	1980	2030

William ORMANDY [3329] (1788-1856)

Joseph ORMANDY [3330] (1790-1860)

Mary WILKINSON [2344] (1791-1848)

Rev. John ORMANDY [2343] (1792-1846)

James ORMANDY [3331] (1794-)

Rev. Thomas ORMANDY [3332] (1796-1878)

George ORMANDY [3333] (1799-1854)

Dr. Isaac ORMANDY [3334] (1801-1855)

Isabella WHINNERAH [5385] (1807-)

William LEWTHWAITE Captain [2951] (1812-1858)

Dorothy ORMANDY [2950] (1819-1889)

Mary Ann ORMANDY [2822] (1820-1872)

Thomas ORMANDY [2341] (1823-1864)

Juliann ORMANDY [2823] (1825-)

Sarah JONES [2342] (1825-1872)

John ORMANDY [2952] (1828-1829)

Harrison Wilkinson ORMANDY [2824] (1831-1891)

Margaret ORMANDY [5390] (1833-)

William ORMANDY [5391] (1836-)

George ORMANDY [5392] (1837-)

Mary Ann HUSTON [2340] (1845-1919)

Julia ORMANDY [2354] (1846-)

William Lewithwaite ORMANDY [2339] (1847-1893)

Mary Wilkinson ORMANDY [2353] (1849-1880)

Victoria ORMANDY [2352] (1851-1907)

Richard Francis SAUSE [2578] (1851-1909)

Esther (Hester?) Slee ORMANDY [2351] (1852-)

Johnathan Harrison ORMANDY [2350] (1854-1927)

George Julias ORMANDY [2349] (1857-1885)

James Alma ORMANDY [2348] (1858-1873)

1780	1830	1880	1930	1980	2030

Estimated Birth or Death

Timeline: Descendants of Richard ORMANDY [3923]

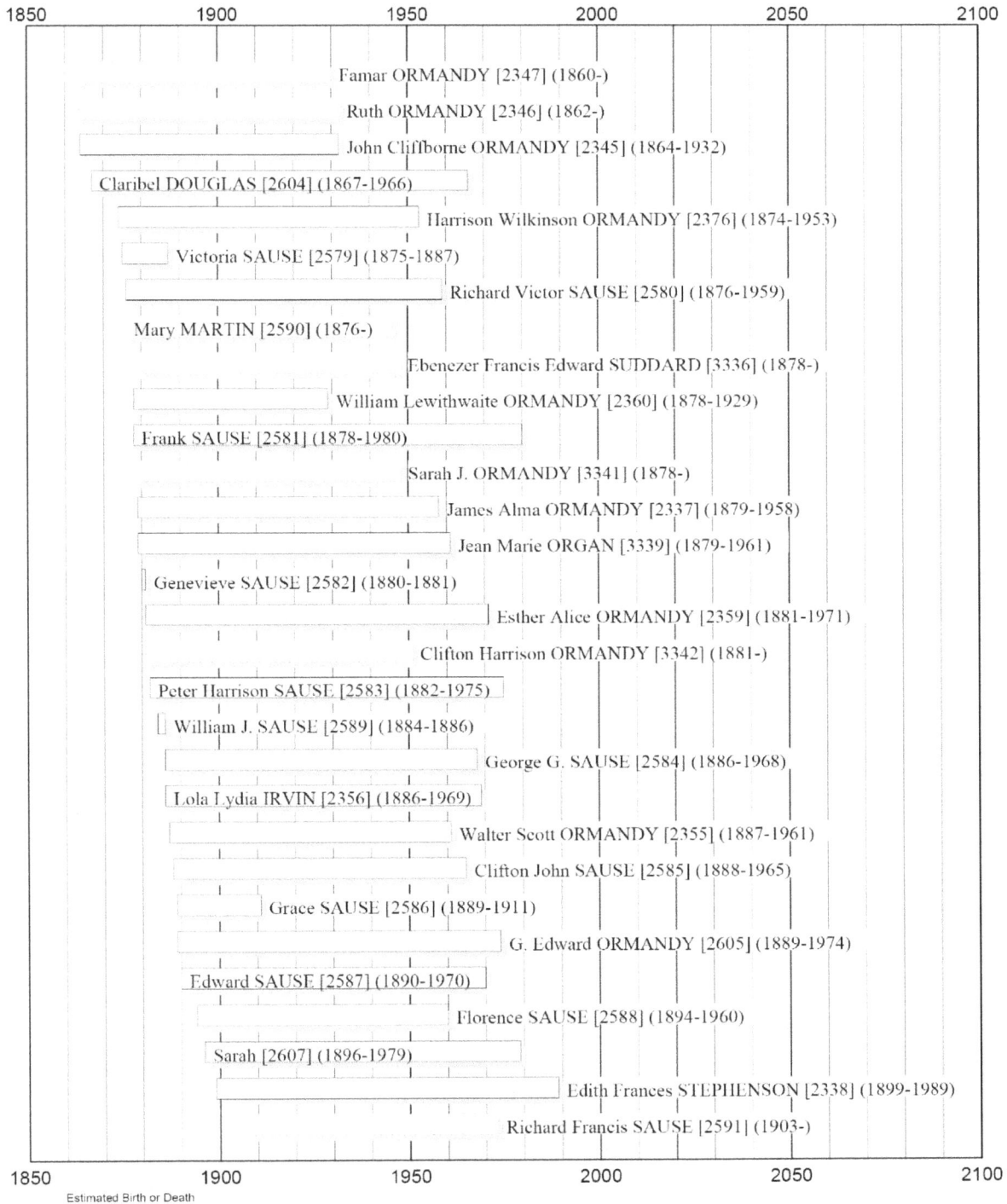

| 1850 | 1900 | 1950 | 2000 | 2050 | 2100 |

Famar ORMANDY [2347] (1860-)

Ruth ORMANDY [2346] (1862-)

John Cliftborne ORMANDY [2345] (1864-1932)

Claribel DOUGLAS [2604] (1867-1966)

Harrison Wilkinson ORMANDY [2376] (1874-1953)

Victoria SAUSE [2579] (1875-1887)

Richard Victor SAUSE [2580] (1876-1959)

Mary MARTIN [2590] (1876-)

Ebenezer Francis Edward SUDDARD [3336] (1878-)

William Lewithwaite ORMANDY [2360] (1878-1929)

Frank SAUSE [2581] (1878-1980)

Sarah J. ORMANDY [3341] (1878-)

James Alma ORMANDY [2337] (1879-1958)

Jean Marie ORGAN [3339] (1879-1961)

Genevieve SAUSE [2582] (1880-1881)

Esther Alice ORMANDY [2359] (1881-1971)

Clifton Harrison ORMANDY [3342] (1881-)

Peter Harrison SAUSE [2583] (1882-1975)

William J. SAUSE [2589] (1884-1886)

George G. SAUSE [2584] (1886-1968)

Lola Lydia IRVIN [2356] (1886-1969)

Walter Scott ORMANDY [2355] (1887-1961)

Clifton John SAUSE [2585] (1888-1965)

Grace SAUSE [2586] (1889-1911)

G. Edward ORMANDY [2605] (1889-1974)

Edward SAUSE [2587] (1890-1970)

Florence SAUSE [2588] (1894-1960)

Sarah [2607] (1896-1979)

Edith Frances STEPHENSON [2338] (1899-1989)

Richard Francis SAUSE [2591] (1903-)

| 1850 | 1900 | 1950 | 2000 | 2050 | 2100 |

Estimated Birth or Death

Timeline: Descendants of Richard ORMANDY [3923]

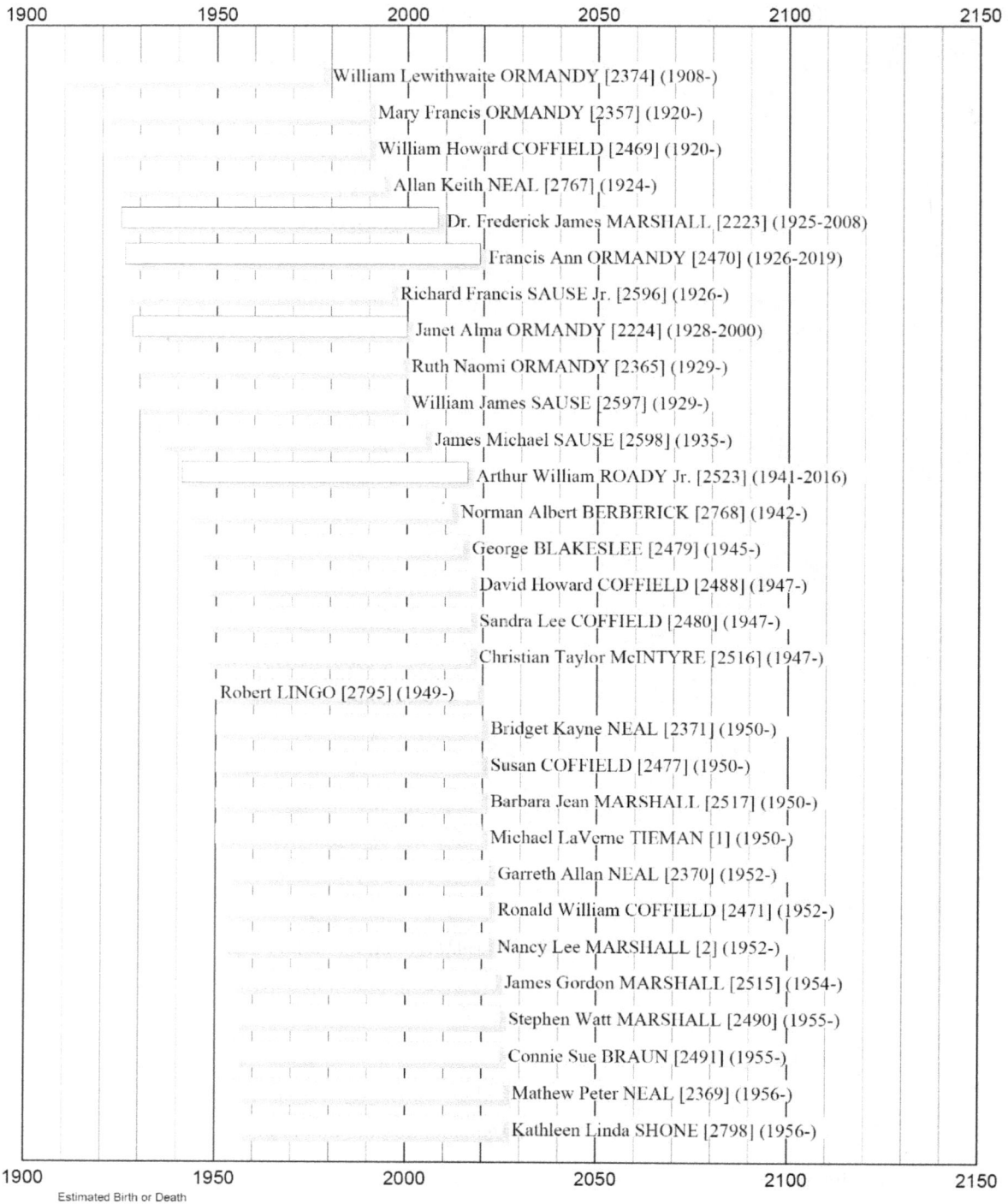

1900	1950	2000	2050	2100	2150

William Lewithwaite ORMANDY [2374] (1908-)

Mary Francis ORMANDY [2357] (1920-)

William Howard COFFIELD [2469] (1920-)

Allan Keith NEAL [2767] (1924-)

Dr. Frederick James MARSHALL [2223] (1925-2008)

Francis Ann ORMANDY [2470] (1926-2019)

Richard Francis SAUSE Jr. [2596] (1926-)

Janet Alma ORMANDY [2224] (1928-2000)

Ruth Naomi ORMANDY [2365] (1929-)

William James SAUSE [2597] (1929-)

James Michael SAUSE [2598] (1935-)

Arthur William ROADY Jr. [2523] (1941-2016)

Norman Albert BERBERICK [2768] (1942-)

George BLAKESLEE [2479] (1945-)

David Howard COFFIELD [2488] (1947-)

Sandra Lee COFFIELD [2480] (1947-)

Christian Taylor McINTYRE [2516] (1947-)

Robert LINGO [2795] (1949-)

Bridget Kayne NEAL [2371] (1950-)

Susan COFFIELD [2477] (1950-)

Barbara Jean MARSHALL [2517] (1950-)

Michael LaVerne TIEMAN [1] (1950-)

Garreth Allan NEAL [2370] (1952-)

Ronald William COFFIELD [2471] (1952-)

Nancy Lee MARSHALL [2] (1952-)

James Gordon MARSHALL [2515] (1954-)

Stephen Watt MARSHALL [2490] (1955-)

Connie Sue BRAUN [2491] (1955-)

Mathew Peter NEAL [2369] (1956-)

Kathleen Linda SHONE [2798] (1956-)

1900	1950	2000	2050	2100	2150

Estimated Birth or Death

Timeline: Descendants of Richard ORMANDY [3923]

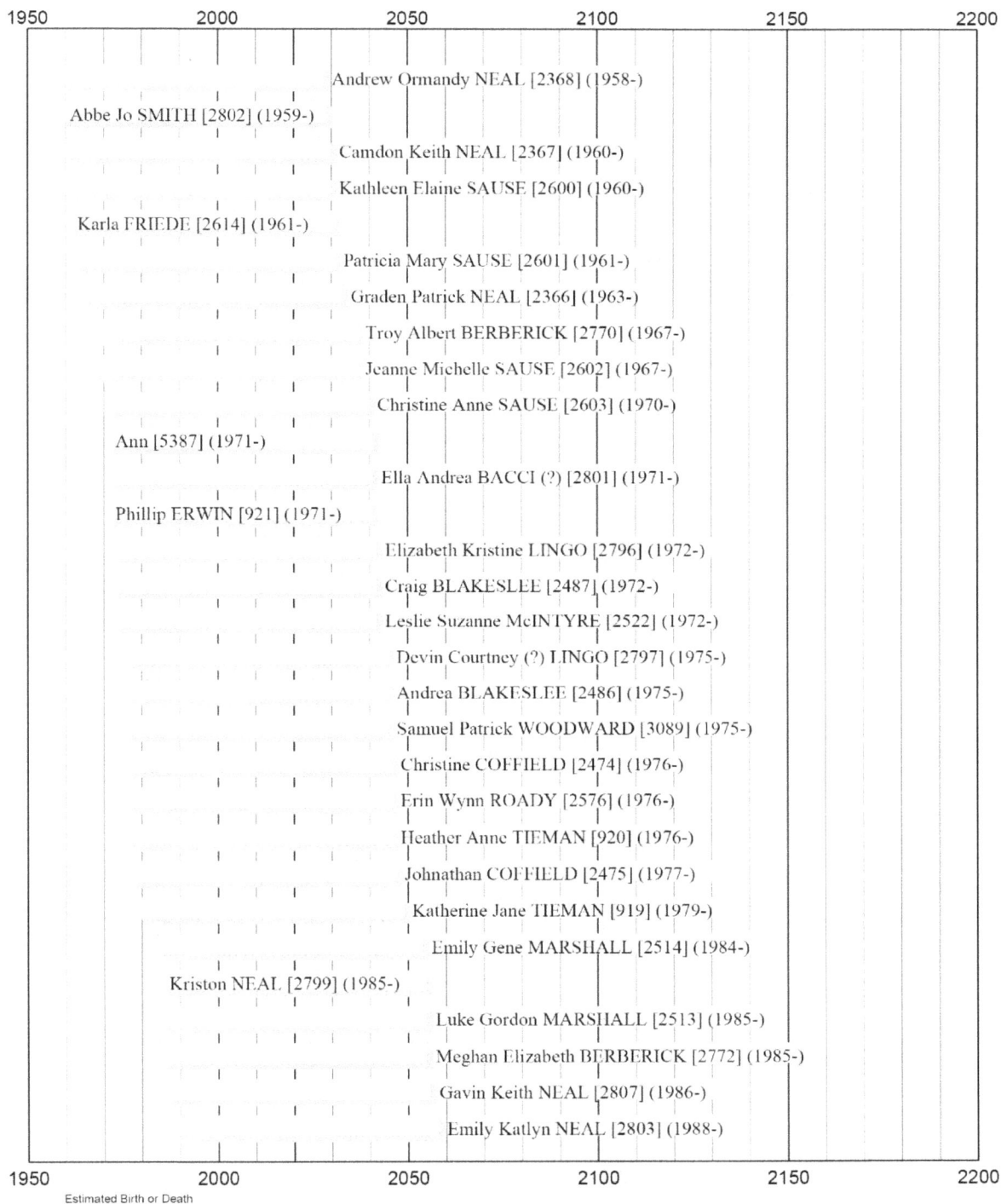

1950	2000	2050	2100	2150	2200

Andrew Ormandy NEAL [2368] (1958-)

Abbe Jo SMITH [2802] (1959-)

Camdon Keith NEAL [2367] (1960-)

Kathleen Elaine SAUSE [2600] (1960-)

Karla FRIEDE [2614] (1961-)

Patricia Mary SAUSE [2601] (1961-)

Graden Patrick NEAL [2366] (1963-)

Troy Albert BERBERICK [2770] (1967-)

Jeanne Michelle SAUSE [2602] (1967-)

Christine Anne SAUSE [2603] (1970-)

Ann [5387] (1971-)

Ella Andrea BACCI (?) [2801] (1971-)

Phillip ERWIN [921] (1971-)

Elizabeth Kristine LINGO [2796] (1972-)

Craig BLAKESLEE [2487] (1972-)

Leslie Suzanne McINTYRE [2522] (1972-)

Devin Courtney (?) LINGO [2797] (1975-)

Andrea BLAKESLEE [2486] (1975-)

Samuel Patrick WOODWARD [3089] (1975-)

Christine COFFIELD [2474] (1976-)

Erin Wynn ROADY [2576] (1976-)

Heather Anne TIEMAN [920] (1976-)

Johnathan COFFIELD [2475] (1977-)

Katherine Jane TIEMAN [919] (1979-)

Emily Gene MARSHALL [2514] (1984-)

Kriston NEAL [2799] (1985-)

Luke Gordon MARSHALL [2513] (1985-)

Meghan Elizabeth BERBERICK [2772] (1985-)

Gavin Keith NEAL [2807] (1986-)

Emily Katlyn NEAL [2803] (1988-)

1950	2000	2050	2100	2150	2200

Estimated Birth or Death

Timeline: Descendants of Richard ORMANDY [3923]

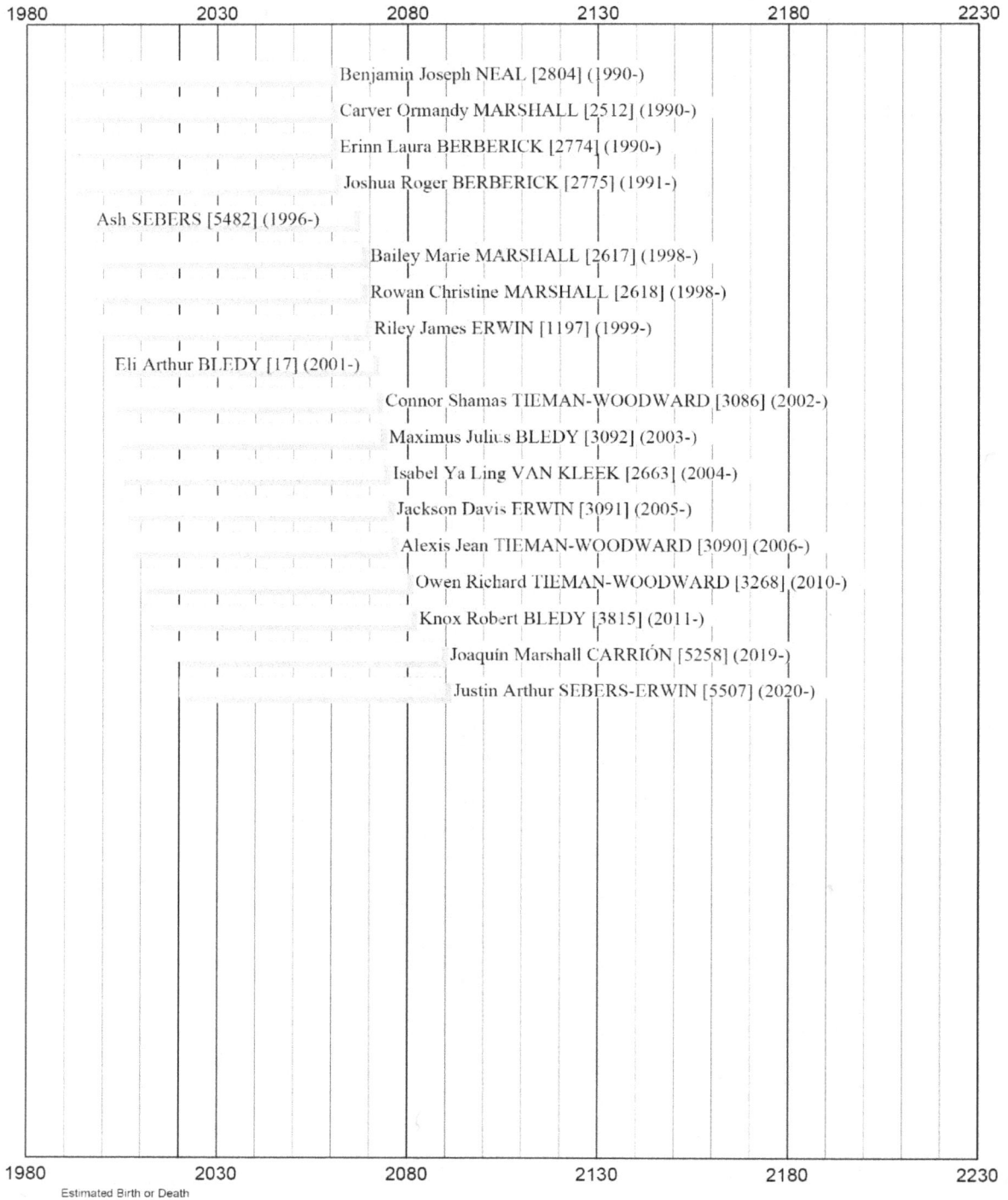

1980	2030	2080	2130	2180	2230

Benjamin Joseph NEAL [2804] (1990-)

Carver Ormandy MARSHALL [2512] (1990-)

Erinn Laura BERBERICK [2774] (1990-)

Joshua Roger BERBERICK [2775] (1991-)

Ash SEBERS [5482] (1996-)

Bailey Marie MARSHALL [2617] (1998-)

Rowan Christine MARSHALL [2618] (1998-)

Riley James ERWIN [1197] (1999-)

Eli Arthur BLEDY [17] (2001-)

Connor Shamas TIEMAN-WOODWARD [3086] (2002-)

Maximus Julius BLEDY [3092] (2003-)

Isabel Ya Ling VAN KLEEK [2663] (2004-)

Jackson Davis ERWIN [3091] (2005-)

Alexis Jean TIEMAN-WOODWARD [3090] (2006-)

Owen Richard TIEMAN-WOODWARD [3268] (2010-)

Knox Robert BLEDY [3815] (2011-)

Joaquín Marshall CARRIÓN [5258] (2019-)

Justin Arthur SEBERS-ERWIN [5507] (2020-)

1980	2030	2080	2130	2180	2230

Estimated Birth or Death

First Generation Richard Ormandy Timeline 1635

		Ormandy Family 1635-2020				
Year		**Rulers**	**World History**	**U.S. History**	**Science/Technology**	**Art**
1630		King Charles I rules 1629			micrometer 1636	
	Richard Ormandy 1635-1706	Queen Christina of Sweden 1632				
1640		Louis XIV of France 1643	English Civil War 1642		barometer 1643	
			Portugal independence 1640			
			War Venice/Turks 1645			
			30 Years War Ended 1648			
1650					pendulum clock 1656	
1660			New York founded (1664)			
			Great Fire of London (1666)		reflecting telescope 1668	Rococo
1670					calculating machine 1671	
			Russo-Turkish War 1678		pocket watch 1675	
1680		Peter the Great of Russia 1682				
			Eng. Constitu. monarchy 1689		pressure cooker.(1679)	
1690						
					steam pump 1698	
1700			Great Britain formed 1707			piano 1709
1710		King Fred. William I Prussia 1713		Tuscarora War (1711)		

First Generation
Richard Ormandy 1635-1706

Richard ORMANDY was born in 1635 in Broughton In Furness, Lancashire, England and died on 6 Apr 1706 in Broughton In Furness, Lancashire, England at age 71. Richard married **Elizabeth ATKINSON**, on 19 Feb 1670 in Broughton In Furness, Lancashire, England. Elizabeth was born on 30 Aug 1639 in Lancaster, Lancashire, England and died 10 Oct 1699. **Children**: Easter, John, Sarah, **William,** Elizabeth.

Family Lore has this line going back to Sir John Ormandy Vicar of Old Church Holy Trinity (Church of England), Millom England before 1066. To date I cannot find any info on Sir John.

Holy Trinity Church is a medieval building situated next to Millom Castle near the town of Millom, Cumbria, England. It is an active Anglican parish church in the deanery of Furness, the archdeaconry of Westmorland and Furness, and the diocese of Carlisle. Its benefice is united with those of St George (in the center of Millom), St Anne, Thwaites, and St Luke, Haverigg. The church is recorded in the National Heritage List for England as a designated Grade I listed building. Worship has taken place at this site for over 1000 years.

The earliest parts of the church are the nave and chancel, which date from the 12th century. The south aisle was added in the early 13th century and was rebuilt in a more elaborate style in about 1335 as the Huddlestone Chapel. Some details were restored in the 19th century, and the south porch was added in 1906. More drastic alterations were carried out in 1930 by Hicks and Charlewood of Newcastle, which included making the chancel wider. During this work, and incorporated into the northeast corner of the chancel, were part of a cross-shaft dating probably from the 10th or 11th century, and another ancient boss. Also, at this time a west gallery was installed.

Millom Castle is an ancient building at Millom in Cumbria. It is a Grade I listed building and scheduled ancient monument. A manor on the site was granted to Godard de Boyvill, owner of the Manor of Millom, in around 1134. The manor came into the Hudleston family's ownership in around 1240 when de Boyvill's granddaughter married into the Hudleston family. John Hudleston was given a license to crenellate in 1335. The great tower dates from the 16th or 17th century but was badly damaged by a cannon attack in 1648 during the English Civil War. By 1739 the castle walls were in dilapidated condition. The great tower is now used as a farmhouse.

Photos

Millom Castle

Millom Castle Holy Trinity Church

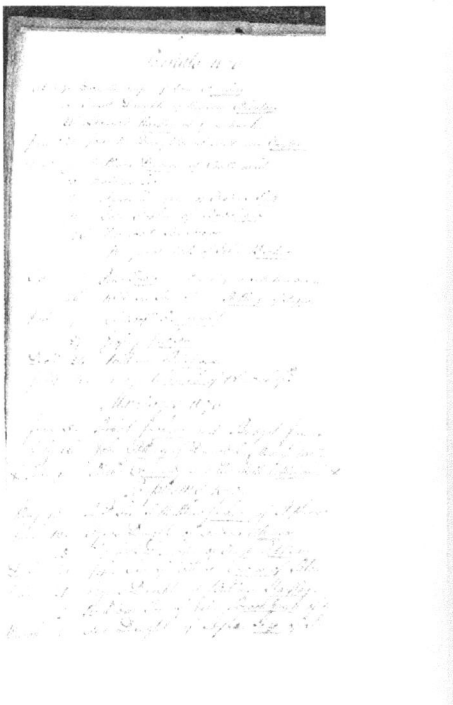

Richard & Elizabeth Marriage Record

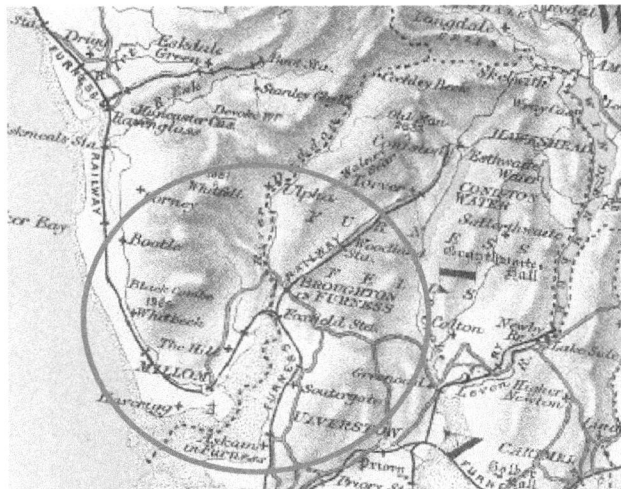

Broughton In Furness and Millom

1600's Map detail of Broughton In Furness and Millom

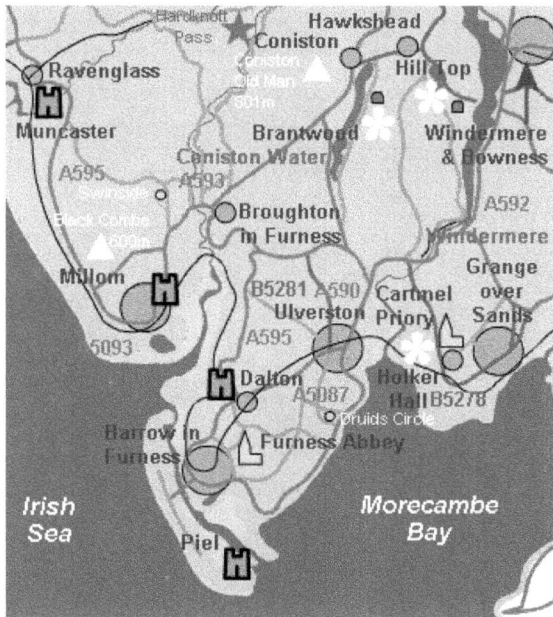

Map of castles in Broughton In Furness area

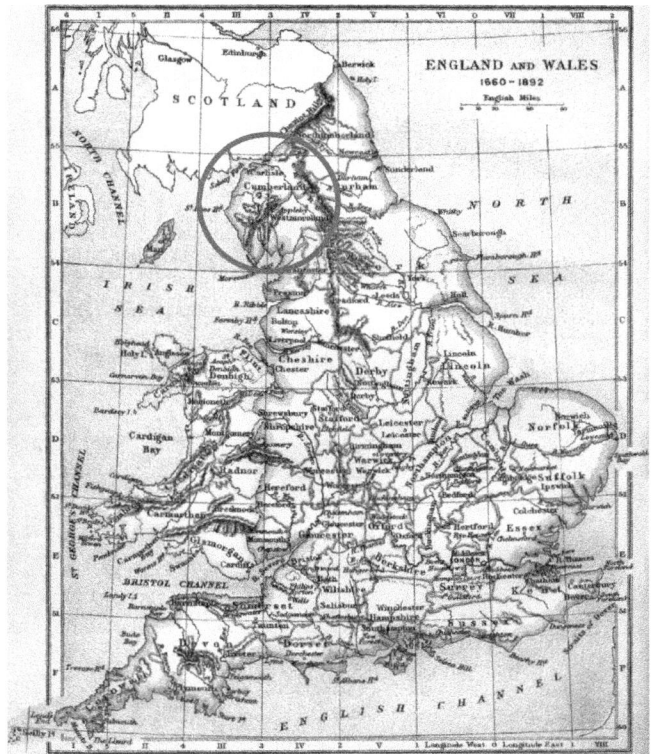

Second Generation William Ormandy Timeline 1680-1766

		Ormandy Family 1635-2020				
Year		**Rulers**	**World History**	**U.S. History**	**Science/Technology**	**Art**
1670					calculating machine 1671	
			Russo-Turkish War 1678		pocket watch 1675	
1680		Peter the Great of Russia 1682				
			Eng. Constitu. monarchy 1689		pressure cooker.(1679)	
1690						
					steam pump 1698	
1700			Great Britain formed 1707			piano 1709
1710		King Fred. William I Prussia 1713		Tuscarora War (1711)		
				City of New Orleans (1718)		
1720	William Ormandy 1680-1766	Card. Fleury governs France 1726	Persia's dynasty fell 1722		Coffee planted in Brazil 1727	
1730						
1740		Frederick The Great Russia1740	Prussia attacks Austria 1740			
		Elizabeth I of Russia 1741	First Saudi State (1744)			
1750			7 Years War 1756-1763			
			Battle of Quebec(1759)			
1760		Catherine II - Rus. 1762	Stamp Act(1765)		Industrial Revolution 1760	
		George III - Eng. 1760				
					Steam engine 1769	
1770		Louis XVI -Fr. 1774		Boston Tea Party (1773)		

Second Generation
William Ormandy 1680-1766

William ORMANDY was born in 1680 in Broughton In Furness, Lancashire, England, was christened on 18 Oct 1680 in Broughton In Furness, Lancashire, England, and died 01 Jun 1766 (?1746) in Aldingham, Lancashire, England at age 66. William married **Bridget ADDISON** on 16 Sep 1716 at St. Mary, Augustine Ch. Broughton in Furness. Bridget was born in Aulthurstide, England, died on 12 Jan 1766 in Broughton In Furness, Lancashire, England, and was buried on 12 Jan 1766 in Broughton In Furness, Lancashire, England. **Children:** John, Anne, Richard, Betty, James, Bridget, **Thomas.**

Aldingham parish, composed of a single township of the same name, occupies a pleasant position on the southeast side of Low Furness overlooking Morecambe Bay. The surface is undulating, being highest in the north, where 400 ft. above sea level is attained on the border of Birkrigg; in the northern half also at the coast it rises steeply from the sea, 200 ft. being attained a quarter to half a mile from the shore. The southern end is flat and low near the shore, but to the north-west, on the border of Dalton, rises to 214 ft. above sea level at Scarbarrow. The two portions are known as Upper and Lower Aldingham.

Photos

St Mary Magdalene's Church, Broughton-in-Furness

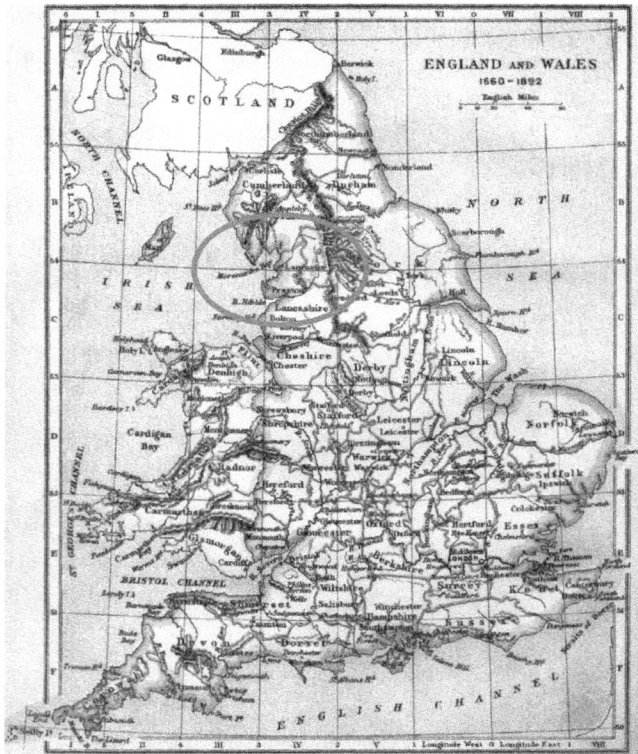

Broughton In Furness and Millom

Third Generation Thomas Ormandy Timeline 1717-1776

Year		Rulers	World History	U.S. History	Science/Technology	Art
		Ormandy Family 1635-2020				
1710		King Fred. William I Prussia 1713		Tuscarora War (1711)		
				City of New Orleans (1718)		
1720		Card. Fleury governs France 1726	Persia's dynasty fell 1722		Coffee planted in Brazil 1727	
1730						
	Thomas Ormandy 1717-1776					
1740		Frederick The Great Russia1740	Prussia attacks Austria 1740			
		Elizabeth I of Russia 1741	First Saudi State (1744)			
1750			7 Years War 1756-1763			
			Battle of Quebec(1759)			
1760		Catherine II - Rus. 1762	Stamp Act(1765)		Industrial Revolution 1760	
		George III - Eng. 1760				
					Steam engine 1769	
1770		Louis XVI -Fr. 1774		Boston Tea Party (1773)		
					Submarine 1776	
				American Revolution		
1780					Bifocals 1784	Neoclassicism
				U.S. Independence 1783	1st Parachute 1783	*Federalist Pub. 1788*

Third Generation
Thomas Ormandy 1717-1776

Thomas ORMANDY a butcher, was christened on 17 Jun 1717 in Broughton In Furness, Lancashire, England, died in Dec 1776 in Gleaston Castle, Lancashire, England at age 59, and was buried on 20 Dec 1776 in Gleaston Castle, Lancashire, England. Thomas married **Jane STANLEY**, daughter of **Joseph STANLEY** , on 24 Nov 1744 in Broughton In Furness, Lancashire, England. Jane was born on 13 Jan 1717/1719 in St. Mary Magdalene, Broughton In Furness, England and died on 29 Apr 1803 in Burried, St. Cuthberts Ch. Aldingham, Lancs. Eng. at age 86. **Children: Thomas,** Ann, William Addison, William, Jane, Richard, Joseph, John, James, Bridget, Catherine, Anne.

Gleaston Castle is a medieval building in a valley about 1 kilometer (0.62 mi) north-east of the village of Gleaston. The village lies between the towns of Ulverston and Barrow-in-Furness in the Furness peninsula, Cumbria, England. Gleaston Castle has a quadrilateral plan, with a tower at each corner. The largest of these, the north-west tower, probably housed a hall.

The castle was most likely built for John Harington, 1st Baron Harington in the 14th century, replacing nearby Aldingham Motte. Gleaston Castle descended through the Harrington family until 1458 when it passed to William Bonville through marriage and was subsequently abandoned. The castle passed to the Grey family until Henry Grey, 1st Duke of Suffolk was executed for treason in 1554. As a result, Gleaston Castle became royal property before it was bought by the Preston family in the 17th century, and then passed to the Cavendish family.

As the castle was disused from the mid-15th century it fell into dilapidation, and antiquarian depictions from the 18th century show Gleaston in a state of ruin. Though it is not open to the public, it has been the subject of historical and archaeological investigation in the 20th and 21st centuries.

Photos

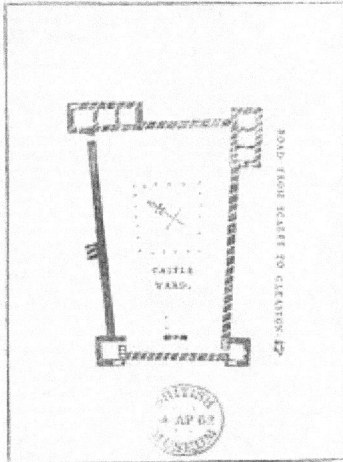

Gleaston Castle

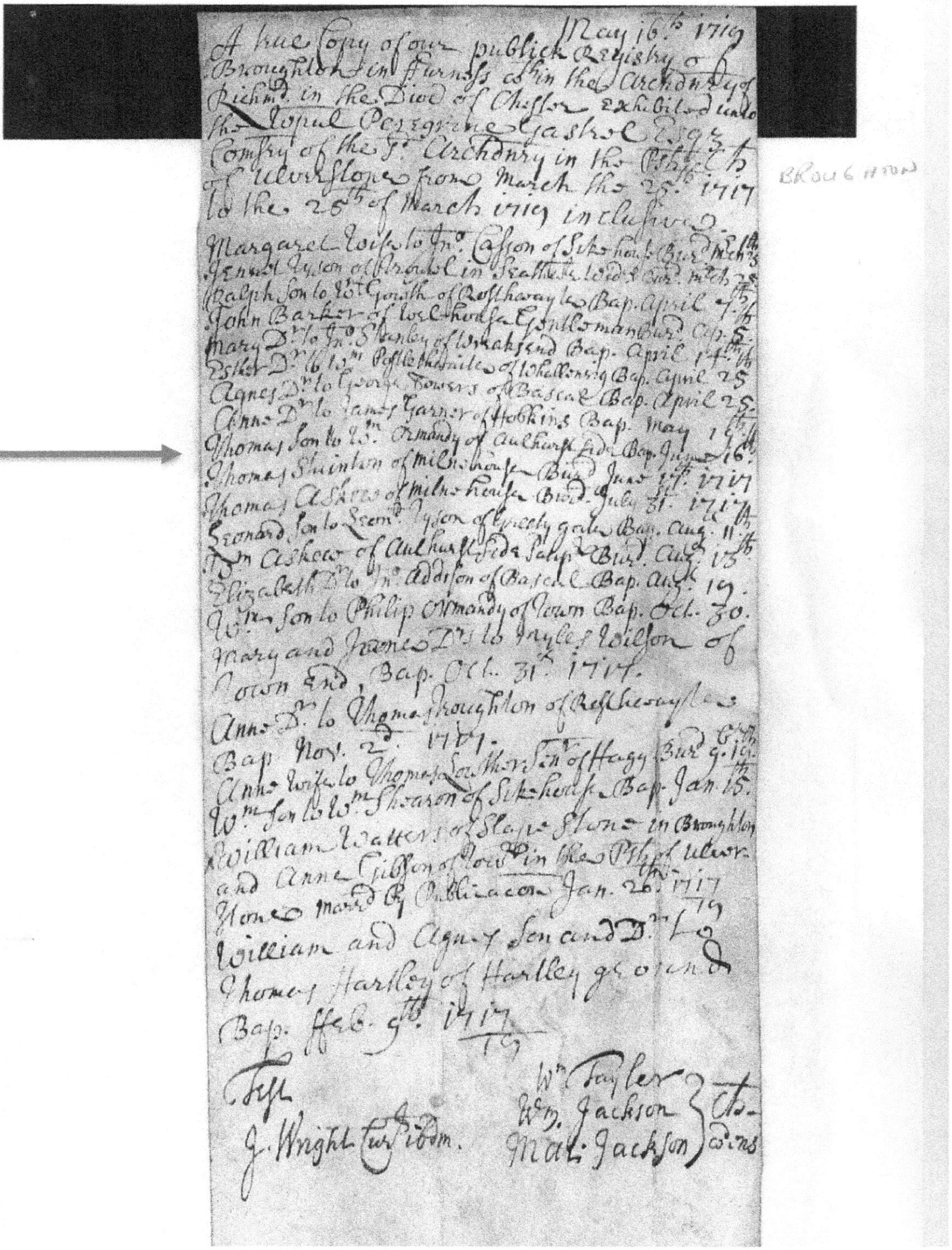

Baptism Record for Thomas Ormandy

Marriage Record of Thomas Ormandy to Jane Stanley

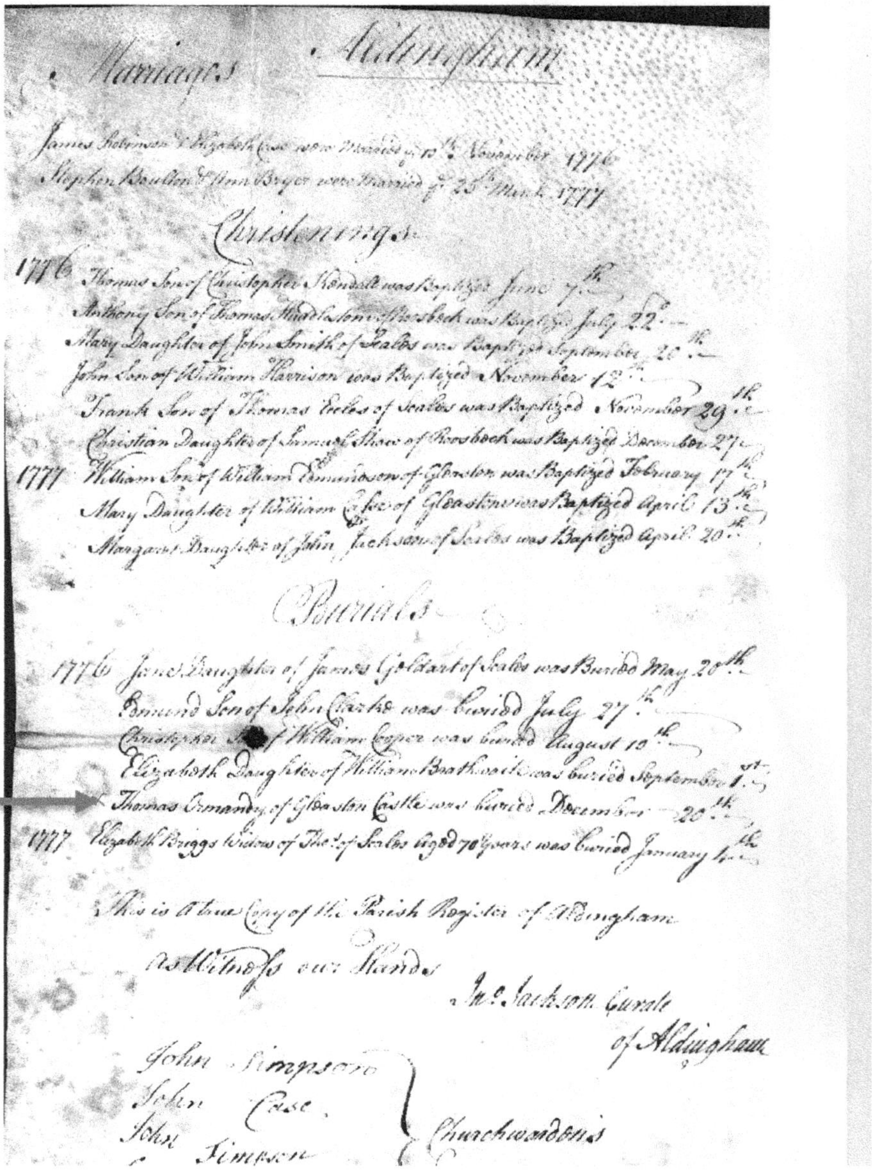
Marriages Aldingham

James Robinson & Elizabeth Case were Married ye 10th November 1776
Stephen Boulton & Ann Bryer were Married ye 25th March 1777

Christenings

1776 Thomas Son of Christopher Kendall was Baptized June 7th
Anthony Son of Thomas Middleton of Roosbeck was Baptized July 22d
Mary Daughter of John Smith of Scales was Baptized September 20th
John Son of William Harrison was Baptized November 12th
Frank Son of Thomas Eccles of Scales was Baptized November 29th
Christian Daughter of Samuel Shaw of Roosbeck was Baptized December 27th
1777 William Son of William Edmundson of Gleaston was Baptized February 17th
Mary Daughter of William Case of Gleaston was Baptized April 13th
Margaret Daughter of John Jackson of Scales was Baptized April 20th

Burials

1776 Jane Daughter of James Goldart of Scales was Buried May 20th
Edmund Son of John Clarke was buried July 27th
Christopher Son of William Cooper was buried August 10th
Elizabeth Daughter of William Braithwaite was buried September 1st
Thomas Ormandy of Gleaston Castle was buried December 20th
1777 Elizabeth Briggs Widow of Thos of Scales Aged 70 years was buried January 4th

This is a true Copy of the Parish Register of Aldingham
As Witness our Hands
Jno Jackson Curate of Aldingham

John Simpson
John Case
John Simpson
Churchwardens

Burial Record of Thomas Ormandy

Fourth Generation Thomas Ormandy Timeline 1749-1827

Year		Ormandy Family 1635-2020				
		Rulers	**World History**	**U.S. History**	**Science/Technology**	**Art**
1740		Frederick The Great Russia1740	Prussia attacks Austria 1740			
		Elizabeth I of Russia 1741	First Saudi State (1744)			
1750			7 Years War 1756-1763			
			Battle of Quebec(1759)			
1760		Catherine II - Rus. 1762	Stamp Act(1765)		Industrial Revolution 1760	
		George III - Eng. 1760				
					Steam engine 1769	
1770		Louis XVI -Fr. 1774		Boston Tea Party (1773)		
					Submarine 1776	
				American Revolution		
1780					Bifocals 1784	Neoclassicism
				U.S. Independence 1783	1st Parachute 1783	Federalist Pub. 1788
		Carlos IV - Sp. 1788				
				Constitution Ratified 1788	Steamboat 1786	
	Thomas Ormandy 1749-1827					
		Frederick Wm. II - Ger. 1786				
		Pres. George Washington 1789	French Revolution	Irish Catholics Migration		
1790		Pres. John Adams 1797	Canada Act 1791	Vermont 1791	Gas Turbine 1791	Rights of Man 1791
		Paul - Rus. 1796	France/Netherlands	Kentucky 1792	Cotton Gin 1793	
				Fugitive Slave Act 1793		
				Tennessee 1796		
				Ohio 1803		
1800		Pres. Thomas Jefferson 1801	Irish Potato Famine	Lib. Of Congress 1800	Electric Cell 1800	Romanticism
		Ferdinand VII - Sp. 1808	Battle of Trafalgar	Lousiana Purchase 1803		Webster Dictionary 1806
		Napolean - Fr. 1804	Peninsular War in Spain	Louis & Clark Exp. 1804	1st Submarine 1801	Fifth Symphony 1808
		Alexander I - Rus. 1801		African Slaves Act 1808	Oil lamp 1804	
		Pres. James Madison1809		Lousiana 1812	Braille 1809	
1810		Pres. James Monroe 1817	British American War	Indiana 1816	1st Photograph 1814	
		Louis XVIII -Fr. 1814	Napolean defeated	Mississippi 1817	Steam Locomotive 1814	
				Illinois 1818	Stethoscope 1819	
				Alabama 1819	Erie Canal 1817	
				Maine 1820		
1820		Pres. J. Q. Adams 1825	Peru Freedom	Missouri 1821	Microphone 1827	Hudson River Sch. 1825
		George IV - Eng. 1820	Greek War of	Monroe Doctrine 1823	Typewriter 1829	Audubon
		Charles X - Fr. 1824	Independance			
		Nicholas I - Rus. 1825	Spanish Revolution			
			Russia/Turkey	Arkansas 1836		
		Pres. Andrew Jackson 1829	Uruguay Freedom	German Migration		
1830		William IV - Eng. 1830		Michigan 1837	Sewing Machine 1830	Hunchback of ND 1831

Fourth Generation
Thomas Ormandy 1749-1827

Rev. Thomas ORMANDY was born on 11 Jun 1749 in Broughton In Furness, Lancashire, England, died on 8 May 1827 in Aldingham, Lancashire, England at age 77, and was buried on 8 May 1827 in St. Cuthberts Church Aldingham, Lancashire. England. Thomas married **Dorothy BOLTON**, daughter of **William BOULTON**, on 23 Jul 1785-26 in Aldingham, Lancashire, England. Dorothy was born in 1759 in Walney Island Lancs. England., died in Mar 1821 in Aldingham, Lancashire, England at age 62, and was buried on 13 Mar 1821 in St. Cuthberts Church, Aldingham, Lancashire, England. **Children:** Anne, William, Joseph, **John**, James, Thomas, Eleanor, George, Isaac.

Rev. Thomas Ormandy of Aldingham 1796 (now Cumbria) P.C. of Wintbeck 1850-78. Parish Marriage records show date of marriage 26 Jun 1785 and wife's last name BOLTON. Marriage License dated 23 Jul 1785 and wife's last name BOULTON

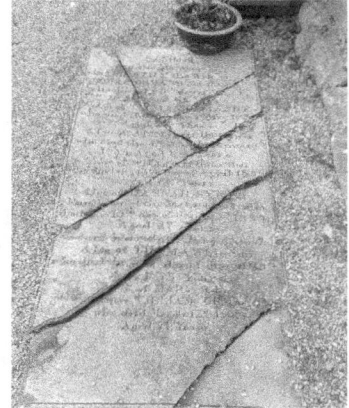

He worked as a Vicar of Old Church of the Holy Trinity at Millom, England.

Photos

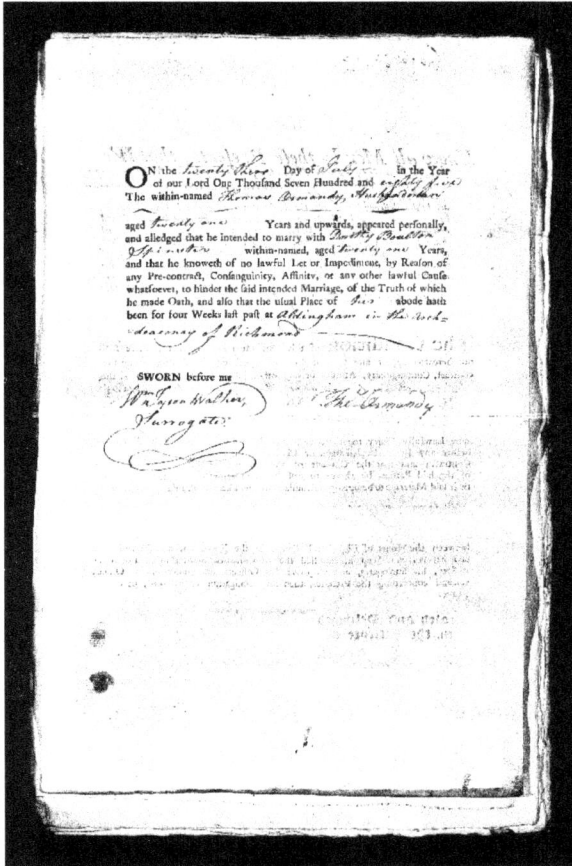

Marriage Record

Old Church of the Holy Trinity at Millom, England.

Whitbeck

Broughton In Furness and Millom

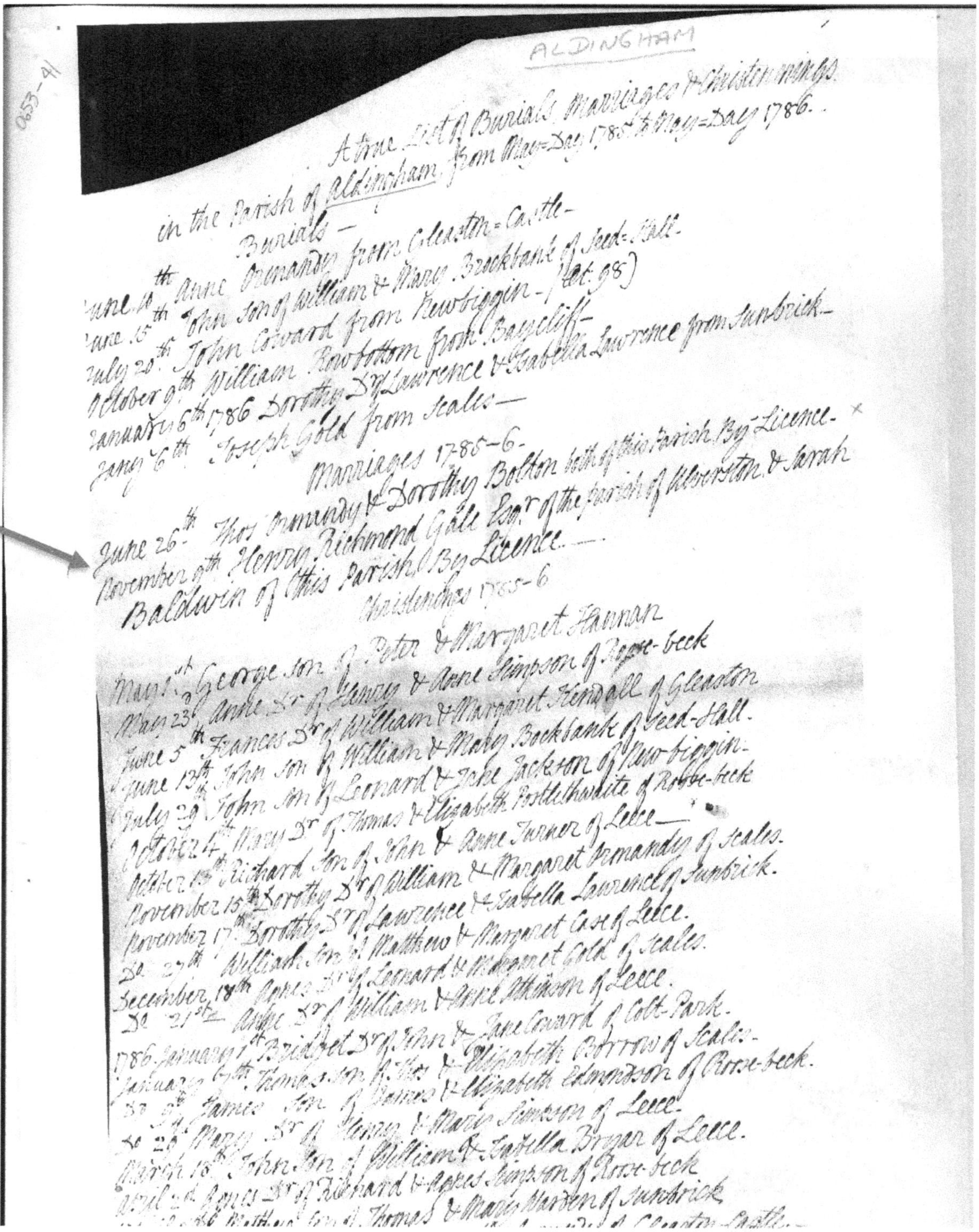

Marriage Record of Thomas Ormandy to Dorothy Bolton

Page 12.

BURIALS in the Parish of _Aldingham_
in the County of _Lancaster_   in the Year 18_26_

Name.	Abode.	When buried.	Age.	By whom the Ceremony was performed.
William Geldart No. 145.	Scales	1826 May 29	70 years	Thos Ormandy Curate.
Margaret Clayton No. 146.	Gleaston	1826 November 4	65 years	Thos Ormandy Curate
William Kendall No. 147.	Gleaston	1826 December 11	71 years	Thos Ormandy Curate
George Postlethwaite No. 148.	Ulverston	1827 January 15	81 years	Thos Ormandy Curate
Elizabeth Barton No. 149.	Sykes House in Dalton	1827 March 18	72 years	Thos Ormandy Curate
Jane Newby No. 150.	Urswick	1827 April 5	39 years	Thos Ormandy Curate
Thomas Ormandy No. 151.	Bayclift	1827 May 8	77	John Stonard Rector.
Jane Mount	Bayclift	1827 October 5	20 years	Thos Orm... Curate

Burial Record of Thomas Ormandy

Fifth Generation John Ormandy Timeline 1792-1846

		Ormandy Family 1635-2020				
Year		**Rulers**	**World History**	**U.S. History**	**Science/Technology**	**Art**
1790		Pres. John Adams 1797	Canada Act 1791	Vermont 1791	Gas Turbine 1791	*Rights of Man 1791*
	John Ormandy 1792-1846	Paul - Rus. 1796	France/Netherlands	Kentucky 1792	Cotton Gin 1793	
				Fugitive Slave Act 1793		
				Tennessee 1796		
				Ohio 1803		
1800		Pres. Thomas Jefferson 1801	Irish Potato Famine	Lib. Of Congress 1800	Electric Cell 1800	Romanticism
		Ferdinand VII - Sp. 1808	Battle of Trafalgar	Lousiana Purchase 1803		*Webster Dictionary 1806*
		Napolean - Fr. 1804	Peninsular War in Spain	Louis & Clark Exp. 1804	1st Submarine 1801	Fifth Symphony 1808
		Alexander I - Rus. 1801		African Slaves Act 1808	Oil lamp 1804	
		Pres. James Madison1809		Lousiana 1812	Braille 1809	
1810		Pres. James Monroe 1817	British American War	Indiana 1816	1st Photograph 1814	
		Louis XVIII -Fr. 1814	Napolean defeated	Mississippi 1817	Steam Locomotive 1814	
				Illinois 1818	Stethoscope 1819	
				Alabama 1819	Erie Canal 1817	
				Maine 1820		
1820		Pres. J. Q. Adams 1825	Peru Freedom	Missouri 1821	Microphone 1827	Hudson River Sch. 1825
		George IV - Eng. 1820	Greek War of	Monroe Doctrine 1823	Typewriter 1829	Audubon
		Charles X - Fr. 1824	Independance			
		Nicholas I - Rus. 1825	Spanish Revolution			
			Russia/Turkey	Arkansas 1836		
		Pres. Andrew Jackson 1829	Uruguay Freedom	German Migration		
1830		William IV - Eng. 1830		Michigan 1837	Sewing Machine 1830	*Hunchback of ND 1831*
		Queen Victoria 1837			Calculator 1835	*Oliver Twist 1837*
		Isabel II- Sp. 1833		Mormons 1830		
		Pres. M. Van Buren 1837		Trail of Tears 1838	Telegraph 1837	
		Louis-Philippe- Fr. 1830	Britian/China -Opium	Florida 1845	Bicycle 1839	
1840		Pres. Harrison & Tyler 1841	Britian Factory Act	Texas 1845	Anesthetic 1842	Edgar A. Poe
		Pres. James Polk 1845	U.S./ Mexico	Iowa 1846		
		Pres. Taylor & Fillmore 1849	Communist Manifesto	California Gold Rush 1848		*3 Muskateers 1844*
				Wisconsin 1848		
				California 1850		Karl Marx
1850		Louis Napolean III - Fr. 1852	Crimean War 1853-56	Minnesota 1858	Jeans 1850	Realism

Fifth Generation
John Ormandy 1792-1846

Rev. John ORMANDY was born on 5 Apr 1792 in Aldingham, Lancashire, England and died on 16 May 1846 in Thwaites Chapel In Millom, Cumberland, England at age 54. John married **Mary WILKINSON**, daughter of **John WILKINSON** and **Julia HARRISON** on 14 Feb 1819 in Greystoke, Cumberland, England. Mary was born in 1791 in Thorpe, Derbyshire, England, was christened on 14 Apr 1791 in Thorpe, Derbyshire, England, died in 1848 in Twaites Chapel, Millom, Cumberland, England at age 57, and was buried on 31 Dec 1848 in Twaites Chapel, Millom, Cumberland, England. **Children:** Dorothy, Mary Ann, **Thomas**, Juliann, John, Harrison.

Priest at Greystoke 1815-1822. Vicar 1822-1846 of Thwaites Chapel In Millom, Cumberland, England.

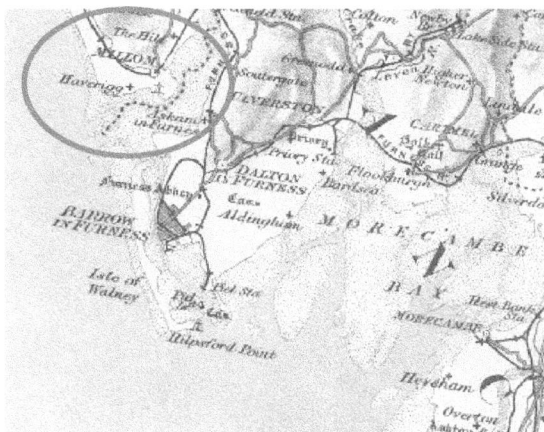

"**THWAITES**, a chapelry in the parish of Millom, ward of Allerdale-above-Derwent, county Cumberland, 4 miles from Broughton, in Lancashire, its post town, and 10 S.E. of Ravenglass. The chapelry includes the hamlets of Duddon Bridge, Hall Thwaites, and Lady Hall. The living is a perpetual curacy in the diocese of Carlisle, value £115, in the patronage of landowners. The church is dedicated to St. Anne. There is a Druidical temple at Swineside, about 2 miles from the church." [Description(s) from *The National Gazetteer of Great Britain and Ireland* (1868) - Transcribed by Colin Hinson ©2003]

St Anne's Church is in the village of Thwaites, Cumbria, England. It is an active Anglican parish church in the deanery of Millom, the archdeaconry of Furness, and the diocese of Carlisle. Its benefice is united with those of St George, Millom, Holy Trinity, Millom, and St Luke, Haverigg. The church is recorded in the National Heritage List for England as a designated Grade II listed building.

The church replaced a chapel of ease (A chapel of ease is a church building other than the parish church, built within the bounds of a parish for the attendance of those who cannot reach the parish church conveniently), on the other site of the road, which was built in 1721 and consecrated in 1725. This church was built in 1853, and designed by the Lancaster architect E. G. Paley, at a cost of £1,678 (equivalent to £150,000 as of 2018). It was consecrated on 16 June 1854 by the bishop of Chester.

Photos

Census Record Rev. John Ormandy

Counties in England

Baptism Record of John Ormandy

Page 55.

0653-38

BURIALS in the Parish of _Chapelry of Thwaites_ in the County of _Cumberland_ in the Year 1846				
Name.	Abode.	When Buried.	Age.	By whom the Ceremony was performed.
Elizabeth Hodgin No. 257.	High Stile Dunnerdale	January 10th	24	John Ormandy Curate
William Rickthay No. 258.	Orchard head Broughton	April 29th	84	John Ormandy Curate
Rev. John Ormandy Incumbent No. 259.	Bridge End	May 10	54	Henry Pickthall, Vicar of Millom.
Joseph Shepherd. No. 260.	Bridge End.	June 12.	24.	W. Williamson, Officiating Minister.
Margaret Bowes. No. 261.	Fenwick.	July 29.	68.	W. Williamson Officiating Minister
John Mather - No. 262.	High Bridge End.	August 2nd	38.	W. Williamson Officiating Minister.
Ellen Kitchen No. 263.	Strands	September 28	87	Henry Pickthall Vicar of Millom
Henry H. Harrison	Frying	Novr 2	26.	W. Williamson Officiating

Burial Record of Rev. John Ormandy

Sixth Generation Thomas Ormandy Timeline 1823-1864

Year	Rulers	World History	U.S. History	Science/Technology	Art
	Ormandy Family 1635-2020				
1820	Pres. J. Q. Adams 1825	Peru Freedom	Missouri 1821	Microphone 1827	Hudson River Sch. 1825
	George IV - Eng. 1820	Greek War of	Monroe Doctrine 1823	Typewriter 1829	Audubon
	Charles X - Fr. 1824	Independance			
	Nicholas I - Rus. 1825	Spanish Revolution			
		Russia/Turkey	Arkansas 1836		
	Pres. Andrew Jackson 1829	Uruguay Freedom	German Migration		
1830	William IV - Eng. 1830		Michigan 1837	Sewing Machine 1830	*Hunchback of ND 1831*
	Queen Victoria 1837			Calculator 1835	*Oliver Twist 1837*
	Isabel II- Sp. 1833		Mormons 1830		
	Pres. M. Van Buren 1837		Trail of Tears 1838	Telegraph 1837	
	Louis-Philippe- Fr. 1830	Britian/China -Opium	Florida 1845	Bicycle 1839	
1840	Pres. Harrison & Tyler 1841	Britian Factory Act	Texas 1845	Anesthetic 1842	Edgar A. Poe
	Pres. James Polk 1845	U.S./ Mexico	Iowa 1846		
	Pres. Taylor & Fillmore 1849	Communist Manifesto	California Gold Rush 1848		*3 Muskateers 1844*
			Wisconsin 1848		
			California 1850		Karl Marx
1850	Louis Napolean III - Fr. 1852	Crimean War 1853-56	Minnesota 1858	Jeans 1850	Realism
	Pres. Franklin Pierce 1853	Britain/China 1856	Oregon 1859	Pasteurisation 1856	*Scarlet Letter 1850*
	Pres. J. Buchanan 1857			Smith & Wesson 1854	*Moby Dick 1851*
	Alexander II - Rus. 1855			Darwin 1859	*Walden 1854*
			Kansas 1861		*Leaves of Grass 1855*
1860	Pres. Abraham Lincoln 1861	U.S. Civil War 1861-65	U.S. Civil War 1861-65	Dynamite 1867	
			West Virginia 1863		*War & Peace 1865*
			Emancipation Proc. 1863		

(left margin, vertical text: Thomas Ormandy 1823-1864)

Sixth Generation
Thomas Ormandy 1823-1864

Thomas ORMANDY was born on 10 Aug 1823 in Twaites Chapel, Millom, Cumberland, England and died on 7 Mar 1864 in Cahaba, Alabama at age 40. The cause of his death was Pneumonia while prisoner of war 15 Apr 1864 Cahaba, Alabama. Thomas married **Sarah JONES**, in Aug 1845 in London, England. Sarah was born on 22 Aug 1825 in Chippenham, Wiltshire, England, died on 6 Aug 1872 in Astoria, Queens, New York, USA at age 46, and was buried on 8 Aug 1872 in Long Island City, Queens, New York, USA. **Children:** Julia, **William,** Mary, Victoria, Esther, Johnathan, George, James, Famar, Ruth, John.

Became an Indentured Servant in 14 May 1839 to Isaac Ormandy of Liverpool a surgeon, he agreed to apprentice for 5 years in the Art of Pharmacy and Surgery and the business thereof.

War Department Adjutant General's Office Washington, Feby 14, 1882 Respectfully returned to the Commissioner of Pensions. Thomas Ormandy, (?), Company "E", 178 Regiment New York Volunteers, was enrolled on the 23rd day of March 1863, at New York, N.Y., and is reported: on rolls to Dec 31, 1863 present. Jany & Feby 1864 absent without leave. March & April 1864 deserted from Sherman Expeditions Feb 19, 1864. May & June 1864 name not (?). July & Aug 1864 Absent Captured by Enemy, Sherman Raid, (?), - Same report to April 30, 1865. May & June 1865 Died at Cahaba, Ala March 7, 1864. (?), Returned report him died April 15, 1864 at Cahawba of pneumonia.

Prisoner of War Records show him admitted to Hospital at Cahaba Ala., date not given, and died March 7, 1864, of Pneumonia, Capture not given. (Signature) Assistant Adjutant General.

Cahaba prison was located near Selma, Alabama, in the center of the now-vanished town of Cahawba which was the state capital of Alabama from 1820 to 1826. The prison was located in a cotton warehouse on the banks of the Alabama River and was in operation intermittently from 1862 to April 1865. More than 9,000 men were imprisoned at Cahaba over that time period. At its peak in 1864 and 1865, 3,000 men were housed there in with an average living space of only six square feet, by far the most crowded of any prison, north or south. Conditions were harsh, but thanks to a humane prison director and the kindnesses of town people, fewer than 250 soldiers died there.

Cahaba Prisoner of War Camp

Confederate 1863-1865 Selma, Alabama

In January 1864, Confederate authorities decided to establish a permanent prison facility at the unfinished red-brick cotton warehouse at Cahaba, Alabama. They acquired the warehouse for the use as a prison for captured Union prisoners in the summer of 1862. Col. Samuel M. Hill originally owned the warehouse and had constructed the building as part of a complex to provide storage for the Cahaba, Marion, and Greensborough Railroad. The railroad failed in the 1850's and the warehouse was abandoned.

The place had been used as a gathering point for the military district's political and Union prisoners for several months, starting in late 1863. The prison was located on the on the central east end of the city on the banks of the Alabama and Cahaba Rivers. The prison was initially built to hold 500 prisoners. It held over 5,000 Union soldiers between 1863 and 1865.

The prison was 15,000 sq. feet, covered by a leaky roof with 1,600 feet of open space in its center and was surrounded by a tall brick wall. The building had 4 open windows and the floor was bare earth. A 12-foot-high wide-plank fence was built around the 1/3-acre site. Inside the building, bunks, 5 tiers high, were erected along the walls and would hold 432 men. By the end of March 1864, 660 prisoners were held at the prison.

The prison yard, enclosed by a fence, was about 35x46 feet and could be used by the prisoners during the daytime. It also served as the cook yard. Guards patrolled on an elevated walkway around the outside of the fence. Two small cannons protruded out of 2 portholes in the north end of the stockade wall. The walls of the warehouse were about 14 feet high and measured 193x116 feet on the outside.

By May 1864, there were 1,500 prisoners, and the prison was ordered to be closed. The prisoners healthy enough to travel were transferred to Andersonville Prison. When Andersonville became too overcrowded, Cahaba Prison was reopened. By September, there were 2,500 prisoners and that number eventually climbed to 3,000.

There were 2 co-commanders at the prison, with Capt. H.A.M. Henderson sharing command with Lt. Col. Sam Jones. Henderson took charge of the prison facilities, while Jones directed the prison's guards. The prison guard totaled 179 troops, with a number of them coming from established Alabama reserves

Life & Conditions:

Prisoners were contained in old decrepit buildings which held no provisions for bedding. Instead, prisoners slept on bare floors with one fireplace in the building to keep them warm. There was not any way to heat the building so open fires were allowed on the floor.

The water supply came from an open trench that ran from an artesian well, which had become extremely polluted by the sewer runoff from the town and the prison itself. The well was located 200 yards away, outside the prison wall. According to stories told, the river often flooded and covered the floors of the buildings in waters running 1-4 feet deep.

Rations were the standard issue of raw meat and cornmeal. The prisoners were required to do their own cooking.

The commanding officer at Cahaba Prison was Capt. H. A. M. Henderson. He was a Methodist minister. Due to his overseeing of this prison, prisoners were treated fairly, and the death rate was extremely low in comparison to most other prison camps. Due to an increasing rate of sickness, a hospital was established at the Bell Tavern Hotel, 2 blocks away from the prison. The prevailing diseases were scurvy, dysentery, and chronic diarrhea. There were problems with lice, rats, and dysentery. However, Cahaba had access to ample medical supplies, firewood, and food. This contributed to the substantially lower death rate among Cahaba prisoners.

Aftermath:

The Union prisoners from Cahaba prison were to be transferred back to the Federal government. Their trip home ended up in a disaster. It became known as the "Sultana Disaster".

In the early morning hours of April 27, 1865, the steamboat Sultana exploded on the Mississippi River near Memphis, Tennessee. The Sultana was crowded with former Union prisoners-of-war from

Cahaba Prison and was carrying over 2,000 people. Of these, 1,500 or more were killed either by the explosion, the subsequent fire, or drowning.

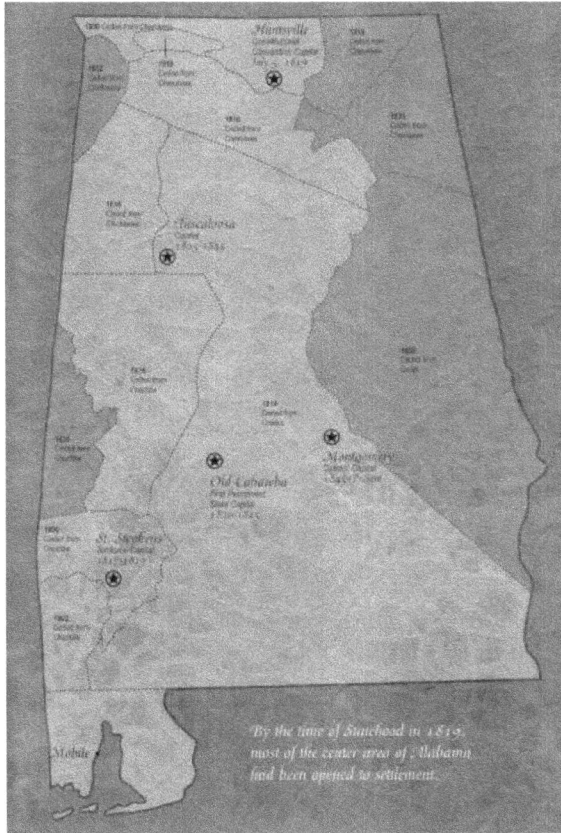

Cahaba letter (Submitted by Jim Sause)

Description Confederacy, Castle Morgan, Cahaba Ala., oatmeal paper Prisoner cover bearing U.S. 1861 3¢ rose tied by grid cancels, addressed to Lieut. Wilkins, 17th Ill. Vol. Inf. at Vicksburg Miss., matching "Old Point Comfort Va. Apr 18" dcds, endorsed "By flag of truce", original one-page letter datelined "Cahaba Military Prison, Cahaba, Ala. March 12 64" from Lieut. E.E. Ryan of same unit as addressee his cover shows no Confederate postal markings and was either hand carried to the Old Point Comfort, Va. transfer point, perhaps by another POW being exchanged or released, or sent inside another envelope franked with Confederate postage, the outer envelope being discarded at the transfer point. The Confederate Military Prison at Cahaba was also known as Castle Morgan. This is a little-known prison but was actually more crowded and congested than Andersonville. Lt. Ryan was captured as a POW while leading a foraging party near Meridian, Miss. on Feb. 15, 1864. He was first confined at Cahaba Military Prison and was later transferred to Camp Oglethorpe with a brief stop through Andersonville. He was subsequently transferred to Savannah and then Charleston where he was under the fire of the Union bombardment of the city as a POW. He survived and was exchanged in September 1864. During his time as POW, Lt. Ryan kept a detailed diary that was later published. Accompanying this letter is a lengthy article entitled "Cahaba to Charleston: The Prison Odyssey of Lt. Edmund Ryan.". The letter is written on a small piece of lined notebook paper and says, in part, "Lieut. Wilkins, I cannot depict to you the horror of being closely confined in prison day after day and week after week. We have one consolation and that is that we are well treated by the officers of the prison."

Photos

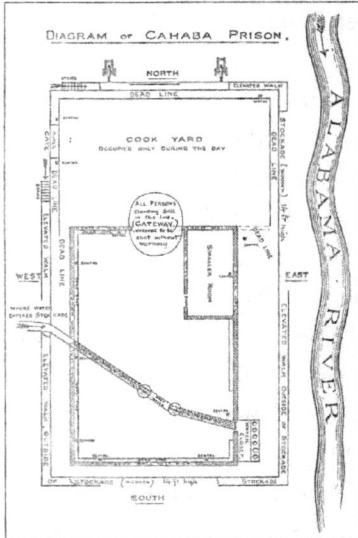

Cahaba Prison

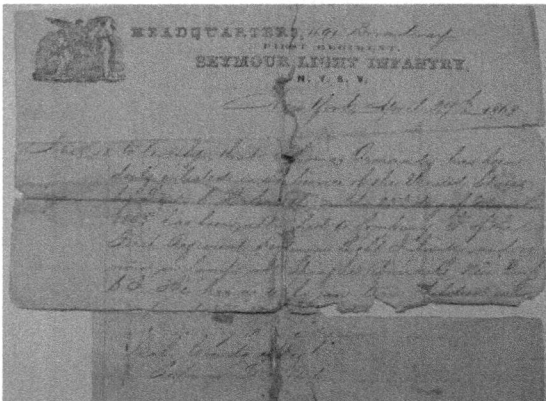

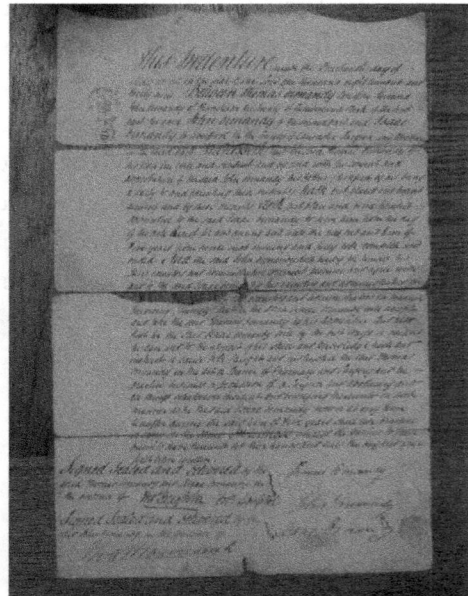

Military Papers – Sign up   His Indenture Papers

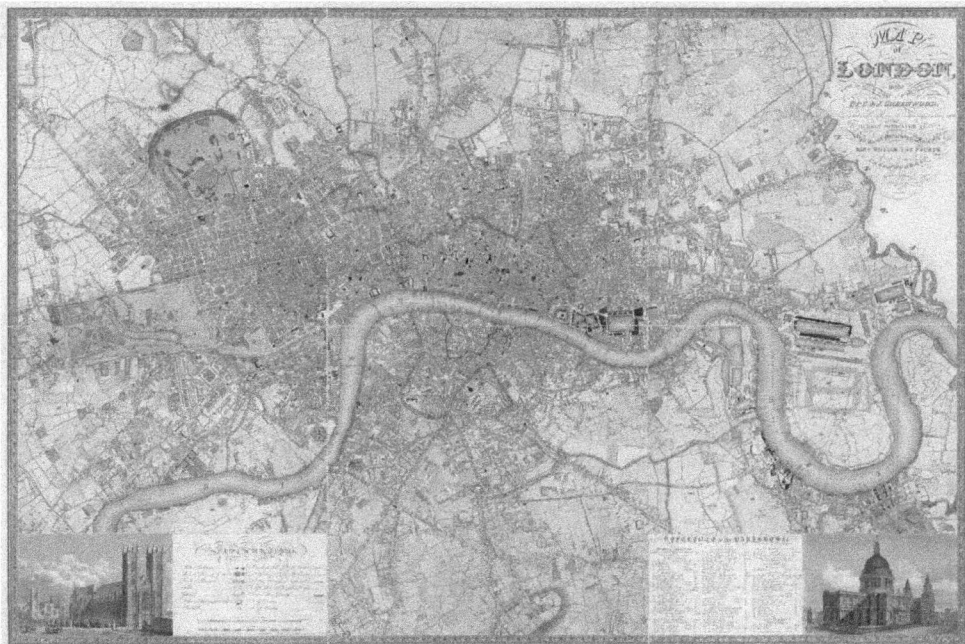

Seventh Generation William Ormandy Timeline 1847-1893

Year	Rulers	World History	U.S. History	Science/Technology	Art
	Ormandy Family 1635-2020				
			Wisconsin 1848		
			California 1850		Karl Marx
1850	Louis Napolean III - Fr. 1852	Crimean War 1853-56	Minnesota 1858	Jeans 1850	Realism
	Pres. Franklin Pierce 1853	Britain/China 1856	Oregon 1859	Pasteurisation 1856	*Scarlet Letter 1850*
	Pres. J. Buchanan 1857			Smith & Wesson 1854	*Moby Dick 1851*
	Alexander II - Rus. 1855			Darwin 1859	*Walden 1854*
			Kansas 1861		*Leaves of Grass 1855*
1860	Pres. Abraham Lincoln 1861	U.S. Civil War 1861-65	U.S. Civil War 1861-65	Dynamite 1867	
			West Virginia 1863		*War & Peace 1865*
			Emancipation Proc. 1863		
			Nevada 1864		Dostoevsky
			Navajo Long Walk 1864-68		
			Lincoln Assassinated 1865		
			South Reconstruction 1865		
			Nebraska 1867		
	Pres. Lincoln & Johnson 1865			Tungsten Steel 1868	
	Pres. Ulysses S. Grant 1869		Brooklyn Bridge 1872	Suez Canal 1869	
1870		Franco-Prussian War	Colorado 1876	Color Photo 1873	Impressionism 1874
	Pres. R. Hayes 1877	Unification of Germany	Little Big Horn 1876	Telephone 1876	Lewis Carroll
	Amadeo I - Sp. 1870	Russo-Turkish War ends	Danish, Icelandic,		Wagner
	Pres. Diaz -Mex.	War in Pacific 1879	Norwegian, Swedish	Record Player 1877	Gilbert & Sullivan
	Alfonso XII - Sp. 1874	Triple Alliance 1882	Migration	Light Bulb 1879	
1880			North Dakota 1889		1st US Film 1889
	Alexander III - Rus. 1881		South Dakota 1889	Freud 1899	
			Montana 1889	Rabies Vaccine 1885	
	Pres. Garfield & Arthur 1881		Washington 1889	1st Motion Picture	
	Pres. G. Cleveland 1885			Camera 1889	
	Alfonso XIII - Sp. 1886				
	Pres. B. Harrison 1889		Wyoming 1890	CP Railway opens 1885	
1890	Pres. G. Cleveland 1893	Chili Civil War 1891	Utah 1896	Telegraph 1895	*Time Machine 1895*
	Nicholas II - Rus. 1894	Modern Olympics 1896	Wounded Knee 1890	X-Rays Discovered 1895	
	Pres. W. McKinley 1897	Spanish/American 1898		Radium/Polonium	
			Eastern Europe, Italian	Discovered 1898	
1900	Pres. McKinley & Roosevelt 1901	Titanic Sinks 1912	Migration	1st Airplane 1903	Expressionism

(Vertical label spanning rows 1860–1880: William Ormandy 1847-1893)

Seventh Generation
William Ormandy Timeline 1847-1893

William Lewithwaite ORMANDY a clerk, was born on 26 Oct 1847 in London, England, died on 1 Apr 1893 in Mt. Zion, Oregon at age 45, and was buried in 1893 in Portland, Multnomah, Oregon, USA. William married **Mary Ann HUSTON**, on 24 Dec 1873 in New York, New York, USA. Mary was born on 18 Feb 1845 in Londonderry, Northern Ireland, died on 17 Sep 1919 in Portland, Multnomah, Oregon, USA at age 74, and was buried on 19 Sep 1919 in Portland, Multnomah, Oregon, USA. **Children:** Harrison, William, **James,** Esther, Walter.

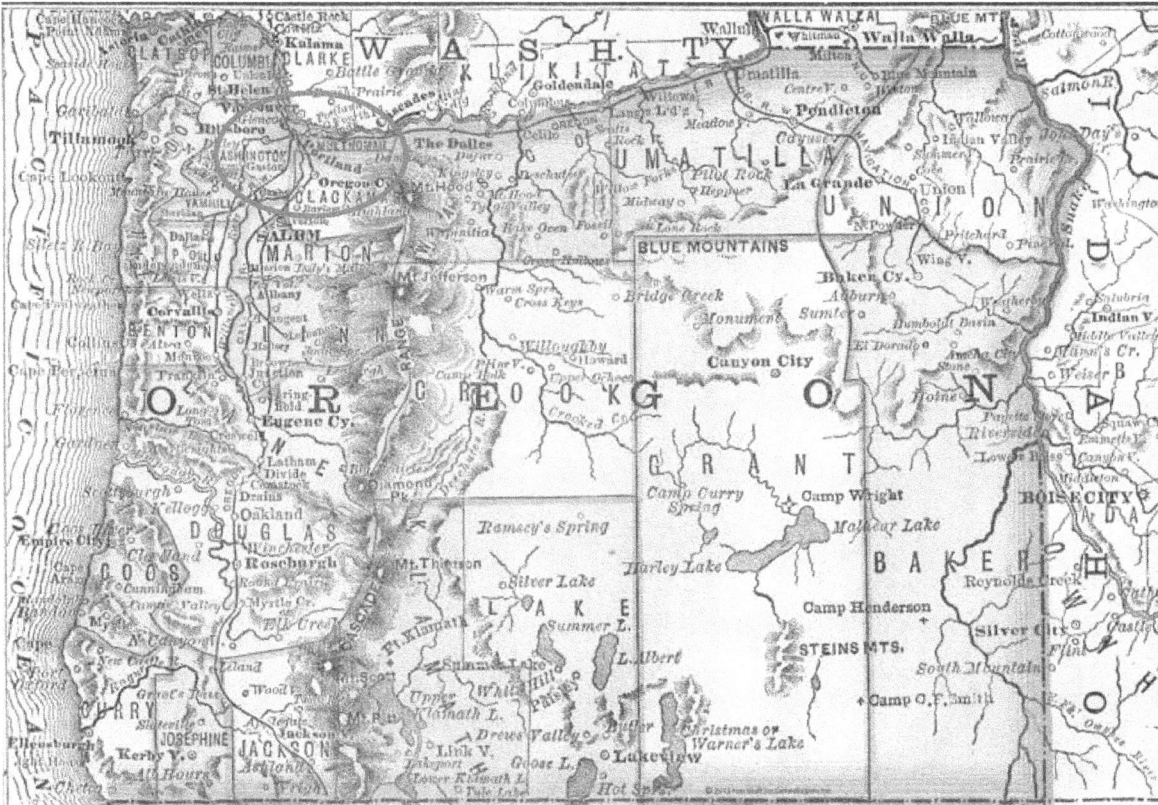

Photos

Headstone

Naturalization Papers

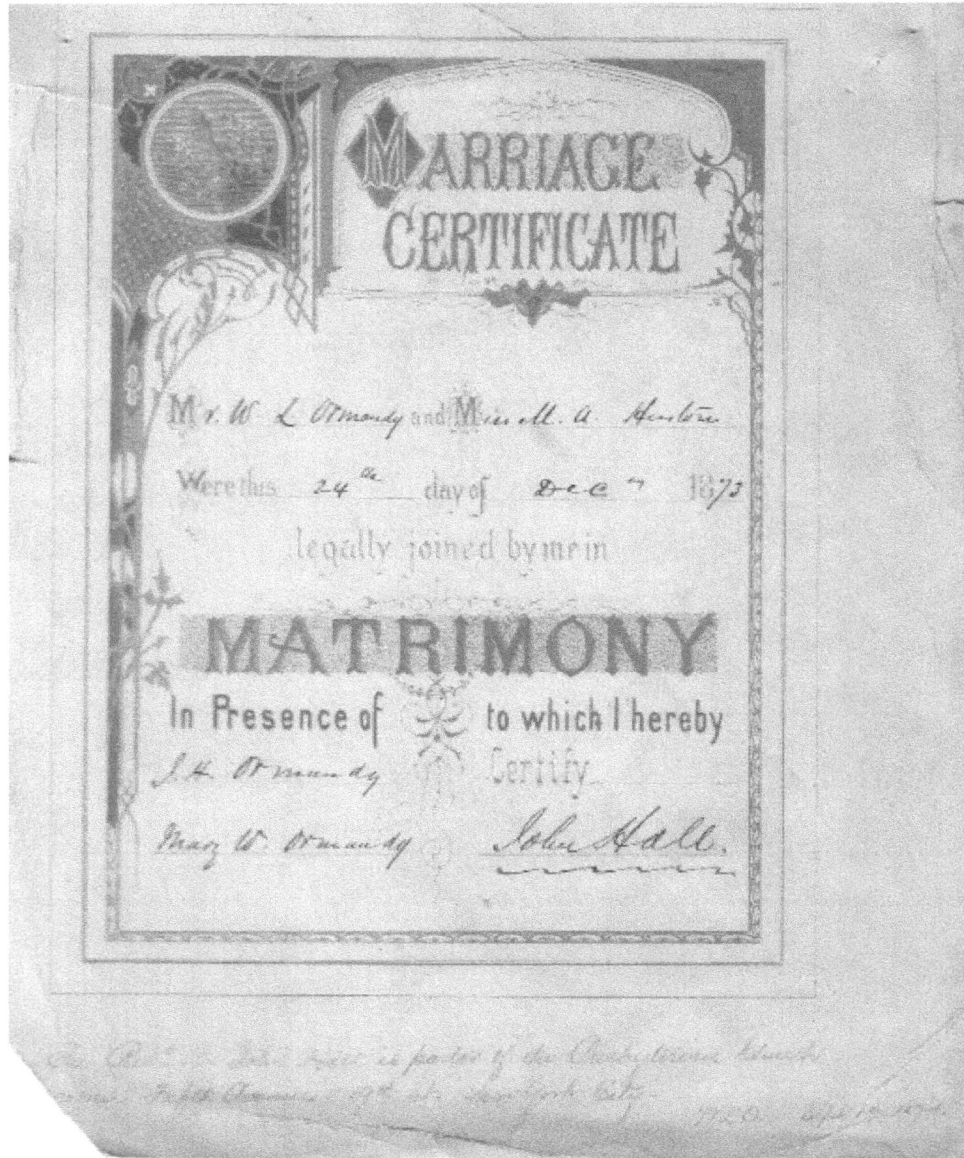

Eighth Generation James Alma Ormandy
Timeline 1879-1958

	Ormandy Family 1635-2020				
Year	**Rulers**	**World History**	**U.S. History**	**Science/Technology**	**Art**
	Alfonso XII - Sp. 1874	Triple Alliance 1882	Migration	Light Bulb 1879	
1880			North Dakota 1889		1st US Film 1889
	Alexander III - Rus. 1881		South Dakota 1889	Freud 1899	
			Montana 1889	Rabies Vaccine 1885	
	Pres. Garfield & Arthur 1881		Washington 1889	1st Motion Picture	
	Pres. G. Cleveland 1885			Camera 1889	
	Alfonso XIII - Sp. 1886				
	Pres. B. Harrison 1889		Wyoming 1890	CP Railway opens 1885	
1890	Pres. G. Cleveland 1893	Chili Civil War 1891	Utah 1896	Telegraph 1895	*Time Machine* 1895
	Nicholas II - Rus. 1894	Modern Olympics 1896	Wounded Knee 1890	X-Rays Discovered 1895	
	Pres. W. McKinley 1897	Spanish/American 1898		Radium/Polonium	
			Eastern Europe, Italian	Discovered 1898	
1900	Pres. McKinley & Roosevelt 1901	Titanic Sinks 1912	Migration	1st Airplane 1903	Expressionism
	Pres. T. Roosevelt 1905	Boxer Rebellion 1900	Tribes become US Cit. 1901		Cubism 1907
	Edward VII -Eng. 1901	Russo/Japanese War	McKinley Assassinated 1901		Jack London
	Ferdinand of Bulgaria 1908	Russia Revolution	Forest Conservation 1902		
		Young Turk Revolution	NAACP 1909		
			Oklahoma 1907		
	Pres. William Taft 1909		New Mexico 1912		
1910	Pres. Woodrow Wilson 1913	World War I 1914	Arizona 1912	Theory of Relativity 1916	Stravinsky
	George V - Eng. 1910		Select. Service Draft 1917		
			18th Ammend. No Alcohol		
1920	Mussolini - Italy 1922	Hague Court 1920	19th Ammend. Women Vote		James Joyce
	Pres. C. Coolidge 1925	Spain Dictatorship			T.S. Eliot
		Stalin Expands Russia	Stock Market Crash 1929		Disney 1st Cartoon 1924
	Pres. Herbert Hoover 1929		New Deal 1933		Surrealism 1924
1930	Pres. F. D. Roosevelt 1933	World War II 1939		Plastics 1937	Hitchcock
	Edward VIII - Eng. 1936				
	George VI - Eng. 1936		Social Security 1935		
	Hitler - Germany 1933	Spain Civil War	Marshall Plan 1947		Faulkner
1940	Pres. Roosevelt & Truman 1945	United Nations 1945		Radar 1940	Hemmingway
	Pres. Harry S. Truman 1949	A-Bomb of Japan 1945		Transistor 1948	Sartre
	Gandhi Assass. 1948	NATO 1949			Jazz
		India Freedom 1947	Asian Migration		
1950	Charles de Gaulle France 1958	Korean War 1950	Blacks Boycott Buses 1955	Sputnik - 1957	Abstract Expressionism
	Elizabeth II - Eng. 1952	Argentine Military 1955	School Segregation 1955	H Bomb 1951	
			Alaska 1959	DNA 1953	
	Pres. D. Eisenhower 1953		Hawaii 1959		
	Khrushchev - Russia		Peace Corps 1961		
1960	Pres. Kennedy & Johnson 1961/63	Vietnam War 1964	Civil Rights Move. 1960-65	Laser 1960	Pop Art

(Left margin vertical label: James Ormandy 1879-1958)

Eighth Generation
James Alma Ormandy 1879-1958

James Alma ORMANDY was born on 12 Nov 1879 in Pleasant Valley, Pawnee, Kansas, USA, was christened on 5 Jun 1881, died on 12 Sep 1958 in Portland, Multnomah, Oregon, USA at age 78, and was buried on 14 Sep 1958 in Riverview Cemetery, Portland, Oregon. James married **Edith Frances STEPHENSON**, daughter of **Franklin David STEPHENSON** and **Lucile Adelaide SMOOT** on 14 Mar 1925 in Portland, Multnomah, Oregon, USA. Edith was born on 19 Jun 1899 in Walla Walla, Walla Walla, Washington, USA, died on 14 Jul 1989 in Portland, Multnomah, Oregon, USA at age 90, and was buried in Riverview Cemetery, Portland, Oregon. **Children:** Francis, **Janet.**

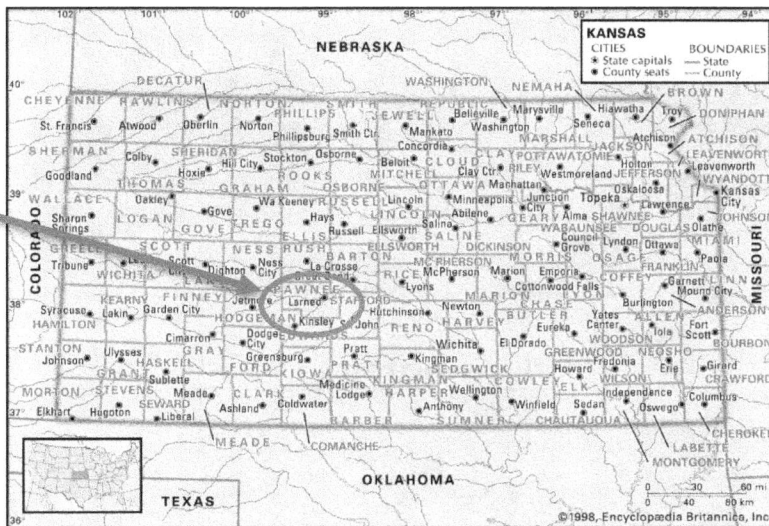

"Ormandy, Former SP Passenger Agent, Dies"

James A. Ormandy, general passenger agent for the Southern Pacific railroad in Portland from 1923 to 1949, died at Emanuel hospital Saturday night.

He was 78. Born in Larned, Kansas, Ormandy came to Portland as a boy and attended the Harrison Street grammar institute. His first job was as a Western Union Messenger, delivering telegrams at 2 cents each.

With experience in telegraphy picked up as a Western Union boy, Ormandy began his railroad career at 17.

Ormandy was a former president of the Oregon Advertising club, a member of the board of directors of the Portland Chamber of Commerce and Rose Festival, an honorary member of the Portland Passenger Assoc., and a member of the Arlington club, Shrine and Masonic lodge.

He is survived by his wife, Edith of 117 NW Trinity Pl.; two daughters, Mrs. Janet Marshall of Chicago, and Mrs. Frances Ann Coffield of Newberg; a sister, Alice Ormandy and a brother, Walter, both of Portland, and eight grandchildren.

The service will be at 11 am Tuesday in the chapel of Trinity Episcopal Church.

Photos

Jim Ormandy

Jim Ormandy Family

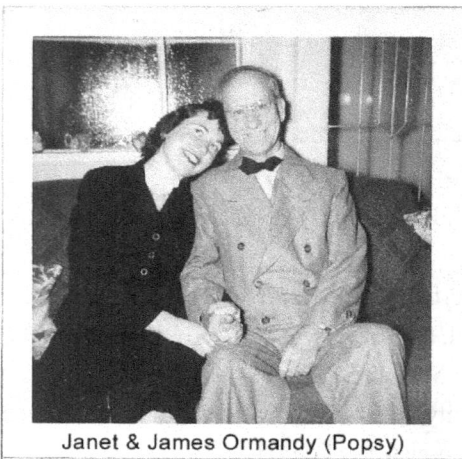

Janet & James Ormandy (Popsy)

Washington

In the Name of the Father, and of the Son, and of the Holy Ghost. Amen.

We do Certify: That, after the example of the Holy Apostles, and in accordance with the universal practice of the Holy Catholic Church, by the laying on of our hands, we did administer

to _____ *Edith Ormandy* _____

—THE SACRAMENTAL RITE OF—

CONFIRMATION

wherein were conveyed the SEVENFOLD GIFTS of the HOLY SPIRIT, which administration

was upon ___ *Sunday, March thirty-first* ___ 19 ⁵⁷

in ___ *Trinity Episcopal* ___ Church, *Portland* ___ Oregon

RT. REV. _____
                          Bishop

Presented by the Rev. _____

In the Name of the Father, and of the Son, and of the Holy Ghost. Amen.

We do Certify: That, after the example of the Holy Apostles, and in accordance with the universal practice of the Holy Catholic Church, by the laying on of our hands, we did administer

to _____ *James A. Ormandy* _____

—THE SACRAMENTAL RITE OF—

CONFIRMATION

wherein were conveyed the SEVENFOLD GIFTS of the HOLY SPIRIT, which administration

was upon ___ *Sunday, March thirty-first* ___ 19 ⁵⁷

in ___ *Trinity Episcopal* ___ Church, *Portland* ___ Oregon

RT. REV. _____
                          Bishop

Presented by the Rev. _____

4 A   Oregon Journal MONDAY, SEPT. 15, 1958

Ormandy, Former SP Passenger Agent, Dies

James A. Ormandy, general passenger agent for the Southern Pacific railroad in Portland from 1923 to 1949, died at Emanuel hospital Saturday night. He was 78.

Born in Larned, Kas., Ormandy came to Portland as a boy and attended the Harrison Street grammar institute. His first job was as a Western Union messenger, delivering telegrams at 2 cents each.

With experience in telegraphy picked up as a Western Union boy, Ormandy began his railroad career at 17.

ORMANDY was a former president of the Oregon Advertising club, a member of the board of directors of the Portland Chamber of Commerce and Rose Festival, an honorary member of the Portland Passenger Assn. and a member of the Arlington club, Shrine and Masonic lodge.

He is survived by his wife, Edith of 117 NW Trinity pl.; two daughters, Mrs. Janet Marshall of Chicago and Mrs. Frances Ann Coffield of Newberg; a sister, Alice Ormandy, and a brother, Walter, both of Portland, and eight grandchildren.

J. P. Finley & Son mortuary is in charge of the funeral arrangements. The service will be at 11 a. m. Tuesday in the chapel of Trinity Episcopal church.

Obituary for James Ormandy

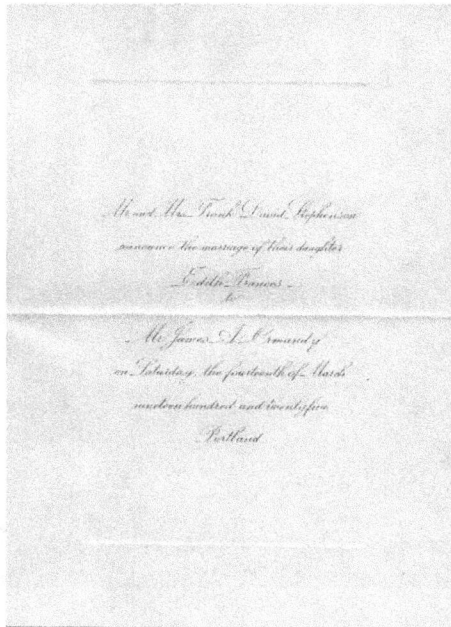

Marriage Announcement

Ninth Generation Janet Alma Ormandy Timeline 1928-2000

		Ormandy Family 1635-2020				
Year		**Rulers**	**World History**	**U.S. History**	**Science/Technology**	**Art**
1920		Mussolini - Italy 1922	Hague Court 1920	19th Ammend. Women Vote		James Joyce
		Pres. C. Coolidge 1925	Spain Dictatorship			T.S. Eliot
			Stalin Expands Russia	Stock Market Crash 1929		Disney 1st Cartoon 1924
		Pres. Herbert Hoover 1929		New Deal 1933		Surrealism 1924
1930		Pres. F. D. Roosevelt 1933	World War II 1939		Plastics 1937	Hitchcock
		Edward VIII - Eng. 1936				
		George VI - Eng. 1936		Social Security 1935		
		Hitler - Germany 1933	Spain Civil War	Marshall Plan 1947		Faulkner
1940		Pres. Roosevelt & Truman 1945	United Nations 1945		Radar 1940	Hemmingway
		Pres. Harry S. Truman 1949	A-Bomb of Japan 1945		Transistor 1948	Sartre
		Gandhi Assass. 1948	NATO 1949			Jazz
			India Freedom 1947	Asian Migration		
1950		Charles de Gaulle France 1958	Korean War 1950	Blacks Boycott Buses 1955	Sputnik - 1957	Abstract Expressionism
	Janet (Ormandy) Marshall 1928-2000	Elizabeth II - Eng. 1952	Argentine Military 1955	School Segregation 1955	H Bomb 1951	
				Alaska 1959	DNA 1953	
		Pres. D. Eisenhower 1953		Hawaii 1959		
		Khrushchev - Russia		Peace Corps 1961		
1960		Pres. Kennedy & Johnson 1961/63	Vietnam War 1964	Civil Rights Move. 1960-65	Laser 1960	Pop Art
		Pres. L. Johnson 1965	Brazil Military 1964	Kennedy Assass. 1963		Bob Dylan
		Pres. Richard Nixon 1969		Anti War Dem. 1965-70		Beatles
		Brezhnev - Russia 1964				1968 Movie *2001*
				Hippies 1966-69	US -Moon Landing 1969	
				Many Cultures Migration		
1970		Juan Carlos- Sp. 1975		War Powers Act 1973	Personal Computer 1978	Post Modern
		Pres. Nixon & Ford 1973/74		Nixon Resigns 1973-74	Viking I & II on Mars	Solzhenitsyn
		Pres. Jimmy Carter 1977		Wounded Knee 1973		*Star Wars 1977*
				Feminism 1970's		Punk Rock
				War on Drugs 1980's		
1980		Pres. Ronald Reagan 1981	Berlin Wall Down 1989		CD, VCR & Cable	Rap
		Pres. George Bush 1989		Welfare Reform 1996	Ozone Hole 1987	
1990		Pres. W. Clinton 1993	Gulf War 1991	Land on Mars 1997	World Wide Web 1993	
			Soviet Union Breakup 1991	Inter. Space Station 1998		
			Cold War Over	Longest Robust Economy 1997		
			Germany United 1990			
2000		Pres. G. W. Bush 2001	War on Terror 9/11/2001		Animals Cloned 2000	

Ninth Generation
Janet Alma Ormandy 1928-2000

Janet Alma ORMANDY was born on 20 Feb 1928 in Portland, Multnomah, Oregon, USA, was christened in Feb 1947 in Corvallis, Benton, Oregon, USA, died on 7 Mar 2000 in Portland, Multnomah, Oregon, USA at age 72, and was buried in Portland, Multnomah, Oregon, USA. Janet married **Dr. Frederick James MARSHALL**, son of **Leslie Frederick MARSHALL** and **Robertha Josephine WATT** on 21 Aug 1948 in Portland, Multnomah, Oregon, USA. Frederick was born on 11 Feb 1925 in Vancouver, British Columbia, Canada, was christened on 12 Apr 1925 in Vancouver, B.C., Canada, died on 24 Jan 2008 in Portland, Multnomah, Oregon, USA at age 82, and was cremated on 23 Feb 2008 in Portland, Multnomah, Oregon, USA. **Children:** Barbara, **Nancy**, Gordon, Stephen.

Janet Marshall

Known as "Muzzy2" by grandchildren/great-grandchildren and the "outlaws", (Art, Michael, Connie and Karla). "Muzzy I" was Jan's grandmother's name instead of grandma. She was a teacher in her early married life.

Christmas Day, 1934 - At Portland, Oregon

To Mr. St. Nick Santa Claus-

The Santa Claus Angel records herein the doings of one little girl. Her name as given to her by her worthy parents is Janet Ormandy - sometimes called Janety Panety the Pooleykobook.

Princess Janet had one high adventure. Tis meat you should know of it Dear Santa. It happened in thus wise. The month was September - just when the heat of summer turns toward the cool blasts of winter and all things stand betwix and between so to speak. The place was the Indian Reservation and the horse was that beast called Old Blue. And the hills and canyons of the Warm Springs river still resound with the War Hoops of this tiny maid as she dashed hither and yon on the hurricane deck of the Blue nag.

Janet has treated her dog Princess with forthought and consideration; tho her Mother and Father have not always been treated so gently.

But when it comes to book learning the little Princess hath done exceedingly well. The Dutch Twins with the adventures of Kit and Kat are as past time and figures and Indian myths have passed without struggle. Of course sometimes she must stand in a corner to think things over and to see Ted daily that's not to be thought of.

Me thinks Santa Claus might well admonish the little maid to quarrel the less with the big sister and look to it that she minds her saintly mother and her devoted Mary.

When this has been done me thinks she should have her presents and wishes with a big kiss on each rosy red cheek for many, many Christmases as happy and free from care; and that light hearted she may go tripping through life bringing happiness to all around her.

-The Recording Angel-

Janet Ormandy Marshall -Obit

Janet Ormandy Marshall died March 7, 2000, surrounded by her loved ones.

She was born in Portland February 20, 1928 the second daughter of James and Edith Ormandy. She met her husband F. James Marshall (Jim) fifty-four years ago. He had come to Portland from Vancouver, Canada, to attend dental school after the war. His mother, Bertha and her mother, Edith who had been Camp Fire Girls together 30 years earlier, arranged a blind date. Jan said "yes" to a marriage proposal six weeks later.

After they married in 1948, she attended night school to complete her degree from Oregon State University and graduated in 1949 with a degree in Home Economics. Jan was Mrs. "Marshmallow" to her students when she taught kindergarten for a year to put Jim through his last year at dental school. She is a lifelong alum of the Gamma Phi Beta Sorority.

Jan and Jim raised four children while living in Vancouver, B.C., Chicago, IL, Winnipeg, Manitoba, Pittsburgh, PA and Columbus, OH, before returning to Portland in 1972.

Back "home" Jan discovered the pleasures of competitive tennis and volunteered at William Temple House for eight years as a lay counselor. She acted as "den mother" to Jim's graduate students. Over the years, she soared with the birds flying in a glider and a helicopter and taking single-engine flying lessons.

The joy and wonder of Jan's life will continue through her husband of fifty-two years, Jim; daughters, Barbara and Nancy; sons Gordon and Stephen. Their spouses, Arthur, Michael, Karla and Connie; grandchildren, Leslie, Erin, Heather, Katie, Emily, Luke, Carver, Bailey and Rowan; great grandson Riley; sister, Fran Coffield; nieces, nephews, cousins and good friends too numerous to count. One of her special gifts was the ability to make everyone who came to her home feel like they were a member of the family and her friend.

There will be a memorial service Saturday, March 18th at 2:00 pm at St. Luke Lutheran Church in SW Portland. In lieu of flowers, the family requests donations to William Temple House and the American Cancer Society.

Photos

Sorority Party - center back - Janet Ormandy & Jim Marshall

Janet Ormandy

Edith, Janet, Jim Ormandy 1958

Janet Ormandy Marshall 1948

January 31, 2000 Jim & Jan Marshall - Jan died two months later.

Janet Ormandy & ?

Janet Ormandy

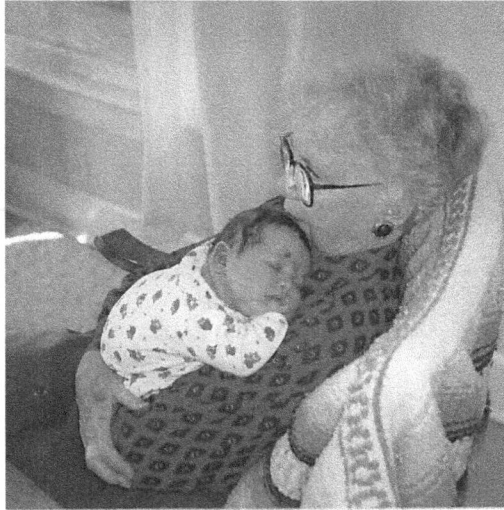

1999 - Janet (Muzzy2) Marshall and Riley Erwin

Jim & Jan Marshall 1947

Nancy, Janet, Bar, Gordon & Steve Marshall 1958

Tenth Generation Nancy Lee (Marshall) Tieman
Timeline 1952

Year	Ormandy Family 1635-2020 Rulers	World History	U.S. History	Science/Technology	Art
1950	Charles de Gaulle France 1958	Korean War 1950	Blacks Boycott Buses 1955	Sputnik - 1957	Abstract Expressionism
	Elizabeth II - Eng. 1952	Argentine Military 1955	School Segregation 1955	H Bomb 1951	
			Alaska 1959	DNA 1953	
	Pres. D. Eisenhower 1953		Hawaii 1959		
	Khrushchev - Russia		Peace Corps 1961		
1960	Pres. Kennedy & Johnson 1961/63	Vietnam War 1964	Civil Rights Move. 1960-65	Laser 1960	Pop Art
	Pres. L. Johnson 1965	Brazil Military 1964	Kennedy Assass. 1963		Bob Dylan
	Pres. Richard Nixon 1969		Anti War Dem. 1965-70		Beatles
	Brezhnev - Russia 1964				1968 Movie *2001*
			Hippies 1966-69	US -Moon Landing 1969	
			Many Cultures Migration		
1970	Juan Carlos- Sp. 1975		War Powers Act 1973	Personal Computer 1978	Post Modern
	Pres. Nixon & Ford 1973/74		Nixon Resigns 1973-74	Viking I & II on Mars	Solzhenitsyn
	Pres. Jimmy Carter 1977		Wounded Knee 1973		*Star Wars 1977*
			Feminism 1970's		Punk Rock
			War on Drugs 1980's		
1980	Pres. Ronald Reagan 1981	Berlin Wall Down 1989		CD, VCR & Cable	Rap
	Pres. George Bush 1989		Welfare Reform 1996	Ozone Hole 1987	
1990	Pres. W. Clinton 1993	Gulf War 1991	Land on Mars 1997	World Wide Web 1993	
		Soviet Union Breakup 1991	Inter. Space Station 1998		
		Cold War Over	Longest Robust Economy 1997		
		Germany United 1990			
2000	Pres. G. W. Bush 2001	War on Terror 9/11/2001		Animals Cloned 2000	
				Drones Fight War 2004	
			Global Recession Crisis 2008/9		
	Pres. B. Obama 2009		Affordable Care Act 2010		
2010	Philip VI - Sp. 2014				David Fincher
2016	Pres. D Trump 2016				
2020	Pres. J. Biden 2021			Covid 19 World Pandemic	

Nancy (Marshall) Tieman 1952 -

Tenth Generation
Nancy Lee (Marshall) Tieman1952

Nancy Lee MARSHALL was born on 5 Mar 1952 in Vancouver, British Columbia, Canada. Nancy married **Michael LaVerne TIEMAN**, son of **Malcolm Laverne TIEMAN** and **Doris Earline MORRILL** on 16 Jun 1972 in Columbus, Franklin, Ohio, USA. Michael was born on 20 Aug 1950 in Keokuk, Lee, Iowa, USA and was christened on 31 Dec 1950 in Keokuk, Lee, Iowa, USA. **Children:** Heather, Katherine.

Dictated by Nancy in April 2019

"I was born 5 March 1952, 2nd daughter of 4 children to Jim and Jan Marshall. We lived in Vancouver, British Columbia the first 5 years of my life. After my brothers were born, we had a young woman from the unwed mother's home take care of us children.

We moved from the small house up to the boulevard before I went to pre-school. Dad decided he wanted to go back to school to get a master's degree in Dentistry so he could practice other than general practice, and we moved to Chicago, Illinois. I started kindergarten and first grade. Under the bushes in the yard I had my first kiss with a boy pronounced Hale, but his name was Hal.

Outside in our backyard in Maywood, Illinois Dad also built us a skating rink both winters we were there. The teenagers from the church across the street came and ice skated with us kids.

The summer between his two years at Northwestern University we took driving a trip to New York City to see Mum's aunt, Aunt Marion, and see a number of sights before driving back to Chicago.

The next year Dad and Mum did not have enough money for tuition, but he got a grant from the American Govt. as a Canadian and as long as he promised to work somewhere in the world as an educator for one year, he did not have to pay it back.

After he graduated, we then moved to Winnipeg, Manitoba so he could start working as a professor at the University of Manitoba's Dental School. He became the chairman of the Endodontics Department. We lived there for six years grades 2 thru grade 7 and we went to Queenstown Elementary School where every winter they built a skating rink on the school grounds with a warming hut so that we could ice skate after school and in the evening with lights on and music.

I was in Brownies and Girl Guides and moved onto the Junior High.

My sister Barbara and I went to art school once a week on Saturdays downtown Winnipeg we took the bus down and took the bus home and would stop at the Hudson Bay store waiting for our bus and go to the hat department and try on hats and giggle. During grade 7 we used to have to take the bus to another school so that we could do home economics both cooking and sewing.

Part of my education at Queenstown included doing an IQ test by myself sitting in the nurse's office with no answer on what my IQ was but my parents were told I could go to college. And then in grade 4 I was taken out of school once a week to go to a special ed class, (I figured it out as an adult) to work on spelling with a teacher that was in a wheelchair and it was the only year in my life I passed spelling. This was the beginning of the understanding that I was dyslexic and different from my siblings in how I learned and processed.

After grade 7 we moved to Pittsburg, Pennsylvania where Dad became the chairman of the Endodontics department at the Dental School at the University of Pittsburg.

In 8th grade I took the school bus to and from the Jr. High and in that fall, Mum and I went to get material for my home economics project and were in a car accident where I had a tooth knocked out and Dad came to the hospital in Pittsburg run by the nuns and he demanded to use the dental chair to put my tooth back in but they were not going to allow it because he didn't have privileges, well guess what, Dad won.

That summer we joined the community swimming pool that was just behind our house and had a fabulous time continued through 9th grade. We also went on a camping trip borrowing friends tent trailer leaving Barbara to work in Pittsburg for those summer months we were gone. We went all the way to Key West on the Florida Keys and back driving past Columbus Ohio on our way back to Pittsburg. The next year in the summer between 9th grade and 10th grade we were again on the move to Columbus Ohio so that Dad could start teaching at the Ohio State University Dental School.

Barbara and I started at Upper Arlington High School for 10th and 12th grades and we registered as students 2000 and 2001. This school did not use school buses but carpooling.

Between 10th grade and 11th grade I got to come out to the west coast to visit grandparents and cousins. I spent almost two months on the west coast and saw my grandmother Dede and her husband Freeman, went out to Newberg to visit with Auntie Fran and Uncle Bill and cousins as I had my driver's license that summer Suzie let me drive the pickup truck which was so much fun. Then up to Canada to Vancouver to be with Grannie and Pop, Uncle Bob and Auntie Jerry, Uncle Don and Auntie Diane, and Auntie Jane. Spent weeks and weeks on my grandfather's boat the Jaro, with my cousin Liese. At one point we wanted to go waterskiing with boys that had a ski boat when we were up near Seashelt, up past Powell River, but Grannie wouldn't let us go water skiing with them because she considered them the local scum. Cousin Liese now has her summer home on the island up where we were and is part of the local scum.

Had to work off that trip at $1/hr. for the ticket and by Thanksgiving after painting the stairs to the basement it turned out I had been dealing with walking pneumonia most of my trip and so I spent a number of days at home on large doses of antibiotics.

During my senior year at Upper Arlington High School I wanted to date but wasn't and my girlfriend set me up on a blind date that was an absolute disaster. I told my Mum that the movie "Bullet" with Steve McQueen was good even though it opened in a bloody scene of a murder.

I finally asked God to put the right man in my life. Soon after I was able to get a job at Buckeye Mart which was a box store, so that I could earn money for spending when I went to Europe with the Study Abroad 6 week tour for Humanities and met the man I was to be with at Buckeye Mart. Girlfriends had given me as a joke a bride's magazine and after the first date I opened up the magazine and said yup.

Then I left for Europe with the Foreign Study League for 6 weeks. We stayed in Florence and did a side trip to Rome, then on to Germany and stayed outside of Munich and toured in Germany. We studied politics and art and religion in all of the countries. Headed to France and stopped for 1 night in Nancy France and then to staying just outside of Paris and fell in love with Paris. Then on to the Netherlands and stayed halfway between Amsterdam and Rotterdam. From there we took the ferry across the English Channel and stayed an hour out of London. My parents set it up so I could spend a weekend with my Grandmother's (Grannie Bertha Watt Marshall) cousin in Cobble Kent and their son who worked at Lloyd's of London with his father. I was taken in the back way so I could look down on Lloyd's of London trading floor as women were not allowed to go in 1970. We then went sailing on the Thames and I had my first mixed drink, Gin and Tonic which I still love to this day then home. Crazy fast but wonderful.

I started at Ohio State planning to do Dental Hygiene and continued dating Michael, being very careful not to push and expect more from him as we got to know each other. Went out for New Year's Eve and told him the relationship was great the way it was and found out later he was looking for diamonds since September. He asked me sometime at the end of January what I would say if he asked me to marry him and I told him to ask.

On Valentine's Day in '71 he asked. And we were engaged, and we planned a wedding for the summer of '72.

Dual US and Canadian Citizen, 1970 became US citizen, Canadian from father, US from mother.

EDUCATION: 1994 - Portland State University, Portland, OR Master of Science in Education: Counseling. Member of Chi Sigma Iota, Counseling Academic and Professional Honor Society.

1994 - Good Samaritan Ministries, Beaverton, OR, Certificate of Christian Counseling.

1994 - National Certified Counselor

1990 - Portland State University, Portland OR, Bachelor of Science in Psychology.

1972 - Ohio State University, Columbus, OH, Graduated Dental Hygienist.

PROFESSIONAL MENTAL HEALTH THERAPIST EXPEREANCE

2007-2011 Clatsop Behavioral Healthcare, OR Children Therapist Worked with teenagers and their families, on issues of abuse, anxiety and depression.

2004-2006 Clatsop Behavioral Healthcare, OR Crisis Therapist: Conducted mental health assessments and coordinated placements for at risk patients at the two county hospitals and jail

2001-2002 Columbia River Mental Health, Vancouver, WA Children Therapist Worked in the clinic with teenagers and their families, on issues of abuse, anxiety and depression. School therapist at the Washington State School for the Blind working with behavioral problems as well as mental health issues.

1998- 1999 Columbia River Mental Health, Vancouver, WA Day Treatment Therapist Worked in a classroom setting with students that have learning disabilities as well behavior disabilities. Oregon Branch of the International Dyslexia Association, Portland, OR. Facilitator for the Adult Support Group. Arranged monthly meetings with speakers and facilitated discussions around key topics.

1997-1998 Portland State University, Portland, OR Supervisor- Counselors in training/Practicum. Observed client sessions, debriefed students and gave written assessments.

1993-1997 Good Samaritan Ministries, Beaverton, OR Counselor. Worked in a clinic setting with issues of sexual/physical abuse, depression, suicidal ideation, marriage/relationship difficulties, adoption and loss and grief problems.

1973-1993 Dental Hygienist, private practice and taught at the Oregon Health & Science University, Portland, Oregon

DNA GENETIC ANCESTRY TEST RESULTS

74% Great Britain - Primarily located in: England, Scotland, Wales Also found in: Ireland, France, Germany, Denmark, Belgium, Netherlands, Switzerland, Austria, Italy

The history of Great Britain is often told in terms of the invasions with different groups of invaders displacing the native population. The Romans, Anglo-Saxon, Vikings and Normans have all left their mark on Great Britain both politically and culturally. However, the story of Great Britain is far more complex than the traditional view of invaders displacing existing populations. In fact modern studies of British people tend to suggest the earliest populations continued to exist and adapt and absorb the new arrivals.

18% Ireland - Primarily located in: Ireland, Wales, Scotland Also found in: France, England

Ireland is in the eastern part of the North Atlantic Ocean, directly west of Great Britain. A variety of internal and external influences have shaped Ireland as we know it today. Ireland's modern cultural remains deeply rooted in the Celtic culture that spread across much of Central Europe and into the British Isles. Along with Wales, Scotland, and a handful of other isolated communities within the British Isles, Ireland remains one of the last holdouts of the ancient Celtic languages that were once spoken throughout much of Western Europe. And though closely tied to Great Britain, both geographically and historically, the Irish have fiercely maintained their unique character through the centuries.

5% Scandinavian - Primarily located in: Sweden, Norway, Denmark Also found in: Great Britain, France, Germany, Netherlands, Belgium, the Baltic States, Finland

Scandinavia is perched atop northern Europe, its natives referred to throughout history as "North Men." Separated from the main European continent by the Baltic Sea, the Scandinavians have historically been renowned seafarers. Their adventures brought them into contact with much of the rest of Europe, sometimes as feared raiders and other times as well-traveled merchants and tradesmen.

As the glaciers retreated from northern Europe, roaming groups of hunter-gatherers from southern Europe followed reindeer herds inland and marine resources along the Scandinavian coast. Neolithic farmers eventually settled the region beginning about 6,000 years ago.

The Goths, originally from southern Sweden, wandered south around the 1st century B.C., crossed the Baltic Sea, and settled in what is now eastern Germany and Poland. In 410 A.D., forced west by the invading Huns, the Goths sacked Rome, contributing to the decline and fall of the Western Roman Empire.

Photos

Nancy 1970 London, England

Graduation from Ohio State 1972

Steve, Barb, Nancy
& Gordon Marshall

1967

2006 - Michael & Nancy Tieman with grandkids
Riley Erwin, Connor & Alexis Woodward-Tieman
& Jackson Erwin

1957 - Gordon, Barbara, Nancy & Steve Marshall
with grandmother "Dede"

Nancy and Michael 2016 In Venice, Italy

Nancy & Michael
2017 Cannon Beach

Michael, Courage and Nancy
Nov 2012, Dedicating "Courage" to Nancy's Mum at OHSU

Nancy & Michael 2016 Cooking Classes in Florence, Italy

2016 new coat Florence, Italy   2015 in Cannon Beach

1970 in Columbus, Ohio   Heather, Katie and Nancy 1980

Sister Barbara and Nancy 1954

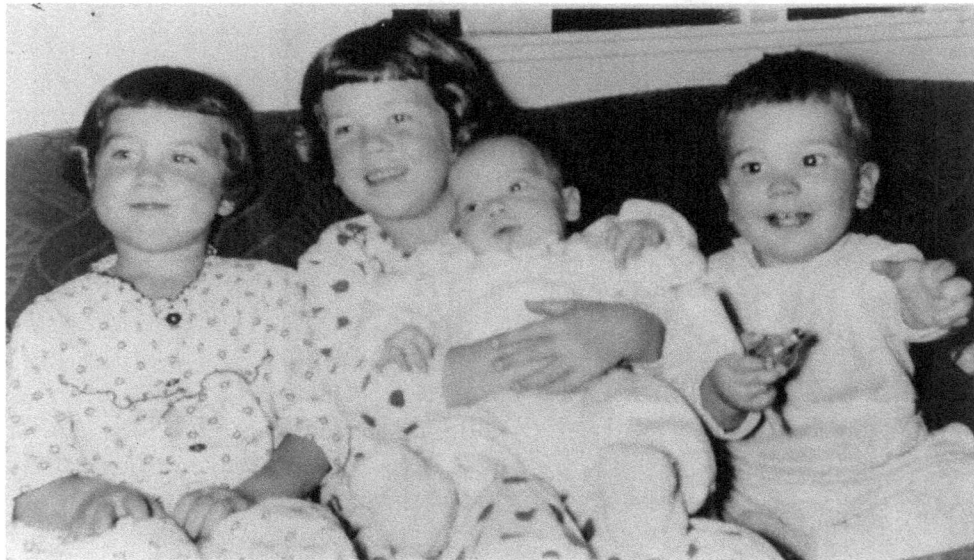

1955/56 Nancy, Barbara, Stephen and Gordon

Gordon Marshall, Edith (Dede) Stephensen, Nancy & Stephen Marshall

Nancy Marshall 1966

Barb & Nancy Marshall 1959

Jan, Nancy, Barb, Gordon, Steve Marshall 1960

Nancy Marshall H.S. Graduation 1970

Nancy Marshall 1957

June 16, 1972 Michael & Nancy Tieman

2003 - Playing at the beach with Nana.
Katie Tieman, Riley Erwin, Nancy (Nana) Tieman, Connor Tieman, Heather Erwin

June 16, 1972 Nancy & Michael Tieman are official with their parents

LaVerne and Doris Tieman, Michael & Nancy Tieman, Jan & Jim Marshall

Jim, Nancy & Barb Marshall 1952

Nancy, Katie and Heather 1979

2002 - Nancy & Michael Tieman in their front yard at Cannon Beach Oregon

11th Generation Timeline 1976

Year			Ormandy Family 1635-2020				
			Rulers	**World History**	**U.S. History**	**Science/Technology**	**Art**
1970			Juan Carlos- Sp. 1975		War Powers Act 1973	Personal Computer 1978	Post Modern
			Pres. Nixon & Ford 1973/74		Nixon Resigns 1973-74	Viking I & II on Mars	Solzhenitsyn
			Pres. Jimmy Carter 1977		Wounded Knee 1973		*Star Wars 1977*
					Feminism 1970's		Punk Rock
					War on Drugs 1980's		
1980			Pres. Ronald Reagan 1981	Berlin Wall Down 1989		CD, VCR & Cable	Rap
			Pres. George Bush 1989		Welfare Reform 1996	Ozone Hole 1987	
1990	Heather (Tieman) Erwin 1976-	Katherine Tieman 1979-	Pres. W. Clinton 1993	Gulf War 1991	Land on Mars 1997	World Wide Web 1993	
				Soviet Union Breakup 1991	Inter. Space Station 1998		
				Cold War Over	Longest Robust Economy 1997		
				Germany United 1990			
2000			Pres. G. W. Bush 2001	War on Terror 9/11/2001		Animals Cloned 2000	
						Drones Fight War 2004	
					Global Recession Crisis 2008/9		
			Pres. B. Obama 2009		Affordable Care Act 2010		
2010			Philip VI - Sp. 2014				David Fincher
2016			Pres. D Trump 2016				
2020			Pres. J. Biden 2021			Covid 19 World Pandemic	

11th Generation 1976

Heather Anne TIEMAN was born on 17 May 1976 in North Vancouver, British Columbia, Canada and was christened in 1976 in North Vancouver, British Columbia, Canada. Heather married **Phillip ERWIN**, son of **Sidney Fred ERWIN** and **Judith Lee BENSCOTER** on 22 Jun 1996 in Lake Oswego, Clackamas, Oregon, USA. Phillip was born on 30 May 1971 in Boise, Ada, Idaho, USA. **Children:** Riley, Jackson.

Katherine Jane TIEMAN was born on 25 Jun 1979 in North Vancouver, British Columbia, Canada. Katherine married **Shawn SCHULBERG**, on 4 Nov 2000 in Portland, Multnomah, Oregon, USA. The marriage ended in divorce. **Children** Connor. Katherine next married **Samuel Patrick WOODWARD**, son of **Gary Milton WOODWARD** and **(Rosa) Yung-Mei KAU** on 25 Jul 2009 in Portland, Multnomah, Oregon, USA.[187] Samuel was born on 16 Sep 1975 in T'ai-Pei, Taiwan, Rep. of China. **Children:** Alexis, Owen.

12th Generation 1999

Year	Riley Erwin 1999-	Connor Tieman 2002-	Jack Erwin 2005-	Alexis Tieman-Woodward 2006-	Owen Tieman-Woodward 2010-	Ormandy Family 1635-2020				
						Rulers	World History	U.S. History	Science/Technology	Art
1990						Pres. W. Clinton 1993	Gulf War 1991	Land on Mars 1997	World Wide Web 1993	
							Soviet Union Breakup 1991	Inter. Space Station 1998		
							Cold War Over	Longest Robust Economy 1997		
							Germany United 1990			
2000						Pres. G. W. Bush 2001	War on Terror 9/11/2001		Animals Cloned 2000	
									Drones Fight War 2004	
								Global Recession Crisis 2008/9		
						Pres. B. Obama 2009		Affordable Care Act 2010		
2010						Philip VI - Sp. 2014				David Fincher
2016						Pres. D Trump 2016				
						Pres. J. Biden 2021			Covid 19 World Pandemic	
2020										

12th Generation 1999

Riley James ERWIN was born on 27 Sep 1999 in Portland, Multnomah, Oregon, USA and was christened in 2000 in Portland, Multnomah, Oregon, USA. **Children: Justin**

Jackson Davis ERWIN was born on 26 Jul 2005 in Portland, Multnomah, Oregon, USA and was christened in Oct 2005 in Portland, Multnomah, Oregon, USA.

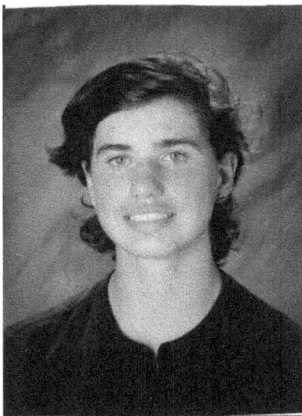

Connor Shamas TIEMAN-WOODWARD was born on 28 Oct 2002 in Portland, Multnomah, Oregon, USA.

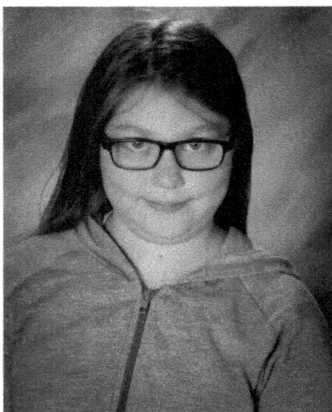

Alexis Jean TIEMAN-WOODWARD was born on 12 Nov 2006 in Portland, Multnomah, Oregon, USA.

Owen Richard TIEMAN-WOODWARD was born on 18 Feb 2010 in Portland, Multnomah, Oregon, USA.

13th Generation 2020

Year		Ormandy Family 1635-2020				
		Rulers	World History	U.S. History	Science/Technology	Art
2016		Pres. D Trump 2016				
2020	Justin Sebers Erwin 2020 -	Pres. J. Biden 2021			Covid 19 World Pandemic	

13th Generation 2020

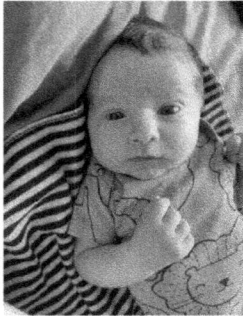

Justin Arthur SEBERS-ERWIN was born on 30 Aug 2020 in Stanwood, Washington, USA to **Riley James ERWIN** and **Ashley SEBERS.**

Source Citations

1. O653-29 Ormandy/Miliss Tree.
2. O653-47 Richard Ormandy 1635 - Marriage - Parish Records.
3. HY-0001 Brighton in Furness, Lancashire, England - History.
4. MP-0001 Millom, England 1805 - Map.
5. MP-0009 Cumberland, England 1646 - Map.
6. MP-0010 England 1598 - Map.
7. MP-0011 Cumberland, England 1607 - Map.
8. O653-8 Hauptman's Family Tree (Name: Michael A. Hauptman;).
9. O653-44 Thomas Ormandy 1717 - Baptism - Parish Records.
10. HY-0002 Millom, Cumberland, England - History.
11. O653-43 Bridget Ormandy - Burial - Parish Records.
12. O653-6 Corres. of Ormandy/Wilkinson Line. Jim M. Sause
13. O653-31 T. Ormandy 1749- England Select Births & Christenings 1538-1975, FHL Film Number: 0844819IT2.
14. O653-45 Thomas Ormandy/Jane Stanley Marriage - Parish Records.
15. O653-46 Thomas Ormandy 1717 - Burial - Parish Records.
16. O653-48 Thomas Ormandy/Stanley Lancashire, England, Extracted Parish Records.
17. "O653-50 Tombstone - Thomas & Dorothy Ormandy," database.
18. "O653-51 Land Deed - Thomas Ormandy," database.
19. O653-33 T. Ormandy/Boulton 1785 Marriage Register.
20. O653-32 T. Ormandy 1749- England Select Death & Burials 1538-1991, FHL Film Number: 1040315.
21. O653-30 T. Ormandy 1749- Lancashire England Extracted Parish Records, Parish Register, 1634-1812.
22. O635-40 John Ormandy 1792- Baptism - Parish Records.
23. O635-41 Thomas Ormandy/Dorothy Bolton - Marriage - Parish Records.
24. O653-42 Dorothy Ormandy - Burial - Parish Records.
25. England Select Births & Christenings, 1538-1975, William A. Ormandy (N.p.: n.p., n.d.).
26. Burials 1750 - 1800 from the Bishop's Transcripts, Page 66, Entry 11 Ormandy William A (N.p.: n.p., n.d.).
27. Baptisms 1673 - 1796, Page 69, Entry 8 William A Ormandy b1751 (N.p.: n.p., n.d.).
28. England Select Deaths & Burials 1538-1991 Jane Ormandy d1753 (N.p.: n.p., n.d.).
29. England Select Deaths & Burials 1538-1991 Richard Ormandy d1817 (N.p.: n.p., n.d.).
30. Ormandy, Joseph 1834 Burial Record (N.p.: n.p., n.d.).
31. England & Wales Marriage Records 1538-1988, Ormandy, Joseph Marriage Record (N.p.: n.p., n.d.).
32. England & Wales Marriages 1538-1988 James Ormandy (N.p.: n.p., n.d.).
33. Burials 1827 - 1831 from the Bishop's Transcripts, Entry 1080 James Ormandy (N.p.: n.p., n.d.).
34. Marriages 1750-1780 from the Bishop's Transcripts, Page 31, Entry 19 James Ormandy (N.p.: n.p., n.d.).

35. Baptisms 1673 - 1796, Page 71, Entry 7 James Ormandy b1753 (N.p.: n.p., n.d.).

36. England Select Births & Christenings 1538-1975 Anne Ormandy b1745 (N.p.: n.p., n.d.).

37. O653-10 England & Wales Census, 1841, John Ormandy.

38. Marriages 1813 - 1825 from the Bishop's Transcripts, Page 32, Entry 95 Ormandy, William 1788 (N.p.: n.p., n.d.).

39. Burials 1821 - 1877 from the Bishop's Transcripts, Page 57 & 58, Entry 459 William Ormand (N.p.: n.p., n.d.).

40. 1851 census of England Ormandy, William b1788; PRO HO 107.

41. UK & Ireland Find A Grave 1300's - Current William Ormandy d1856.

42. English & Wales National Probate Calendar, 1858-1995, Joseph Ormandy 1860 (N.p.: n.p., n.d.).

43. England, Select Births & Christenings, 1538-1975 Joseph Ormandy 1790 (N.p.: n.p., n.d.).

44. 1841 census of England Ormandy, Joseph; PRO HO 107.

45. England, Select Marriages, 1538-1973 John Ormandy m1819 (N.p.: n.p., n.d.).

46. O653-9 England & Wales Census 1851, John Ormandy.

47. O653-11 England Births & Christenings, 1538-1975, Thomas Ormandy, Indexing Project #- C05832-1 System Orgin - England-ODM Film #-90668.

48. O653-5 Corres. of Sir John Ormandy. Unknown

49. O653-18 Rev. John Ormandy Death Certificate Index.

50. O653-19 Bulmer's History and Directory Of Cumberland 1901.

51. O653-35 Juliana Ormandy - Baptism - Parish Records.

52. O653-36 John Ormandy 1828 - Baptism- Parish Records.

53. O653-38 Rev. John Ormandy - Burial - Parish Records.

54. O635-39 Mary Ormandy - Burial - Parish Records.

55. England Select Births & Christening 1538-1975 James Ormandy 1778 (N.p.: n.p., n.d.).

56. England Select Births & Christenings, 1538-1975 Thomas Ormandy 1796 (N.p.: n.p., n.d.).

57. Ormandy_George_1851Census; PRO HO 107.

58. 1841 census of England Ormandy, Isaac; PRO HO 107.

59. Ormandy, Isaac Marriage Record.

60. Ormandy Isaac 1851 census of England; PRO HO 107.

61. Liverpool, England, Church of England Marriages and Banns, 1754-1932 Ormandy, Dorothy (N.p.: n.p., n.d.).

62. England, Select Births and Christenings, 1538-1975 Dorothy Ormandy (N.p.: n.p., n.d.).

63. England & Wales, Civil Registration Death Index, 1837-1915 Dorothy Ormandy (N.p.: n.p., n.d.).

64. England Select Marriages 1538-1973 Mary Anne Ormandy (N.p.: n.p., n.d.).

65. England & Wales National Probate Calendar Mary Anne Ormandy (N.p.: n.p., n.d.).

66. England, Select Births and Christenings, 1538-1975 Ormandy, Mary Ann (N.p.: n.p., n.d.).

67. O653-1 William Lewthwaite Ormandy Family Bible - Original (Name: Original 1872;).

68. M624-8 Marshall Ancestry Charts.

69. O653-16 T. Ormandy War Pensions Records.

70. O653-12 Indenture - Thomas Ormandy.

71. O653-14 Civil War Enlistment Papers - T. Ormandy, Headquarters, 491, Broadway (?); First Regiment; Seymour Light Infantry; N.Y.S.V; New York, April 29th 1863.

72. O653-15 Civil War Military Records Thomas Ormandy, Ormandy, Thomas pg1581.

73. O654-49 UK Census 1861, Thomas Ormandy, Civil Parish; Ulverston; Town; Ulverston; County; Lancashire; Country: England; Ecclesiastical Parish: Holy Trinity; Registration District: Ulverston; Sub-registration District: Ulverston; Piece; 3168; Folio:71; Pages 2-3 Household Schedule #: 7.

74. O653-34 T. Ormandy 1823- Civil War Records & Profiles 1861-1865.

75. England Select Marriages 1538-1973 Julia Ormandy (N.p.: n.p., n.d.).

76. O653-37 John Ormandy 1828 - Burial - Parish Records.

77. England Select Marriages 1538-1973 Ormandy, Harrison W b1832 (N.p.: n.p., n.d.).

78. UK, Apprentices Indentured in Merchant Navy, 1824-1910 Ormandy, Harrison b1832 (N.p.: n.p., n.d.).

79. England & Wales Civil Registration Death Index 1837-1915 Ormandy, Harrison b1832 (N.p.: n.p., n.d.).

80. O653-13 Marriage Certificate - Ormandy & Huston.

81. O653-17 Ormandy/Sause Line Email.

82. O653-7 Corres. of Ormandy/Griswold Line. Ruth Neal

83. 1930 U.S. census, population schedule; digital images; citing National Archives and Records Administration microfilm T626.

84. 1940 U.S. census, population schedule; digital images; citing National Archives and Records Administration microfilm T627.

85. M624-3 Corres. Marshall Line (Name: Janet (Ormandy) Marshall;).

86. S530-1 Corres. Smoot Ancestry (Name: unknown;).

87. O653-3 Obit-James A. Ormandy (Name: Newspaper;).

88. S315-1 Birth Certificate Edith Francis Stephenson (Name: Original;).

89. S315-2 Obit Edith Stephenson Essex (Name: Newspaper;).

90. S530-2 Smoot Ancestor Chart.

91. S315-4 Corres. of Stephenson Family (Name: Gerald Stephenson; Date: 1990;).

92. O653-2 In Memory - Esther Alice Ormandy.

93. O653-4 Obit-Esther A. Ormandy (Name: Newspaper;).

94. 1940 U.S. census, population schedule; digital images; citing National Archives and Records Administration microfilm T627.

95. Oregon Death Index 1898-2008 Ormandy, Walter S (N.p.: n.p., n.d.).

96. U.S. WWII Draft Cards Young Men, 1940-1947 Ormandy, William L b1908 (N.p.: n.p., n.d.).

97. S315-20 1880 US Census Dr. AC Stephenson (N.p.: n.p., n.d.).

98. S315-5 Bureau of Pensions, Wash. D.C., Marian Stephenson Patmore (Name: photocopy;).

99. S315-3 Military Records - revolutionary Descent from Lt. Casparus Pruyn.

100. F432-1 Bureau of Pensions Report - James Fletcher - A certified copy of the bureau Bureau of Pensions National No. 86360 (Name: Bureau of Pensions; Location: Washington, D.C; Date: 1777;).

101. S530-3 Smoot Pedigree Chart - Family Search Ancestral Files, A collection of genealogical information taken from Pedigree Charts and Family Group Records submitted to the Family History Dept. since1978. Submitters: J.E. Daniel, C.E. Bauer, S.L. Smoot, Z.H. White.
102. From Individual.
103. M624-10 Marshall Family Chart (Name: Bob Marshall; Date: 2008;).
104. B600-1 Braun Family Line - 2008, Database online. Connie Braun
105. M624-38 Source from Geraldine Beverly (Nesbit) Marshall.
106. M624-43 Janet (Ormandy) Marshall Death Certif. (Intercranial Hemorrhage).
107. M624-42 F James and Janet Marshall Marriage Certif.
108. M624-9 Obit - F. James Marshall (Oregonian Newspaper; Portland, Oregon; 2008;).
109. M624-21 Baptism Certificate - Frederick James Marshall (Name: St. George's Church, Vancouver, British Columbia, Easter Day 1925;).
110. M624-22, My Glengarry Dr. F. James Marshall (Cannon Beach, OR, Michael Tieman Publishing, 2007).
111. M624-23 Interview with F. James Marshall 1998.
112. M624-39 F. James Marshall US Naturalization Papers (Columbus, OH).
113. M624-40 F James Marshall Death Certificate - Orig.
114. M624-41 F James Marshall Cert. of Birth.
115. M624-44 F James Marshall WWII Discharge Papers.
116. W300-1 Obit Bertha Watt Marshall (Name: Newspaper;).
117. M624-4 British Columbia Canada Birth Index 1872-1903 Leslie Marshall (Name: British Columbia, Vital Statistics Agency; Location: British Columbia, Canada;), Registration #: 1899-09-198639 BCA #: B13815 GSU#: 2134885.
118. M624-12 1901 Canada Census - Leslie Marshall.
119. M624-14 1919 Passenger List - Les Marshall (Name: Seattle Passenger and Crew Lists 1882-1957 - Name: Leslie F. Marshall Arrival Date: Oct 1919 Age:20 Estimated Birth Year: 1899 Birthplace: Canada Last Residence: CAN Gender: Male Race/Nationality: English Port of Arrival: Seattle, Washington Port of Departure: Vancouver, British Columbia Line# 11 Microfilm Roll# M1383_42; Location: Seatte Washington;).
120. M624-13 1911 Canada Census - Les Marshall (Name: Census of Canada 1911, Page # 29; Family# 296, Name: Leslie Marshall, Marital Status: Single, Age: 11, Birth Date: Aug 1899, Birthplace: British Columbia, Relationship to Head of House: Son, Father's Name: Fred J. Marshall, Mother's Name: Fanny Marshall; Location: Tribal: English, Province: British Columbia, District: Vancouver, District #: 12, Sub-District: Vancouver City, Sub-District #: 41, Place of Habitation: 2335 Lanel; Date: Vancouver, British Columbia, Canada1911;).
121. M624-15 British Columbia Death Index 1872-1990 - Leslie Marshall (Name: British Columbia, Canada, Death Index 1872-1990; Location: Birth Year: about 1900, Death Age: 71, Date Death: 30 Nov 1971, Death Location: Vancouver, Registration #: 1971-09-016851, BCA#: B13314, GSU#: 2034297;).
122. M624-45 Leslie Frederick Marshall Birth Certificate.
123. M624-46 Leslie Frederick Marshall Death Certificate.

124. W300-8 1920 census Bertha Watt.
125. W300-16 1901 Scotland Census Bertha Watt.
126. W300-6 Encyclopedia Titanic, Bertha Watt.
127. W300-22 Titanic Passenger List - Robertha Watt.
128. W300-23 Titanic Story written by Robertha Watt.
129. M624-47 Robertha (Watt) Marshall Death Certificate.
130. M624-1 Marriage Notice Barbara Marshall/McIntyre (Name: Newspaper; Location: Columbus, Ohio;).
131. Source From Janet O. Marshall.
132. R300-16 Arthur Roady Marriage Index.
133. Source from Barbara Jean (Marshall) Roady.
134. M624-5 Copy of Canadian Birth Certificate - Nancy Lee Marshall (Name: British Columbia Division of Vital Statistics; Location: Vancouver, British Columbia, Canada; Date: March 13, 1952;).
135. M624-6 Christening Papers - Nancy Lee Marshall.
136. M624-7 U.S. Passport - Nancy L. (Marshall) Tieman (Date: Issued 25 APR 2008;).
137. T500-16 Marriage Certificate Michael Tieman & Nancy Marshall (Name: State of Ohio;).
138. M624-20 US Certificate of Citizenship -Nancy Marshall (Name: Application # A19 583 620, Certificate # 35294; Date: Issued on 13 FEB 1974, but became a U.S. citizen on date of birth5 MAR 1952;).
139. M624-17 Nancy Marshall Wedding Announcement (Name: Newspaper; Location: Columbus, Ohio; Date: 1972;).
140. M624-18 Nancy Marshall Engagement Announcement.
141. M624-19 Registration of Live Birth - Nancy Marshall (Name: Dept. of Health & Welfare Division of Vital Statistics Victoria, BC- Certified A True Photographic Print of the Original Registration #52-09-004896; Date: 18 Mar 1952;).
142. M624-16 Certificate of Canadian Citizenship - Nancy Marshall (Name: Nancy Lee Tieman;).
143. M624-24 Nancy Marshall Ohio State Admission.
144. T500-51 Nancy (Marshall) Tieman Portland State Admittance.
145. T500-13 Copy of State of Iowa Birth Certificate, - Michael L. Tieman (Name: State of Iowa;).
146. T500-14 U.S. Passport - Michael Tieman (Name: US Government;).
147. T500-6 Marquis Who's Who In The West 1989- Michael Tieman (Name: 23rd Edition;).
148. T500-20 Verne Tieman life History (Name: Verne Tieman;).
149. T500-21 Michael Tieman Bio (Name: Michael Tieman;).
150. T500-34 Birth Registration, Michael Tieman.
151. T500-35 Canada Immigration, Michael Tieman.
152. HY-0016 Keokuk, Lee Co., Iowa - History.
153. T500-63 Michael L. Tieman Birth Announcement, Daily Gate City Newspaper, Keokuk, Iowa.
154. B600-6 1940 Federal Census, C. Braun.
155. R300-11 1920 U.S. Census Harvey A Roady.

156. R300-12 1930 U.S. Census - Arthur W. Roady.

157. R300-14 1940 U.S. Census - Arthur W. Roady.

158. T500-23 US WWII Army Enlistment Records 1938-1946, LaVerne Tieman.

159. T500-24 1930 US Census, LaVerne Tieman.

160. T500-27 Iowa Births & Christenings Index 1857-1947 - Malcolm Tieman.

161. T500-15 1930 US Census - Malcolm Tieman, April 10, 1930 - Sheet #14B, Enumeration Dist. #56-17, Supervisor's Dist. #15, Keokuk Township, Lee Co. Iowa.

162. T500-37 WWII Separation Papers, LaVerne Tieman.

163. T500-42 LaVerne Tieman Marriage Announcement.

164. S360-2 Ancestor Chart - Starr (Name: Amy Starr; Date: 1992;).

165. T500-46 LaVerne Tieman National Thespian Certif.

166. T500-44 1940 U.S. Census Malcolm Tieman, April 12, 1940, Sheet #12B, S.D.#1, E.D. 56-17, Keokuk, Lee Co. Iowa.3rd Ward.

167. T500-53 LaVerne Tieman WWII Honoree.

168. T500-50 LaVerne & Doris Tieman Marriage License.

169. T500-58 Birth Certificate (Orig) M. LaVerne Tieman, Dept of Vital Statistics, State of Iowa, County of Lee, City of Keokuk, Index # 05C-1451, Registered # 1725.

170. T500-59 Death Certificate (Orig), M. LaVerne Tieman, Ohio Dept. of Heath, Vital Statistics, Certificate of Death, Reg. Dist. # 77, Primary Reg. Dist. #7705.

171. T500-60 Military Papers, WWII, M. LaVerne Tieman, Greetings letter (Orig), Report for Induction letter (orig), Special Orders #162 (Orig), Honorable Discharge Certif.(Orig).

172. M640-20 Copy of Newspaper Death Notice - Doris E. (Morrill) Tieman (Date: 2003;).

173. T500-3 Tieman/Morrill 1989 (Name: Unknown;).

174. M640-40 Doris Morrill Birth Registration.

175. M640-41 Doris Morrill Birth Certificate.

176. M640-47 1930 United States Federal Census, Don Morrill (Name: Ancestry.com Operations Inc; Location: Provo, UT, USA; Date: 2002;). United States of America, Bureau of the Census. Fifteenth Census of the United States, 1930. Washington, D.C.: National Archives and Records Administration, 1930. T626, 2,667 rolls.

177. M640-48 1940 United States Federal Census, Don Morrill (Name: Ancestry.com Operations, Inc; Location: Provo, UT, USA; Date: 2012;). United States of America, Bureau of the Census. Sixteenth Census of the United States, 1940. Washington, D.C.: National Archives and Records Administration, 1940. T627, 4,643 rolls.

178. M640-46 Iowa, State Census Collection, 1836-1925, Don Morrill (Name: Ancestry.com Operations Inc; Location: Provo, UT, USA; Date: 2007;). Microfilm of Iowa State Censuses, 1856, 1885, 1895, 1905, 1915, 1925 as well various special censuses from 1836-1897 obtained from the State Historical Society of Iowa via Heritage Quest.

179. M640-16 Corresp. Doris (Morrill) Tieman (Name: Letter;).

180. T500-67 Doris (Morrill) Tieman Orig Death Certif.

181. M640-143 U.S., World War II Cadet Nursing Corps Card Files, 1942-1948 Doris Morrill (Name: Ancestry.com Operations, Inc; Location: Provo, UT, USA; Date: 2011;), National Archives and Records Administration; Washington, D.C; Cadet Nurse Corps Files, compiled 1943 - 1948, documenting the period 1942 -1948; Box #: 204.

182. T500-17 Copy of Canadian Birth Abroad Certificate - Heather A. Tieman.

183. Source From Nancy L. (Marshall) Tieman.

184. E300-1 Source From Book from Judy Erwin.

185. Source From Heather A. (Tieman) Erwin.

186. T500-18 Copy of Canadian Birth Abroad Certificate - Katherine J. Tieman.

187. W500-2 Marriage Certificate Sam Woodward/ Katie Tieman.

188. W500-1 Sam Woodward's family tree - Mother's side (Name: Sam's Mother, Rosa; Date: 2008;). Rosa's Chinese family history

189. T500-45 Katie Tieman Baptism Papers.

190. Source From Katherine J. Tieman.

191. B600-5 1930 Federal Census, C. Braun.

192. W600-1 1930 US Census, Nancy L. Wisecarver.

193. "W500-3 Find a Grave - Gary Woodward Family," database.

Genealogy Summary - Ormandy
First Generation

1. Richard ORMANDY [3923],[1,2,3,4,5,6,7,8] son of **ORMANDY** [5170], was born in 1635 in Broughton In Furness, Lancashire, England and died on 6 Apr 1706 in Broughton In Furness, Lancashire, England at age 71.

General Notes: Family Lore has this line going back to Sir John Ormandy Vicar of Old Church Holy Trinity (Church of England), Millom England before 1066. To date I cannot find any info on Sir John.

1st Lord of Millom Castle, Sir Richard Huddleston (c.1198-1250)
2nd Lord of Millom Castle, SIR JOHN, LORD OF MILLOM (c.1222-1252);
     m: abt.1239 Joan de Boyville

Holy Trinity Church is a medieval building situated next to Millom Castle near the town of Millom, Cumbria, England. It is an active Anglican parish church in the deanery of Furness, the archdeaconry of Westmorland and Furness, and the diocese of Carlisle. Its benefice is united with those of St George (in the centre of Millom), St Anne, Thwaites, and St Luke, Haverigg. The church is recorded in the National Heritage List for England as a designated Grade I listed building. Worship has taken place at this site for over 1000 years.

The earliest parts of the church are the nave and chancel, which date from the 12th century. The south aisle was added in the early 13th century and was rebuilt in a more elaborate style in about 1335 as the Huddlestone Chapel. Some details were restored in the 19th century and the south porch was added in 1906. More drastic alterations were carried out in 1930 by Hicks and Charlewood of Newcastle, which included making the chancel wider. During this work, and incorporated into the northeast corner of the chancel, were part of a cross-shaft dating probably from the 10th or 11th century, and another ancient boss. Also at this time a west gallery was installed.

Millom Castle is an ancient building at Millom in Cumbria. It is a Grade I listed building and scheduled ancient monument. A manor on the site was granted to Godard de Boyvill, owner of the Manor of Millom, in around 1134. The manor came into the Hudleston family's ownership in around 1240 when de Boyvill's granddaughter married into the Hudleston family. John Hudleston was given a license to crenellate in 1335. The great tower dates from the 16th or 17th century but was badly damaged by a cannon attack in 1648 during the English Civil War. By 1739 the castle walls were in dilapidated condition. The great tower is now u sed as a farmhouse.

Broughton in Furness is mentioned in the Domesday Book as one of the townships forming the Manor of Hougun held by Tostig Godwinson, Earl of Northumbria. Dating from around the eleventh century, the original settlement grew to become the local market town for both fishing and agriculture. Wool was particularly important for the town's development. The town was given a charter in 1575.

Market Square was formally laid out in 1760 by John Gilpin Sawrey, the Lord of the Manor, who lived at Broughton Tower, a large mansion just a short distance from the Square. In the 1990s the A595 road was diverted in an attempt to improve the environment of the town and help it retain its rural feel.

Richard married **Elizabeth ATKINSON** [3924][1,2,9] [MRIN: 1390], daughter of **ATKINSON** [5171], on 19 Feb 1670 in Broughton In Furness, Lancashire, England. Elizabeth was born on 30 Aug 1639 in Lancaster, Lancashire, England and died on 10 Oct 1699 in England at age 60.

General Notes: Lancaster is a city in northwest England. On a hilltop, the medieval Lancaster Castle has antique furniture, 19th-century prison cells and views of the River Lune. Lancaster City Museum features displays on the city's history and its army regiment in a Georgian building. William son Park offers woodland walks, a butterfly house and coastal views. The city's seafaring past is explored at Lancaster Maritime Museum.

Children from this marriage were:

+   2   F   i.   **Easter ORMANDY [5393]** was born in 1672 and died in 1686 at age 14.

+   3   M   ii.   **John ORMANDY [5394]** was born in 1677.

+   4   F   iii.   **Sarah ORMANDY [5395]** was born in 1679.

+   5   M   iv.   **William ORMANDY [3324]**[1,4,5,6,7,10,11,12,13] was born in 1680 in Broughton In Furness, Lancashire, England, was christened on 18 Oct 1680 in Broughton In Furness, Lancashire, England, and died 01 Jun 1766 (?1746) in Aldingham, Lancashire, England at age 66.

     William married **Bridget ADDISON** [3325][1,10,14] [MRIN: 1170] (d. 12 Jan 1766) on 16 Sep 1716 in Broughton In Furness, Lancashire, England.

+   6   F   v.   **Elizabeth ORMANDY [5396]**[15] was christened on 20 Nov 1774 in Bristol, Gloucestershire, England.

Second Generation

2. Easter ORMANDY [5393] (*Richard [3923]* [1]) was born in 1672 and died in 1686 at age 14.

3. John ORMANDY [5394] (*Richard [3923]* [1]) was born in 1677.

4. Sarah ORMANDY [5395] (*Richard [3923]*[1]) was born in 1679.

5. William ORMANDY [3324][1,4,5,6,7,10,11,12,13] (*Richard [3923]*[1]) was born in 1680 in Broughton In Furness, Lancashire, England, was christened on 18 Oct 1680 in Broughton In Furness, Lancashire, England, and died 01 Jun 1766 (?1746) in Aldingham, Lancashire, England at age 66.

General Notes: Broughton in Furness is mentioned in the Domesday Book as one of the townships forming the Manor of Hougun held by Tostig Godwinson, Earl of Northumbria. Dating from around the eleventh century, the original settlement grew to become the local market town for both fishing and agriculture. Wool was particularly important for the town's development. The town was given a charter in 1575.

Market Square was formally laid out in 1760 by John Gilpin Sawrey the Lord of the Manor, who lived at Broughton Tower, a large mansion just a short distance from the Square. In the 1990s the A595 road was diverted in an attempt to improve the environment of the town and help it retain its rural feel.

Aldingham parish, composed of a single township of the same name, occupies a pleasant position on the southeast side of Low Furness overlooking Morecambe Bay. The surface is undulating, being highest in the north, where 400 ft. above sea level is attained on the border of Birkrigg; in the northern half also at the coast it rises steeply from the sea, 200 ft. being attained a quarter to half a mile from the shore. The southern end is flat and low near the shore, but to the north-west, on the border of Dalton, rises to 214 ft. above sea level at Scarbar row. The two portions are known as Upper and Lower Aldingham.

William married **Bridget ADDISON** [3325][1,10,14] [MRIN: 1170], daughter of **ADDISON** [5172], on 16 Sep 1716 in Broughton In Furness, Lancashire, England. Bridget was born in Aulthurstide, England, died on 12 Jan 1766 in Broughton In Furness, Lancashire, England, and was buried on 12 Jan 1766 in Broughton In Furness, Lancashire, England.

Children from this marriage were:

+ 7 M i. **Thomas ORMANDY [3123]**[1,3,5,10,11,16,17,18,19,20] was born in Jun 1717 in Broughton In Furness, Lancashire, England, was christened on 17 Jun 1717 in Broughton In Furness, Lancashire, England, died in Dec 1776 in Gleaston Castle, Lancashire, England at age 59, and was buried on 20 Dec 1776 in Gleaston Castle, Lancashire, England.

   Thomas married **Jane STANLEY** [3323][1,10,18,21] [MRIN: 1096] (b. Between 13 Jan 1717 and 1719, d. 29 Apr 1803) on 24 Nov 1744 in Broughton In Furness, Lancashire, England.

+ 8 M ii. **John ORMANDY [5397]**[21] was born on 12 Aug 1719 in Broughton In Furness, Lancashire, England and died in 1763 in Dalton in Furness, Lancashire, England at age 44.

+ 9 M iii. **Richard ORMANDY [5398]** was born in 1723 and died in 1801 at age 78.

+ 10 F iv. **Anne ORMANDY [5399]**[21] was born on 10 Mar 1726 in Broughton In Furness, Lancashire, England and died on 24 Apr 1726 in Broughton In Furness, Lancashire, England.

+ 11 F v. **Betty ORMANDY [5400]** was born on 9 Apr 1727 in Broughton In Furness, Lancashire, England.

+ 12 M vi. **James ORMANDY [5401]** was born on 30 Mar 1729 in Broughton In Furness, Lancashire, England and died in Nov 1804 in Broughton In Furness, Lancashire, England at age 75.

+ 13 F vii. **Bridget ORMANDY [5402]**[21] was born on 26 May 1733 in Broughton In Furness, Lancashire, England and died on 4 Apr 1734 in Broughton In Furness, Lancashire, England.

6. Elizabeth ORMANDY [5396][15] (*Richard [3923]* [1]) was christened on 20 Nov 1774 in Bristol, Gloucestershire, England.

Third Generation

7. Thomas ORMANDY [3123][1,3,5,10,11,16,17,18,19,20] (*William [3324]*[5], *Richard [3923]*[1]) was born in Jun 1717 in Broughton In Furness, Lancashire, England, was christened on 17 Jun 1717 in Broughton In Furness, Lancashire, England, died in Dec 1776 in Gleaston Castle, Lancashire, England at age 59, and was buried on 20 Dec 1776 in Gleaston Castle, Lancashire, England.

General Notes: 24 Nov 1744 Thomas Ormandy, Church Town, Broughton, Kirkby Irelith, butcher & Jane Stanley, Broughton. Bn: Richard Lowther, Torver, yeo. At Broughton.

Book: Lancaster Marriage Bonds (Marriage Bond)

Collection: Lancashire, Westmorland: - Marriage Bonds, Deaneries of Lonsdale Kendal Furness Copeland and Amounderness (Archdeaconry of Richmond) 1739-1745

Gleaston Castle is a medieval building in a valley about 1 kilometer (0.62 mi) north-east of the village of Gleaston. The village lies between the towns of Ulverston and Barrow-in-Furness in the Furness peninsula, Cumbria, England. Gleaston Castle has a quadrilateral plan, with a tower at each corner. The largest of these, the north-west tower, probably housed a hall.

The castle was most likely built for John Harington, 1st Baron Harington in the 14th century, replacing nearby Aldingham Motte. Gleaston Castle descended through the Harrington family until 1458 when it passed to William Bonville through marriage and was subsequently abandoned. The castle passed to the Grey family until Henry Grey, 1st Duke of Suffolk was executed for treason in 1554. As a result, Gleaston Castle became royal property before it was bought by the Preston family in the 17th century, and then passed to the Cavendish family.

As the castle was disused from the mid-15th century it fell into dilapidation, and antiquarian depictions from the 18th century show Gleaston in a state of ruin. Though it is not open to the public, it has been the subject of historical and archaeological investigation in the 20th and 21st centuries.

Thomas married **Jane STANLEY** [3323][1,10,18,21] [MRIN: 1096], daughter of **Joseph STANLEY** [3925], on 24 Nov 1744 in Broughton In Furness, Lancashire, England. Jane was born between 13 Jan 1717 and 1719 in St. Mary Magdalene, Broughton In Furness, England and died on 29 Apr 1803 Buried, St. Cuthberts Ch. Aldingham, Lancs. England.

Children from this marriage were:

+ 14 F i. **Catherine ORMANDY [3934]** was born in 1745 in Broughton In Furness, Lancashire, England.

+ 15 F ii. **Anne ORMANDY [3935]**[22] was born on 15 Nov 1745 in Broughton In Furness, Lancashire, England and died on 18 Jun 1785 at age 39.

+   16   F   iii.   **Bridget ORMANDY [3933]** was born on 16 Sep 1747 in Broughton In Furness, Lancashire, England and died on 27 Sep 1748 at age 1.

+   17   M   iv.   **Rev Thomas ORMANDY [2619]**[1,10,16,17,23,24,25,26,27,28,29] was born on 11 Jun 1749 in Broughton In Furness, Lancashire, England, died on 8 May 1827 in Aldingham, Lancashire, England at age 77, and was buried on 8 May 1827 in St. Cuthberts Church Aldingham, Lancashire. England.

       Thomas married **Dorothy BOLTON** [3322][1,10,23,26,27,28,30] [MRIN: 844] (b. 1759, d. Mar 1821) on 23 Jul 1785-26 Jun 1785 in Aldingham, Lancashire, England.

+   18   F   v.   **Ann ORMANDY [3326]**[10] was born in 1751.

+   19   M   vi.   **William Addison ORMANDY [3932]**[31,32,33] was born on 25 Aug 1751 in Broughton In Furness, Lancashire, England and died on 14 Dec 1797 in Aldingham, Lancashire, England at age 46.

+   20   M   vii.   **William ORMANDY [3327]**[10] was born in 1753.

+   21   M   viii.   **James ORMANDY [3931]**[34,35,36,37] was born on 3 Nov 1753 in Broughton In Furness, Lancashire, England.

       James married **Jane ATKINSON** [5384][36,38] [MRIN: 2098] on 25 Nov 1780 in St Mary, Dalton in Furness, Lancashire, England.

+   22   F   ix.   **Jane ORMANDY [3930]**[39] was born on 20 Aug 1755 in Broughton In Furness, Lancashire, England and was buried on 23 Dec 1813 in Dalton in Furness, Lancashire, England.

+   23   M   x.   **Richard ORMANDY [3929]**[40] was born in 1757 in Broughton In Furness, Lancashire, England and was buried on 31 Aug 1817 in Lancashire, England.

+   24   M   xi.   **Joseph ORMANDY [3928]**[38,41] was born in 1759 in Broughton In Furness, Lancashire, England and was buried on 2 Nov 1834 in Standish. Lancashire, England.

       Joseph married **Isabella CHARNOCK** [5386][38] [MRIN: 2102] on 5 Nov 1775 in Dalton in Furness, Lancashire, England.

+   25   M   xii.   **John ORMANDY [3927]** was born on 13 Jan 1762 and died on 20 Jan 1826 at age 64.

8. John ORMANDY [5397][21] (*William [3324]*[5]*, Richard [3923]*[1]) was born on 12 Aug 1719 in Broughton In Furness, Lancashire, England and died in 1763 in Dalton in Furness, Lancashire, England at age 44.

9. Richard ORMANDY [5398] (*William [3324]*[5]*, Richard [3923]*[1]) was born in 1723 and died in 1801 at age 78.

10. Anne ORMANDY [5399][21] (*William [3324]*[5]*, Richard [3923]*[1]) was born on 10 Mar 1726 in Broughton In Furness, Lancashire, England and died on 24 Apr 1726 in Broughton In Furness, Lancashire, England.

11. Betty ORMANDY [5400] (*William [3324]*[5]*, Richard [3923]*[1]) was born on 9 Apr 1727 in Broughton In Furness, Lancashire, England.

12. James ORMANDY [5401] (*William [3324]*[5]*, Richard [3923]*[1]) was born on 30 Mar 1729 in Broughton In Furness, Lancashire, England and died in Nov 1804 in Broughton In Furness, Lancashire, England at age 75.

13. Bridget ORMANDY [5402][21] (*William [3324]*[5]*, Richard [3923]*[1]) was born on 26 May 1733 in Broughton In Furness, Lancashire, England and died on 4 Apr 1734 in Broughton In Furness, Lancashire, England.

Fourth Generation

14. Catherine ORMANDY [3934] (*Thomas [3123]*[7], *William [3324]*[5], *Richard [3923]*[1]) was born in 1745 in Broughton In Furness, Lancashire, England.

Figure 199.
Maid in Sacque, Apron, and Clogs. Middle Eighteenth Century.

15. Anne ORMANDY [3935][22] (*Thomas [3123]*[7], *William [3324]*[5], *Richard [3923]*[1]) was born on 15 Nov 1745 in Broughton In Furness, Lancashire, England and died on 18 Jun 1785 at age 39.

Figure 199.
Maid in Sacque, Apron, and Clogs. Middle Eighteenth Century.

16. Bridget ORMANDY [3933] (*Thomas [3123]* [7], *William [3324]* [5], *Richard [3923]* [1]) was born on 16 Sep 1747 in Broughton In Furness, Lancashire, England and died on 27 Sep 1748 at age 1.

Maid in Sacque, Apron, and Clogs. Middle Eighteenth Century.

17. Rev Thomas ORMANDY [2619] [1,10,16,17,23,24,25,26,27,28,29] (*Thomas [3123]* [7], *William [3324]* [5], *Richard [3923]* [1]) was born on 11 Jun 1749 in Broughton In Furness, Lancashire, England, died on 8 May 1827 in Aldingham, Lancashire, England at age 77, and was buried on 8 May 1827 in St. Cuthberts Church Aldingham, Lancashire. England.

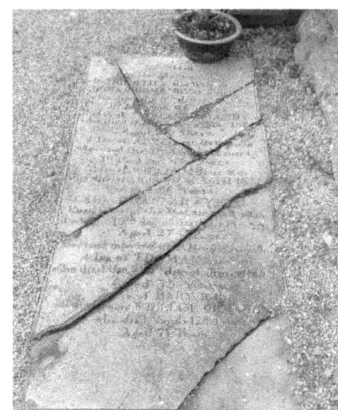

> General Notes: O653-6 Rev. Thomas Ormandy of Aldingham 1796 (now Cumbria) P.C. of Wintbeck 1850-78

> O635-41 Parish Marriage records show date of marriage 26 Jun 1785 and wife's last name BOLTON.

> O653-33 Marriage License dated 23 Jul 1785 and wife's last name BOULTON

> Occupation: Vicar of Old Church of the Holy Trinity at Millom, England.

Thomas married **Dorothy BOLTON** [3322] [1,10,23,26,27,28,30] [MRIN: 844], daughter of **William BOULTON** [3936], on 23 Jul 1785-26 Jun 1785 in Aldingham, Lancashire, England. Dorothy was born in 1759 in Walney Island Lancs. England, died in Mar 1821 in Aldingham, Lancashire, England at age 62, and was buried on 13 Mar 1821 in St. Cuthberts Ch. Aldingham, Lancs., Eng.

Children from this marriage were:

+ 26 F i. **Anne ORMANDY [3328]** [1,10,42] was born on 18 Apr 1786 in Gleaston Castle, Lancashire, England and died in Jun 1867 in Ulverston, Lancashire, England at age 81.

+ 27 M ii. **William ORMANDY [3329]**[1,10,43,44,45,46] was born on 20 Apr 1788 in Aldingham, Lancashire, England and died on 16 Apr 1856 in Gleaston Castle, Lancashire, England at age 67.

William married **Mary ALLONBY** [2429][43,45] [MRIN: 2097] on 30 Aug 1823 in Holy Trinity, Colton, Lancashire, England.

+ 28 M iii. **Joseph ORMANDY [3330]**[1,10,21,47,48] was born on 28 Apr 1790 in Gleaston Castle, Lancashire, England, was christened on 30 May 1790 in Lancashire, England, and died on 5 Jan 1860 in Lancaster, Lancashire, England at age 69.

Joseph had a relationship with **Ann** [5387][48] [MRIN: 2103]. (b. 1971)

+ 29 M iv. **Rev. John ORMANDY [2343]**[1,10,16,26,42,49,50,51,52,53,54,55,56,57] was born on 5 Apr 1792 in Aldingham, Lancashire, England[42] and died on 16 May 1846 in Thwaites Chapel In Millom, Cumberland, England at age 54.

John married **Mary WILKINSON** [2344][10,16,42,50,54,55,57,58] [MRIN: 843] (b. 1791, d. 1848) on 14 Feb 1819 in Greystoke, Cumberland, England.

+ 30 M v. **James ORMANDY [3331]**[1,10,59] was born on 29 Jun 1794 and was christened on 26 Jul 1795 in St Cuthbert, Aldingham, Lancashire, England.

+ 31 M vi. **Rev. Thomas ORMANDY [3332]**[1,10,60] was born on 11 Dec 1796 in Aldingham, Lancashire, England and died on 6 Mar 1878 in Buried At Whitbeck Church Yard, Cumberland, England at age 81.

Thomas married **Eleanor KENDALL** [5382] [MRIN: 2083] on 27 Dec 1836 in St Cuthbert, Aldingham, Lancashire, England.

+ 32 M vii. **George ORMANDY [3333]**[1,10,61] was born on 18 Aug 1799 in St Cuthbert, Aldingham, Lancashire, England, died on 12 May 1854 at age 54, and was buried in Pennington in Furness, Lancashire, England.

George married **Isabella WHINNERAH** [5385][61] [MRIN: 2100] (b. 1807) on 9 Oct 1828 in Bootle, Cumberland, England.

+ 33 M viii. **Dr. Isaac ORMANDY [3334]**[1,10,62,63,64] was born on 5 Jul 1801 in Gleaston Castle, Lancashire, England and died on 19 Jan 1855 in Cumbria, Lancashire, United Kingdom at age 53.

Isaac married **Anne KITTY** [5383][62,63,64] [MRIN: 2099] on 7 Feb 1832 in Liverpool, Lancashire, England.

18. Ann ORMANDY [3326][10] (*Thomas [3123]* [7], *William [3324]* [5], *Richard [3923]* [1]) was born in 1751.

FIGURE 199.
Maid in Sacque, Apron, and Clogs. Middle Eighteenth Century.

19. William Addison ORMANDY [3932][31,32,33] (*Thomas [3123]* [7], *William [3324]* [5], *Richard [3923]* [1]) was born on 25 Aug 1751 in Broughton In Furness, Lancashire, England and died on 14 Dec 1797 in Aldingham, Lancashire, England at age 46.

> General Notes: Baptism: 25 Aug 1751 St Mary Magdalene, Broughton in Furness, Lancashire, England
> William Addison Ormandy - Son of Thos. Ormandy
> Source: LDS Film 1040308

20. William ORMANDY [3327][10] (*Thomas [3123]* [7], *William [3324]* [5], *Richard [3923]* [1]) was born in 1753.

21. James ORMANDY [3931][34,35,36,37] (*Thomas [3123]* [7], *William [3324]* [5], *Richard [3923]* [1]) was born on 3 Nov 1753 in Broughton In Furness, Lancashire, England.

Friesischer Bürger aus Westerland auf Sylt.

> Source: LDS Film 1040308
> Burial: 5 Sep 1829 Priory Church of St Mary and St Michael, Cartmel, Lancashire, England
> James Ormandy -
> Age: 75
> Abode: Pit Farm
> Buried by: P. Richardson
> Register: Burials 1827 - 1831 from the Bishop's Transcripts, Entry 108 0
> Source: LDS Film 1040490

James married **Jane ATKINSON** [5384][36,38] [MRIN: 2098] on 25 Nov 1780 in St Mary, Dalton in Furness, Lancashire, England.

22. Jane ORMANDY [3930][39] (*Thomas [3123]* [7], *William [3324]* [5], *Richard [3923]* [1]) was born on 20 Aug 1755 in Broughton In Furness, Lancashire, England and was buried on 23 Dec 1813 in Dalton in Furness, Lancashire, England.

FIGURE 199.
Maid in Sacque, Apron, and Clogs. Middle Eighteenth Century.

> FHL Film Number: 1471899

23. Richard ORMANDY [3929][40] (*Thomas [3123]* [7], *William [3324]* [5], *Richard [3923]* [1]) was born in 1757 in Broughton In Furness, Lancashire, England and was buried on 31 Aug 1817 in Lancashire, England.

Friesischer Bürger aus Westerland auf Sylt.

> FHL Film Number: 1040315

24. Joseph ORMANDY [3928][38,41] (*Thomas [3123]*[7], *William [3324]*[5], *Richard [3923]*[1]) was born in 1759 in Broughton In Furness, Lancashire, England and was buried on 2 Nov 1834 in Standish, Lancashire, England.

Joseph married **Isabella CHARNOCK** [5386][38] [MRIN: 2102] on 5 Nov 1775 in Dalton in Furness, Lancashire, England.

25. John ORMANDY [3927] (*Thomas [3123]*[7], *William [3324]*[5], *Richard [3923]*[1]) was born on 13 Jan 1762 and died on 20 Jan 1826 at age 64.

Fifth Generation

26. Anne ORMANDY [3328][1,10,42] (*Thomas (Rev) [2619]* [17], *Thomas [3123]* [7], *William [3324]* [5], *Richard [3923]* [1]) was born on 18 Apr 1786 in Gleaston Castle, Lancashire, England and died in Jun 1867 in Ulverston, Lancashire, England at age 81.

> General Notes: Anne Ormandy - Daughter of Thomas Ormandy & Dorothy
> Abode: Gleaston Castle
> Register: Baptisms 1750 - 1800 from the Bishop's Transcripts, Page 44,
>   Entry 20
> Source: LDS Film 1040315

27. William ORMANDY [3329][1,10,43,44,45,46] (*Thomas (Rev) [2619]* [17], *Thomas [3123]* [7], *William [3324]* [5], *Richard [3923]* [1]) was born on 20 Apr 1788 in Aldingham, Lancashire, England and died on 16 Apr 1856 in Gleaston Castle, Lancashire, England at age 67.

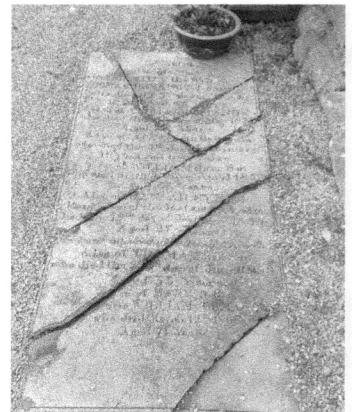

> General Notes: William Ormandy - Gleaston Castle, parish of
> Aldingham
> Mary Allonby - Spinster
> Witness: Joseph Ormandy; George Ormandy; Margaret Turner
> Married by License by: Edward Ellerton
> Register: Marriages 1813 - 1825 from the Bishop's Transcripts, Page 32, Entry 95
>
> Burial: 21 Apr 1856 St Cuthbert, Aldingham, Lancashire, England
> William Ormandy -
> Age: 68
> Abode: Gleaston Castle
> Buried by: J. Macaulay, Rector
> Register: Burials 1821 - 1877 from the Bishop's Transcripts, Page 5 7 & 58, Entry 459
> Source: LDS Film 1040315

William married **Mary ALLONBY** [2429][43,45] [MRIN: 2097] on 30 Aug 1823 in Holy Trinity, Colton, Lancashire, England.

28. Joseph ORMANDY [3330][1,10,21,47,48] (*Thomas (Rev) [2619]* [17], *Thomas [3123]* [7], *William [3324]* [5], *Richard [3923]* [1]) was born on 28 Apr 1790 in Gleaston Castle, Lancashire, England, was christened on 30 May 1790 in Lancashire, England, and died on 5 Jan 1860 in Lancaster, Lancashire, England at age 69.

General Notes Occupation: Husbandman

Notes: Son of Thomas Ormandy of Gleaston-Castle, Husband, son of

Thomas Ormandy of Gleaston-Castle, Husbandman, by Jane his wife, dr. of Joseph Stanley heretofore of Broughton, Skinner & Glover, by Dorothy his wife, dr. of Wm. Bolton of ye Isle of Walney, Husbandman, by Margaret his wife, dr. of Thos.

Richardson of the Old Park in the parish of Dalton, Husbandman.

Register: Baptisms 1750 - 1800 from the Bishop's Transcripts, Page 52, Entry 5

Joseph had a relationship with **Ann** [5387][48] [MRIN: 2103]. No evidence this couple married. Ann was born in 1971.

29. Rev. John ORMANDY [2343][1,10,16,26,42,49, 50,51,52,53,54,55,56,57] (*Thomas (Rev) [2619]* [17], *Thomas [3123]* [7], *William [3324]* [5], *Richard [3923]* [1]) was born on 5 Apr 1792 in Aldingham, Lancashire, England[42] and died on 16 May 1846 in Thwaites Chapel In Millom, Cumberland, England at age 54.

General Notes: O653-6

Priest at Greystoke 1815-1822. PC of Thwaites 1822-1846 of Bridge Edd, Millom

Thwaites is a small village near Duddon Valley and on the edge of the Duddon Estuary in the Lake District National Park in Cumbria, England. The River Duddon flows through the valley, rising in the mountains between Eskdale and Langdale, before flowing into the Irish Sea near Broughton in Furness. In its lower reaches it is bounded by the Furness Fells and Harter Fell.

Thwaites has an impressive sized church for the small population '97 the neighboring villages of The Green, Broad Gate, Hallthwaites and Lady Hall all use St. Anne's Church.

Close by along the Duddon Valley are steep roads leading over the Hard Knott Pass to Eskdale and east over the Wrynose Pass to the Langdale valleys. A less steep pass to Eskdale over Birker Fell leaves the Duddon Valley at Ulpha, with extensive views of the Scafell range. There is also the Corney Fell Road from Duddon Bridge or Broad Gate over to Waberthwaite and Broad Oak near Muncaster Castle.

St. Anne's Church is in the village of Thwaites, Cumbria, England. It is an active Anglican parish church in the deanery of Millom, the archdeaconry of Furness, and the diocese of Carlisle. Its benefice is united with those of St. George, Millom, Holy Trinity, Millom, and St. Luke,

Haverigg. The church is recorded in the National Heritage List for England as a designated Grade II listed building.

The church replaced a chapel of ease (A chapel of ease is a church building other than the parish church, built within the bounds of a parish for the attendance of those who cannot reach the parish church conveniently, on the other site of the road, which was built in 1721 and consecrated in 1725. This church was built in 1853, and designed by the Lancaster architect E. G. Paley, at a cost of £1,678 (equivalent to £150,000 as of 2018). It was consecrated on 16 June 1854 by the bishop of Chester.

1841 Census, Thwaites Vicarage (Y= Born in Cumberland, N= Born elsewhere) John Ormandy Age 45 Male Clerk (In Holy Orders) N Mary Ormandy Age 45 Female Y Mary Ormandy Age 15 Female N Juliann Ormandy Age 15 Female Y Harrison Ormandy Age 10 Male Y Harriett King Age 15 Female   Independent Means N Elizabeth King Age 13 Female Independent Means N

It is suggested that Thomas was 18 at the time and away from home

O653-5 Sir John Ormandy, Vicar of "Old Church of the Holy Trinity" of Millom, England. Either father or uncle of my Grandfather. Old Church of the Holy Trinity was built before 1066AD 1000 AD Millom part of Cumberland and was under Malcom King of Scotland 1031 AD Cumberland under English as part of Earldom of North-Umberland 1100AD Goddarg de Boyville a crusader granted Lordship of Millom. Castle adjoining Old Church of the Holy Trinity build about 1125 AD. One of the de Boyville daughters married an Huddleston who built the Huddleston Chapel now part of the "Old Church of the Holy Trinity"

Baptism: 13 May 1792, Aldingham, Lancashire, England.

Occupation: Vicar, Between 1822 and 1846, Thwaites Chapel In Millom, Cumberland, England.

John married **Mary WILKINSON** [2344][10,16,42,50,54,55,57,58] [MRIN: 843], daughter of **John WILKINSON** [2953][16] and **Julia HARRISON** [2954],[16] on 14 Feb 1819 in Greystoke, Cumberland, England. Mary was born in 1791 in Thorpe, Derbyshire, England, was christened on 14 Apr 1791 in Thorpe, Derbyshire, England, died in 1848 in Twaites Chapel, Millom, Cumberland, England at age 57, and was buried on 31 Dec 1848 in Twaites Chapel, Millom, Cumberland, England.

Children from this marriage were:

+ 34 F   i.   **Dorothy ORMANDY [2950]**[10,16,65,66,67] was born on 11 Jul 1819 in Greystoke, Cumberland, England and died between Jan and Mar 1889 in Ulverston, Lancashire, England.

Dorothy married **William LEWTHWAITE Captain** [2951][16,65] [MRIN: 1034] (b. 1812, d. 1858) on 21 Oct 1843 in Liverpool, Lancashire, England.

+ 35 F   ii.   **Mary Ann ORMANDY [2822]**[10,16,42,68,69,70] was born in 1820 in Formby, Lancashire, England, was christened on 10 Aug 1821 in Formby, Lancashire, England, and died on 13 Oct 1872 in Cumberland, England at age 52.

Mary married **Dennis MELLON** [2949][16,68] [MRIN: 1010] on 9 Nov 1844 in Millom, Cumberland, England.

+ 36 M iii. **Thomas ORMANDY [2341]**[10,16,50,71,72,73,74,75,76,77,78] was born on 10 Aug 1823 in Twaites Chapel, Millom, Cumberland, England[12,50,78] and died on 7 Mar 1864 in Cahaba, Alabama at age 40.

Thomas married **Sarah JONES** [2342][10,16,71,72,73] [MRIN: 842] (b. 22 Aug 1825, d. 6 Aug 1872) in Aug 1845 in London, England.

+ 37 F iv. **Juliann ORMANDY [2823]**[10,16,42,54,79] was born on 26 Aug 1825.

Juliann married **Thomas LAURENCE** [5388][79] [MRIN: 1095] on 19 Apr 1860 in Urswick, Lancashire, England.

+ 38 M v. **John ORMANDY [2952]**[10,16,55,80] was born in 1828 in Twaites Chapel, Millom, Cumberland, England, died in 1829 in Twaites Chapel, Millom, Cumberland, England at age 1, and was buried on 21 Apr 1829 in Twaites Chapel, Millom, Cumberland, England.

+ 39 M vi. **Harrison Wilkinson ORMANDY [2824]**[10,16,42,81,82,83] was born on 29 Apr 1831 in Cumberland, England and died in Mar 1891 in Liverpool, Lancashire, England at age 59.

Harrison married **Elizabeth FINNISWOOD** [5389][81] [MRIN: 2101] on 3 Nov 1868 in Barton, Westmorland, England.

30. James ORMANDY [3331][1,10,59] (*Thomas (Rev) [2619]* [17], *Thomas [3123]* [7], *William [3324]* [5], *Richard [3923]* [1]) was born on 29 Jun 1794 and was christened on 26 Jul 1795 in St Cuthbert, Aldingham, Lancashire, England.

General Notes: Abode: Gleaston Castle
Occupation: Husbandman
Notes: Son of Thomas Ormandy of Gleaston Castle, Husbandman, son of Thomas Ormandy of do, Husbandman, by Jane his wife, dr. of Joseph Stanley heretofore of Broughton, Skinner and Glover, by [Mother's details] Dorothy his wife, dr. of Wm. Bolton of the Isle of Walney, Husbandman, by Margaret his wife, dr. of Thomas Richardson of Old Park in the parish of Dalton, Husbandman.
Baptized by: Mr. Bolton, Curate of Ulpha
Register: Baptisms 1750 - 1800 from the Bishop's Transcripts, Page 61, Entry 6
Source: LDS Film 1040315

31. Rev. Thomas ORMANDY [3332][1,10,60] (*Thomas (Rev) [2619]* [17], *Thomas [3123]* [7], *William [3324]* [5], *Richard [3923]* [1]) was born on 11 Dec 1796 in Aldingham, Lancashire, England and died on 6 Mar 1878 in Buried At Whitbeck Church Yard, Cumberland, England at age 81.

> General Notes: Abode: Gleaston Castle
> Register: Baptisms 1750 - 1800 from the Bishop's Transcripts, Page 64 , Entry 16
> Source: LDS Film 1040315
> Marriage: 27 Dec 1836 St Cuthbert, Aldingham, Lancashire, England
> Thomas Ormandy - Clerk, Bachelor, of this Parish
> Eleanor Kendall - Spinster, of this Parish
> Witness: Joseph Ormandy; Jas. Kendall
> Married by License by: John Stonard, Rector
> Register: Marriages 1821 - 1848 from the Bishop's Transcripts, Page 35 , Entry 104
> Source: LDS Film 1040315

Thomas married **Eleanor KENDALL** [5382] [MRIN: 2083] on 27 Dec 1836 in St Cuthbert, Aldingham, Lancashire, England.

32. George ORMANDY [3333][1,10,61] (*Thomas (Rev) [2619]* [17], *Thomas [3123]* [7], *William [3324]* [5], *Richard [3923]* [1]) was born on 18 Aug 1799 in St Cuthbert, Aldingham, Lancashire, England, died on 12 May 1854 at age 54, and was buried in Pennington in Furness, Lancashire, England.

> General Notes Abode: Gleaston Castle
> Register: Baptisms 1750 - 1800 from the Bishop's Transcripts, Page 67, Entry 12
> Source: LDS Film 1040315
> Name: George Armondy
> Gender: Male
> Marriage Date: 9 Oct 1828
> Marriage Place: Bootle, Cumberland, England
> Spouse: Isabella Whinnerah
> FHL Film Number: 90566
> Burial: Pennington in Furness, Lancashire, England
> 19 Jun 1854 St Michael and the Holy Angels, Pennington in Furness, Lancashire, England
> George Ormandy -
> Age: 70 yrs.
> Abode: Beck Side, Pennington

Buried by: Charles Mortlock, Vicar

Register: Burials 1814 - 1870 from the Bishop's Transcripts, Entry 472

Source: LDS Films 1040309 and 1040491

George married **Isabella WHINNERAH** [5385][61] [MRIN: 2100] on 9 Oct 1828 in Bootle, Cumberland, England. Isabella was born in 1807.

Children from this marriage were:

+ 40 F i. **Margaret ORMANDY [5390]**[61] was born in 1833 in Lancashire, England.

+ 41 M ii. **William ORMANDY [5391]**[61] was born in 1836 in Lancashire, England.

+ 42 M iii. **George ORMANDY [5392]**[61] was born in 1837 in Lancashire, England.

33. Dr. Isaac ORMANDY [3334][1,10,62,63,64] (*Thomas (Rev) [2619]*[17], *Thomas [3123]*[7], *William [3324]*[5], *Richard [3923]*[1]) was born on 5 Jul 1801 in Gleaston Castle, Lancashire, England and died on 19 Jan 1855 in Cumbria, Lancashire, United Kingdom at age 53.

Isaac married **Anne KITTY** [5383][62,63,64] [MRIN: 2099] on 7 Feb 1832 in Liverpool, Lancashire, England.

Sixth Generation

34. Dorothy ORMANDY [2950][10,16,65,66,67] (*John (Rev.) [2343]* [29]*, Thomas (Rev)*
[2619] [17]*, Thomas [3123]* [7]*, William [3324]* [5]*, Richard [3923]* [1]) was born on 11 Jul
1819 in Greystoke, Cumberland, England and died between Jan and Mar 1889 in
Ulverston, Lancashire, England.

General Notes: FHL Film Number: 90623

Name: Dorothy Lewthwaite
Estimated birth year: abt 1822
Registration Year: 1889
Registration Quarter: Jan-Feb-Mar
Age at Death: 67
Registration district: Ulverston
Parishes for this Registration District: View Ecclesiastical Parishes associated with this
Registration District
Inferred County: Lancashire
Volume: 8e
Page: 587

Dorothy married **William LEWTHWAITE Captain** [2951][16,65] [MRIN: 1034], son of
LEWTHWAITE [5175], on 21 Oct 1843 in Liverpool, Lancashire, England. William was born in
1812 and died in 1858 at age 46.

35. Mary Ann ORMANDY [2822][10,16,42,68,69,70] (*John (Rev.) [2343]* [29]*, Thomas*
(Rev) [2619] [17]*, Thomas [3123]* [7]*, William [3324]* [5]*, Richard [3923]* [1]) was born in 1820
in Formby, Lancashire, England, was christened on 10 Aug 1821 in Formby,
Lancashire, England, and died on 13 Oct 1872 in Cumberland, England at age 52.

General Notes: Name: Mary Ann Ormandy
Gender: Female
Baptism Date: 10 Aug 1821
Baptism Place: St. Peter's, Formby, Lancashire, England
Father: John Ormandy
Mother: Mary
FHL Film Number: 1468978
Probate: 9 Aug 1873, Carlisle, Cumberland, England.

Mary married **Dennis MELLON** [2949][16,68] [MRIN: 1010], son of **MELLON** [5173], on 9 Nov 1844 in Millom, Cumberland, England.

36. **Thomas ORMANDY** [2341][10,16,50,71,72,73,74,75,76,77,78] *(John (Rev.) [2343]* [29], *Thomas (Rev) [2619]* [17], *Thomas [3123]* [7], *William [3324]* [5], *Richard [3923]* [1]*)* was born on 10 Aug 1823 in Twaites Chapel, Millom, Cumberland, England[12,50,78] and died on 7 Mar 1864 in Cahaba, Alabama at age 40. The cause of his death was Pneumonia while prisoner of war 15 Apr 1864 Cahaba, Alabama.

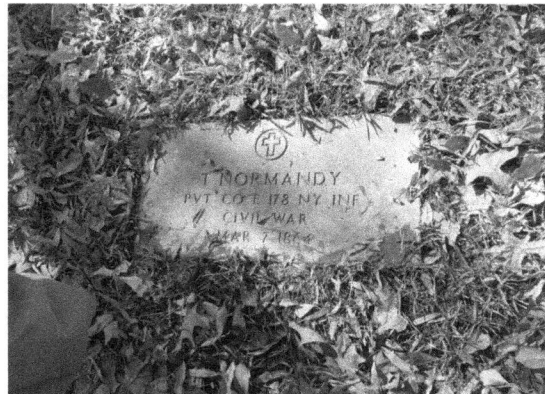

General Notes: O653-1 Ormandy Family Bible

d. Thomas while prisoner of war 15 Apr 1864 Andersonville, Georgia

O653-6 Correspondence Ormandy

Born at Twaites Chapel in Millom, England in Aug 1823. Enrolled in 17 th Regt. of N.Y. Volunteers, Co. E, on March 28, 1863. Mustered in on June 19, 1863 at New Dorp. Staten Island, N.Y. Captured by rebels at battle of Meridien, Miss. In Feb. 1864. Died in prison hospital at Cahaba, Ala. on March 7, 1864. May have been an Abolitionist?

Pension Report states that prisoner of war records show that Thomas died at the Confederate prison hospital in Cahaba, Alabama on March 7, 1 864. He was a member of E Company, 178th Regiment Infantry, New York Volunteers. He was captured during the Meridien, Miss. Campaign, while he was with Sherman's expedition. Thomas mustered into his regiment at New York, Staten Island, NY on 23 Mar, 1863. He was captured about 19 Feb 1864.

War Department Adjutant General's Office Washington, Feby 14, 1882 Respectfully returned to the Commissioner of Pensions. Thomas Ormandy, Company "E", 178 Regiment New York Volunteers, was enrolled on the 23rd day of March, 1863, at New York, N.Y., and is reported: on rolls to Dec 31 1863 present. Jany & Feby 1864 absent without leave. March & April 1864 deserted from Sherman Expeditions Feb 19, 1864. May & June 1864 name not. July & Aug 1864 Absent Captured by Enemy, Sherman Raid, - Same report to April 30, 1865. May & June 1865 Died at Cahaaba, Ala March 7, 1864., Returned report him died April 15, 1864 at Cahawba of pneumonia.

Prisoner of War Records show him admitted to Hospital at Cahaba Ala., date not given, and died March 7, 1864, of Pneumonia, Capture not given. (Signature) Assistant Adjutant General

O653-34 T. Ormandy 1823- Civil War Records & Profiles 1861-1865

Name: Thomas Ormandy Residence: New York City, New York Age at enlistment: 39 Enlistment Date: 23 Mar 1863 Rank at enlistment: Corporal Enlistment place: New York City, New York State Served: New York Was POW: Yes Survived the War: No Service Record: Promoted to Full Private on 15 Dec 1863. Promoted to Full Sergeant on 5 Jul 1863. Enlisted in

Company E, New York 178th Infantry Regiment on 19 Jun 1863. Mustered out on 13 Apr 1864 at Cohawba, AL. Birth Date: about 1824 Sources: New York: Report of the Adjutant-General

O653-14 Civil War Enlistment Papers - T. Ormandy
Headquarters, 491, Broadway (?); First Regiment; Seymour Light Infantry; N.Y.S.V.; New York, April 29th, 1863. This is to certify that Thomas Ormandy has been duly enlisted in the service of the United States by Lieut. S. H. S on the 23rd day of April 1863, has been attached to Company "I" of the First Regiment Seymour Light Infantry, and is now in camp at Sprague Barracks New Dorf S. I. He has a wife and ten children ...

O653-15 Civil War Military Records Thomas Ormandy
Ormandy, Thomas pg1581 M.L.R. 39 Years; Enlisted; 23 March 1863 N.Y . City; Period of Years; 3; Mustered in: 19 June 1863; Company E 178th Infantry Left the Organization: M.R. April 30, '64; Deserted 19 February 1864; Private; Explanation: from Sherman Expedition; M.R. June 30 , '65; Died 13 April 1864; at Cohawba, Ala. final statements forwarded . Remarks: Present M.R. June 30,'63 appointed Sergeant July 5, 1863 vice deserted Aug 31, '63, Oct 31, '63. Private absent without leave M.R. Feb 29, '64 captured by the enemy on Sherman Expedition in Miss. Aug. 31, '64, Oct 31, '64, Dec. 31, '64, Feb 28 '65, Apr. 30, '65 Present reduced to the ranks Aug 5, '63 M.R. Sep 31, '63
Born: England; Age 39 years; Occupation: Clerk; Eyes: Gray; Hair: Brown; Complexion: Light; 5' 8" high

Cahaba letter
Submitted by Jim Sause
Description Confederacy, Castle Morgan, Cahaba Ala., oatmeal paper Prisoner cover bearing U.S. 1861 3¢ rose tied by grid cancels, addressed to Lieut. Wilkins, 17th Ill. Vol. Inf. at Vicksburg Miss., matching " Old Point Comfort Va. Apr 18" dcds, endorsed "By flag of truce", original one-page letter datelined "Cahaba Military Prison, Cahaba, Ala. March 12 64" from Lieut. E.E. Ryan of same unit as addressee his cover shows no Confederate postal markings and was either hand carried to the Old Point Comfort, Va. transfer point, perhaps by another POW being exchanged or released, or sent inside another envelope franked with Confederate postage, the outer envelope being discarded at the transfer point. The Confederate Military Prison at Cahaba was also known a s Castle Morgan. This is a little-known prison but was actually more crowded and congested than Andersonville. Lt. Ryan was captured as a POW while leading a foraging party near Meridian, Miss. on Feb. 15, 1864. He was first confined at Cahaba Military Prison and was later transferred to Camp Oglethorpe with a brief stop through Andersonville. He was subsequently transferred to Savannah and then Charleston where he was under the fire of the Union bombardment of the city as a PO W. He survived and was exchanged in September 1864. During his time a s POW, Lt. Ryan kept a detailed diary that was later published. Accompanying this letter is a lengthy article entitled "Cahaba to Charleston: The Prison Odyssey of Lt. Edmund Ryan.". The letter is written on a small piece of lined notebook paper and says, in part, "Lieut Wilkins, I cannot depict to you the horror of being closely confined in prison day

after day and week after week. We have one consolation and that is that we are well treated by the officers of the prison."

Cahaba Prisoner of War Camp
Union & Confederate Civil War Prisoner of War Records, 1861-1865
[Selma, Alabama POW Camp]
Confederate 1863-1865
Selma, Alabama

In January 1864, Confederate authorities decided to establish a permanent prison facility at the unfinished red-brick cotton warehouse at Cahaba, Alabama. They acquired the warehouse for the use as a prison for captured Union prisoners in the summer of 1862. Col. Samuel M. Hill originally owned the warehouse and had constructed the building as part of a complex to provide storage for the Cahaba, Marion, and Greensborough Railroad. The railroad failed in the 1850's and the warehouse was abandoned.

The place had been used as a gathering point for the military district 's political and Union prisoners for several months, starting in late 1863. The prison was located on the on the central east end of the city on the banks of the Alabama and Cahaba Rivers. The prison was initially built to hold 500 prisoners. It held over 5,000 Union soldiers between 1863 and 1865.

The prison was 15,000 sq. feet, covered by a leaky roof with 1,600 feet of open space in its center and was surrounded by a tall brick wall. The building had 4 open windows and the floor was bare earth. A 12-foot-high wide-plank fence was built around the 1/3-acre site. Inside the building, bunks, 5 tiers high, were erected along the walls and would hold 432 men. By the end of March 1864, 660 prisoners were held at the prison.

The prison yard, enclosed by a fence, was about 35x46 feet and could be used by the prisoners during the daytime. It also served as the cook yard. Guards patrolled on an elevated walkway around the outside of the fence. Two small cannons protruded out of 2 portholes in the north end of the stockade wall. The walls of the warehouse were about 14 feet high and measured 193x116 feet on the outside.

By May 1864, there were 1,500 prisoners, and the prison was ordered to be closed. The prisoners healthy enough to travel were transferred to Andersonville Prison. When Andersonville became too overcrowded, Cahaba Prison was reopened. By September, there were 2,500 prisoners and that number eventually climbed to 3,000.

There were 2 co-commanders at the prison, with Capt. H.A.M. Henderson sharing command with Lt. Col. Sam Jones. Henderson took charge of the prison facilities, while Jones directed the prison's guards. The prison guard totaled 179 troops, with a number of them coming from established Alabama reserves

Life & Conditions:

Prisoners were contained in old decrepit buildings which held no provisions for bedding. Instead, prisoners slept on bare floors with one fireplace in the building to keep them warm. There was not any way to be at the building so open fires were allowed on the floor.

The water supply came from an open trench that ran from an artesian well, which had become extremely polluted by the sewer runoff from the town and the prison itself. The well was located

200 yards away, outside the prison wall. According to stories told, the river often flooded and covered the floors of the buildings in waters running 1-4 feet deep.

Rations were the standard issue of raw meat and cornmeal. The prisoners were required to do their own cooking.

The commanding officer at Cahaba Prison was Capt. H. A. M. Henderson. He was a Methodist minister. Due to his overseeing of this prison, prisoners were treated fairly and the death rate was extremely low in comparison to most other prison camps. Due to an increasing rate of sickness, a hospital was established at the Bell Tavern Hotel, 2 blocks away from the prison. The prevailing diseases were scurvy, dysentery, and chronic diarrhea. There were problems with lice, rats, and dysentery. However, Cahaba had access to ample medical supplies, firewood, and food. This contributed to the substantially lower death rate among Cahaba prisoners.

Aftermath:

The Union prisoners from Cahaba prison were to be transferred back to the Federal government. Their trip home ended up in a disaster. It became known as the "Sultana Disaster".

In the early morning hours of April 27, 1865, the steamboat Sultana exploded on the Mississippi River near Memphis, Tennessee. The Sultana was crowded with former Union prisoners-of-war from Cahaba Prison and was carrying over 2,000 people. Of these, 1,500 or more were killed either by the explosion, the subsequent fire, or drowning.

Occupation: artist.

Thomas married **Sarah JONES** [2342][10,16,71,72,73] [MRIN: 842], daughter of **JONES** [5174], in Aug 1845 in London, England. Sarah was born on 22 Aug 1825 in Chippenham, Wiltshire, England, died on 6 Aug 1872 in Astoria, Queens, New York, USA at age 46, and was buried on 8 Aug 1872 in Long Island City, Queens, New York, USA.

General Notes: O653-6

She proves her marriage for the pension report , by having an attorney in Rome, NY get a signed affidavit from the pastor of the Zion Protestant Episcopal Church in Rome, NY that she and Thomas were married in the parsonage on June 13, 1852!

She also proves she has 8 children under 16 years by producing Baptismal Certificate from Trinity Methodist Episcopal Church in NYC. Baptized 30 Oct 1864: Victoria, Jonathon, James, Tamar, Ruth and John C.

Children from this marriage were:

+ 43 F i. **Julia ORMANDY** [2354][10,16,71] was born on 4 Aug 1846 in Chippenham, Wiltshire, England.

Julia married **Francis Edward SUDDARD** [3335][10] [MRIN: 1171] on 11 Aug 1877 in Hackney, Middlesex, England.

+ 44 M ii. **William Lewithwaite ORMANDY [2339]**[10,16,71,72,84] was born on 26 Oct 1847 in London, England, died on 1 Apr 1893 in Mt. Zion, Oregon at age 45, and was buried in 1893 in Portland, Multnomah, Oregon, USA.

William married **Mary Ann HUSTON** [2340][16,71,72,84] [MRIN: 839] (b. 18 Feb 1845, d. 17 Sep 1919) on 24 Dec 1873 in New York, New York, USA.

+ 45 F iii. **Mary Wilkinson ORMANDY [2353]**[10,16,71] was born on 5 Aug 1849 in Utica, Oneida, New York, USA and died in 1880 in Pawnee, Kansas, USA at age 31.

Mary married **Isaac J. BROOKS** [3337][10] [MRIN: 1172] on 17 Feb 1874 in New York, New York, USA.

+ 46 F iv. **Victoria ORMANDY [2352]**[10,16,71,85] was born 12 Apr 1851(2) in Utica, Oneida, New York, USA, died 15 Apr 1907(2) in New York, New York, USA at age 56, and was buried in St. Raymonds Cem., The Bronx, NY.

Victoria married **Richard Francis SAUSE** [2578][16,85] [MRIN: 847] (b. 10 Apr 1851, d. 8 Mar 1909) about 1874 in New York, New York, USA.

+ 47 F v. **Esther (Hester?) Slee ORMANDY [2351]**[10,16,71] was born on 28 Dec 1852 in Syracuse, Oneida, New York.

Esther had a relationship with **Charles E. ORGAN** [3338] [MRIN: 1173].

+ 48 M vi. **Johnathan Harrison ORMANDY [2350]**[10,16,71] was born on 30 Apr 1854 in Freeport, Stephenson, Illinois, USA and died on 22 Oct 1927 in County Farm, Los Angeles, California at age 73.

Johnathan had a relationship with **Matilda Winifred POOLE** [3340] [MRIN: 1174].

+ 49 M vii. **George Julias ORMANDY [2349]**[10,16,71] was born on 21 Feb 1857 in Lewis, Cass Co., Iowa, USA and died on 15 May 1885 in Canton, China at age 28.

+ 50 M viii. **James Alma ORMANDY [2348]**[10,16,71] was born on 19 May 1858 in London, England and died in 1873 in Memphis, Shelby, Tennessee, USA at age 15.

+ 51 F ix. **Famar ORMANDY [2347]**[10,16,71] was born on 12 Jan 1860 in Ulverston, Lancashire, England.

+ 52 F x. **Ruth ORMANDY [2346]**[10,16,71] was born on 15 Jul 1862 in Carlisle, Cumberland, England.

Ruth married **Walter Scott GRIFFIN** [3343] [MRIN: 1175] on 30 Sep 1882.

+ 53 M xi. **John Cliffborne ORMANDY [2345]**[10,16,71] was born on 14 Jun 1864 in New York, New York, USA and died in 1932 in Whitehall, Washington, New York, USA at age 68.

John married **Claribel DOUGLAS** [2604][16] [MRIN: 846] (b. 13 Nov 1867, d. 1966) on 13 Nov 1887 in Whitehall, Washington, New York, USA.

37. Juliann ORMANDY [2823][10,16,42,54,79] *(John (Rev.) [2343]* [29]*, Thomas (Rev) [2619]* [17]*, Thomas [3123]* [7]*, William [3324]* [5]*, Richard [3923]* [1]*)* was born on 26 Aug 1825.

> General Notes: Baptism Date: 26 Aug 1825
> Baptism Place: Thwaites, Cumberland, England
> Marriage Date: 19 Apr 1860
> Marriage Place: Urswick, Lancashire, England
> Father: John Ormandy
> Spouse: Thomas Laurence
> FHL Film Number: 1040313

Juliann married **Thomas LAURENCE** [5388][79] [MRIN: 1095] on 19 Apr 1860 in Urswick, Lancashire, England.

38. John ORMANDY [2952][10,16,55,80] *(John (Rev.) [2343]* [29]*, Thomas (Rev) [2619]* [17]*, Thomas [3123]* [7]*, William [3324]* [5]*, Richard [3923]* [1]*)* was born in 1828 in Twaites Chapel, Millom, Cumberland, England, died in 1829 in Twaites Chapel, Millom, Cumberland, England at age 1, and was buried on 21 Apr 1829 in Twaites Chapel, Millom, Cumberland, England.

39. Harrison Wilkinson ORMANDY [2824][10,16,42,81,82,83] *(John (Rev.) [2343]* [29]*, Thomas (Rev) [2619]* [17]*, Thomas [3123]* [7]*, William [3324]* [5]*, Richard [3923]* [1]*)* was born on 29 Apr 1831 in Cumberland, England and died in Mar 1891 in Liverpool, Lancashire, England at age 59.

Apprentice Indentured in UK Merchant Navy 03 Jun 1848 on the Queen Ocean at age 16

Harrison married **Elizabeth FINNISWOOD** [5389][81] [MRIN: 2101] on 3 Nov 1868 in Barton, Westmorland, England.

40. Margaret ORMANDY [5390][61] (*George [3333]*[32], *Thomas (Rev) [2619]*[17], *Thomas [3123]*[7], *William [3324]*[5], *Richard [3923]*[1]) was born in 1833 in Lancashire, England.

41. William ORMANDY [5391][61] (*George [3333]*[32], *Thomas (Rev) [2619]*[17], *Thomas [3123]*[7], *William [3324]*[5], *Richard [3923]*[1]) was born in 1836 in Lancashire, England.

42. George ORMANDY [5392][61] (*George [3333]*[32], *Thomas (Rev) [2619]*[17], *Thomas [3123]*[7], *William [3324]*[5], *Richard [3923]*[1]) was born in 1837 in Lancashire, England.

Seventh Generation

43. Julia ORMANDY [2354][10,16,71] (*Thomas [2341]* [36]*, John (Rev.) [2343]* [29]*, Thomas (Rev) [2619]* [17]*, Thomas [3123]* [7]*, William [3324]* [5]*, Richard [3923]* [1]) was born on 4 Aug 1846 in Chippenham, Wiltshire, England.

Julia married **Francis Edward SUDDARD** [3335][10] [MRIN: 1171], son of **SUDDARD** [5176], on 11 Aug 1877 in Hackney, Middlesex, England.

General Notes: According to the marriage records Jim Sause rec'vd from England Julia and Francis Suddard were married Aug 11, 1877 at the Register Office in the District of Hackney, county of Middlesex. Julia is listed as a 30-year-old spinster who has no occupation listed. Francis is a 35-year-old bachelor who works as a teacher. Julia's father is listed as Thomas Ormandy and his occupation is artist.

The child from this marriage was:

+   54   M   i.   **Ebenezer Francis Edward SUDDARD [3336]**[10] was born on 29 Aug 1878 in London, England.

44.   William Lewithwaite ORMANDY [2339][10,16,71,72,84] (*Thomas [2341]* [36]*, John (Rev.) [2343]* [29]*, Thomas (Rev) [2619]* [17]*, Thomas [3123]* [7]*, William [3324]* [5]*, Richard [3923]* [1]) was born on 26 Oct 1847 in London, England, died on 1 Apr 1893 in Mt. Zion, Oregon at age 45, and was buried in 1893 in Portland, Multnomah, Oregon, USA.

General Notes: O653-1

Married Dec 24, 1873, by Revd. Dr. John Hall, pastor of Presbyterian Church, 5th Avenue & 19th Street, New York City. Died William, Mt. Zion n ear Portland, Or April 1st, 1893. Interred in Sylvan Cemetery. Reinterred Riverview Cemetery October 1919

William married **Mary Ann HUSTON** [2340][16,71,72,84] [MRIN: 839], daughter of **HUSTON** [5177], on 24 Dec 1873 in New York, New York, USA. Mary was born on 18 Feb 1845 in Londonderry, Northern Ireland, died on 17 Sep 1919 in Portland, Multnomah, Oregon, USA at age 74, and was buried on 19 Sep 1919 in Portland, Multnomah, Oregon, USA.

General Notes: O653-6 Burial: Riverview Cemetery From obituary:

Funeral services for Mrs. Mary A. Ormandy, a widely known and much-beloved resident of Irvington, were held last Friday at Westminster Church, Dr. Edward H. Pence officiating. Services at Riverview were private. Death took place Wednesday morning at her late residence, 501 Weidler, where she had lived many years. She had been in Oregon since 1889 and in Portland from 1893. Mrs. Ormandy was born in Londonderry, Ireland in February 1845, and came to New York in 1866 and was married to William L. Ormandy in 1873. He died in 1893. The children are: Harry W., William L., Walter L., James A., and E. Alice Ormandy.

Death was caused by paralysis. Mrs. Ormandy was widely known as a work er in charitable enterprises of Westminster, of which she was long a member.

O653-1 Born Feby 8, 1845 near Londonderry, Ireland. Married Dec. 24, 1873 by Revd. Dr. John Hull, pastor of Presbyterian Church 5th Ave. & 19th St. New York City. Died Portland, Or September 17th1919. Interred Riverview Cemetery Portland, Or Sept 19, 1919

Occupation: Charity Worker.

Children from this marriage were:

+ 55 M i. **Harrison Wilkinson ORMANDY [2376]**[71] was born on 14 Oct 1874 in New York, New York, USA, was christened on 14 Feb 1875 in Dr. Halls Church 5Th Ave. & 19Th St., Ny, NY, died on 20 Mar 1953 in Hondo, CA at age 78, and was buried on 25 Mar 1953 in Riverview, Portland Oregon.

+ 56 M ii. **William Lewithwaite ORMANDY [2360]**[71,86] was born on 19 May 1878 in Larned, Pawnee, Kansas, USA, was christened on 5 Jun 1881, and died on 16 Jan 1929 in Portland, Multnomah, Oregon, USA at age 50.

    William married **Birdie Corabell GRISWOLD** [2361][71,86,87] [MRIN: 849] on 4 Jun 1907 in Portland, Multnomah, Oregon, USA.

+ 57 M iii. **James Alma ORMANDY [2337]**[71,72,88,89,90,91,92,93,94] was born on 12 Nov 1879 in Pleasant Valley, Pawnee, Kansas, USA, was christened on 5 Jun 1881, died on 12 Sep 1958 in Portland, Multnomah, Oregon, USA at age 78, and was buried on 14 Sep 1958 in Riverview Cemetery, Portland, Oregon.

    James married **Edith Frances STEPHENSON** [2338][71,72,89,90,91,93,94,95,96,97,98,99,100] [MRIN: 782] (b. 19 Jun 1899, d. 14 Jul 1989) on 14 Mar 1925 in Portland, Multnomah, Oregon, USA.

+ 58 F iv. **Esther Alice ORMANDY [2359]**[71,101,102] was born on 5 Nov 1881 in Pleasant Valley, Pawnee, Kansas, USA, died on 6 Jan 1971 in Gladstone, Clackamas, Oregon, USA at age 89, and was buried on 9 Jan 1971 in Portland, Multnomah, Oregon, USA.

+ 59 M v. **Walter Scott ORMANDY [2355]**[71,103,104] was born on 29 Sep 1887 in Pleasant Valley, Pawnee, Kansas, USA, died on 13 Jul 1961 in Portland, Multnomah, Oregon, USA at age 73, and was buried in 1961 in Portland, Multnomah, Oregon, USA.

Walter had a relationship with **Lola Lydia IRVIN** [2356][103] [MRIN: 848]. (b. 1886, d. 13 May 1969)

45. Mary Wilkinson ORMANDY [2353][10,16,71] *(Thomas [2341]* [36]*, John (Rev.) [2343]* [29]*, Thomas (Rev) [2619]* [17]*, Thomas [3123]* [7]*, William [3324]* [5]*, Richard [3923]* [1]*)* was born on 5 Aug 1849 in Utica, Oneida, New York, USA and died in 1880 in Pawnee, Kansas, USA at age 31.

General Notes: O653-6

In the 1870 census, she is listed as living with her sister Julia and the Lamb family in New York. Her occupation is listed as a dressmaker. In 1874 Mary graduated from the Eclectic Medical School in New York. That same year she married Issac J. Brooks who was studying to become a doctor (student of medicine) marriage certificate. Mara as she was called died in 1880 in Pawnee County Kansas. She and her husband had followed her brothers to Kansas and died of purple fever. This information was found in the AIS Mortality Schedules Index. She was listed as Mary W. Brooks age 29 birth New York.

Mary married **Isaac J. BROOKS** [3337][10] [MRIN: 1172], son of **BROOKS** [5178], on 17 Feb 1874 in New York, New York, USA.

46. Victoria ORMANDY [2352][10,16,71,85] *(Thomas [2341]* [36]*, John (Rev.) [2343]* [29]*, Thomas (Rev) [2619]* [17]*, Thomas [3123]* [7]*, William [3324]* [5]*, Richard [3923]* [1]*)* was born 12 Apr 1851(2) in Utica, Oneida, New York, USA, died 15 Apr 1907(2) in New York, New York, USA at age 56, and was buried in St. Raymonds Cem., The Bronx, NY.

Victoria married **Richard Francis SAUSE** [2578][16,85] [MRIN: 847], son of **SAUSE** [5179], about 1874 in New York, New York, USA. Richard was born on 10 Apr 1851 in New York, New York, USA and died on 8 Mar 1909 in Bronx, Bronx, New York, USA at age 57.

Children from this marriage were:

+ 60 F i. **Victoria SAUSE [2579]**[85] was born in 1875 in New York, New York, USA and died in 1887 in New York, New York, USA at age 12.

+ 61 M ii. **Richard Victor SAUSE [2580]**[85] was born in Apr 1876 in New York, New York, USA and died on 19 Dec 1959 in Staten Island, Richmond, New York, USA at age 83.

    Richard married **Mary MARTIN** [2590][85] [MRIN: 958] (b. Abt 1876) about 1902 in New York, New York, USA.

+ 62 M iii. **Frank SAUSE [2581]**[85] was born on 26 Feb 1878 in New York, New York, USA and died on 15 Feb 1980 in Castle Point Vet Hosp., Beacon, New York, USA at age 101.

+ 63 F iv. **Genevieve SAUSE [2582]**[85] was born in Apr 1880 in New York, New York, USA and died on 3 Sep 1881 in New York, New York, USA at age 1.

+ 64 M v. **Peter Harrison SAUSE [2583]**[85] was born on 9 Sep 1882 in New York, New York, USA and died in Mar 1975 in Cleveland, Cuyahoga, Ohio, USA at age 92.

+ 65 M vi. **William J. SAUSE [2589]**[85] was born on 3 Nov 1884 in New York, New York, USA and died in Jul 1886 in New York, New York, USA at age 1.

+ 66 M vii. **George G. SAUSE [2584]**[85] was born on 30 Aug 1886 in New York, New York, USA and died in Mar 1968 in Souderton, Montgomery, Pennsylvania, USA at age 81.

+ 67 M viii. **Clifton John SAUSE [2585]**[85] was born on 22 Nov 1888 in New York, New York, USA and died on 26 Aug 1965 in Staten Island, Richmond, New York, USA at age 76.

+ 68 F ix. **Grace SAUSE [2586]**[85] was born in Jan 1889 in New York, New York, USA and died in Dec 1911 in New York, New York, USA at age 22.

+ 69 M x. **Edward SAUSE [2587]**[85] was born on 3 Jan 1890 in New York, New York, USA and died in Mar 1970 at age 80.

+ 70 F xi. **Florence SAUSE [2588]**[85] was born in Jan 1894 in New York, New York, USA and died on 12 Jan 1960 at age 66.

47. Esther (Hester?) Slee ORMANDY [2351][10,16,71] *(Thomas [2341]* [36]*, John (Rev.) [2343]* [29]*, Thomas (Rev) [2619]* [17]*, Thomas [3123]* [7]*, William [3324]* [5]*, Richard [3923]* [1]*)* was born on 28 Dec 1852 in Syracuse, Oneida, New York.

General Notes: O653-6 May have been adopted into another family.

Esther had a relationship with **Charles E. ORGAN** [3338] [MRIN: 1173], son of **ORGAN** [5180]. No evidence this couple married.

Their child was:
+   71 F   i.   **Jean Marie ORGAN [3339]** was born on 5 Sep 1879 in Noxon, New York, USA and died on 14 Mar 1961 at age 81.

48. Johnathan Harrison ORMANDY [2350][10,16,71] *(Thomas [2341]* [36]*, John (Rev.) [2343]* [29]*, Thomas (Rev) [2619]* [17]*, Thomas [3123]* [7]*, William [3324]* [5]*, Richard [3923]* [1]*)* was born on 30 Apr 1854 in Freeport, Stephenson, Illinois, USA and died on 22 Oct 1927 in County Farm, Los Angeles, California at age 73.

General Notes: O653-6 Known to be living in Pawnee Kansas 1878-1880

Johnathan had a relationship with **Matilda Winifred POOLE** [3340] [MRIN: 1174], daughter of **POOLE** [5181]. No evidence this couple married.

Their children were:
+   72 F   i.   **Sarah J. ORMANDY [3341]** was born in 1878 in Kansas, USA.
+   73 M   ii. **Clifton Harrison ORMANDY [3342]** was born in Dec 1881 in Kansas, USA.

49. George Julias ORMANDY [2349][10,16,71] *(Thomas [2341]* [36]*, John (Rev.) [2343]* [29]*, Thomas (Rev) [2619]* [17]*, Thomas [3123]* [7]*, William [3324]* [5]*, Richard [3923]* [1]*)* was born on 21 Feb 1857 in Lewis, Cass Co., Iowa, USA and died on 15 May 1885 in Canton, China at age 28.

General Notes: O653-6 Died on board USS Alert in Canton China

50. James Alma ORMANDY [2348][10,16,71] *(Thomas [2341]* [36]*, John (Rev.) [2343]* [29]*, Thomas (Rev) [2619]* [17]*, Thomas [3123]* [7]*, William [3324]* [5]*, Richard [3923]* [1]) was born on 19 May 1858 in London, England and died in 1873 in Memphis, Shelby, Tennessee, USA at age 15.

General Notes: O653-6 May have died in Yellow Fever Epidemic in Memphis, TN

51. Famar ORMANDY [2347][10,16,71] *(Thomas [2341]* [36]*, John (Rev.) [2343]* [29]*, Thomas (Rev) [2619]* [17]*, Thomas [3123]* [7]*, William [3324]* [5]*, Richard [3923]* [1]) was born on 12 Jan 1860 in Ulverston, Lancashire, England.

General Notes: O653-6 Known to have been living in Elizabeth NJ in 1879

52. Ruth ORMANDY [2346][10,16,71] *(Thomas [2341]* [36]*, John (Rev.) [2343]* [29]*, Thomas (Rev) [2619]* [17]*, Thomas [3123]* [7]*, William [3324]* [5]*, Richard [3923]* [1]) was born on 15 Jul 1862 in Carlisle, Cumberland, England.

General Notes: O653-6 Was known to be living in NYC in 1885. Joe Charles Cabbane of St. Louis, MO was legal guardian in 1878.

Ruth married **Walter Scott GRIFFIN** [3343] [MRIN: 1175], son of **GRIFFIN** [5182], on 30 Sep 1882.

53. John Cliffborne ORMANDY [2345][10,16,71] *(Thomas [2341]* [36]*, John (Rev.) [2343]* [29]*, Thomas (Rev) [2619]* [17]*, Thomas [3123]* [7]*, William [3324]* [5]*, Richard [3923]* [1]) was born on 14 Jun 1864 in New York, New York, USA and died in 1932 in Whitehall, Washington, New York, USA at age 68.

John married **Claribel DOUGLAS** [2604][16] [MRIN: 846], daughter of **DOUGLAS** [5183], on 13 Nov 1887 in Whitehall, Washington, New York, USA. Claribel was born on 13 Nov 1867 in Whitehall, Washington, New York, USA and died in 1966 in Whitehall, Washington, New York, USA at age 99.

Children from this marriage were:

+ 74 M i. **C. Harold ORMANDY [2606]**[16] was born in Whitehall, Washington, New York, USA.

> C. married **May COLLINS** [2611] [MRIN: 962] in 1912.

+ 75 M ii. **G. Edward ORMANDY [2605]**[16] was born on 2 Mar 1889 in New York, New York, USA and died on 17 Feb 1974 in Whitehall, Washington, New York, USA at age 84.

> G. had a relationship with **Sarah** [2607] [MRIN: 961]. (b. 1 Jun 1896, d. 25 May 1979)

Eighth Generation

54. Ebenezer Francis Edward SUDDARD [3336][10] (*Julia ORMANDY [2354]* [43]*, Thomas [2341]* [36]*, John (Rev.) [2343]* [29]*, Thomas (Rev) [2619]* [17]*, Thomas [3123]* [7]*, William [3324]* [5]*, Richard [3923]* [1]) was born on 29 Aug 1878 in London, England.

55. Harrison Wilkinson ORMANDY [2376][71] (*William Lewithwaite [2339]* [44]*, Thomas [2341]* [36]*, John (Rev.) [2343]* [29]*, Thomas (Rev) [2619]* [17]*, Thomas [3123]* [7]*, William [3324]* [5]*, Richard [3923]* [1]) was born on 14 Oct 1874 in New York, New York, USA, was christened on 14 Feb 1875 in Dr. Halls Church 5Th Ave. & 19Th St., Ny, NY, died on 20 Mar 1953 in Hondo, CA at age 78, and was buried on 25 Mar 1953 in Riverview, Portland Oregon.

General Notes: O653-1

Harrison Wilkinson Ormandy Born Oct 4, 1874 in 17 Perry St. New York City- Vaccinated Dec 9, 1874 Christened at Dr. Halls Church on 5th Avenue & 19th St. New York, Feb 14. 1875. Died at Hondo, Calf. March 20, 1953 Interred Riverview Cemetery Portland, Oregon, March 25, 1953

56. William Lewithwaite ORMANDY [2360][71,86] (*William Lewithwaite [2339]* [44]*, Thomas [2341]* [36]*, John (Rev.) [2343]* [29]*, Thomas (Rev) [2619]* [17]*, Thomas [3123]* [7]*, William [3324]* [5]*, Richard [3923]* [1]) was born on 19 May 1878 in Larned, Pawnee, Kansas, USA, was christened on 5 Jun 1881, and died on 16 Jan 1929 in Portland, Multnomah, Oregon, USA at age 50.

General Notes: O653-1 William Lewithwaite Ormandy Born May 18, 1878 in Topeka St. Larned Pawnee Co. Kansas. Vaccinated March 2, 1881 Christened June 5, 1881 by Rev. J.C. McElroy Died at Portland, Oregon Portland Sanitarium Jan 16, 1929. Interred Lincoln Memorial Park, Portland, OR

William married **Birdie Corabell GRISWOLD** [2361][71,86,87] [MRIN: 849], daughter of **GRISWOLD** [5184], on 4 Jun 1907 in Portland, Multnomah, Oregon, USA.

Children from this marriage were:

+   76   M   i.   **James Griswold ORMANDY [2375]**.[86]

     James had a relationship with **Eva Van BLARCIONE** [2757][86] [MRIN: 870].

+   77   F   ii.   **Margaret Mary ORMANDY [2373]**.[86]

     Margaret had a relationship with **Leigh SMITH** [2756][86] [MRIN: 868].

+   78   F   iii.   **Phyllis Patricia ORMANDY [2372].**[86]

     Phyllis had a relationship with **Walter PEARSON** [2766][86] [MRIN: 864].

     Phyllis next had a relationship with **Stewart SEELEY** [2789][86] [MRIN: 865].

     Phyllis next had a relationship with **John GAY** [2790][86] [MRIN: 866].

     Phyllis next had a relationship with **Clifford BITTINGER** [2794][86] [MRIN: 867].

+   79   M   iv.   **Donald Harrison ORMANDY [2364].**[86]

     Donald married **Mary** [2765][86] [MRIN: 856] in 1934.

+   80   M   v.   **Robert Mosier ORMANDY [2363].**[86]

     Robert had a relationship with **Helen** [2758][86] [MRIN: 851].

     Robert next had a relationship with **Diane** [2759][86] [MRIN: 852].

     Robert next had a relationship with **Audrey** [2760][86] [MRIN: 853].

     Robert next had a relationship with **Christine** [2761][86] [MRIN: 854].

     Robert next had a relationship with **Kathy** [2762][86] [MRIN: 855].

+   81   F   vi.   **Esther Grace ORMANDY [2362].**[86]

     Esther married **Albert Orman BERBERICK** [2754][86] [MRIN: 850] on 10 Apr 1937.

+   82   M   vii.   **William Lewithwaite ORMANDY [2374]**[86,87,105] was born on 11 Apr 1908 in Portland, Multnomah, OR.

     William had a relationship with **Carol BELLES** [2755][86] [MRIN: 869].

+   83   F   viii.   **Ruth Naomi ORMANDY [2365]**[86] was born on 20 Mar 1929.

     Ruth had a relationship with **Allan Keith NEAL** [2767][86] [MRIN: 857]. (b. 16 Oct 1924)

57. James Alma ORMANDY [2337][71,72,88,89,90,91,92,93,94] (*William Lewithwaite [2339]* [44], *Thomas [2341]* [36], *John (Rev.) [2343]* [29], *Thomas (Rev) [2619]* [17], *Thomas [3123]* [7], *William [3324]* [5], *Richard [3923]* [1]) was born on 12 Nov 1879 in Pleasant Valley, Pawnee, Kansas, USA, was christened on 5 Jun 1881, died on 12 Sep 1958 in Portland, Multnomah, Oregon, USA at age 78, and was buried on 14 Sep 1958 in Riverview Cemetery, Portland, Oregon.

     General Notes: Died at Emmanuel Hospital, Portland Oregon, 12 Sep 1958. Interred Riverview Cemetery, Portland Oregon 14 Sep 1958

     O653-1   James Alma Ormandy Born Nov 12, 1879 in Pleasant Valley Towns hip, Pawnee Co., Kansas. Christened June 15, 81 by Rev. J.C. McElroy. Married to Edith Frances Stephenson at Trinity Episcopal Church Port land, Ore March 14, 1925 by Rev. A.A. Morrison. Died Sept 12/13, 1958

O653-3 "Ormandy, Former SP Passenger Agent, Dies"

James A. Ormandy, general passenger agent for the Southern Pacific railroad in Portland from 1923 to 1949, died at Emanual hospital Saturday night. He was 78.

Born in Larned, Kansas. Ormandy came to Portland as a boy and attended the Harrison Street grammar institute. His first job was as a Western Union Messenger, delivering telegrams at 2 cents each. With experience in telegraphy picked up as a Western Union boy, Ormandy began his railroad career at 17.

Ormandy was a former president of the Oregon Advertising club, a member of the board of directors of the Portland Chamber of Commerce and Rose Festival, an honorary member of the Portland Passenger Assoc., and a member of the Arlington club, Shrine and Masonic lodge.

He is survived by his wife, Edith of 117 NW Trinity Pl.; two daughters, Mrs. Janet Marshall of Chicago and Mrs. Frances Ann Coffield of Newberg; a sister, Alice Ormandy and a brother, Walter, both of Portland, and eight grandchildren.

The service will be at 11 am Tuesday in the chapel of Trinity Episcopal Church.

James married **Edith Frances STEPHENSON** [2338][71,72,89,90,91,93,94,95,96,97,98,99,100] [MRIN: 782], daughter of **Franklin David STEPHENSON** [2377][72,89,95,97,98,106,107,108,109] and **Lucile Adelaide SMOOT** [2378],[72,89,95,97,106,107,108,110,111] on 14 Mar 1925 in Portland, Multnomah, Oregon, USA. Edith was born on 19 Jun 1899 in Walla Walla, Walla Walla, Washington, USA, died on 14 Jul 1989 in Portland, Multnomah, Oregon, USA at age 90, and was buried in Riverview Cemetery, Portland, Oregon.

General Notes: From Jan Marshall:

Worked for Childcraft & World book for about 12 years until her retirement in 1962. She had been an English teacher at the U. of North Dakota for about a year.

Also taught at Gresham High for a year. An active community volunteer, she had served as a reader for Doernbecher Children's Hospital and had made tapes for the blind. She had done volunteer work for the Oregon Historical Society, Girl Scouts, and guide at the Japanese Gardens. She wrote, performed & directed plays that were performed at Portland Civic Theatre.

S315-2 Edith S. Essex

A memorial service for Edith S. Essex of Southwest Portland will be a t 7p.m. Monday in First Christian Church.

She died of causes related to age July 14th in her home. She was 90.

She was born June 19, 1899, in Walla Walla. She had lived in the Portland area since she was a child. Her maiden name was Stephenson. She was a graduate of the University of Washington. She married J.A. Ormandy in 1925. Mr. Ormandy died in1958. She married Freeman Essex in 1967. He died in 1972.

Mrs. Essex had worked for Childcraft and Worldbook for about 12 years until her retirement in 1962. She had been an English teacher at the University of North Dakota for about a year and taught at Gresham High School for a year.

An active community volunteer, she had served as a reader for Doernbecher her Children's Hospital and had made tapes for the blind. She had done volunteer work for the Oregon Historical Society and the Girl Scouts and served as a guide for the Japanese Gardens.

She wrote and directed children's plays that were performed at Portland Civic Theatre and had acted in many productions at the theatre.

Survivors include her daughters, Frances O. Coffield of Newberg and Janet O. Marshall of Lake Oswego; eight grandchildren and 14 great-grandchildren.

Disposition was by cremation.

The family suggests that remembrances be contributions to the Japanese Garden Society.

Occupation: School Teacher.

Children from this marriage were:

+ 84 F i. **Francis Ann ORMANDY [2470]**[71,88,89] was born on 1 Mar 1926 in Portland, Multnomah, Oregon, USA and died on 30 Apr 2019 in Oregon, USA at age 93.

Francis married **William Howard COFFIELD** [2469][71,88] [MRIN: 915] (b. 25 Oct 1920) on 1 Sep 1946 in Portland, Multnomah, Oregon, USA.

+ 85 F ii. **Janet Alma ORMANDY [2224]**[71,72,88,89,112,113,114,115,116,117] was born on 20 Feb 1928 in Portland, Multnomah, Oregon, USA, was christened in Feb 1947 in Corvallis, Benton, Oregon, USA, died on 7 Mar 2000 in Portland, Multnomah, Oregon, USA at age 72, and was buried in Portland, Multnomah, Oregon, USA.

Janet married **Dr. Frederick James MARSHALL** [2223][72,88,112,113,114,115,117,118,119,120,121,122,123,124,125] [MRIN: 3] (b. 11 Feb 1925, d. 24 Jan 2008) on 21 Aug 1948 in Portland, Multnomah, Oregon, USA.

58. Esther Alice ORMANDY [2359][71,101,102] (*William Lewithwaite [2339]* [44], *Thomas [2341]* [36], *John (Rev.) [2343]* [29], *Thomas (Rev) [2619]* [17], *Thomas [3123]* [7], *William [3324]* [5], *Richard [3923]* [1]) was born on 5 Nov 1881 in Pleasant Valley, Pawnee, Kansas, USA, died on 6 Jan 1971 in Gladstone, Clackamas, Oregon, USA at age 89, and was buried on 9 Jan 1971 in Portland, Multnomah, Oregon, USA.

General Notes: O653-2

In Memory of Esther Alice Ormandy Born Pawnee County, Kansas, November 5, 1881 Passed away Portland, Oregon, Services Hustad Funeral Home 7 303 North Leavitt Ave Saturday, January 9th at 2:00 Clergyman Rev. Martin W. Crabb, Pastor Kenton United Presbyterian Church 2115 N. Lombard St., Private Vault Internment Riverview Cemetery

O653-4

Funeral for Miss Esther Alice Ormandy, a retired Portland schoolteacher, will be Saturday at 2pm at the Hustad Funeral Home. Miss Ormandy, who made her home with a nephew at 8505 SE Cason Road, Gladstone, died Wednesday in a Gladstone convalescent hospital. She was 89. She was born in Pawnee

County, Kansas, Nov 5, 1881, and had lived in the Portland area since 1889. She taught elementary grades in the Portland school system until her retirement in 1946. She was a graduate of the University of Oregon where she was a member of Phi Beta Kappa, scholastic honorary. She was also a member of Minerva Chapter, 105, OES, the National Retired Teachers Assoc, the Oregon Retired Teachers Assoc and did volunteer service work for the Salvation Army. Private vault interment will follow the funeral. Miss Ormandy is survived by a number of nieces & nephews.

Occupation: Portland Elementary School Teacher - retired.

EDUC: University of Oregon.

59. Walter Scott ORMANDY [2355][71,103,104] (*William Lewithwaite [2339]* [44]*, Thomas [2341]* [36]*, John (Rev.) [2343]* [29]*, Thomas (Rev) [2619]* [17]*, Thomas [3123]* [7]*, William [3324]* [5]*, Richard [3923]* [1]) was born on 29 Sep 1887 in Pleasant Valley, Pawnee, Kansas, USA, died on 13 Jul 1961 in Portland, Multnomah, Oregon, USA at age 73, and was buried in 1961 in Portland, Multnomah, Oregon, USA.

General Notes: O653-1

Scott Ormandy. Born Sept 29, 1887 on SW 1/4 section 10, Top'n 23 Range 16 in Pleasant Valley township, Pawnee Co. Kansas

Walter had a relationship with **Lola Lydia IRVIN** [2356][103] [MRIN: 848]. No evidence this couple married. Lola was born in 1886, died on 13 May 1969 in Portland, Multnomah, Oregon, USA at age 83, and was buried in Riverview Cem. Portland, Multnomah, Oregon, USA.

General Notes: ORMANDY - Lola, 7657 N Willamette Blvd.; mother of Irvin S. Ormandy; 6 grandchildren, 3 great grandchildren; sister of Alda Ervin. Services Thursday, May 15, at 2 pm, Hustad Funeral Home, 7303 N. Leavitt. Private committal Riverview Cemetery.

[The Oregonian, 14 May 1969, p59]

Their children were:

+ 86 M i. **Irwin Scott ORMANDY [2358]**.[103]
+ 87 F ii. **Mary Francis ORMANDY [2357]** was born in 1920.

60. Victoria SAUSE [2579][85] (*Victoria ORMANDY [2352]*[46]*, Thomas [2341]*[36]*, John (Rev.) [2343]*[29]*, Thomas (Rev) [2619]*[17]*, Thomas [3123]*[7]*, William [3324]*[5]*, Richard [3923]*[1]*)* was born in 1875 in New York, New York, USA and died in 1887 in New York, New York, USA at age 12.

61. Richard Victor SAUSE [2580][85] (*Victoria ORMANDY [2352]*[46]*, Thomas [2341]*[36]*, John (Rev.) [2343]*[29]*, Thomas (Rev) [2619]*[17]*, Thomas [3123]*[7]*, William [3324]*[5]*, Richard [3923]*[1]*)* was born in Apr 1876 in New York, New York, USA and died on 19 Dec 1959 in Staten Island, Richmond, New York, USA at age 83.

Richard married **Mary MARTIN** [2590][85] [MRIN: 958] about 1902 in New York, New York, USA. Mary was born about 1876 in Castleblayney, Monaghan, Ireland.

Children from this marriage were:

+   88   M   i.   **Thomas SAUSE [2592]**.
+   89   F   ii.   **Everline SAUSE [2593]**.
+   90   M   iii.   **Edward SAUSE [2594]**.
+   91   M   iv.   **Richard Francis SAUSE [2591]**[85] was born on 22 May 1903.

            Richard married **Winnifred CURRY** [2595][85] [MRIN: 959] on 16 Jun 1925 in Staten Island, Richmond, New York, USA.

62. Frank SAUSE [2581][85] (*Victoria ORMANDY [2352]*[46]*, Thomas [2341]*[36]*, John (Rev.) [2343]*[29]*, Thomas (Rev) [2619]*[17]*, Thomas [3123]*[7]*, William [3324]*[5]*, Richard [3923]*[1]*)* was born on 26 Feb 1878 in New York, New York, USA and died on 15 Feb 1980 in Castle Point Vet Hosp., Beacon, New York, USA at age 101.

63. Genevieve SAUSE [2582][85] (*Victoria ORMANDY [2352]*[46]*, Thomas [2341]*[36]*, John (Rev.) [2343]*[29]*, Thomas (Rev) [2619]*[17]*, Thomas [3123]*[7]*, William [3324]*[5]*, Richard [3923]*[1]*)* was born in Apr 1880 in New York, New York, USA and died on 3 Sep 1881 in New York, New York, USA at age 1.

64. Peter Harrison SAUSE [2583][85] (*Victoria ORMANDY [2352]*[46]*, Thomas [2341]*[36]*, John (Rev.) [2343]*[29]*, Thomas (Rev) [2619]*[17]*, Thomas [3123]*[7]*, William [3324]*[5]*, Richard [3923]*[1]*)* was born on 9

Sep 1882 in New York, New York, USA and died in Mar 1975 in Cleveland, Cuyahoga, Ohio, USA at age 92.

65. William J. SAUSE [2589][85] (*Victoria ORMANDY [2352]* [46], *Thomas [2341]* [36], *John (Rev.) [2343]* [29], *Thomas (Rev) [2619]* [17], *Thomas [3123]* [7], *William [3324]* [5], *Richard [3923]* [1]) was born on 3 Nov 1884 in New York, New York, USA and died in Jul 1886 in New York, New York, USA at age 1.

66. George G. SAUSE [2584][85] (*Victoria ORMANDY [2352]* [46], *Thomas [2341]* [36], *John (Rev.) [2343]* [29], *Thomas (Rev) [2619]* [17], *Thomas [3123]* [7], *William [3324]* [5], *Richard [3923]* [1]) was born on 30 Aug 1886 in New York, New York, USA and died in Mar 1968 in Souderton, Montgomery, Pennsylvania, USA at age 81.

67. Clifton John SAUSE [2585][85] (*Victoria ORMANDY [2352]* [46], *Thomas [2341]* [36], *John (Rev.) [2343]* [29], *Thomas (Rev) [2619]* [17], *Thomas [3123]* [7], *William [3324]* [5], *Richard [3923]* [1]) was born on 22 Nov 1888 in New York, New York, USA and died on 26 Aug 1965 in Staten Island, Richmond, New York, USA at age 76.

68. **Grace SAUSE [2586]**[85] (*Victoria ORMANDY [2352]* [46]*, Thomas [2341]* [36]*, John (Rev.) [2343]* [29]*, Thomas (Rev) [2619]* [17]*, Thomas [3123]* [7]*, William [3324]* [5]*, Richard [3923]* [1]) was born in Jan 1889 in New York, New York, USA and died in Dec 1911 in New York, New York, USA at age 22.

69. **Edward SAUSE [2587]**[85] (*Victoria ORMANDY [2352]* [46]*, Thomas [2341]* [36]*, John (Rev.) [2343]* [29]*, Thomas (Rev) [2619]* [17]*, Thomas [3123]* [7]*, William [3324]* [5]*, Richard [3923]* [1]) was born on 3 Jan 1890 in New York, New York, USA and died in Mar 1970 at age 80.

70. **Florence SAUSE [2588]**[85] (*Victoria ORMANDY [2352]* [46]*, Thomas [2341]* [36]*, John (Rev.) [2343]* [29]*, Thomas (Rev) [2619]* [17]*, Thomas [3123]* [7]*, William [3324]* [5]*, Richard [3923]* [1]) was born in Jan 1894 in New York, New York, USA and died on 12 Jan 1960 at age 66.

71. **Jean Marie ORGAN [3339]** (*Esther (Hester?) Slee ORMANDY [2351]* [47]*, Thomas [2341]* [36]*, John (Rev.) [2343]* [29]*, Thomas (Rev) [2619]* [17]*, Thomas [3123]* [7]*, William [3324]* [5]*, Richard [3923]* [1]) was born on 5 Sep 1879 in Noxon, New York, USA and died on 14 Mar 1961 at age 81.

72. Sarah J. ORMANDY [3341] (*Johnathan Harrison [2350]* [48]*, Thomas [2341]* [36]*, John (Rev.) [2343]* [29]*, Thomas (Rev) [2619]* [17]*, Thomas [3123]* [7]*, William [3324]* [5]*, Richard [3923]* [1]) was born in 1878 in Kansas, USA.

73. Clifton Harrison ORMANDY [3342] (*Johnathan Harrison [2350]* [48]*, Thomas [2341]* [36]*, John (Rev.) [2343]* [29]*, Thomas (Rev) [2619]* [17]*, Thomas [3123]* [7]*, William [3324]* [5]*, Richard [3923]* [1]) was born in Dec 1881 in Kansas, USA.

74. C. Harold ORMANDY [2606] [16] (*John Cliffborne [2345]* [53]*, Thomas [2341]* [36]*, John (Rev.) [2343]* [29]*, Thomas (Rev) [2619]* [17]*, Thomas [3123]* [7]*, William [3324]* [5]*, Richard [3923]* [1]) was born in Whitehall, Washington, New York, USA.

C. married **May COLLINS** [2611] [MRIN: 962], daughter of **COLLINS** [5185], in 1912.

The child from this marriage was:
+   92   F   i.   **Margaret Claribel ORMANDY [2612]**.
                      Margaret married **Howard M. CLARK** [2613] [MRIN: 964] in Mar 1936.

75. G. Edward ORMANDY [2605] [16] (*John Cliffborne [2345]* [53]*, Thomas [2341]* [36]*, John (Rev.) [2343]* [29]*, Thomas (Rev) [2619]* [17]*, Thomas [3123]* [7]*, William [3324]* [5]*, Richard [3923]* [1]) was born on 2 Mar 1889 in New York, New York, USA and died on 17 Feb 1974 in Whitehall, Washington, New York, USA at age 84.

G. had a relationship with **Sarah** [2607] [MRIN: 961]. No evidence this couple married. Sarah was born on 1 Jun 1896 in Whitehall, Washington, New York, USA and died on 25 May 1979 in Whitehall, Washington, New York, USA at age 82.

Their child was:
+   93   F   i.   **Ruth Mae ORMANDY [2608]**.
                      Ruth married **Lloyd C. LAMPHRON** [2609] [MRIN: 963] in Jul 1935.

Ninth Generation

76. James Griswold ORMANDY [2375][86] (*William Lewithwaite [2360]*[56], *William Lewithwaite [2339]*[44], *Thomas [2341]*[36], *John (Rev.) [2343]*[29], *Thomas (Rev) [2619]*[17], *Thomas [3123]*[7], *William [3324]*[5], *Richard [3923]*[1]).

James had a relationship with **Eva Van BLARCIONE** [2757][86] [MRIN: 870], daughter of **BLARCIONE** [5186]. No evidence this couple married.

Their child was:

+ 94 M   i.   **Ray ORMANDY [2779]**.[86]

Ray had a relationship with **Babe** [2780][86] [MRIN: 998].

Ray next had a relationship with **Jeri** [2781][86] [MRIN: 999].

Ray next had a relationship with **Mary** [2783][86] [MRIN: 1000].

77. Margaret Mary ORMANDY [2373][86] (*William Lewithwaite [2360]*[56], *William Lewithwaite [2339]*[44], *Thomas [2341]*[36], *John (Rev.) [2343]*[29], *Thomas (Rev) [2619]*[17], *Thomas [3123]*[7], *William [3324]*[5], *Richard [3923]*[1]).

Margaret had a relationship with **Leigh SMITH** [2756][86] [MRIN: 868], son of **SMITH** [5188]. No evidence this couple married.

Their children were:

+ 95 M   i.   **Anthony Leigh SMITH [2776]**.[86]

Anthony had a relationship with **Ariel** [2777][86] [MRIN: 996].

+ 96 F   ii.   **Carolyn Marie SMITH [2778]**.[86]

Carolyn had a relationship with **Jason LYNETTE** [2808] [MRIN: 997].

78. Phyllis Patricia ORMANDY [2372][86] (*William Lewithwaite [2360]*[56], *William Lewithwaite [2339]*[44], *Thomas [2341]*[36], *John (Rev.) [2343]*[29], *Thomas (Rev) [2619]*[17], *Thomas [3123]*[7], *William [3324]*[5], *Richard [3923]*[1]).

Phyllis had a relationship with **Walter PEARSON** [2766][86] [MRIN: 864], son of **PEARSON** [5189]. No evidence this couple married.

Their children were:

+ 97 M   i.   **Duke Christian PEARSON [2787]**.[86]

+ 98 F   ii.   **Candace PEARSON [2788]**.[86]

Phyllis next had a relationship with **Stewart SEELEY** [2789][86] [MRIN: 865], son of **SEELEY** [5190]. The marriage ended in divorce. No evidence this couple married.

Phyllis next had a relationship with **John GAY** [2790][86] [MRIN: 866], son of **GAY** [5191]. No evidence this couple married.

Their children were:

+ 99 F i. **Vixen GAY [2791]**.[86]
+ 100 M ii. **Volney GAY [2792]**.[86]
+ 101 F iii. **Niliss (?) GAY [2793]**.[86]

Phyllis next had a relationship with **Clifford BITTINGER** [2794][86] [MRIN: 867], son of **BITTINGER** [5192]. No evidence this couple married.

79. Donald Harrison ORMANDY [2364][86] (*William Lewithwaite [2360]*[56], *William Lewithwaite [2339]*[44], *Thomas [2341]*[36], *John (Rev.) [2343]*[29], *Thomas (Rev) [2619]*[17], *Thomas [3123]*[7], *William [3324]*[5], *Richard [3923]*[1]).

Donald married **Mary** [2765][86] [MRIN: 856] in 1934. The marriage ended in divorce.

80. Robert Mosier ORMANDY [2363][86] (*William Lewithwaite [2360]*[56], *William Lewithwaite [2339]*[44], *Thomas [2341]*[36], *John (Rev.) [2343]*[29], *Thomas (Rev) [2619]*[17], *Thomas [3123]*[7], *William [3324]*[5], *Richard [3923]*[1]).

Robert had a relationship with **Helen** [2758][86] [MRIN: 851]. No evidence this couple married.

Robert next had a relationship with **Diane** [2759][86] [MRIN: 852]. No evidence this couple married.

Robert next had a relationship with **Audrey** [2760][86] [MRIN: 853]. No evidence this couple married.

Robert next had a relationship with **Christine** [2761][86] [MRIN: 854]. No evidence this couple married.

Robert next had a relationship with **Kathy** [2762][86] [MRIN: 855]. No evidence this couple married.

Their children were:

+ 102 F i. **Debbie ORMANDY [2763]**.[86]

+ 103 M ii. **Brett ORMANDY [2764].**[86]

81. Esther Grace ORMANDY [2362][86] (*William Lewithwaite [2360]* [56], *William Lewithwaite [2339]* [44], *Thomas [2341]* [36], *John (Rev.) [2343]* [29], *Thomas (Rev) [2619]* [17], *Thomas [3123]* [7], *William [3324]* [5], *Richard [3923]* [1]).

Esther married **Albert Orman BERBERICK** [2754][86] [MRIN: 850], son of **BERBERICK** [5194], on 10 Apr 1937.

The child from this marriage was:

+ 104 M i. **Norman Albert BERBERICK [2768]**[86] was born on 24 Jul 1942.

Norman married **Georgiana HIGG** [2769][86] [MRIN: 993] in Oct 1966.

82. William Lewithwaite ORMANDY [2374][86,87,105] (*William Lewithwaite [2360]* [56], *William Lewithwaite [2339]* [44], *Thomas [2341]* [36], *John (Rev.) [2343]* [29], *Thomas (Rev) [2619]* [17], *Thomas [3123]* [7], *William [3324]* [5], *Richard [3923]* [1]) was born on 11 Apr 1908 in Portland, Multnomah, OR.

General Notes: WWII Draft

Name: William Lewthwaite Ormandy
Gender: Male
Race: White
Age: 32
Relationship to Draftee: Self (Head)
Birth Date: 11 Apr 1908
Birth Place: Portland, Oregon, USA
Residence Place: Portland, Multnomah, Oregon, USA
Registration Date: 16 Oct 1940
Registration Place: Oregon, USA
Employer: Unemployed
Weight: 135
Complexion: Light
Eye Color: Hazel
Hair Color: Brown
Height: 5 6
Next of Kin: Birdie Cora Belle Ormandy

William had a relationship with **Carol BELLES** [2755][86] [MRIN: 869], daughter of **BELLES** [5187]. No evidence this couple married.

83. Ruth Naomi ORMANDY [2365][86] (*William Lewithwaite [2360]*[56], *William Lewithwaite [2339]*[44], *Thomas [2341]*[36], *John (Rev.) [2343]*[29], *Thomas (Rev) [2619]*[17], *Thomas [3123]*[7], *William [3324]*[5], *Richard [3923]*[1]) was born on 20 Mar 1929.

Ruth had a relationship with **Allan Keith NEAL** [2767][86] [MRIN: 857], son of **NEAL** [5193]. No evidence this couple married. Allan was born on 16 Oct 1924.

Their children were:

+   105   F   i.   **Bridget Kayne NEAL [2371]**[86] was born on 12 Dec 1950.

Bridget had a relationship with **Robert LINGO** [2795][86] [MRIN: 863]. (b. 10 Mar 1949)

+   106   M   ii.   **Garreth Allan NEAL [2370]**[86] was born on 12 Jun 1952.

Garreth had a relationship with **Kathleen Linda SHONE** [2798][86] [MRIN: 862]. (b. 20 Sep 1956)

+   107   M   iii.   **Mathew Peter NEAL [2369]**[86] was born on 30 Sep 1956.

+   108   M   iv.   **Andrew Ormandy NEAL [2368]**[86] was born on 9 Sep 1958.

Andrew had a relationship with **Ella Andrea BACCI (?)** [2801][86] [MRIN: 861]. (b. 21 May 1971)

+   109   M   v.   **Camdon Keith NEAL [2367]**[86] was born on 25 Jul 1960.

Camdon had a relationship with **Abbe Jo SMITH** [2802][86] [MRIN: 860]. (b. 18 Sep 1959)

+   110   M   vi.   **Graden Patrick NEAL [2366]**[86] was born on 19 Jan 1963.

Graden had a relationship with **Carolyn McCANN** [2805][86] [MRIN: 858].

Graden next had a relationship with **Paula Jane** [2806][86] [MRIN: 859].

84. Francis Ann ORMANDY [2470][71,88,89] (*James Alma [2337]*[57], *William Lewithwaite [2339]*[44], *Thomas [2341]*[36], *John (Rev.) [2343]*[29], *Thomas (Rev) [2619]*[17], *Thomas [3123]*[7], *William [3324]*[5], *Richard [3923]*[1]) was born on 1 Mar 1926 in Portland, Multnomah, Oregon, USA and died on 30 Apr 2019 in Oregon, USA at age 93.

Francis married **William Howard COFFIELD** [2469][71,88] [MRIN: 915], son of **COFFIELD** [5195], on 1 Sep 1946 in Portland, Multnomah, Oregon, USA. William was born on 25 Oct 1920.

Children from this marriage were:

+   111   M   i.   **David Howard COFFIELD [2488]**[88] was born on 24 May 1947 in Silverton, Marion, Oregon, USA.

David had a relationship with **Roseanna** [2489] [MRIN: 921].

+ 112 F ii. **Sandra Lee COFFIELD [2480]**[88] was born on 11 Aug 1947 in Silverton, Marion, Oregon, USA.

Sandra had a relationship with **George BLAKESLEE** [2479] [MRIN: 918]. (b. 29 Aug 1945)

Sandra next had a relationship with **Gary BREWER** [2483] [MRIN: 919].

+ 113 F iii. **Susan COFFIELD [2477]**[88] was born on 8 Oct 1950 in Newberg, Yamhill, Oregon, USA.

Susan had a relationship with **Kent KALTENBACHER** [2476] [MRIN: 917].

+ 114 M iv. **Ronald William COFFIELD [2471]**[88] was born on 12 Mar 1952 in Newberg, Yamhill, Oregon, USA.

Ronald had a relationship with **Nancy** [2472] [MRIN: 916].

85. Janet Alma ORMANDY [2224][71,72,88,89,112,113,114,115,116,117] (*James Alma [2337]* [57]*, William Lewithwaite [2339]* [44]*, Thomas [2341]* [36]*, John (Rev.) [2343]* [29]*, Thomas (Rev) [2619]* [17]*, Thomas [3123]* [7]*, William [3324]* [5]*, Richard [3923]* [1]) was born on 20 Feb 1928 in Portland, Multnomah, Oregon, USA, was christened in Feb 1947 in Corvallis, Benton, Oregon, USA, died on 7 Mar 2000 in Portland, Multnomah, Oregon, USA at age 72, and was buried in Portland, Multnomah, Oregon, USA. Another name for Janet was Muzzy.

General Notes: Known as "Muzzy" by grandchildren/great-grandchildren and the "outlaws ", (Art, Michael, Connie and Karla). "Muzzy I" was Jan's grandmother' s name instead of grandma.

Janet Marshall

Christmas Day, 1934 - At Portland, Oregon

To Mr. St. Nick Santa Claus-

The Santa Claus Angel records herein the doings of one little girl. He r name as given to her by her worthy parents is Janet Ormandy - sometimes called Janety Panety the Pooleykobook.

Princess Janet had one high adventure. Tis meat you should know of it Dear Santa. It happened in thus wise. The month was September - just when the heat of summer turns toward the cool blasts of winter and all things stand betwix and between so to speak. The place was the Indian Reservation, and the horse was that beast called Old Blue. And the hills and canyons of the Warm Springs river still resound with the War Hoops of this tiny maid as she dashed hither and yon on the hurricane deck of the Blue nag.

Janet has treated her dog Princess with forthought and consideration; tho her Mother and Father have not always been treated so gently.

But when it comes to book learning the little Princess hath done exceedingly well. The Dutch Twins with the adventures of Kit and Kat are as past time and figures and Indian myths have passed without struggle. Of course sometimes she must stand in a corner to think things over and to see Ted daily that's not to be thought of.

Me thinks Santa Claus might well admonish the little maid to quarrel the less with the big sister and look to it that she minds her saintly mother and her devoted Mary.

When this has been done me thinks she should have her presents and wishes with a big kiss on each rosy red cheek for many, many Christmases as happy and free from care; and that light hearted she may go tripping through life bringing happiness to all around her.

The Recording Angel

Janet Ormandy Marshall -Obit

Janet Ormandy Marshall died March 7, 2000, surrounded by her loved ones.

She was born in Portland February 20, 1928 the second daughter of James and Edith Ormandy. She met her husband F. James Marshall (Jim) fifty -four years ago. He had come to Portland from Vancouver, Canada, to attend dental school after the war. His mother, Bertha and her mother, Edith who had been Camp Fire Girls together 30 years earlier, arranged a blind date. Jan said "yes" to a marriage proposal six weeks later.

After they married in 1948, she attended night school to complete her degree from Oregon State University and graduated in 1949 with a degree in Home Economics. Jan was Mrs. "Marshmallow" to her students when she taught kindergarten for a year to put Jim through his last year at dental school. She is a lifelong alum of the Gamma Phi Beta Sorority.

Jan and Jim raised four children while living in Vancouver, B.C., Chicago, IL, Winnipeg, Manitoba, Pittsburgh, PA and Columbus, OH, before returning to Portland in 1972.

Back "home" Jan discovered the pleasures of competitive tennis and volunteered at William Temple House for eight years as a lay counselor. She acted as "den mother" to Jim's graduate students. Over the years, she soared with the birds flying in a glider and a helicopter and taking single-engine flying lessons.

The joy and wonder of Jan's life will continue through her husband of fifty-two years, Jim; daughters, Barbara and Nancy; sons Gordon and Stephen. Their spouses, Arthur, Michael, Karla and Connie; grandchildren, Leslie, Erin, Heather, Katie, Emily, Luke, Carver, Bailey and Rowan; great grandson Riley; sister, Fran Coffield; nieces, nephews, cousins and good friends too numerous to count. One of her special gifts was the ability to make everyone who came to her home feel like they were a member of the family and her friend.

There will be a memorial service Saturday, March 18th at 2:00 pm at St. Luke Lutheran Church in SW Portland. In lieu of flowers, the family requests donations to William Temple House and the American Cancer Society.

Occupation: Teacher.

Janet married **Dr. Frederick James MARSHALL** [2223][72,88,112,113,114,115,117,118,119,120,121,122,123,124,125] [MRIN: 3], son of **Leslie Frederick MARSHALL** [2225][72,113,115,119,126,127,128,129,130,131,132,133,134] and **Robertha Josephine WATT** [2226],[72,113,115,119,126,135,136,137,138,139,140] on 21 Aug 1948 in Portland, Multnomah, Oregon, USA. Frederick was born on 11 Feb 1925 in Vancouver, British Columbia, Canada, was christened on 12 Apr 1925 in Vancouver, B.C., Canada, died on 24 Jan 2008 in Portland, Multnomah, Oregon, USA at age 82, and was buried on 23 Feb 2008 in Portland, Multnomah, Oregon, USA.

MY GLENGARRY

My Glengarry was a "bra wee cap" as my Scottish Granny Watt would say. We first became paired when I joined the Seaforth Highlander Cadet Battalion. We are still together today, some 55 years later. There were various additional caps along the way but "my Glengarry" brings back the best memories.

At the start I was part of the Signals platoon under Sgt. Maj. Ross Duncanson. Later on I became a Sgt. myself, but only after I had spent many long hours down at the old Hotel Vancouver (taken over during the war as Pacific Coast Army Headquarters) learning the Morse Code and other Signal necessities. My "wee cap" and I also spent many Friday afternoons getting polished and "spiffed up " for Friday night parades. I even modified the cap badge so that the antlers on the stag's head showed up more like the cast silver badges that officers wore. It was seldom out of my hands except for the time at Cadet Camp in Duncan, Vancouver Island, when I trusted it to a good friend while I won 50 cents on a dare and jumped/dived naked out of my kilt, off the nearby railroad bridge. Not a great example for a sergeant to make, next day the bridge was "off limits". That camp experience was also notable for our delayed return home to Vancouver, necessitated by the AWOL activities of Canadian Home Defense troops slated to go to the Aleutians.

Shortly after summer camp the "wee cap" went with me into the Canadian Army. Where we were to spend a year in the #2 Canadian Army University Training program in preparation for Officers Selection and Training. Basic training, however, came first and this was accomplished at Wetaskawin, Alberta. "Wee Cap" was kept stowed away all this time and also through the year that followed in barracks while we "learned a pre-officer education" at the University of British Columbia. "Wee Cap" was replaced by a sharp pointed slim cap with two brass buttons (the buttons were only there to polish during all the training time and all through the year that followed in while we "learned to be officers" at the University of British Columbia. We were marched to classes from our huts buried deeply in the woods of the University development lands (Acadia Camp - later to become student housing). The advantage of being far from sight meant that when we staged our "in house " water fights or sneaked into the Universities experimental chicken farms to enhance our rather mundane Army grub we weren't easily detected. On being suspected of "chicken raiding" we were merely asked to return the identification tags. "No names no pack drill". The thrilling highlight of this posting was my session with "mumps". Everyone one in camp seemed to get this dread disease sooner or later but I got mine just before Christmas. If my Dad hadn't had pull at the Infectious Disease Hospital in Vancouver and got me released early none of my hut-mates would have had Christmas Leave. Not a good public relations problem.

At the end of our year on campus "wee cap" and I went on leave, hitch hiked to Boeing Field in Seattle, where we talked our way onto a Flying Fortress (enroute to Spokane Washington). Sitting in the nose blister, bumping up and down was very hard on my airworthiness and I didn't enjoy all of the trip.

Next day it was off to Sacramento in a twin-engine Lockheed Hudson coastal command plane. "Wee cap" and me in my Army shorts and puttees caused truly noticeable stares as we explored the downtown. The next morning we were to continue on to Los Angeles, but our plane was "injured " in the night so the next best trip was in a small twin-engine, 6 passenger plane that took us to Palm Springs. All that we remember of that stop was a very small public library and an even smaller Town Hall, except for a plane smoking/burning up on the far side of the airfield. In retrospect it may have been the testing of one the early jets.

The next stop was Long Beach, reached by a DC-3, where I turned in my parachute before going on to Hollywood, the Stage Door Canteen, Breakfast at Sardies and other attractions. There "Wee Cap" and me in my summer uniform weren't so out of place.

Returning north on the ground wasn't so easy and we resorted to hitchhiking by big trucks. To my discomfort later on I indulged in Boston cream pie for dessert (in the desert south of San Francisco, I did visit the Stage Door Canteen in San Francisco but by the time I got to friends in Eugene I came down with a violent case of food poisoning. First, I was in a civilian hospital for IV therapy and then to Camp Adair (near Corvallis) by military ambulance and a 7 day stay. On being wheeled into the ward I was greeted by a fellow patient asking the nurse "what have you got there sister - a stiff!", I was not in good shape and to this day I eat no more Boston Cream pie. Although I missed my buddies next move, I did catch up with them in Camrose, Alberta.

With this move, the "Wee Cap" was stowed away again as we endured another Basic Infantry Training at course. Here we met a group of # 2 CAU T members from the U of Alberta. We didn't have much in common. They played bridge, in their spare time, we drank beer. The most unusual thing of notice during this time was to be on leave in Edmonton and be directed by "locals" to wait for a "Blue" streetcar, they were all painted red. Then if you were lucky you would find out that the colour referred to a small card at the front on the roof. It was great to be a greenhorn along with the many Americans there as they stopped off on their way to building the Alcan highway.

The "wee cap" remained stowed away through my next two training locations, Advanced Infantry Training at Curry Barracks (Calgary, Alberta) and Embarkation Preparation at Debert. Nova Scotia. Calgary was OK because it was my pal John Rudolph's hometown, and he had a sister and she had girlfriends. It was a notable trip by troop train from Calgary to Debert. Four days and three nights with meals served into our aluminum mess tins (this guaranteed instant cooling) and one blanket, no mattress, or other amenities. I remember the emptiness of the countryside. The railroads didn't get rich on the land that was their bonus for building them thus the barrenness. Debert was a bit of a surprise, the "beautiful Annapolis Valley" was anything but, rain and mud predominated. We were glad when we took off for Halifax and our trip overseas, although that voyage was less than a desirable experience. At Debert I added a third cap to my collection, an Army Beret- khaki in color. This traveled with me through the remaining time in service and even into the time after graduation when I joined the Reserve s as a dental officer (Captain, yet!). However, on leave later on I was able to exchange the beret for my "wee cap", my Glengarry.

7,000 give or take a few, boarded the RMS Andes, for an unescorted high-speed trip to England, into the teeth of a howling "North Atlantic November Winter Storm" leaving Halifax at mid-night. My smartest move on boarding was to pick a hammock for sleeping, at least I wasn't a target as were those who slept on the deck. Our quarters were " A deck aft" as far down as one could go and as far back -

this produced some very violent motions for the ship and noticeable reactions on those of us stationed there. We were to have had two meals per day. I had only "one" after I went in for breakfast the first day and was served "stewed liver and rice" into aluminum mess tins that guaranteed the food was cold. For the next 5 days I survived on crackers and sardines bought in the canteen. I still can't eat sardines.

When we arrived off the south coast of Ireland, we were met by two destroyers and escorted up the Irish Sea to the mouth of the Mersey River on our way to debarkation in Birmingham. We saw many little light s through the fog. They turned out to be markers on AA stations in sitting on wooden piles in the middle of the river. The next sight was a fully lighted hospital ship on its way home - welcome to the war!

A short ride by Canadian standards finally delivered us to Aldershot, an army base since Queen Victoria's days and it looked the part. Our mess hall was the original horse stables. We trained hard for a month, then the first shoe fell and 9 of us were detached for Infantry Signals training and we didn't go to Italy along with those we had trained with in Calgary. The other shoe fell when the records office burn t down and we were lost to "general fatigues" for 9 weeks. This consisted mostly of shoveling coal and trucking it all over southern England (by 1945 the English railway system was all but warn out). However once in a while we worked in the Officers Mess where we got fed better than the others (as an example of rationing, it was an egg per man per month perhaps and they were generally served Sunday morning when everyone was away on leave).

During this time my buddy John Rudolph and I were able to sneak out the back door of the barracks "so to speak" and visit, down in Dartford , Kent with mothers cousin Joe Ballantyne (he was a high-up member of Lloyd's of London). We'd go out shooting rabbits in the nearby fields and bring back whatever we could add to the ration pot. We were there for Christmas '44 and on Boxing Day enjoyed a roast leg of pork (the animal had slipped in his pen and broke a leg so it had to be put down - or so the neighboring farmer claimed). Where the turkey for Christmas day came from, I never heard. It was here that I first met his daughter Betty when she was home from her war work. There was coal for central hot water heat for their 14-room country home and I don' t know where that came from either - there was rationing and a war on! A V-1 bomb actually landed in their back yard and when they told the story, they had trouble remembering the day, ha!

We finally got to the Signals School and two days later I fell off an obstacle in training and ended up in hospital for several weeks (they couldn't find a fracture) but even the weight of the bed clothes was painful so there I stayed for "observation" - if they could have stopped the pain with local anesthesia I would have finished the course). This hospital session was followed by a Convalescent Depot and that was where I was when VE Day happened. That was quite a night, I was able to connect with my buddy, John Rudolph and a bottle of Demerara Rum that we brought with us from Canada. Along with Devon (hard) cider chasers we danced on the village green (Farnborough) that night in spite of my gimpy ankle. Ah youth!

Shortly thereafter I was able to wangle a leave and see some of Britain, visit a few relatives and wear my Glengarry while I traveled, ending up in Scotland, where such regalia comes from. My first stop was Birmingham, mother's other cousin Jack Ballantyne, where there were two daughters but there was only time to visit a very large "bath house " and have a swim. I visited a few pubs in Edinburgh but finally ended up near the original Seaforth Barracks and visited a friend of mother's from her school days. There were two daughters there Beth (who visited us here with her husband) and --------? That was a fun stop. After Edinburgh I went on to Aberdeen (and as I remember Inverurie) where I met another distant relative and. Peggy Anderson (I've forgotten her husband's name and he's the relative) Most of us have visited Peggy in the recent past. On my way back to Farnborough I stopped in Glasgow on a dreary rainy night and the pubs were closed, a notable trip.

From my time in Britain I always thought that the British pub system should have been exported to Canada, it seemed like such a sensible way to drink.

On my return to the Convalescent Depot, with VE Day come and gone, everyone was talking about going home (some of the troops had been abroad for five years) some were talking about the Army of Occupation (for at least a year) we were all counting our "points". I knew that with the few points I had I was headed for the occupation so when the Army "bribed me" I volunteered to go to Japan (the bribe was $100 and a month's leave. I was a bit delayed in leaving for home however, because there were riots in Aldershot when the 5 year men weren't sent home ahead of those going to Japan so the "powers that be" decided to expedite their return. We sailed at last on the Isle de France from Guerich Scotland, in beautiful sunny weather and had a smooth sail to Halifax along with General Crerar and his alleged 10 tons of liberated memorabilia plus the flag of the Canadian First Army.

We arrived to much fanfare, everyone figuring that the Canadian Army had done a good job that this time would last. Certainly my train trip back to Vancouver was much different than when I left for Overseas. The beds/berths had mattresses, sheets, pillows and blankets, we ate in dining cars and not out of mess tins. When we arrived at the Great Northern depot on Main Street, we debarked, and I walked out towards the street for at least a block and never saw a family member. I wasn't expecting a hero's welcome, but I did expect some of the family to be there. Finally I was stopped by Ernie and Wanda Baxter, I had passed the entire family with a large kit bag over one shoulder covering my face and a large Tam-o-shanter headdress covering the other side - the reunion was worth the wait. Shortly thereafter, we were on the Jaro and cruising off Vancouver Island. The next day we visited Yellow Point, where Marjorie Greene was working for the summer and took her out for the day, Marjorie had been my last date before overseas. While we were off in the canoe, Dad came to the door of the Jaro and fired off a clip of ammunition from his 32 automatic. Figuring that something was afoot we returned to find out that "Harry" had dropped the bomb and VJ had resulted. I periodically remember "Harry" in my prayers to this day. Especially after visiting in Japan and seeing what an invasion would have had to do.

I seem to remember that my Glengarry had one more outing when we went to the Armistice Day parade, November 11th, 1945. For sure my "wee cap" has been kept safely at hand to remind me of our travels, how it all started, how it continued and how it was completed.

Obit, Oregonian Newspaper, Portland, Oregon
Dr. F. James 'Jim' Marshall
Frederick James "Jim" Marshall, DMD, was born Feb. 11, 1925, to Les and Bertha Marshall in Vancouver, B.C. He was joined by brothers Bob and Don and sister Jane. One of Jim's claims to fame was that his mother, Bertha, and his grandmother, Elizabeth, survived the sinking of the Titanic in 1912. His life was shaped by family, hard work and the love of boating on the family yacht, the "Jaro."

In grade 11, he joined the Seaforth Cadets and later went on to Canadian Army camp and then to officers training at the University of British Columbia. Jim was sent to Great Britain in World War II and was on leave at home when VJ Day was declared. After the war he attended dental school in Portland, where he met the love of his life, Janet "Jan" Ormandy. After only six weeks, they were "promised" to each other and married in 1948. Jim graduated from dental school in 1949 and they moved to Vancouver, B.C., where Jim joined his father's dental practice.

In 1957 with a wife, four kids and a dog, Jim went back to school at the University of Illinois for a master's degree and in 1959 began a long and successful career as an educator and mentor to dental student s at the University of Manitoba, the University of Pittsburgh and the Ohio State University before finally coming full circle to teach at the Dental School in the Oregon Health Sciences University in 1972. Jim retired in 1990 but continued to work a half day each week at the school. Jim was a leader in his field and a member of numerous dental societies.

Jim lost his beloved Jan eight years ago but has been active in the Kiwanis Club and his church, has traveled the world, bicycled the back roads, indulged his life-long passion for learning and knowledge and enjoyed his family and friends.

Jim died Jan. 24, 2008, fiercely loved and respected by all who knew him. He is survived by his daughters, Barbara and Nancy, and their spouses, Arthur and Michael; sons, Gordon and Stephen and their spouses, Karla and Connie; nine grandchildren, Leslie, Erin, Heather, Katie, Emily, Luke, Carver, Rowan and Bailey; seven great grandchildren, Isabell, Eli, Max, RJ, Jackson, Connor and Alexis; his brothers, Bob and Don; and the extended Marshall and Ferguson families. Jim was a loving patriarch to his family, friends and colleagues around the world and he will be profoundly missed.

A celebration of Jim's life will be held at noon Saturday, Feb. 23, 20 08, at St. Luke Lutheran Church in Southwest Portland. A private interment at Riverview Cemetery will take place prior to the service.

In lieu of flowers, the family suggests contributions to the Mt. Hood Kiwanis Camp for Adults and Children with Disabilities, an organization dear to Jim's heart.

Noted events in his life were:
Occupation: Professor Of Endodontics.
EDUC: MS, DMD.
Membership: Masonic Order.
Military: Joined Canadian Army, 27 Jul 1943, Vancouver, B.C., Canada. Discharged 4 Oct 1945
Naturalized: 13 May 1969, Columbus, Franklin, Ohio, USA.

Children from this marriage were:

+ 115 F i. **Barbara Jean MARSHALL [2517]**[88,112,113,141,142,143] was born on 19 Mar 1950 in Vancouver, British Columbia, Canada.

Barbara married **Christian Taylor McINTYRE** [2516][113,141,142,144] [MRIN: 930] (b. 3 Feb 1947) on 29 Dec 1970 in Columbus, Franklin, Ohio, USA.[141]

Barbara next married **Arthur William ROADY Jr.** [2523][72,112,113,142,143,144] [MRIN: 932] (b. 24 Feb 1941, d. 30 May 2016) on 27 Sep 1975 in Portland, Multnomah, Oregon, USA.

+ 116 F ii. **Nancy Lee MARSHALL [2]**[72,88,112,113,142,145,146,147,148,149,150,151,152,153,154,155,156] was born on 5 Mar 1952 in Vancouver, British Columbia, Canada.[145]

Nancy married **Michael LaVerne TIEMAN** [1][89,112,113,148, 150,151,157,158,159,160,161,162,163,164,165,166] [MRIN: 1] (b. 20 Aug 1950) on 16 Jun 1972 in Columbus, Franklin, Ohio, USA.[148]

+ 117 M iii.   **James Gordon MARSHALL [2515]**[88,112,113,141] was born on 10 Jun 1954 in Vancouver, British Columbia, Canada.

James married **Karla FRIEDE** [2614][112,113,142] [MRIN: 929] (b. 14 Jan 1961) on 22 Apr 1994 in Hawaii, USA.

+ 118 M iv.   **Stephen Watt MARSHALL [2490]**[88,112,113,114,141,167] was born on 6 Sep 1955 in Vancouver, British Columbia, Canada.

Stephen married **Connie Sue BRAUN** [2491][112,113,114] [MRIN: 922] (b. 5 Apr 1955) on 4 Aug 1978 in Columbus, Franklin, Ohio, USA.

86. Irwin Scott ORMANDY [2358][103] (*Walter Scott [2355]* [59]*, William Lewithwaite [2339]* [44]*, Thomas [2341]* [36]*, John (Rev.) [2343]* [29]*, Thomas (Rev) [2619]* [17]*, Thomas [3123]* [7]*, William [3324]* [5]*, Richard [3923]* [1]).

87. Mary Francis ORMANDY [2357] (*Walter Scott [2355]* [59]*, William Lewithwaite [2339]* [44]*, Thomas [2341]* [36]*, John (Rev.) [2343]* [29]*, Thomas (Rev) [2619]* [17]*, Thomas [3123]* [7]*, William [3324]* [5]*, Richard [3923]* [1]) was born in 1920.

88. Thomas SAUSE [2592] (*Richard Victor SAUSE [2580]* [61]*, Victoria ORMANDY [2352]* [46]*, Thomas [2341]* [36]*, John (Rev.) [2343]* [29]*, Thomas (Rev) [2619]* [17]*, Thomas [3123]* [7]*, William [3324]* [5]*, Richard [3923]* [1]).

89. Everline SAUSE [2593] (*Richard Victor SAUSE [2580]* [61]*, Victoria ORMANDY [2352]* [46]*, Thomas [2341]* [36]*, John (Rev.) [2343]* [29]*, Thomas (Rev) [2619]* [17]*, Thomas [3123]* [7]*, William [3324]* [5]*, Richard [3923]* [1]).

90. Edward SAUSE [2594] (*Richard Victor SAUSE [2580]* [61]*, Victoria ORMANDY [2352]* [46]*, Thomas [2341]* [36]*, John (Rev.) [2343]* [29]*, Thomas (Rev) [2619]* [17]*, Thomas [3123]* [7]*, William [3324]* [5]*, Richard [3923]* [1]).

91. Richard Francis SAUSE [2591][85] (*Richard Victor SAUSE [2580]* [61]*, Victoria ORMANDY [2352]* [46]*, Thomas [2341]* [36]*, John (Rev.) [2343]* [29]*, Thomas (Rev) [2619]* [17]*, Thomas [3123]* [7]*, William [3324]* [5]*, Richard [3923]* [1]) was born on 22 May 1903.

Richard married **Winnifred CURRY** [2595][85] [MRIN: 959], daughter of **William CURRY** [3860] and **Marie DENKER** [3861], on 16 Jun 1925 in Staten Island, Richmond, New York, USA.

Children from this marriage were:

+ 119 M i. **Richard Francis SAUSE Jr. [2596]**[85] was born on 18 May 1926 in Staten Island, Richmond, New York, USA.

+ 120 M ii. **William James SAUSE [2597]**[85] was born on 2 Jul 1929 in Staten Island, Richmond, New York, USA.

+ 121 M iii. **James Michael SAUSE [2598]**[85] was born on 2 Nov 1935 in Staten Island, Richmond, New York, USA.

James married **Elaine RIVETT** [2599][85] [MRIN: 960] in 1959.

92. Margaret Claribel ORMANDY [2612] (*C. Harold [2606]*[74], *John Cliffborne [2345]*[53], *Thomas [2341]*[36], *John (Rev.) [2343]*[29], *Thomas (Rev) [2619]*[17], *Thomas [3123]*[7], *William [3324]*[5], *Richard [3923]*[1]).

Margaret married **Howard M. CLARK** [2613] [MRIN: 964], son of **CLARK** [5197], in Mar 1936. Howard was buried in Morningside Cem., Hartford, NY.

Noted events in his life were:

Occupation: Dairy Farmer in Hartford, NY.
EDUC: Trinity School and City College.

93. Ruth Mae ORMANDY [2608] (*G. Edward [2605]*[75], *John Cliffborne [2345]*[53], *Thomas [2341]*[36], *John (Rev.) [2343]*[29], *Thomas (Rev) [2619]*[17], *Thomas [3123]*[7], *William [3324]*[5], *Richard [3923]*[1]).

Ruth married **Lloyd C. LAMPHRON** [2609] [MRIN: 963], son of **LAMPHRON** [5198], in Jul 1935.

The child from this marriage was:

+ 122 M i. **David L. LAMPHRON [2610]**.

Tenth Generation

94. Ray ORMANDY [2779][86] (*James Griswold [2375]*[76], *William Lewithwaite [2360]*[56], *William Lewithwaite [2339]*[44], *Thomas [2341]*[36], *John (Rev.) [2343]*[29], *Thomas (Rev) [2619]*[17], *Thomas [3123]*[7], *William [3324]*[5], *Richard [3923]*[1]).

Ray had a relationship with **Babe** [2780][86] [MRIN: 998]. No evidence this couple married.

Ray next had a relationship with **Jeri** [2781][86] [MRIN: 999]. No evidence this couple married.

Their child was:

+ 123 M i. **Michael ORMANDY [2782]**.[86]

Ray next had a relationship with **Mary** [2783][86] [MRIN: 1000]. No evidence this couple married.

Their children were:

+ 124 F i. **Melise ORMANDY [2784]**.[86]
+ 125 F ii. **Vanessa ORMANDY [2785]**.[86]
+ 126 M iii. **Robert Mosier ORMANDY [2786]**.[86]

95. Anthony Leigh SMITH [2776][86] (*Margaret Mary ORMANDY [2373]*[77], *William Lewithwaite [2360]*[56], *William Lewithwaite [2339]*[44], *Thomas [2341]*[36], *John (Rev.) [2343]*[29], *Thomas (Rev) [2619]*[17], *Thomas [3123]*[7], *William [3324]*[5], *Richard [3923]*[1]).

Anthony had a relationship with **Ariel** [2777][86] [MRIN: 996]. No evidence this couple married.

96. Carolyn Marie SMITH [2778][86] (*Margaret Mary ORMANDY [2373]*[77], *William Lewithwaite [2360]*[56], *William Lewithwaite [2339]*[44], *Thomas [2341]*[36], *John (Rev.) [2343]*[29], *Thomas (Rev) [2619]*[17], *Thomas [3123]*[7], *William [3324]*[5], *Richard [3923]*[1]).

Carolyn had a relationship with **Jason LYNETTE** [2808] [MRIN: 997], son of **LYNETTE** [5199]. No evidence this couple married.

General Notes: William Ormandy line from Esther Berberick

97. Duke Christian PEARSON [2787][86] (*Phyllis Patricia ORMANDY [2372]*[78], *William Lewithwaite [2360]*[56], *William Lewithwaite [2339]*[44], *Thomas [2341]*[36], *John (Rev.) [2343]*[29], *Thomas (Rev) [2619]*[17], *Thomas [3123]*[7], *William [3324]*[5], *Richard [3923]*[1]).

98. Candace PEARSON [2788][86] (*Phyllis Patricia ORMANDY [2372]*[78], *William Lewithwaite [2360]*[56], *William Lewithwaite [2339]*[44], *Thomas [2341]*[36], *John (Rev.) [2343]*[29], *Thomas (Rev) [2619]*[17], *Thomas [3123]*[7], *William [3324]*[5], *Richard [3923]*[1]).

99. Vixen GAY [2791][86] (*Phyllis Patricia ORMANDY [2372]*[78], *William Lewithwaite [2360]*[56], *William Lewithwaite [2339]*[44], *Thomas [2341]*[36], *John (Rev.) [2343]*[29], *Thomas (Rev) [2619]*[17], *Thomas [3123]*[7], *William [3324]*[5], *Richard [3923]*[1]).

100. Volney GAY [2792][86] (*Phyllis Patricia ORMANDY [2372]*[78], *William Lewithwaite [2360]*[56], *William Lewithwaite [2339]*[44], *Thomas [2341]*[36], *John (Rev.) [2343]*[29], *Thomas (Rev) [2619]*[17], *Thomas [3123]*[7], *William [3324]*[5], *Richard [3923]*[1]).

101. Niliss (?) GAY [2793][86] (*Phyllis Patricia ORMANDY [2372]*[78], *William Lewithwaite [2360]*[56], *William Lewithwaite [2339]*[44], *Thomas [2341]*[36], *John (Rev.) [2343]*[29], *Thomas (Rev) [2619]*[17], *Thomas [3123]*[7], *William [3324]*[5], *Richard [3923]*[1]).

102. Debbie ORMANDY [2763][86] (*Robert Mosier [2363]*[80], *William Lewithwaite [2360]*[56], *William Lewithwaite [2339]*[44], *Thomas [2341]*[36], *John (Rev.) [2343]*[29], *Thomas (Rev) [2619]*[17], *Thomas [3123]*[7], *William [3324]*[5], *Richard [3923]*[1]).

General Notes: adopted

103. Brett ORMANDY [2764][86] (*Robert Mosier [2363]*[80], *William Lewithwaite [2360]*[56], *William Lewithwaite [2339]*[44], *Thomas [2341]*[36], *John (Rev.) [2343]*[29], *Thomas (Rev) [2619]*[17], *Thomas [3123]*[7], *William [3324]*[5], *Richard [3923]*[1]).

104. Norman Albert BERBERICK [2768][86] (*Esther Grace ORMANDY [2362]*[81], *William Lewithwaite [2360]*[56], *William Lewithwaite [2339]*[44], *Thomas [2341]*[36], *John (Rev.) [2343]*[29], *Thomas (Rev) [2619]*[17], *Thomas [3123]*[7], *William [3324]*[5], *Richard [3923]*[1]) was born on 24 Jul 1942.

Norman married **Georgiana HIGG** [2769][86] [MRIN: 993], daughter of **HIGG** [5203], in Oct 1966.

The child from this marriage was:

+ 127 M i. **Troy Albert BERBERICK [2770]**[86] was born on 19 Jun 1967.

Troy had a relationship with **Cathi KNUTSON** [2771][86] [MRIN: 994].

Troy married **Katherine TULLY** [2773][86] [MRIN: 995] on 9 Mar 1990.

105. Bridget Kayne NEAL [2371][86] (*Ruth Naomi ORMANDY [2365]* [83]*, William Lewithwaite [2360]* [56]*, William Lewithwaite [2339]* [44]*, Thomas [2341]* [36]*, John (Rev.) [2343]* [29]*, Thomas (Rev) [2619]* [17]*, Thomas [3123]* [7]*, William [3324]* [5]*, Richard [3923]* [1]) was born on 12 Dec 1950.

Bridget had a relationship with **Robert LINGO** [2795][86] [MRIN: 863], son of **LINGO** [5200]. No evidence this couple married. Robert was born on 10 Mar 1949.

Their children were:

+ 128 F i. **Elizabeth Kristine LINGO [2796]**[86] was born on 24 Sep 1972.
+ 129 M ii. **Devin Courtney (?) LINGO [2797]**[86] was born on 11 Jul 1975.

106. Garreth Allan NEAL [2370][86] (*Ruth Naomi ORMANDY [2365]* [83]*, William Lewithwaite [2360]* [56]*, William Lewithwaite [2339]* [44]*, Thomas [2341]* [36]*, John (Rev.) [2343]* [29]*, Thomas (Rev) [2619]* [17]*, Thomas [3123]* [7]*, William [3324]* [5]*, Richard [3923]* [1]) was born on 12 Jun 1952.

Garreth had a relationship with **Kathleen Linda SHONE** [2798][86] [MRIN: 862], daughter of **SHONE** [5201]. No evidence this couple married. Kathleen was born on 20 Sep 1956.

Their children were:

+ 130 M i. **Kacy Garrith NEAL [2800]**.[86]
+ 131 F ii. **Kriston NEAL [2799]**[86] was born in Nov 1985.

107. Mathew Peter NEAL [2369][86] (*Ruth Naomi ORMANDY [2365]* [83]*, William Lewithwaite [2360]* [56]*, William Lewithwaite [2339]* [44]*, Thomas [2341]* [36]*, John (Rev.) [2343]* [29]*, Thomas (Rev) [2619]* [17]*, Thomas [3123]* [7]*, William [3324]* [5]*, Richard [3923]* [1]) was born on 30 Sep 1956.

108. Andrew Ormandy NEAL [2368][86] (*Ruth Naomi ORMANDY [2365]* [83]*, William Lewithwaite [2360]* [56]*, William Lewithwaite [2339]* [44]*, Thomas [2341]* [36]*, John (Rev.) [2343]* [29]*, Thomas (Rev) [2619]* [17]*, Thomas [3123]* [7]*, William [3324]* [5]*, Richard [3923]* [1]) was born on 9 Sep 1958.

Andrew had a relationship with **Ella Andrea BACCI (?)** [2801][86] [MRIN: 861]. No evidence this couple married. Ella was born on 21 May 1971.

109. Camdon Keith NEAL [2367][86] (*Ruth Naomi ORMANDY [2365]* [83]*, William Lewithwaite [2360]* [56]*, William Lewithwaite [2339]* [44]*, Thomas [2341]* [36]*, John (Rev.) [2343]* [29]*, Thomas (Rev) [2619]* [17]*, Thomas [3123]* [7]*, William [3324]* [5]*, Richard [3923]* [1]) was born on 25 Jul 1960.

Camdon had a relationship with **Abbe Jo SMITH** [2802][86] [MRIN: 860], daughter of **SMITH** [5202]. No evidence this couple married. Abbe was born on 18 Sep 1959.

Their children were:

+ 132 F i. **Emily Katlyn NEAL [2803]**[86] was born on 7 Jun 1988.

+ 133 M ii. **Benjamin Joseph NEAL [2804]**[86] was born on 15 Jun 1990.

110. Graden Patrick NEAL [2366][86] (*Ruth Naomi ORMANDY [2365]* [83], *William Lewithwaite [2360]* [56], *William Lewithwaite [2339]* [44], *Thomas [2341]* [36], *John (Rev.) [2343]* [29], *Thomas (Rev) [2619]* [17], *Thomas [3123]* [7], *William [3324]* [5], *Richard [3923]* [1]) was born on 19 Jan 1963.

Graden had a relationship with **Carolyn McCANN** [2805][86] [MRIN: 858], daughter of **McCANN** [5207]. No evidence this couple married.

General Notes: William Ormandy line from Ruth Neal

Graden next had a relationship with **Paula Jane** [2806][86] [MRIN: 859]. No evidence this couple married.

Their child was:

+ 134 M i. **Gavin Keith NEAL [2807]**[86] was born on 22 Apr 1986.

111. David Howard COFFIELD [2488][88] (*Francis Ann ORMANDY [2470]* [84], *James Alma [2337]* [57], *William Lewithwaite [2339]* [44], *Thomas [2341]* [36], *John (Rev.) [2343]* [29], *Thomas (Rev) [2619]* [17], *Thomas [3123]* [7], *William [3324]* [5], *Richard [3923]* [1]) was born on 24 May 1947 in Silverton, Marion, Oregon, USA.

David had a relationship with **Roseanna** [2489] [MRIN: 921]. No evidence this couple married.

112. Sandra Lee COFFIELD [2480][88] (*Francis Ann ORMANDY [2470]* [84], *James Alma [2337]* [57], *William Lewithwaite [2339]* [44], *Thomas [2341]* [36], *John (Rev.) [2343]* [29], *Thomas (Rev) [2619]* [17], *Thomas [3123]* [7], *William [3324]* [5], *Richard [3923]* [1]) was born on 11 Aug 1947 in Silverton, Marion, Oregon, USA.

Sandra had a relationship with **George BLAKESLEE** [2479] [MRIN: 918], son of **BLAKESLEE** [5204]. The marriage ended in divorce. No evidence this couple married. George was born on 29 Aug 1945.

Their children were:

+ 135 M i. **Jack BLAKESLEE [2481]**.
+ 136 M ii. **Craig BLAKESLEE [2487]** was born on 27 Feb 1972.
+ 137 F iii. **Andrea BLAKESLEE [2486]** was born on 13 Feb 1975.

Sandra next had a relationship with **Gary BREWER** [2483] [MRIN: 919], son of **BREWER** [5205]. No evidence this couple married.

113. Susan COFFIELD [2477][88] (*Francis Ann ORMANDY [2470]*[84], *James Alma [2337]*[57], *William Lewithwaite [2339]*[44], *Thomas [2341]*[36], *John (Rev.) [2343]*[29], *Thomas (Rev) [2619]*[17], *Thomas [3123]*[7], *William [3324]*[5], *Richard [3923]*[1]) was born on 8 Oct 1950 in Newberg, Yamhill, Oregon, USA.

Susan had a relationship with **Kent KALTENBACHER** [2476] [MRIN: 917], son of **KALTENBACHER** [5196]. No evidence this couple married.

Their child was:

+ 138 M i. **Chris KALTENBACHER [2478]**.

114. Ronald William COFFIELD [2471][88] (*Francis Ann ORMANDY [2470]*[84], *James Alma [2337]*[57], *William Lewithwaite [2339]*[44], *Thomas [2341]*[36], *John (Rev.) [2343]*[29], *Thomas (Rev) [2619]*[17], *Thomas [3123]*[7], *William [3324]*[5], *Richard [3923]*[1]) was born on 12 Mar 1952 in Newberg, Yamhill, Oregon, USA.

Religion: Mormon.

Ronald had a relationship with **Nancy** [2472] [MRIN: 916]. No evidence this couple married.

Their children were:

+ 139 F i. **Grace COFFIELD [2473]**.
+ 140 F ii. **Christine COFFIELD [2474]** was born in Feb 1976.
+ 141 M iii. **Johnathan COFFIELD [2475]** was born in Feb 1977.

115. Barbara Jean MARSHALL [2517][88,112,113,141,142,143] (*Janet Alma ORMANDY [2224]*[85], *James Alma [2337]*[57], *William Lewithwaite [2339]*[44], *Thomas [2341]*[36], *John (Rev.) [2343]*[29], *Thomas (Rev) [2619]*[17], *Thomas [3123]*[7], *William [3324]*[5], *Richard [3923]*[1]) was born on 19 Mar 1950 in Vancouver, British Columbia, Canada.

General Notes: M624-1

Miss Barbara Jean Marshall became the bride of S.Sgt. Christian Taylor McIntyre on Dec 29 in Covenant Presbyterian Church. The Rev. Francis Park III performed the 7:30 p.m. ceremony. The bride is the daughter of Dr. and Mrs. Frederick James Marshall, 2345 Pinebrook Rd., and the bridegroom is the son of Mr. and Mrs. James W. McIntyre of Friedens, Pa. Miss Nancy Lee Marshall was her sister's maid of honor. Bridesmaids were the bridegroom's sister Miss Keri McIntyre of Friedens Pa., and Miss Cathy McIntyre, the bridegroom's cousin of Pittsburgh, Pa.

Malinda Schettler was flower girl. Richard McIntyre of Friedens, was best man. Seating guests were the bride's brothers, Gordon and Stephen Marshall. Following a reception at the church, the couple left for a wed ding trip in northern Ohio. They will reside in Beaufort, S.C., where the bride is employed by Garland Knitting Mills and her husband is stationed with the Marine Corps. Both attend the University of South Carolina branch at Beaufort.

Barbara married **Christian Taylor McINTYRE** [2516][113,141,142,144] [MRIN: 930], son of **James Wilbert McINTYRE** [2518][141] and **Barbara BURNS** [2519],[141] on 29 Dec 1970 in Columbus, Franklin, Ohio, USA.[141] The marriage ended in divorce. Christian was born on 3 Feb 1947 in Pittsburgh, Allegheny, Pennsylvania, USA.

Noted events in his life were:
Military: S. Sgt, Marine Corps: Beaufort, Beaufort, South Carolina, USA.
The child from this marriage was:

+ 142 F   i.   **Leslie Suzanne McINTYRE [2522]**[113,142,144] was born on 22 Aug 1972 in Meyersdale, Somerset, Pennsylvania, USA.

Leslie married **Craig VAN KLEEK** [2621][113] [MRIN: 1097] on 13 Mar 1999.

Barbara next married **Arthur William ROADY Jr.** [2523][72,112,113,142,143,144] [MRIN: 932], son of **Arthur William ROADY** [2526][72,144,168,169,170] and **Argyll Jean SMITH** [2527],[72,144,170] on 27 Sep 1975 in Portland, Multnomah, Oregon, USA. Arthur was born on 24 Feb 1941 in Yamhill, Oregon, USA and died on 30 May 2016 in Vancouver, , WA at age 75.

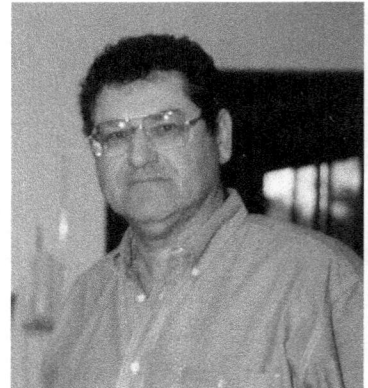

General Notes: In Memoriam
Arthur William Roady Jr., born February 24, 1941 in Yamhill, OR, to father Arthur Sr. and mother Argyll Smith, passed away unexpectedly May 30, 2016.

In Arthur's early years, he led a gypsy life, living with various relatives from Oregon to Colorado. He joined the Army at the age of 17, eventually serving as a Military Police Officer. He served at the Dugway Proving Grounds, in post-war Korea, in Vietnam during the war and in Italy, hauling spent nuclear warheads. He was stationed in Norway as part of the security detail at the US Embassy, and eventually at the United States Disciplinary Barracks in Fort Leavenworth, Kansas.

He retired from the military in 1974, and luckily decided to take a drafting course at Portland Community College where he met his future wife Barbara Jean Marshall. Arthur, Barbara and her daughter Leslie, age 3, became a family on September 27, 1975. They were married at the Pioneer Church in Sellwood, followed by a potluck reception in the park. The groom wore a blue polyester leisure suit and the bride wore a handmade dress. The flower girl (Leslie), wore a bad attitude. A year later, they welcomed second daughter Erin.

In 1975, Arthur began work at OHSU as a security guard and in 1977 decided to use his military police experience and served as one of a two- man police force in Walport, OR. However, working long nights alone without backup was difficult for Arthur, who struggled quietly throughout his life with PTSD. He decided that working in the outdoors would b e a good change for him.

The family moved to foothills of the Ochoco Mountains east of Prineville, OR where he worked on the 200,000-acre Grindstone Ranch. He spent long days doing physical labor - plowing fields, mending fencing and avoiding the sometimes-wandering Longhorn cattle. He loved it. A back injury and subsequent surgery forced the family to leave the ranch life behind and move back toward Portland to Lake Oswego.

Arthur was admitted to the Oregon National Guard and worked as a technician at Camp Withycombe - National Guard Base until 1993, when he had surgery to remove his colon. Subsequently, he worked as a civilian technician for the State of Oregon at Camp Withycombe until his 2003 retirement. In 2008 he was diagnosed with Lung Cancer but after having a portion of his lung removed, he was cancer free.

Arthur had a number of hobbies and adventures in his lifetime. He loved golf. He became a cross-country skier while in Norway. He was passionate about fly-fishing and tied his own flies. Feathers were often aloft as doors opened and closed. He reveled in retirement, taking time to read, nap, go to the movies and walk the dog. He explored his surprising artistic talents. He took up photography, created gorgeous landscapes with pastels and painted with oils outdoors on sunny days. He sculpted pottery and hand carved wooden duck and cork decoys.

He loved sharing his paintings with his granddaughter, Izzy, golfing with friends and family, taking grandsons Eli and Max to the movies and Knox to McDonalds for fries and ice cream. He was the best "snuggler " and the kindest man we knew.

The role of grandfather fit him like a glove.

He was a storyteller like no other, and an amazing, cherished friend. He was honest, loving and fiercely protective of those he loved and was loved fiercely in return by all who knew him.

He was preceded in death by most of his extended family and his grands on Rian James Van Kleel, as well as his beloved Basset Hound, Hercules.

He is survived by his wife, Barbara, daughters Leslie and Erin, sons-in-law Aaron and Craig, and his adored grandchildren Izzy, Eli, Max and Knox.

We will forever feel his loving arms around us.

The child from this marriage was:

+ 143 F i. **Erin Wynn ROADY [2576]**[112,113,142,144] was born on 1 Aug 1976 in Portland, Multnomah, Oregon, USA.

Erin married **Aaron BLEDY** [2809][113,144] [MRIN: 10] on 19 Feb 2000 in Las Vegas, Clark, Nevada, USA.

116.   Nancy Lee MARSHALL [2][72,88,112,113,142,145,146,147,148,149,150,151,152,153,154,155,156] (*Janet Alma ORMANDY [2224]* [85]*, James Alma [2337]* [57]*, William Lewithwaite [2339]* [44]*, Thomas [2341]* [36]*, John (Rev.) [2343]* [29]*, Thomas (Rev) [2619]* [17]*, Thomas [3123]* [7]*, William [3324]* [5]*, Richard [3923]* [1]) was born on 5 Mar 1952 in Vancouver, British Columbia, Canada.[145] Another name for Nancy is Nana.

General Notes: Nancy Lee (Marshall) Tieman
Dictated by Nancy in April 2019

"I was born 5 March 1952, 2nd daughter of 4 children to Jim and Jan Marshall. We lived in Vancouver, British Columbia the first 5 years of my life. After my brothers were born, we had a young woman from the unwed mother's home take care of us children.

We moved from the small house up to the boulevard before I went to pre-school. Dad decided he wanted to go back to school to get a master' s degree in Dentistry so he could practice other than general practice, and we moved to Chicago, Illinois. I started kindergarten and first grade. Under the bushes in the yard I had my first kiss with a boy pronounced Hale, but his name was Hal.

Outside in our backyard in Maywood, Illinois Dad also built us a skating rink both winters we were there. The teenagers from the church across the street came and ice skated with us kids.

The summer between his two years at Northwestern University we took driving a trip to New York City to see Mum's aunt, Aunt Marion, and see a number of sights before driving back to Chicago.

The next year Dad and Mum did not have enough money for tuition, but he got a grant from the American Govt. as a Canadian and as long as he promised to work somewhere in the world as an educator for one year , he did not have to pay it back.

After he graduated, we then moved to Winnipeg, Manitoba so he could start working as a professor at the University of Manitoba's Dental School. He became the chairman of the Endodontics Department. We lived there for six years grades 2 thru grade 7 and we went to Queenstown Elementary School where every winter they built a skating rink on the school grounds with a warming hut so that we could ice skate after school and in the evening with lights on and music.

I was in Brownies and Girl Guides and moved onto the Junior High.

My sister Barbara and I went to art school once a week on Saturdays downtown Winnipeg we took the bus down and took the bus home and would stop at the Hudson Bay store waiting for our bus and go to the hat department and try on hats and giggle. During grade 7 we used to have to take the bus to another school so that we could do home economics both cooking and sewing.

Part of my education at Queenstown included doing an IQ test by myself sitting in the nurse's office with no answer on what my IQ was but my parents were told I could go to college. And then in grade 4 I was taken out of school once a week to go to a special ed class, (I figured it out as an adult) to work on spelling with a teacher that was in a wheelchair and it was the only year in my life I passed spelling . This was the beginning of the understanding that I was dyslexic and different from my siblings in how I learned and processed.

After grade 7 we moved to Pittsburg, Pennsylvania where Dad became the chairman of the Endodontics department at the Dental School at the University of Pittsburg.

In 8th grade I took the school bus to and from the Jr. High and in that fall, Mum and I went to get material for my home economics project and were in a car accident where I had a tooth knocked out and Dad came to the hospital in Pittsburg run by the nuns and he demanded to use the dental chair to put my tooth back in but they were not going to allow it because he didn't have privileges, well guess what, Dad won.

That summer we joined the community swimming pool that was just behind our house and had a fabulous time continued through 9th grade. We also went on a camping trip borrowing friends tent trailer leaving Barbara to work in Pittsburg for those summer months we were gone. We went all the way to Key West on the Florida Keys and back driving past Columbus Ohio on our way back to Pittsburg. The next year in the summer between 9th grade and 10th grade we were again on the move to Columbus Ohio so that Dad could start teaching at the Ohio State University Dental School.

Barbara and I started at Upper Arlington High School for 10th and 12th grades and we registered as students 2000 and 2001. This school did not use school buses but carpooling.

Between 10th grade and 11th grade I got to come out to the west coast to visit grandparents and cousins. I spent almost two months on the west coast and saw my grandmother Dede and her husband Freeman, went out to Newberg to visit with Auntie Fran and Uncle Bill and cousins as I had my driver's license that summer Suzie let me drive the pickup truck which was so much fun. Then up to Canada to Vancouver to be with Grannie and Pop, Uncle Bob and Auntie Jerry, Uncle Don and Auntie Diane, and Auntie Jane. Spent weeks and weeks on my grandfather's boat the Jaro, with my cousin Liese. At one point we wanted to go waterskiing with boys that had a ski boat when we were up near Seashelt, up past Powell River, but Grannie wouldn't let us go water skiing with them because she considered them the local scum. Cousin Liese now has her summer home on the island up where we were and is part of the local scum.

Had to work off that trip at $1/hr. for the ticket and by Thanksgiving after painting the stairs to the basement it turned out I had been dealing with walking pneumonia most of my trip and so I spent a number of days at home on large doses of antibiotics.

During my senior year at Upper Arlington High School I wanted to date but wasn't and my girlfriend set me up on a blind date that was an absolute disaster. I told my Mum that the movie "Bullet" with Steve McQueen was good even though it opened in a bloody scene of a murder.

I finally asked God to put the right man in my life. Soon after I was able to get a job at Buckeye Mart which was a box store, so that I could earn money for spending when I went to Europe with the Study Abroad 6 week tour for Humanities and met the man I was to be with at Buckeye Mart. Girlfriends had given me as a joke a bride's magazine and after the first date I opened up the magazine and said yup.

Then I left for Europe with the Foreign Study League for 6 weeks. We stayed in Florence and did a side trip to Rome, then on to Germany and stayed outside of Munich and toured in Germany. We studied politics and art and religion in all of the countries. Headed to France and stopped for 1 night in Nancy France and then to staying just outside of Paris and fell in love with Paris. Then on to the Netherlands and stayed halfway between Amsterdam and Rotterdam. From there we took the ferry across the English Channel and stayed an hour out of London. My parents set it up so I could spend a weekend with my Grandmother's (Grannie Bertha Watt Marshall) cousin in Cobble Kent and their son who worked at Lloyd's of London with his father. I was taken in the back way so I could look down on Lloyd's of London trading floor as women were not allowed to go in 1970. We then went sailing on the Thames and I had my first mixed drink, Gin and Tonic which I still love to this day then home. Crazy fast but wonderful.

I started at Ohio State planning to do Dental Hygiene and continued dating Michael, being very careful not to push and expect more from him as we got to know each other. Went out for New Year's Eve and told him the relationship was great the way it was and found out later he was looking for diamonds since September. He asked me sometime at the end of January what I would say if he asked me to marry him and I told him to ask.

On Valentine's Day in '71 he asked. And we were engaged, and we planned a wedding for the summer of '72.

Dual US and Canadian Citizen, 1970 became US citizen, Canadian from father, US from mother.

EDUCATION: 1994 Portland State University, Portland, OR Master of Science in Education: Counseling. Member of Chi Sigma Iota, Counseling Academic and Professional Honor Society.

1994 Good Samaritan Ministries, Beaverton, OR, Certificate of Christi an Counseling.

1994 National Certified Counselor

1990 Portland State University, Portland OR, Bachelor of Science in Psychology.

1972 Ohio State University, Columbus, OH Graduated Dental Hygienist.

PROFESSIONAL MENTAL HEALTH THERAPIST EXPEREANCE:

2007-2011 Clatsop Behavioral Healthcare, OR Children Therapist Worked with teenagers and their families, on issues of abuse, anxiety and depression.

2004-2006 Clatsop Behavioral Healthcare, OR Crisis Therapist: Conducted mental health assessments and coordinated placements for at risk patients at the two county hospitals and jail.

2001-2002 Columbia River Mental Health, Vancouver, WA Children Therapist Worked in the clinic with teenagers and their families, on issues of abuse, anxiety and depression. School therapist at the Washington State School for the Blind working with behavioral problems as well as mental health issues.

1998- 1999 Columbia River Mental Health, Vancouver, WA Day Treatment Therapist Worked in a classroom setting with students that have learning disabilities as well behavior disabilities. Oregon Branch of the International Dyslexia Association, Portland, OR. Facilitator for the Adult Support Group. Arranged monthly meetings with speakers and facilitated discussions around key topics.

1997-1998 Portland State University, Portland, OR Supervisor-Counselors in training/Practicum. Observed client sessions, debriefed students and gave written assessments.

1993-1997 Good Samaritan Ministries, Beaverton, OR Counselor. Worked in a clinic setting with issues of sexual/ physical abuse, depression, suicidal ideation, marriage/relationship difficulties, adoption and loss and grief problems.

1973-1993 Dental Hygienist, private practice and taught at the Oregon Health & Science University, Portland, Oregon

DNA GENETIC ANCESTRY TEST RESULTS

74% Great Britain - Primarily located in: England, Scotland, Wales Also found in: Ireland, France, Germany, Denmark, Belgium, Netherlands, Switzerland, Austria, Italy

The history of Great Britain is often told in terms of the invasions with different groups of invaders displacing the native population. The Romans, Anglo-Saxon, Vikings and Normans have all left their mark on Great Britain both politically and culturally. However, the story of Great Britain is far more complex than the traditional view of invaders displacing existing populations. In fact modern studies of British people tend to suggest the earliest populations continued to exist and adapt and absorb the new arrivals.

18% Ireland - Primarily located in: Ireland, Wales, Scotland Also found in: France, England

Ireland is located in the eastern part of the North Atlantic Ocean, directly west of Great Britain. A variety of internal and external influences have shaped Ireland as we know it today. Ireland's modern cultural remains deeply rooted in the Celtic culture that spread across much of Central Europe and into the British Isles. Along with Wales, Scotland, and a handful of other isolated communities within the British Isles, Ireland remains one of the last holdouts of the ancient Celtic languages that were once spoken throughout much of Western Europe. And though closely tied to Great Britain, both geographically and historically, the Irish have fiercely maintained their unique character through the centuries.

5% Scandinavian - Primarily located in: Sweden, Norway, Denmark Also found in: Great Britain, France, Germany, Netherlands, Belgium, the Baltic States, Finland

Scandinavia is perched atop northern Europe, its natives referred to throughout history as "North Men." Separated from the main European continent by the Baltic Sea, the Scandinavians have historically been renowned seafarers. Their adventures brought them into contact with much of the rest of Europe, sometimes as feared raiders and other times as well-traveled merchants and tradesmen.

As the glaciers retreated from northern Europe, roaming groups of hunter-gatherers from southern Europe followed reindeer herds inland and marine resources along the Scandinavian coast. Neolithic farmers eventually settled the region beginning about 6,000 years ago.

The Goths, originally from southern Sweden, wandered south around the 1st century B.C., crossed the Baltic Sea, and settled in what is now eastern Germany and Poland. In 410 A.D., forced west by the invading Huns, the Goths sacked Rome, contributing to the decline and fall of the Western Roman Empire.

Religion: Protestant.

EDUC: BS/MS.

Naturalization: Portland, Multnomah, Oregon, USA.[147]

Occupation: Ohio/British Columbia/Washington, Between 1973 and 2011, Oregon.

Education: Ohio State - Dental Hygiene Degree, 1973, Columbus, Franklin, Ohio, USA.

Emigration: 14 Jan 1974, Vancouver, British Columbia, Canada.

Immigration: 20 Aug 1986, Portland, Multnomah, Oregon, USA.

Graduation: Portland State University, BS & MS, 1992, Portland, Multnomah, Oregon, USA.

Nancy married **Michael LaVerne TIEMAN** [1][89,112,113,148,150,151,157,158, 159,160,161,162,163,164,165,166] [MRIN: 1], son of **Malcolm Laverne TIEMAN** [26][112,160,171,172,173,174,175,176,177,178,179,180,181,182,183,184] and **Doris Earline MORRILL** [27],[112,160,176,177,181,185,186,187,188,189,190,191,192,193,194] on 16 Jun 1972 in Columbus, Franklin, Ohio, USA.[148] Michael was born on 20 Aug 1950 in Keokuk, Lee, Iowa, USA[157] and was christened on 31 Dec 1950 in Keokuk, Lee, Iowa, USA. Other names for Michael are MT, Papa.

General Notes: How it all started:

My quest for Nancy and my history, or roots, began innocently enough, Christmas, 1982.

Nancy's grandmother, Dede, gave us a book for Christmas titled *The History of Our Family.* A book of empty pages with headings like: Our Children, Husband's Parents' Family and Where Our Ancestors Have Lived. As Nancy and I started to fill it out, we found that we knew almost nothing of our family from before our great-grandparents, and my family when I asked, would tell me nothing.

I am an artist, and artists are a curious lot by nature, and we love knowledge. So, there it is, I was hooked.

First, my quest was who were my great-grandparents and where did they come from? All I knew was that they came from Prussia in the early 1800's and that because they were of German descent living in the U.S. during two great wars, the past was never talked about. I then took it upon myself to try and fill in the blanks. First, I talked to my parents, and great aunts, as no one else would tell me squat. I began to fill in names of ancestors, and some questionable dates. As time went on, I spent many hours in the archives and library of the Mormon Church. I was lucky that we lived in cities that had local libraries of the main church.

Back then, I had to search actual books and newspapers and hundreds of rolls of film, searching out our ancestors and records of birth and census' and maybe even a parish record. It took a long time back then in the 80's, and money as I had to order the loan of papers and actual records and books from the Mormon Church archives in Salt Lake City. Which I could only look at in their library. Anything I wanted copies of, I had to pay to copy and get their permission. Their genealogical library is extensive, the largest in the world, and in the case of Prussia, they had the only info as most of it was destroyed in the wars.

My list of ancestors started to become impressive. Then I asked, "Who were these people?" I started to collect stories from our relatives about the families. Oh, the stories I heard when the family finally decided to share. Some info turned out accurate as I researched, others, not so much. Like all families we were descended from kings and leading scholars and vice presidents and famous inventors. Or, so the stories went on that were handed down.

Then with the stories, I became interested in the towns and farms and countries our ancestors came from. What was Millom, England like in the 1600's when Nancy's ancestors lived there? So, I looked into the town histories, and when was Prussia a country, country histories, and maps of the periods when our ancestors lived. Plot maps where I actually found our family names. Curious more, what did my ancestors wear and eat in the 18th century on their farms and what did they grow? What church did they attend and why were there no birth record in a particular period of the 1600's but there were baptism records instead? How did my family name change from Thiemann to Tiemann to Tieman?

Because of that book and asking who was the great grandfather I never knew, this project has now over 5800 people in our two families, over 1500 source documents dating back to the 1600's (some originals pre-19th century), and a collection of over 2000 original photos some dating back to the beginning of photography.

I hope you enjoy reading and searching this project of mine, this labor of love.

When my friends have asked me why I do this, why am I so interested in the past, that only the future is important? I ask them to tell me about their grandparents, and halfway through their memories, they begin to understand that their stories and memories of their families might die with them, and that I never had any.

-Michael Tieman, 10 Mar. 2015-

Memories:

Sister, Beverly Dianne Tieman Starr, 2009

My brother, Michael La Verne, was born Aug. 20, 1950 and according to the stories our mother told, he had his days and nights mixed up until he was about 6 mos. old when he slept through the night. He had a lot of curls and looks like dad. He couldn't say my name and called me "Bebe" which is what I have my grandkids call me.

I mostly remember having to always take him with me growing up no matter where I went. I'm sure he loved going to my friends' house and watch us play! I vowed if I ever had kids they wouldn't have to go everywhere together like we did. The time I rubbed his face in the snow and he got frostbite on his cheeks it was because I was mad at mom for making me take him to the library with me. Since she worked nights, she napped in the daytime and I suppose it was more convenient for her if he was with me. I picked on him a lot as long as he was littler than me ("point to your head and say your initials"). Once he got taller I didn't do it as often!

He called himself "the Ketchup Kid" and ate ketchup sandwiches sometimes…ick. Probably while he was wearing his twin gun holsters and the coon skin Davy Crockett cap!

Our Great Aunts Maggie (11/28/12-6/02/07) and Thelma (09/12/07-09/18/97) Tieman lived with my Great Grandmother Anna (Sommer) Tieman (5/01/1876-06/15/63) near us at 1628 Palean St. I remember Great Grandma's beautiful long white hair that Maggie did up in a braided coiled bun for her. She sure looked like the German housewife then! (Great Grandma was born in Dresden, Germany). In nice weather Maggie would wash the hair and Great Grandma would sit in the backyard in the sun and Maggie would brush and brush it until it was almost dry and then she would braid it up for the week.

Michael and I spent many Saturdays with them and we learned how to make the yummy cinnamon/sugar coffee cake on the big black wood stove in their kitchen. It would rise overnight and be baked for Sunday breakfast the next morning. They made soap from lye and left over soap scraps and they had the prettiest china and vases in their dining room. Years later I got the Havilland china Thelma collected over the years and still cherish it and use it.

I mostly remember what the little white house and neighborhood looked like from the years Michael and I returned and spent summers with Grandma (NaNaw) and Don Morrill after we had moved away. Our first train ride alone was from Elgin to Keokuk in 1959. We were told NOT to get off the train for any reason until we arrived. Along the way, the train hit a stalled car sitting on the tracks. Michael decided he needed to see what was going on and got off with the engineer. I let him go, because I was told not to leave. No one was hurt and the engineer brought Michael back to his seat and of course I couldn't wait to tell on him! Probably was the highlight of my summer.

We had our first TV in 1954. Michael watched "Howdy Doody" and "Daniel Boone" and we watched "Capt. Kangaroo". Michael had a coon skin cap like Daniel Boone that he wore everywhere, even to bed until it had a life (and smell) of its own. He loved his double holster Roy Rogers six shooters and we watched "Hopalong Cassidy" and "the Rifleman". When we wanted "color" on our TV we put a blue sky and green grass plastic across the screen so we could watch "Bonanza". Very high tech. Westerns were popular and "Gunsmoke" was all that Grandpa Don would watch.

Michael and I walked 3 or 4 blocks to Blackhawk School where my best friends were Sylvia Sieferman, Marjorie Lehman and Cheryl Frye. Lehman' s lived across the street from the school and her little brother was also my brother's friend. I taught myself one weekend to ride Michael's bike because I never had one of my own. Guess it was a boy thing.

A tornado went down across the street from us one night, and a big tree fell across the driveway putting a huge tree limb through our parents' bedroom window. I don't remember this but Michael does and dad confirmed his memory.

Grandpa Don had given gave Michael a yellow tom cat that they named Nicky (St. Nicholas) at Christmas. He lived to be a was a very old cat with more than 9 lives fighting all the time, scarred, chewed up, bringing home dead mice and live baby rabbits to show us. He brought a baby rabbit into the house once and let it go. Mom caught it and put it in a shoe box on top of the floor register to keep it warm. She gave it a baby bottle of milk every few hours. It lived until the night she worked and dad wouldn't get up every 2 hours to feed it. Nicky never looked at it again once it was in the house. Once he brought in the live mouse and it ran under the upright piano, she and Michael had to corner it and catch it. After that she never let Nicky in the door a gain without having him open his mouth to be sure there wasn't a tail hanging out of it.

Nicky even survived having his tail amputated for cancer. Mom had said she thought he was mostly embarrassed, and he wouldn't go out of the house for weeks afterwards. We had him a long time (over 10 years) and we took him on our many moves as dad got transferred to a new town every 2 years.

Dad was transferred again Dec.15, 1958 to Elgin, Illinois near Chicago when I was in 6th grade. Connie was 4 mos. old and the house we moved to was so cold on moving day that she got pneumonia. Mom had to find a pediatrician right away practically before the movers left. We lived at 360 Congdon Street in a house that none of us really remember any inside details about. It was yellow and had an enclosed front porch. Michael and I remember there was a dog next door and that our driveway was higher than the neighbors'. I remember the dog was a Boston bulldog and he remembers it was a boxer. Dad also said it was a boxer, so now I've been wrong at least once.

We went to Coleman Elementary school and had a very long cold walk (20 below zero) where the snowbanks were so high at the intersections that cars had red flags on their antenna to be seen. Girls were not all owed to wear pants to school, so I wore slacks under my dress and took them off and on to walk to and from home. The school sat way back from the road across a big field and a long sidewalk that had no cover from the snow, nor freezing wind, nor rain. It seemed like it went on forever. I went to Larsen Jr. high 7th and half of 8th grade before Dad was transferred to Akron, Ohio in Feb. 1960, and I went to Perkins Jr. High there.

We took family vacations to Chicago to the Brookfield Zoo in 1959 and Springfield, Ill in 1960. We went to the Wisconsin Dells and saw the Indian pageantry one summer. 1961 was our first trip to Niagara Falls NY and Canada. Michael and Dad went to the Cave of the Winds and mom, dad and Connie went on the "Maid of the Mist" boat tour leaving Michael and I on the Canadian side with the car. He and I still wonder what we would have done in Canada, with a car and no parents if the boat sank?

Grandma Alta died in June and in July Maggie and Thelma took Michael and I on my "pre high school graduation" trip to Colorado. We drove out there in their 1959 gray Plymouth at about 40 MPH. When it was Thelma's turn to drive, Maggie would watch the speedometer and often lean up over the back seat and tell her to slow down. Thelma became "deaf" during most of this back seat driving. I don't remember how many days it must have taken us to get there at that speed on 2 lane roads, but I do remember the corn fields in Iowa and the wheat fields in Kansas that never ended. My brain goes numb now just thinking about it.

Part of our trip we met and stayed with Mrs. Beck in Evergreen, CO. She had worked for our dad in Akron. She and her husband had retired there and it was way up in the mountains with no one around them. It was beautiful. I loved driving along the roads beside the Colorado River running along beside us.

We stayed overnight at Estes State Park on the Continental Divide where there was still snow on the ground and we made snowballs. We took a bus ride around the area and saw tufted black squirrels and a black bear beside the road.

We also went to the Garden of the Gods Amphitheater where Maggie bemoaned the fact she would miss the Beatles performing there later in the summer. She was crazy about the Beatles (not my favorite) and liked the play/movie "Jesus Christ Superstar" music.

Colorado Springs was beautiful, and the Air Force Academy and Cathedral were fantastic.

We spent time in downtown Denver but missed Pike's Peak because the car wouldn't have made it up there! It was a memorable trip with them and I know we all had fun.

Dad had already been transferred to Zanesville, OH with Buckeye Mart 6 mos. before I graduated, but the 3 of us stayed in Akron in order for me to finish school. We all joined him in Zanesville where I spent the summer waiting to return to Akron to go to nurses' training and Michael went to high school one month before Buckeye Mart transferred dad to Columbus, Ohio. Zanesville's claim to fame was the "Y" bridge over the river which we lived near. I only remember the house was brick and I was counting the days until I left for Akron.

May 4, 1970 was the Kent State Ohio Riot and shooting of 2 students on campus by the Ohio National Guard. They were protesting President Nixon invading Cambodia in the ongoing Vietnam War. Kent was close to Youngstown where we had lived so we were alarmed at what happened. The war protests had escalated around the country. I found out decades later that Michael had taken part in some of them.

August 1971 Michael was coming to Rochester from Columbus, and Mom and Dad and Connie were coming from MA. for his 21st birthday and we were all in a car accident. Mom and I were hurt the worst and were in the hospital for a while. I had surgery on my face and she had a broken pelvis. She saved Amy by pushing her in between the seats when the car was coming at us. Connie and Amy were taken care of by our friends, Bev and Ed Huber. Dad, Michael and Bill sort of looked after each other.

June 16, 1972 Michael married Nancy Marshall in Columbus, OH. They had met at Buckeye Mart where they both worked for Dad. They moved to Vancouver, British Columbia in 1973 where he started an art design business.

Michael and Nancy had Heather in 1976 and Kate in 1979 and they were in the United States again but still up in the Northwest in Washington state and then Oregon. He worked on the Expo '86 while doing advertising and graphic design.

On July 29, 2008 my dear, kind, smart sister Connie Sue lost her 6-year battle with breast cancer. She had all the radiation and chemo a human can have, and it still took her. It was the day before her 25th wedding anniversary and a week before her 50th birthday.

She had told us in Feb. that there was nothing more they could do for her and she had 6 months.

Michael and I decided it was important to have a family reunion in Dallas in March while she was still able to travel. He and Nancy came from Oregon, Connie, John and dad came from Ohio, and she was able to be with us and her dear nieces and great niece and nephew and to meet Blake. She adored the little kids and was always a special aunt to Amy and Nicole. We laughed, played games, ate good food, and hugged and loved each other a lot. She enjoyed the spring flowers at the Dallas Arboretum, and I polished her nails, and trimmed her hair and we played Scrabble. She kept saying it was the sister things we never got to do before.

She never cried even when those of us around her were. Hugging everyone goodbye at the airport was one of the hardest things I've ever done; knowing it was a final goodbye. We all suddenly knew what it meant to want more time together

Michael had silver bracelets made for each of us with "love never fails" on the outside and our initials on the inside. I had them made for Amy and Nicole and we all wear them when we feel especially close to Connie.

She went on hospice in April and they kept her comfortable and active up until a week before she suddenly declined. It was just the 6 months. I was lucky enough to get to Ohio from Dallas in time to spend he r last 12 hrs. with her. She was unconscious, but the experts say the person knows we were there loving them to the end.

Michael was enroute from Oregon, and he had to hear my phone message when he changed planes in Chicago that she was gone. I felt terrible leaving him that message he would receive all alone.

Connie took one last breath, two tears rolled down her face, and she was at peace. Dad was holding her hand, and John and I were in the room with them.

Michael has been dealing with his grief in an artistic way. He said you came to him in a dream on your birthday and inspired him to do a sculpture. He named her "Courage" which is such a loving and accurate tribute to you. He hopes there will be many of her in public places and that she can give people a connection and comfort. John has purchased the first one for the cancer center in Akron in your memory and there will be a book telling the journey of "Courage". You would be so proud; but then you guided him to do this.

I went to Cannon Beach, OR for the first time in the 30+years that Michael and Nancy have lived on the west coast to the first public showing of the sculpture as it was started. John and I will return May 1, 2009 to see the unveiling of the finished piece and send her on her journey for you.

Michael Tieman, 2014 - Just a few memories from my past not covered by Beverly.

Summers as a kid:

A few weeks each summer, when Don had to work when Beverly and I were there, Don would take me to work with him some days. These were special to me because he was a typesetter at the local newspaper, The Daily Gate City in Keokuk Iowa. I was five and he would take me to his station and put me on a stool so I could reach the counter and help him set type for that days newspaper.

At that time, type was set by hand, each letter, one at a time. I would stand on my tip toes in my younger years, so I could reach the California Job Case (collectors now buy the empty cases and hang them on the wall). The case was a large wooden drawer, one drawer for each type style, (font), and it would be sectioned off into compartments, each compartment would contain metal slugs, each compartment was a single letter. I had to learn the position of each letter in the case, because the typesetter's job was to set the story in metal type as fast as possible. I can still remember how Don's hands would fly over the case, picking up the letters and placing them in the metal chase, building the story character by character, line by line until the story was completed. Did I say that the type was set upside down and backwards? That was so that when it was printed, it came out right. Don had a great vocabulary and could spell any word given to him, because the typesetter also had to proofread the story. Throughout my 40 plus years career in advertising, I proofread everything by reading it upside down and backwards and taught others to do the same.

One-year Don and Alta came to spend Christmas with us and brought me my own Case complete with metal type, a chase, typesetting rulers, spacers and carriers with ink and a tapping block. I could and did print my own papers over the years. How cool is that?

Unfortunately, we moved a lot, and to move this case and type, I put the slugs into their own envelope and sealed them and put them into a metal wastepaper basket. Then I waited as the movers came to pick up our belongings. There was always one smart ass mover who saw the basket with envelopes in it and would come along arms full with other boxes and go to pick up the basket with one hand. And fall down. The basket never moving. It had to have at least 50lbs. of metal in the basket. I know, I was a pill, but it was funny.

After several moves, mom made me get rid of the whole setup rather than move it again. I was heartbroken. Can you imagine how much that whole setup would sell for now? And the memories, I bet I could still set type by hand, a little slower maybe, but I still got it.

There would be other days when Don and I would go fishing on the Mississippi river. Now, this was the summer, in Iowa, on the river during the heat of the day, and I was sitting on the rocks on the bank of the river. The temps were in the triple digits, with 100% humidity. Don would take me to a favorite spot. Don and I would climb down the rocks to the river and fish for catfish.

And there is a science to fishing for catfish. I used a casting reel filled with 50lb. test line, a two-foot-long 35lb. test leader with a 2 oz. lead sinker and a treble hook. The hook is baited with a special " very stinky" paste. Normally you just wrap the hook with a ball of the paste, but the Mississippi is fast with strong currents which easily take off the bait, so us "locals" had a trick, we would put a kernel of Green Giant Nibblets Corn on each hook before we put on the paste . It held the paste on the hooks longer and if the paste came off, we could still fish for carp with the corn. In the next paragraph, I will explain the politics of fishing the Mississippi river. Anyhow, come lunch time we would go back to the car, I would have cold hot dogs and a warm Pepsi, Don would have a cold beer. Hummmmm. After lunch I would go back fishing and Don would stay in the car and drink and listen to the radio. At about 3ish, we would pack up and go home. Always with fish. We then had one more stop to make, two if we caught carp.

The politics of fishing the Mississippi river from when I fished it from 1954-61. If you were white, you fished on the rocks on the steep river banks by the dam spillway. And, you fished for catfish, which could weigh as much as 300lbs. If you were black, you fished farther downstream, and you fished for carp, considered a trash fish. If Don and I caught a carp, we were to stop off downstream to where the n***** * were and trade our carp for a catfish if they had one. If they didn't have any, we just gave them our carp. A white man never ate carp.

The stop Don and I always did after fishing was to go into town to the Moose lodge and sit at the bar. I would sit on the bar stool and order my usual from the bartender, a bottle of cold Pepsi and a chocolate Hershey bar. Don's order was a can of Blatz beer, or two. The bartender was the most happy, carefree man that everyone liked as a friend. As long as he was in his place, behind the bar serving white folks. Yes, Leroy was black. A small man, with stark white hair and when he smiled he had some yellow teeth, and the bloodiest gums. His smile was all teeth and gums from ear to ear.

Back to the way of the world in Iowa on the Mississippi river in the 50's and 60's. Leroy was everyone's friend when he was in his place behind the bar. When Don and I would pass Leroy, or any other blacks, on the streets of Keokuk, we never spoke, and as we came near them, they would get off the sidewalk and walk in the gutter until we were past . I did not know anything else as I was under 11.

When my dad was a kid in Keokuk, he would sneak away from his block, and go play with the little black boys. His mom would find him and beat him all the way home. The next day he would do the same, as did she.

Later in life I remembered all of this and did what I could to right these wrongs.

December 1, 1969 First Draft Lottery since 1942

This was the US military draft lottery to see what your chances were of being drafted and sent to Viet Nam. All men born in 1944 - 1950 were in the lottery. Needless to say, that was me. I can still recall that lottery night. I was working at a retail store, Buckeye Mart in Columbus Ohio., Dad was the manager of the store, and when it came time for the lottery draw 366 blue capsules with a birthdate on it were put in a roll cage and spun. All of the young men/boys who worked in the store with me were huddled around the TV displays as the lottery was televised live.

It is hard to describe those minutes as we watched, waiting to hear our destiny, holding your breath as the hand went into the cage, the knot in your stomach, the tightness in the chest, standing there with the boys you have been working with and know. If the next number was not your birthdate, you breathed a quick sigh of relief, and then held your breath as they drew the next number. The first 125 numbers were to be drafted immediately. As the lottery continued, I saw my co-worker s/friends stiffen as their number was drawn, close their teary eyes and quietly walk out of the store, I never saw any of them again. After the first 125 were drawn, the few of us left, had hope. Then my birthdate was drawn, #344 out of 366. I was relieved, elated, happy, sad, all of the emotions washed over me like a tidal wave.

For the first time since the first number was drawn, I became aware of someone standing behind me. I looked around and it was dad. With tears in his eyes, he smiled, turned around and walked away, back to work. We never spoke of it, but to this day I still wonder what would have happened if my number would have been the first ones drawn? If I had decided to escape the draft and go to Canada, instead of serve, would this man, my father, who lied about his polio handicap so he could fight in WWII and proud to have served, would he understand and support my decision?

As a side note, in Dec.1971 before Nancy and I were married, I received a "Greetings" draft notice to report for military service. It seems that in their books I had lost my student deferment and had to stand the draft. The problem was, I was still a student in college. Now at this time in the war, most college professors would do almost anything to help you keep your student deferment to stay out of Nam, so I was at a loss as to why I lost mine.

Nancy and I went down to the Selective Service offices to speak to someone, hoping to clear up the mistake. We got a very nice older woman and when she looked into it, they had made a mistake and I was still deferred as a student. But… Here it comes; I had an option of keeping my deferment or give it up and stand the draft. I thought I am not crazy; no way am I standing the draft.

Then the lady behind the desk said she had a son and would tell him to stand the draft and here was the reason. It was December and because of the way the original law was written and for this year only, if I stood the draft it would only be until the end of the year, less than 30 days away. Then if my number was not called, I would get a 1H deferment - Registrant not currently subject to processing for induction. She pointed out that I was in the Ohio State University draft pool and they had never called numbers over 125 and mine was 344.

So I signed away my student deferment and stood the draft until the end of the month. But, neither Nancy nor I got much sleep in Dec., but what a New Year's Eve party we had. After that year, the law was changed so you had to stand the draft for 12 full months, I skated on that one let me tell you,

I loved it when I got my new draft card with the 1H status in Jan., but I still had a draft card burning when I no longer became eligible for military service, at age 35.

May 6, 1970 - The Ohio State Campus Riots - newspaper article

"Acting on a recommendation by Ohio Gov. James A Rhodes, Ohio State University closed its doors in mid-quarter on May 6, 1970. The 45,000 students on the riot-racked Columbus campus were told to leave the university by noon the next day.

In the spring of 1970, women were demanding equal rights, blacks were pressing for equal representation, and young people were calling for an end to the Vietnam War. Put these issues on a college campus and combine them with an overwhelmed OSU administration, confused by the wants of a younger generation, and you've got yourself a riot. In early May, riots raged on more than 100 U.S. campuses, as students protested the escalation of the Vietnam War into Cambodia.

At Kent State University, an ROTC building was torched. On May 3, Gov. Rhodes called the demonstrators "the worst type of people we harbor in America" and ordered the Ohio National Guard to restore order at Kent State. Guardsmen killed four people the next day.

Kent State immediately closed, but Ohio State remained open. Amid chants of "Shut it down," protesting OSU students blocked entrances to several buildings on May 5, but dispersed after Guardsmen forced them away.

On May 6, protesters mobbed Ohio State President Novice G. Fawcett's campus home and the school's administration building. Troops with rifles and bayonets drove them back to the Oval. Shortly before 3 p.m., a fire broke out at Hayes Hall, where, according to some reports, protesters threw stones at firefighters.

Fearing what he called "further disruptions and violence," Fawcett said at 5:30 p.m., "I am closing the university until further notice." More than 80 colleges across the country closed that day in the face of growing protests over the war and the Kent State killings.

Ohio State reopened on May 19. In a letter to parents and students, Fawcett wrote: "In the days ahead we will work toward improved student-faculty-administration relationships.'"

This is what I saw firsthand as a student photographer covering the OS U riots:

I must confess this was not my first protest march, and the marches of the previous month of April at OSU and other Ohio university campuses were bloody and tension filled.

The initial reason for the march this day was to protest the unfair treatment of blacks, women, and of course the war, especially the bombing of Cambodia. The campus, city and state police were very undisciplined at that time. Some of the National Guard, however, made honest attempts to curb the violence. In at least one instance that I observed, National Guard officers who tried to calm things down were chastised by their superiors.

I was in a crowd of people, taking photos, not the entire crowd was students by the way, when all of a sudden there was a rush of National Guard in front of me and tear gas cans being thrown. I can still smell the acrid odor of tear gas. Confusion followed and somehow, I was pushed forward into the arms of a National Guard soldier. I had my Nikon in front of my face at the time and I suppose his natural reaction was to push it. Unfortunately, by doing so he broke my nose and camera.

I was with my friend Dale and he grabbed me and we had to break into a dead run to avoid being trampled by a large group of students charging down a side street from the Oval. They were also being forced back by tear gas and armed police.

Our only thought now was escape. They had closed the campus so we could not get out. I lived off-campus, quite a distance from campus, but fortunately Dale had an apartment on campus, just a few streets away. Like everyone else we had no idea what was going to happen next, so we ran from alley to alley, street to street to safety, away from the gas.

Dale and I waited in his apartment with all the curtains closed until night. I had to get off campus and back to the safety of home.

This is what a scared, bloodied twenty-year-old does in a riot when reason fails.

We snuck out of Dale's safe apartment into the dark night. No, it was not a dark stormy night like in books, but it was dark. We snuck from alley to alley listening to the noise and chatter from the police radios, trying to stay clear of them.

My last memory of that day was as we were almost free, slowly sneaking around; I turned into the last alley to freedom and came face to face with a young National Guard soldier holding his rifle with bayonet in my face. We both froze. I don't know who was more scared, him or me. Here he was in a faintly lit alley, facing two kids, and me with blood down the front of my shirt from my nose. You know what they say about time stopping and you see flashbacks of your life? Nope. Time did stop though, for how long I don't know. Was his gun loaded like at Kent state? Then in that moment, the young man dropped his gun from my face, turned around and walked out of the alley. I don't recall the rest, but I did find my car and got home safely.

That was my "oh shit, what if" moment, hopefully never to be repeated.

Every now and again I wonder what happened to that young man. Did he end up in Nam? Did he survive to tell his version of the Ohio State riots to his kids and grandkids?

And I thank God for people who have a moment of reason, when the rest of the world is going to hell around them.

Here is a sidebar to these riots. I had met Nancy the month before this, and her father was the head of the endodontics school at Ohio State. During the closure of the school, the professors at OSU had fire watch at the school at night, just in case anything happened. Neither Nancy nor I ever told her father that I was on the other side of the barricades during that time.

June 12, 1972 - I survived my honeymoon!

Yes, your wedding day is meant to be special and memorable, as is your honeymoon. You should remember it fondly as you grow old. It should not be a survival class where your life is in danger and you are escaping death, not once, but three times. Fortunately for us our honeymoon was only a long weekend.

Since both Nancy and I were still in school, I was doing summer school classes to finish up my BFA, we had to be married on a Friday and our honeymoon was a room at a state park resort Fri night/Sat/Sun/Mon then back to school.

It all started to go south on us when my best friend and Best Man in my wedding, Dale, decided to trick out my car, a '66 Cuda. Fill it with popcorn and cheese on the muffler as well as balloons and tin cans. When I heard about the plans, I decided to hide the car a couple blocks away and we could make our escape from there.

Escaping Death #1: Dale followed us in his VW bug as we ran to the car and started to drive away. He drove like a crazy man driving straight at us, trying to catch us, and finally trying to run us off the road several times until I could get around him and escape. I have no idea how many trees and cars we narrowly missed. He was a maniac.

Escaping Death #2: Driving the narrow country roads at night on our way to the state park. Nancy and I were coming around a curve and out jumped a deer. I steered left and we just missed her, it was so close we found deer tail hair in the passenger side mirror.

Escaping Death #3: I confess I cannot swim. Many times in my life I tried, even took swimming lessons once as a young tike. I had a scar in the middle of my chest for many years where a lifeguard at Boy Scout camp pushed a metal pole into me to save me from what he thought was drowning. He hit me so hard he succeeded in taking my breath away and I sank like a rock in the pool.

Not to digress, Nancy on the other hand swims like a fish. So, here we are at the resort, out in the lake, close to shore and I am out only as far as I can touch bottom. When my new bride comes up to me and tells me it is ok to come out a bit farther with her. I am young and in love and of course out I go to my wife. And down I drop under water struggling to live. Nancy does grab me and pulls me to where I can a gain touch bottom. Seems she was treading water but thought I was tall enough to touch bottom. My question was if you are treading water how can you tell how far away the bottom is?

We survived our honeymoon and have now been married 48 years. Who knew?

And now I pass the torch.

I will now let my wife and daughters and our grandkids tell their stories and hopefully I am in a lot of them. Let me just say that in Nancy and my 48 years together, we have had our joys and sorrows like every family.

The sorrows of almost losing our daughters in a car accident when Heather was in High school; losing both Nancy's parents and mine; the death of my younger sister to cancer; the death of some of our friends; three times we lost almost everything we had because of business and life's bad rolls, but we fought back and in the end succeeded.

The joys keep coming every day, but include for me; Nancy as my friend , sole mate and wife; our kids Heather and Katie as we watched them grow up and are now wives and mothers with their own family; our son in laws Phillip and Sam and grandkids Riley, Jack, Connor, Alexis and Owen and us being part of their lives; our being able to retire and travel and see the world and the beauty it holds; and for me, being an artist and capturing the celebration of life in my work.

Our family stories will continue, and hopefully will be not only passed down verbally but also written down so that our descendants will know us better and see they are made up of all of us who came before.

My hope is that someone in our family will take an interest in all of this genealogy and will pick up this history of the Tieman-Marshall Family and carry on, adding new members and filling in the gaps of the older ones.

Marquis Who's Who In The West (23rd Edition)
Tieman, Michael LaVerne, graphic design executive; b. Keokuk, Iowa, Aug 20, 1950; s. Malcolm LaVerne and Doris Earline (Morrill) T.; m. Nancy Lee Marshall, June 16, 1972; children: Heather Anne, Katherine Jane. BFA, Columbus Coll. Art and Design, 1972. Art dir. Kersker Advt., Columbus, Ohio. 1969-72: graphic designer The Studio, Inc., Columbus, 1972-74; sr. art dir. Cockfield & Brown Advt., Vancouver,

B.C., Can., 1974-75; ptnr., graphic designer Designers West. Ltd., Vancouver. 1975-78; owner, graphic designer Tieman & Friends, North Vancouver. 1978-86 ; ptnr., art dir. Printpac Mktg., Ltd., Richmond, B.C., 1978-81; sr. a rt dir. McKim Advt., Ltd., Vancouver, 1981-84; sr. graphic designer EX PO 86, Vancouver 1984-86; exec. graphic designer Gilchrist & Assoocs., Inc., Portland, Oreg., 1986-. Recipient First Pl. Presentation Folders award Lithographers & Printing House Craftsmen, 1990. Cert. of Merit Award Printing Industries Am., 1988, First Pl. Ann. Report award Internat. Fedn. Advt. Agys. 1985, PRSA, 1987; named World's Best 30 Second Comedy Spot, Hollywood Radio & TV Soc., 1981. Mem. Nat. Geog. Soc., Am. Inst. Graphic Artists, The Smithsonian Assoc. (Nat.) New England Hist. Geneal. Soc., Trout Unlimited. Friends of the Zoo. Avocations: painting, photography, fly-fishing, reading, computer graphics. Home: 1426 Greentree Cir., Lake Oswego, OR 97034 Office: Gilchrist & Assoc. 815 SE 2nd Ste 300 Portland, OR 97204 503-243-1030.

Places Lived:

1950-55 - Keokuk, Iowa, USA; 1955-58 - Freeport, Illinois, USA; 1958-6 0 - Elgin, Illinois, USA; 1960-65 - Akron, Ohio, USA; 1965-65 - Zanesville, Ohio, USA; 1965-73 - Columbus, Ohio, USA; 1973-86 - North Vancouver, British Columbia, Canada; 1986-96 - Lake Oswego, Oregon, USA; 199 6-2002 - Camas, Washington, USA; 2002-15 - Cannon Beach, Oregon, USA,2015-present - Beaverton, Oregon, USA

Places Visited:

1988 - Hong Kong, Tokyo, Japan(airport); 1998 - Hong Kong, Shenzhen, China, Seoul, Korea (airport); 2000 - London, England, Paris, France; 2011 -Tuscany area of Italy including Pisa, Rome, Florence, Cinque Terre, Carrara, Munich, Germany(airport); 2012- California car trip; Napa Valley and vineyards, San Francisco; 2013 - France; Paris, Avignon, many hill towns of Provence area, Nice. Italy; five towns of Cinque Terre , Siena, many small towns in Tuscany.; 2014- National Parks car trip Utah/Arizona; Zion, Grand Canyon, Bryce, Arches, Canyonlands; 2015 - M A -Boston, (Our homestead in Kittery, Eliot, N. Berwick Maine), Portsmouth, Glouster, Salem, Plymouth, Provincetown, Lexington, Concord, Providence RI, 2016 -Italy with our daughters; Small towns in Tuscany area of Italy including Pisa, Rome, Florence, Cinque Terre, 2017 - California car trip to Sonoma and Napa Valley and vineyards and up the Oregon Coast, 2018 - Car trip to South Dakota/Montana/Idaho/; Black Hills, Mt. Rushmore, Yellowstone, Craters of the Moon, Grand Tetons,

Emigrated to Canada in 1973 with wife, Nancy. Returned to US in 1986 with Nancy and two children, Heather and Katherine.

2002 - Michael started his own gallery/studio with wife Nancy in April 2002, Artists Gallerie, LLC. The gallery was opened in Cannon Beach, Oregon and represented twelve national and international artists, but after five years the falling economy forced it to close. The company continues as an Internet based company selling the paintings and sculptures of Michael throughout the world.

Professional Summary (2010) - A seasoned professional with 40 plus years' experience in and solid understanding of strategic marketing and communications as a graphic designer/art director. Demonstrated ability to select, train and retain self-motivated, highly creative employees. Skilled in branding and marketing strategy, creation and execution of packaging, advertising, collateral, direct marketing, multimedia, environmental and interactive design, web site design and coding experience.

Accomplishments - Creative Director: - provide inspiration and motivation - insist on high quality standards - help make the company a positive, challenging place to work - provide mentorship - solutions provider - know and understand strategy and good creative - help the team develop smart solutions that are exciting and successful and that are on target and strategy - develop budgets and schedules...and meet them - work with production managers to seek the most effective solutions - keep current with technology, and help educate the team - strategy and marketing planning and concept development to insure a consistently excellent product brand and corporate image - media strategy, research and development of media plans. Graphic Designer / Art Director : - concepts - branding - design - graphics - exhibits - packaging - environmental and industrial graphics - print and TV advertising - art direction - marketing strategies - scheduling and production supervision - supervision of teams of writers, designers and production coordinators, art directed photographers and illustrators.

Computer Skills - PC and Macintosh platforms,

Professional Experience - MT Studios, Portland OR, Camas WA, & Cannon Beach, OR, 1993 - 2007 Owner; The Bernhardt Agency, Portland, O R, 1999 - 2001 Partner/V.P. Marketing/Creative Director; Tripwire Security Systems, Portland, OR, 1997-1999 Vice President Marketing ; Online Interactive Network Corporation, Portland, OR, 1997-199 9 President ; Internet World Broadcasting Corp. Portland, OR, 1995- 1997 VP/CD; Gilchrist & Associates, Inc., Portland, OR, 1986-1995 Co - Creative Director; The 1986 World Exposition, Vancouver, Canada , 1984-1986 Sr. Graphic Designer ; McKim Advertising, Ltd., Vancouver, Canada, 1981-1984 Sr. Art Director ; Tieman & Friends, Ltd. , Vancouver, Canada, 1976-1981 CEO/ CD; Cockfield & Brown, Vancouver, Canada, 1973-1976 Sr. Art Director

Education - Bachelor of Fine Arts in Advertising Design, 1972 Columbus College of Art & Design, Columbus, Ohio

Professional Accomplishments - Throughout the years I have won numerous international awards for my designs, print and TV ads.-These include: International Federation of Advertising Agencies, Creativity (New York), International Broadcasting

Award (Hollywood), One Show (Vancouver), Graphic Designers of Canada, Art Directors Club (Toronto), Art Directors Club (LA.), Printing Industries of America, Lithographers & Printing House Craftsmen. -Listed in "Sterling's Who's Who" (in the West).

-Focused on bringing the first Tripwire Intrusion Detection software product to market, including: corporate and product branding, product strategy, positioning, and lead generation programs. Co. was sold in 2011 when my stock was bought back.

-Designed initial web site, collateral, packaging, national ads, trade show booths, and international sales materials for Intrusion.com.

-Supervised the completion of art/programming and bringing to market the first full CD/Internet virtual game "Piggyland" in 1998.

-Designed original Wendy's hamburger chain logo and sign, in store marketing/menus/collateral and interior designs of stores 1971

About Michael Tieman the painter/sculptor/writer

As Michael Tieman sees it, "The role of an artist from the dawn of time has been as a visual storyteller. The stories my paintings and sculptures tell are ones of confidence, strength, passion, playful sophistication and the celebration of life."

Tieman has sketched and painted since childhood and has spent over five decades as a working artist, both as a graphic designer and a fine artist. Following the encouragement of a friend and gallery owner, Michael recently expanded his talents into sculptures cast in bronze. Tieman's sculptures are unique in that they are a combination of traditional figurative sculpture and his Impressionistic painting style. "I create my bronze sculpture as a three dimensional painting; texture is the impasto brushstroke, color is the play of light and shadows a cross the surfaces, and detail is the free style movement of the impressionist style. My ladies have a face with a chiseled jaw and high cheekbones, producing great shadows, and the athletic body and proud confidence of an Amazon warrior."

Sculpture "Courage", Donated to Summa Health System's Cancer Clinic in Akron, Ohio

On July 29, 2009 in Akron, Ohio, "Courage" a 36" tall bronze sculpture standing in tribute to those who have, who are, and who will fight Cancer is being donated to the new Summa Health System's Jean B. and Milton N. Cooper Cancer Center, Akron City Hospital, Akron, Ohio.

"Courage" is a limited-edition bronze and is the creation of Pacific Northwest sculptor and painter Michael Tieman. Cancer has hit home hard with Michael as his older sister Beverly Starr is a 13-year survivor of breast cancer, but his younger sister Connie Sue Drotos recently lost her battle with the disease.

The first 36" sculpture "Courage" in the limited edition has been purchased by Connie's husband of 25 years, John Drotos, and he is dedicating it to the Cancer clinic where Connie had treatments for six years. With the purchase of "Courage" there is also a cash donation of $5000 which goes to the Cancer Support Services department of the

Cancer Center. Connie's family will be present at the dedication ceremonies in Akron July 29th and will include husband John Drotos, her father LaVerne Tieman, sister Beverly Starr, brother Michael Tieman and his wife Nancy.

"Courage is dedicated to the women in my family who have battled breast cancer; my mother-in-law Jan Marshall (Muzzy), my aunt Pat Wetzel, my sister Beverly Starr, and my younger sister Connie Sue Drotos, who after a courageous six year battle with breast Cancer died on July 29 , 2008." - Michael Tieman

The Dream

"In July of 2008, after a courageous six-year battle with breast cancer, my younger sister died, one week shy of her 50th birthday and the day before her 25th wedding anniversary," says Tieman. "Since then I have had the same re-occurring dream. I am on a scaffold built around a piece of white marble 15' tall, and I am carving a figure titled " Courage" - she has a bald head wrapped in cloth, piercing eyes, a firm jaw, taunt body and feet apart yet firmly planted. The people battling cancer have an inner strength and courage as they not only face an uncertain future, but they also have to take their treatments knowing it will make them feel worse. Week after week they look forward to this pain in the hope that eventually it will be gone. There is a look of courage in their eyes I cannot describe with words, it's not entirely defiant (Cancer will not win), but with grace with a quiet determination. That is the courage I need to capture.

In the dream I can only sense the figure; all I can really see is the head. I am carving with a chisel and hammer, no power tools, and I can see my scarred swollen hands and feel the pain in them as I continuously strike the chisel. Yet, there are many unanswered questions; why is the stone exactly 15' tall, why can't I see the entire figure? I am carving the stone by looking at a maquette of the piece but how do I know it is exactly 36" tall since I can only see the head?

The Promise

"People who saw me building the clay sculpture "Courage" November 8th and 9th during my demo at the 2008 Stormy Weather Arts Festival expressed a need for the piece to be seen and touched … now", says Tieman. " So I am casting "Courage" in a limited-edition bronze available in three sizes, 9' high heroic size, 36" high and 18" high maquettes. With up to half of the sale price being donated directly to a local hospital or Cancer center's Cancer Support Services, the daily support and comfort services for those who come to these facilities to battle Cancer. The book "The Building of Courage" (published by Michael Tieman Publishing), which originally was to be made to accompany each sculpture will now be published in a larger edition for people who want the book so they can be connected to "Courage". Because of the requests from survivors, Michael has also cast the butterfly necklace on "Courage" in silver and is being sold to raise funds for Cancer Support Services.

"Courage" Butterfly Necklace

"Butterflies were a favorite of my sister Connie; she said they brought her peace, freedom and hope. At the cemetery after her internment ceremony, her husband John who brought several Mylar butterfly balloons, walked to the little lake alone and released the butterflies as he had promised her. We silently watched as the wind suddenly came up and the butterflies took flight.

Slowly they rose into the air and maneuvered themselves up and around the clouds, staying in sight and staying in the clear blue sky. Up and up they drifted, slowly they left our sight and sailed to the heavens. So of course I had to have a butterfly on 'Courage'."

Books Written, Designed, and or Published By Michael Tieman Publishing:
Ancestors & Descendants of Michael Tieman & Nancy Marshall Vols. I-V – 2019/2020 (paperback) Author: Michael Tieman
Our Mayflower Families, Fuller, Tilley, Howland Vols. I - II 2020 -(paperback) Author: Michael Tieman
Morrell Descendants in America - 2019 (paperback) Author: Michael Tieman
We Started as Farmers in Prussia - 2019 (paperback) Author: Michael Tieman
Oregon Revolutionary War Muster Roll-2018 (paperback) Author: Michael Tieman
Behind the Bronze - My Sculpture- (paperback) Author, artist: Michael Tieman
Behind the Paint - New England 2015- (paperback) Author, artist: Michael Tieman
Behind the Paint - National Parks 2014- (paperback) Author, artist: Michael Tieman
Behind the Paint - France & Italy 2013 - (paperback) Author, artist: Michael Tieman
Behind the Paint - Italy 2011 - (paperback) Author, artist: Michael Tieman
The Building of "Courage" - (hardcover and paperback) Author: Michael Tieman
The Poet - (hardcover) Author: David Sweet
My Glengarry - (hardcover) Author: Dr. F. James Marshall

1/31/2016

Today found sources from the NEHS and Mayflower publications proving " SOURCES" that my father's mother's mother (SOUTH) is a direct line to the Fuller and Lathrop families that came over on the Mayflower in 1620. I also have a copy of the Mayflower Descendants Application approved for a Fuller, proving our lineage.

DNA GENETIC ANCESTRY TEST RESULTS

68% European West - Primarily located in: Belgium, France, Germany, Netherlands, Switzerland, Luxembourg, Liechtenstein Also found in: England, Denmark, Italy, Slovenia, Czech Republic

The Europe West region is a broad expanse stretching from Amsterdam's sea-level metropolis to the majestic peaks of the Alps. Geographically dominated by France in the west and Germany in the east, it includes several nations with distinct cultural identities. From the boisterous beer gardens of Munich to the sun-soaked vineyards of

Bordeaux and the alpine dairy farms of Switzerland, it is a region of charming cultural diversity.

23% Ireland - Primarily located in: Ireland, Wales, Scotland, Also found in: France, England

Ireland is located in the eastern part of the North Atlantic Ocean, directly west of Great Britain. A variety of internal and external influences have shaped Ireland as we know it today. Ireland's modern cultural remains deeply rooted in the Celtic culture that spread across much of Central Europe and into the British Isles. Along with Wales, Scot land, and a handful of other isolated communities within the British Isles, Ireland remains one of the last holdouts of the ancient Celtic languages that were once spoken throughout much of Western Europe. And though closely tied to Great Britain, both geographically and historically, the Irish have fiercely maintained their unique character thro ugh the centuries.

5% Italy/Greece

The 1970's
· Viet Nam war continues, I was in the draft lottery in 1969, #344 out of 366 (see bio above)
· I met Nancy at Buckeye Mart in Upper Arlington, OH. She was a new cashier and I worked in the Photography Dept.
Had our first date April 3, 1970, pizza and pool.
· MT in Ohio State Riots in May 1970 (see bio above)
· We became engaged Feb 14, 1971 in Upper Arlington, OH
· We married June 16, 1972 in Columbus, OH (see bio above)
· I graduated June 1972 from Columbus College of Art & Design with a BFA in Columbus, OH.

I went to school to learn how to be an art director in an ad agency, while working full time as an art director in an ad agency. Crazy right?

During those school years I worked to put myself through school as my parents would not pay for me to become a "poor artist". So I worked full time at the ad agency M-F from 6:30 am-12:30 then to school classes from 1-4, back to the agency until 6pm, then night classes 7-10pm. Weekends and nights I did not have night classes I worked at Buckeye Mart twenty hrs./wk. My entire career I always had a full-time job at an agency and freelanced at night with my own clients.

The school classes were in a few small "almost" condemned buildings, the dorms being a bit better. We were still the best art college east of the Mississippi, CCAD and Pratt fought as to who was the best each year. CCAD has since built a huge school campus taking up a large section of that area of downtown with modern dorms and four multi story buildings housing modern classrooms and equipment. What a change.

·Nancy Graduated from Ohio State University School Dental Hygiene June 1973, Columbus, OH

·The day after I was let go from my job at The Studio, (the owner's friend dropped in some money to keep it going and took my job in return), we went to west coast Aug 1973 as a graduation present from Nancy's parents, came home and decided we were moving to the west coast.

·Moved to BC Oct 8, 1973, Canadian Thanksgiving to Grannie's apartment in Arbutus, BC. Nancy sponsored me as she was "going home" to Canada.

·Nancy started work as Dental Hygienist in Vancouver, BC, her father a sked a past student of his to hire Nancy as a "favor", but it turned out that there was a lack of DH in Vancouver and she could have walked into any dental practice and commanded a job with big money. Oh well, it got us there, and she did move on to another practice later on.

·Moved to rental home in east side of Vancouver Dec 1973

·I went to work at Cockfield & Brown finally in 1974 when I became a landed immigrant. Had a job at JW Thompson Advertising (world's largest ad agency) in Oct. 1973, but it took so long to get immigration papers that I lost that job. The Canadian gov't decided that they would grant amnesty to all of the U S draft dodgers that went to Canada, and they put all of them ahead of me trying to get in legally.

·Moved to second house in North Vancouver in 1974

·Heather was born in May 17,1976 in North Vancouver, BC

·Moved to first house we owned in North Vancouver on 15th St. Aug 1977

·I started a new co. in 1975 when Cockfield & Brown Advertising went out of business

·1978 partner bugged out with money. I lost the company but repaid all the outstanding company debts in two years.

·Katie was born June 25, 1979 in North Vancouver, BC

·My parents came to Canada in 1976 for Heather's christening

Work:

1969-72   Art Director, Kersker Inc., Columbus. OH
1972-74   Graphic Designer, The Studio, Inc., Columbus, OH
1974-75   Sr. Art Director, Cockfield & Brown Advt., Vancouver, B.C., Canada
1975-78   Ptnr., Graphic Designer Designers West. Ltd., Vancouver, B.C., Canada
1978-86   Owner, Graphic Designer, Tieman & Friends, Vancouver, B.C., Canada
1978-81   Ptnr., Art Director, Printpac Mktg., Ltd., Richmond, B.C., Canada

Lived:

1965-73 - Columbus, Ohio, USA.
1973-86 - North Vancouver, British Columbia, Canada.

Travel:

1973 West Coast- Oregon, Washington, Vancouver, Gibsons & Mission B.C. Canada

1977 Ohio Christmas

The 1980's

·Left Expo 86 in June and came to Portland Oregon to work, lived with Nancy's parents

Funny story. Friday, the day before I came down to Portland, I went to my Canadian bank and got a stack of $50 US bills so I could pay for things down here until I could set up bank accounts, etc.. Monday, my first day in US and first day on my new job, I come back from lunch and there waiting for me was my new boss flanked by two Secret Service agents. I had paid my mo. parking that morning with a $50 bill, seems it was counterfeit and the parking lot called the Feds. It was an interesting and long interview as I explained that my Canadian bank gave me the money on Friday and I still had the receipt. They would check it out and took all my "funny money" as evidence. Oh, and don't leave town until they tell me. Oh, did I say that I had given my in-laws several bills to pay my room & board that morning also? How to make friends and impress my new boss. In a strange country with no money and the Feds watching me. Long story short, it was eventually resolved in my favor. The money I was reimbursed by the bank only because one of our good friends (still a good friend) worked at the bank and put pressure on them to pay us back as it was their fault.

Another funny story from this event. I was working with this same agency in 1993 when our client, Intel asked us to come to NASA Ames with them to install their very first parallel Supercomputer. My boss and I went down along with several Intel high ups and super scientists, and our client contact who was an ex-Navy SEAL. We were all subject to background checks and given security clearances accordingly. My boss and I panicked, me with a Secret Service file for counterfeiting. I was doomed. Well, seems that I was given a higher security clearance than everyone else and they had to be accompanied on base by a NASA employee or me. Talk about a pissed off client with questions about who I was. Still makes me smile. But it just reinforces my youngest daughter's idea that I was a spy. Love her imagination.

·Moved to Portland Aug 20, 1986, rented a house in Lake Oswego girls went to grades 2 and 5
·My parents came to see us Dec 1986
·We bought a house in Jan 1987
·Connie was married to John Drotos in Jul 1983

Work:
1986-95   Co-Creative Director, Gilchrist & Associates, Inc., Portland, OR
1984-86   Sr. Graphic Designer The 1986 World Exposition, Vancouver, Canada
1981-84   Sr. Art Director, McKim Advertising, Ltd., Vancouver, Canada

1976-81   CEO/ CD, Tieman & Friends, Ltd., Vancouver, Canada

Lived:
1973-86 - North Vancouver, British Columbia, Canada
1986-96 - Lake Oswego, Oregon, USA

Travel:
1983 - Ohio
1984 - Banff, Alberta, Canada
1988 - Hong Kong, Tokyo, Japan(airport)
1989 - Disneyland

The 1990's
·Nancy turns 40 in March 1992 and we had a big party.
·Kids car accident March 1992, almost loss both of them. They were in the hospital for a while then at home recuperating.
·Heather graduated 1994 from Lake Oswego High School, Lake Oswego, OR
·Katie graduated in 1997 from Lake Oswego High School, Lake Oswego, OR
·My great aunt Thelma Tieman died 18 Sep1997 in Keokuk, IA
·Nancy graduated with BS in Psychology at Portland State in June 1990
·Nancy graduated with MS in Education; Counseling 1994 from Portland State University
·Heather went to U of Idaho in Moscow 1994 graduated with Honors Dec 1998
·My grandmother Viola Tieman died 22 Mar 1995
·Heather married June 1996 to Phillip Erwin in Lake Oswego, OR
·Katie went to Washington State in Pullman in 1997
·We moved to Camas WA in Dec 1997
·Phillip moved in with us Dec 1997 in Camas, WA to work while Heather finished school
·Heather and Phillip moved to Portland June 1998
·Heather's first child Riley Erwin born 27 Sep 1999 Portland, OR
·Our 25th ann. June 16,1997
·Katie left WS in 1999 and became engaged to Shawn Schulberg

Work:
1986-95   Co-Creative Director, Gilchrist & Associates, Inc., Portland, OR
1993-2007 Owner, MT Studios, Portland OR, Camas WA, & Cannon Beach, OR
1995-97   President, Internet World Broadcasting Corp. Portland, OR
1997-99   Partner/V.P. Marketing/Creative Director, Tripwire Security Systems, Portland, OR   1997-99   Vice President Marketing, Online Interactive Network Corporation, Portland, OR
1999-2001 Partner; The Bernhardt Agency, Portland, OR,

Lived:

1986-96 - Lake Oswego, Oregon, USA

1996-2002 - Camas, Washington, USA

Travel:

1998 - Hong Kong, Shenzhen, China, Seoul, Korea (airport); Nancy and my first intercontinental trip

The 2000's

·Nancy's mother, Janet Ormandy Marshall died March 7, 2000

·Katie married Shawn 4 Nov 2000, Portland, OR, Katie kept her maiden name Tieman

·To Iowa for Aunt Pat & Wally Wetzel's 50th ann. Dec. 2000

·Sep 11, 2001 happened 9/11

·Lost job in 2001 and in April 1, 2002 we started our own art gallery in Cannon Beach, OR moved there in June

·Connor Tieman born 28 Oct 2002, Portland, OR

·Katie graduated 2004 from Western Culinary Institute, Cordon Bleu with Honors, Portland, OR

·Katie married 25 July 2009 to Sam Woodward

·Moved Artists Gallerie to new downtown location in 2005

·MT Studios and personal Bankrupt in 2007

·My great aunt Maggie Tieman died 2 Jun 2007, Keokuk, IA

·My mother Doris Tieman died 9 Mar 2003, Akron, OH

·Nancy's father F. James Marshall died 24 Jan 2008, Portland, OR

·My sister Connie Sue Drotos died 29 Jul 2008

·Jackson Erwin was born 26 Jul 2005

·Alexis Tieman-Woodward was born 12 Nov 2006

·Dedicated 36" bronze Courage in July 2009 Summa Health System's Jean B. and Milton N. Cooper Cancer Center, Akron City Hospital, Akron, Ohio, to my sister Connie

·Started working for Haystack Gallery and Cannon Beach newspaper in 2007

·Published my first book "Courage" as Michael Tieman Publishing 2009

Work:

1993 - 2007   MT Studios, Portland OR, Camas WA, & Cannon Beach, OR

1999 - 2001 Partner/V.P. Marketing/Creative Director The Bernhardt Agency, Portland, OR

2002 - Present   Owner, Artists Gallerie, LLC; Michael Tieman Publishing, Cannon Beach, OR

2007-14 Sales, Haystack Gallery, Cannon Beach, OR

Lived:

1996-2002 - Camas, Washington, USA
2002-15 - Cannon Beach, Oregon, USA

Travel:
2000 - London, England, Paris, France

The 2010's
·Owen Tieman-Woodward born 18 Feb 2010, Portland, OR
·My dad M. LaVerne Tieman died in 5 Jan 2011, Stow, OH
·Nancy retired in 2011
·Tripwire was bought out in 2011 by a German company. Our retirement money - I worked at five start-ups in my career, this was the only one that paid off.
·Donated 36" "Courage" to Knight Cancer Center Oregon Health Sciences University in memory of Nancy's mother Janet O. Marshall 9 Nov 2012
·I retired Dec 29, 2013
·We bought and moved into a townhouse in Beaverton, OH in Aug 2015
·Published eight new books this decade as Michael Tieman Publishing

Work:
2002 - Present - Owner; Artists Gallerie, LLC; Michael Tieman Publishing, Cannon Beach and Beaverton, OR
2007-14 Sales, Haystack Gallery, Cannon Beach, OR

Lived:
2002-2015 - Cannon Beach, Oregon, USA
2015-present - Beaverton, Oregon, USA

Travel:
2011 - Tuscany area of Italy including Pisa, Rome, Florence, Cinque Terre, Carrara, Munich, Germany(airport)
2012- California car trip; Napa Valley and vineyards, San Francisco
2013 - France; Paris, Avignon, many hill towns of Provence area, Nice. Italy; five towns of Cinque Terre, Siena, many small towns in Tuscany.
2014- National Parks car trip Utah/Arizona; Zion, Grand Canyon, Bryce , Arches, Canyonlands;
2015 - MA -Boston, (Our homestead in Kittery, Eliot, N. Berwick Maine), Portsmouth, Glouster, Salem, Plymouth, Provincetown, Lexington, Concord, Providence RI;
2016 -Italy with our daughters; Small towns in Tuscany area of Italy including Pisa, Rome, Florence, Cinque Terre
2017 - California car trip to Sonoma and Napa Valley and vineyards and up the Oregon Coast
2018 - Car trip to South Dakota/Montana/Idaho/; Black Hills, Mt. Rushmore,

Yellowstone, Craters of the Moon, Grand Tetons,

2020 The Year of the COVID-19 Global Pandemic

March 21, 2020

So, how is my family doing?

We are all staying home unless we have to go out. Social Distancing 3' -6' apart, wash your hands for 20 secs. often, sneeze in your sleeve, don't touch your face with your hands, Grandparents stay away from your kids and grandkids.

Our daughter Heather went to the fabric store and bought fabric and elastic and she and Nancy are sewing masks for OHSU hospital nurses and doctors because Oregon is not getting PPE from the Feds. Making 30 at a time, then taking them to OHSU. The hospital staff is reusing what they have for 5 days before replacing them.

Our rich country cannot get the supplies we need because of the Federal Govt. incompetence. The local and state governments have to do it themselves and we as individuals have to help. Our state Govt is also buying up and leasing hotels and building temp. shelters to bed the upcoming onslaught of cases. Very little testing in Oregon, hundreds per day to very needy vs. Japan that was testing 10,000 per day to everyone. National testing so far since Jan is at 15,000+ TOTAL nationwide. Trump has promised 4million+ testing kits for the last 2 weeks, nothing is arriving at the state level. Tens of millions of masks and PPE for health professionals and first responders promised, we are making them for the hospitals ourselves since nothing has arrived. Promises, but no action.

Just a few more promises from Trump that are not being done: The Army Corps of Engineers to immediately build hospital units. Not deployed. Two Navy Hospital ships are "on their way to help, one to New York and one to California". Three weeks plus away as they are under repair and there is no staff aboard.

In a time of National crises and especially in a global pandemic we need leaders that we can trust, Trump cannot tell the truth as is obvious at his daily press conferences when he declares all of these great things he is doing then immediately after he talks, in the same press conference the experts we can trust have to "walk back" what he said and tell us the facts. While he is standing behind them.

The economy, as you can tell by the headlines below is tanking. The stock market in the last week+ lost 9,000 points. Everything we gained since Trump took over as President was lost. Massive layoffs and small business closures as business have to close down during the "Shutdown" and stay at home orders. Only food stores, pharmacies and essential lifesaving business are open. Restaurants and bars are closed unless they can sell take out, but soon they will have to close as Oregon is looking into a statewide shutdown like New York, California, Illinois and Connecticut.

Schools are closed in Oregon for at least 6 weeks, they are talking about closing the rest of the school year. Across the country some states have already closed school for the year, some not. The kids who need the schools to get fed breakfast and lunches, now all kids can go to the schools and get a "grab and go" bag. Our daughter Katie is a "Lunch Lady" at an elementary school and she is working putting the meals together. The kids are being taken care of by each district no matter what the national govt does. Some districts in Washington state, the school bus drivers are delivering the food to the kids at their bus stops. People helping people has become the new norm. How cool is that.

All of us old people, 60+ and those with compromised immune systems have been ordered to "stay at home" away from people as we are most at risk of dying. That is Nancy. She is 68 and has Ankylosing Spondylitis and she is taking 2 hr. infusions at a clinic every 8 weeks to keep it from spreading. She is taking drugs to kill most of her immune system. Kind of at the top of the list for risk.

All flights out of the US are cancelled, The US boarders with Canada and Mexico are closed except to restricted traffic. Globally, countries have closed their boarders and ordered their citizens to Shelter in Place".

In all countries including US, sporting events, meetings, corp. events, concerts, parades and crowds of over ten people are all cancelled until at least June 1. They are talking about postponing the Tokyo Olympics until next year.

So, how is my family doing again? We are all fine. We have 2 weeks of food supplies, so we do not have to go to the grocery stores often, which most stores are supplied you just have to see what is available ... but there is food, no problem. We have things to do to keep us occupied and we talk on the phone to our kids every day. We will get through this and come out stronger on the other side.

News Headlines for March 21, 2020
> State health officials signal a new phase of pandemic response
> In hard-hit areas, testing restricted to health care workers, hospital patients
> Shutting down the city that never sleeps
> The scene in New York captures an unimaginable week as the city became a new epicenter of America's epidemic.
> Cases surge at senior care centers, hitting 73 facilities in 22 states, Post review finds
> As of Friday evening, at least 55 coronavirus deaths occurred among people living in elder care facilities. The number is likely higher because official counts often omit a description of the person's last place of residence.
> Rescue bill could inject more than $2 trillion into U.S. economy, top White House adviser says
> Hospitals warn of shortages, closures without emergency aid
> Stay home or carry on? Americans want to sacrifice for others but disagree on what's right.
> How you can help: What to do for nonprofits, local businesses and seniors
> Trump deceives while lawmakers' cash out. It's the 'story of life.'
> Trump is 'nasty' in a crisis and 'terrible' in his response to it
> Pop-country singer of 'The Gambler' who dominated 1970s music charts dies at 81

Laid-off restaurant workers face uncertain futures with looming rent and plenty of worry

The new sick leave law doesn't help the workers that need it most

U.S. intelligence reports from January and February warned about a likely pandemic

Over 2K retired medical workers volunteer to help, NYC mayor says

White House won't say when healthcare workers can expect to have additional supplies

'What do we have to lose?': Trump continues to promote untested drug treatments for coronavirus

Trump: 'I don't know' if family business will receive government assistance

Trump's tone veers wildly under pressure from coronavirus

New York State declared 'major disaster,' coronavirus cases now top 10,000

'Stressed and panicked': California tests out strict limits on daily life previously unimaginable

As Congress debates who gets a check, some experts say: Make it universal

Coronavirus economic relief package could total $2 trillion, Kudlow says

Gupta stunned by Trump-Fauci difference at briefing

President Trump made false claims about possible treatments for the coronavirus, and expert Dr. Anthony Fauci had to tamp down optimism about the treatments at a press conference.

Trump denies a shortage of coronavirus tests. See Fauci's answer

President Donald Trump told reporters there was not a wide-spread shortage of coronavirus tests in the US. Later in the White House briefing, top infectious disease expert Dr. Anthony Fauci said in reality the US is behind on testing capabilities because many Americans don't have easy access to tests.

Calling All People Who Sew: You Can Help Make Masks For 2020 Healthcare Worker PPE Shortage

A complete timeline of the coronavirus pandemic

December 31, 2019
Chinese Health officials inform the WHO about a cluster of 41 patients with a mysterious pneumonia. Most are connected to Huanan Seafood Wholesale Market.
January 1, 2020
Huanan Seafood Wholesale Market closes.
January 7, 2020
Chinese authorities identify a new type of coronavirus (called novel coronavirus or CoVid-19).
January 11, 2020
China records its first death.
January 13, 2020
First coronavirus case outside of China is reported in Thailand.
January 20, 2020

First US case is reported: a 35-year-old man in Snohomish County, Washington.

January 23, 2020

Wuhan is placed under quarantine; Hubei province follows within days.

January 30, 2020

WHO declares a global public-health emergency.

January 31, 2020

President Trump bans foreign nationals from entering the US if they were in China within the prior two weeks.

February 2, 2020

First death outside China is recorded in the Philippines.

February 7, 2020

Chinese whistleblower Li Wenliang dies.

February 8, 2020

US citizen dies in Wuhan - first death of an American citizen.

February 9, 2020

Death toll in China surpasses that of the 2002-2003 SARS epidemic, with 811 deaths recorded.

February 11, 2020

WHO announces that the new coronavirus disease will be called "COVID-19."

February 12, 2020

Coronavirus cases start to spike in South Korea.

February 19, 2020

Iran outbreak begins.

February 21, 2020

Italy outbreak begins.

February 29, 2020

US reports first death on American soil.

March 8, 2020

Italy places all 60 million residents on lockdown.

March 11, 2020

WHO declare the outbreak a pandemic

President Trump bans all travel from 26 European countries.

March 13, 2020

A US national emergency is declared over the novel coronavirus outbreak.

March 17, 2020

A leaked federal plan warns the new coronavirus pandemic "will last 18 months or longer" and may come in "multiple waves" of infections.

Italy reports 475 COVID-19 deaths, the highest single-day death toll for any country since the outbreak began.

March 19, 2020

Globally, authorities report more than 240,000 confirmed cases of COVID19, with about 145,000 being active and ongoing cases, roughly 85,00 0 recoveries, and 10,000 deaths.

Nearly all US states declare a state of emergency.

Coronavirus cases in US
Confirmed cases of novel coronavirus as of Saturday, March 21, 2020.
Alabama: 124
Alaska: 14
Arizona: 63 (including one death)
Arkansas: 100
California: 1,077 (including 24 deaths)
Colorado: 363 (including four deaths)
Connecticut: 194 (including four deaths)
Delaware: 39
District of Columbia: 77 (including one death)
Florida: 557 (including 11 deaths)
Georgia: 507 (including 14 deaths)
Guam: 12
Hawaii: 37
Idaho: 31
Illinois: 585 (including five deaths)
Indiana: 79 (including three deaths)
Iowa: 45
Kansas: 44 (including one death)
Kentucky: 63 (including two deaths)
Louisiana: 585 (including 16 deaths)
Maine: 56
Maryland: 190 (including two deaths)
Massachusetts: 413 (including 1 death)
Michigan: 549 (including three deaths)
Minnesota: 138 (including one death)
Mississippi: 140 (including one death)
Missouri: 73 (including three deaths)
Montana: 21
Nebraska: 38
Nevada: 109 (including two deaths)
New Hampshire: 55
New Jersey: 890 (including 11 deaths)
New Mexico: 43
New York: 10,356 (including 53 deaths)
North Carolina: 184
North Dakota: 26
Ohio:169 (including one death)
Oklahoma: 49 (including one death)
Oregon: 114 (including three deaths)

Pennsylvania: 268 (including one death)
Puerto Rico: 14
Rhode Island: 54
South Carolina: 125 (including one death)
South Dakota: 14 (including one death)
Tennessee: 228
Texas: 202 (including five deaths)
US Virgin Islands: 3
Utah: 112
Vermont: 29 (including two deaths)
Virginia: 152 (including two deaths)
Washington: 1,524 (including 83 deaths)
West Virginia: 8
Wisconsin: 206 (including four deaths)
Wyoming: 22

NBC News Headlines April 3, 2020
Coronavirus cases top 1 million globally
U.S. economy lost over 700,000 jobs in March, ending decadelong streak of employment gains
Out of work because of coronavirus, struggling to file for unemployment
Some dial their state offices hundreds of times while others are met with frozen websites.
Trump admin's lack of a unified national strategy will cost lives, experts say
Empty beds: Hospital ship deployed to NYC with 1,000 bed capacity is only treating 20 patients
Supreme Court cancels courtroom argument for rest of the term
Fauci: 'I don't understand' why all states are not under stay-at-home orders
White House expected to urge Americans in virus hot spots to wear face coverings
Firm under sanctions made Russian ventilators shipped to U.S.
Trump says no one could have predicted coronavirus. But two administration officials said in 2019 that the threat of a pandemic kept them up at night.
Unprecedented unemployment could bring Medicaid to the brink. Experts are sounding the alarm.
Houston hasn't reported a surge of virus cases. But its hospitals tell a different story.
A little-known industry lent billions to U.S. small businesses. Now the bills are due.
Banks warn of 'utter chaos' in new small business lending program
Watch sailors cheer Navy captain relieved of command after raising alarm on coronavirus
Homework? Sign in. Playdate? Log on. For kids during the pandemic, life is digital.
Israel locks down ultra-Orthodox city hit hard by coronavirus
Projected ventilator demand 'outstrips the capacity' of national stockpile, FEMA tells Congress

European countries develop new ways to tackle domestic violence during lockdowns

DOJ's coronavirus response could lead to lasting reforms - or scary power grabs

As Wuhan starts to open up, American expat warns U.S. that lockdowns are just beginning

Pictures show huge temporary mortuary being built in London

Detroit, on the brink of recovery, reels as coronavirus claims lives

Farmworkers fight for safety amid pandemic with little protection from employers

For Biden, Trump is his own worst enemy in coronavirus crisis

'Lean on Me' singer Bill Withers dies at 81

Army Corps of Engineers commander talks about setting up 'pop-up' hospitals

Many Americans may have to wait months for coronavirus relief checks

One nursing home offers grim advice: Take your loved ones home

'Fearing the worst': Arizona sends in National Guard to help stricken Navajo Nation

Could presidential vote be done by mail?

Democratic Party delays July convention until August over coronavirus concerns

Doctors in Britain 'desperate' for safety equipment as they battle pandemic

These states have the most coronavirus cases. See the day-by-day break down.

NBC News Headlines April 6, 2020

Acting Navy secretary rips into ousted captain who raised alarm over COVID-19 outbreak

Dow closes with gain of more than 1,600 points

Top Trump aide says Fauci's caution on possible coronavirus treatment warrants a 'second opinion'

Many Americans won't get coronavirus checks. Here's a look at who is ineligible.

Jared Kushner's shadowy coronavirus task force reveals true danger of nepotism

British Prime Minister Boris Johnson transferred to intensive care unit

Hospitals fear people at risk due to supply shortages and confusing gov't guidance, watchdog report finds

Wisconsin Gov. suspends in-person voting for Tuesday primary amid coronavirus

Xerox plans to make low cost, disposable ventilators

U.S. deaths near 10,000 as medical officials warn worst is yet to come

Trump's use of medical stockpile veers from past administrations leaving state in the lurch

ANALYSIS: Two months in, Trump's coronavirus response creates more chaos

ANALYSIS: Sanders risks his movement's clout by staying in the race against Biden too long

Inspector general fired by Trump defends flagging Ukraine whistleblower complaint

Trump defends decision to fire inspector general, calls him a 'disgrace'

Trump just dealt a brutal blow to federal oversight - as Republicans do nothing

Fauci: 'We are struggling' to get the coronavirus outbreak under control

Surgeon general says this week will be 'Pearl Harbor moment' for coronavirus

China is encouraging herbal remedies to treat COVID-19. But scientists warn against it.

May1, 2020

So, how is my family doing now?

March 23 Oregon Governor issued her Stay at Home order.

Since Nancy and I are retired and have been for 6 years, our daily routine has not changed much. I go down to my studio and work and Nancy is upstairs on the other two floors. With a 3-story home and over 2100' no problem. Things would have been different if we were still living in Cannon Beach.

If we still had a business in CB, we like everyone else there would be in dire straits. How to pay rent and get income to live when the town is closed to all outsider traffic. Glad Nancy and I do not have to go through that daily anguish. We are retired and on Social Security, a guaranteed income base that pays most of our expenses.

Our kids and grandkids are still doing ok, just tired of being cooped up and working from home. Nancy and I have a daily walk of 1.5 miles we do and have since Nancy got sick years ago. She has to do it to control the pain levels. We are over 60 and Nancy has a compromised immune system, so when we go out, we wear masks. In fact, in Oregon you are supposed to wear masks in public and keep 6' apart. We pass people on our walk along a paved path 4 people wide who run or walk in groups with no masks and they do not walk in single file when passing people to keep the 6' distance. Again, the rules do not apply to them, so they endanger us all.

Funny thing happened the other day on our walk we passed a family and as we passed we heard the little boy, maybe pre-school age say to a friend as he passed "I'll see you on Zoom tomorrow". A new normal, video conferencing play dates.

My SAR group has been using Zoom since we cannot meet in person. I think it may become one of our new normal as well. A good way to get people together from all over the state without the travel.

Tomorrow the National SAR is supposed to decide about canceling the National Congress in Richmond VA. Over 250 old men, I have planned to go with Nancy, getting on planes for hours to get to a 5 day meeting in confined rooms and committee meetings, then sitting down in a banquet room eating and drinking with 8 people per table. I hope they cancel.

*Here is gov't promise vs. reality: We are entitled to the $1200 each from the Feds. It is supposed to be put into our bank account because we have direct deposit on our 2018 IRS tax report. To be done April 3. If not that way, since we have direct deposit with our Social Security checks each month, it could also be given to us that way. Everyone else will have checks mailed to them starting in May. Get online to find out about the money. Reality, when I finally got the online system to work to find out about our stimulus checks, I had to fill out a form and our checks will be mailed to us after May 1. So much for automatic deposits. If I believed the Feds and did not check, would we have ever gotten our checks?

*Gov't promise vs. reality: PPP loans to small business will bail them out for 6 months and keep them in business. $3.8B PPP forgivable loans to small business in Oregon out of $349B. 18,732 loans were given out there are 320,019 small business in Oregon. In Cannon Beach when we left in 2015 there were 235 small businesses, from the CB city info web page one business got the loan. Seems that 47 "publicly owned" companies in the US received billions of dollars, several got the money then claimed bankruptcy which was not illegal.

Today as the first part of re-opening Oregon is opening: elective surgery in hospitals, restaurants, breweries and wineries with social distancing and 50% max occupancy.

Oregon re-opening Phase I - no date as to when it will begin.

Phase One would still call for all vulnerable people to stay home, minimize non-essential travel and encourage working from home. The draft proposal discourages social gatherings of more than 10 people. The proposal indicates that not all eight types of businesses would open in Phase One. For instance, large venues are "likely" to remain closed during the initial phase, and visitors would be prohibited from going to hospitals and care facilities, according to the draft. While schools remain closed, as in under the federal framework (center column), Oregon would look to open some childcare facilities.

Officials are trying to figure out how certain industries could reopen with strong social distancing and sanitation measures in place. Rural parts of Oregon with fewer COVID-19 cases might be able to reopen parts of the economy sooner. After lifting some restrictions in Phase One, state officials would look at whether there is a re-emergence of coronavirus illness over 14 days. "If there's not, we can move to Phase Two, which is a further lifting of restrictions,"

One of the things I cannot believe is that Trump signed an Order that meat processing plants had to stay open. This after they are known as one of the top 3 places with high covid cases, along with nursing homes and veteran homes. The CDC and OSHA who normally check business and give them guidelines they have to adhere to or be closed down, issued suggestions to meat producers where they could improve to protect their workers and cut the rate of disease in their facilities. When Trump signed the order, the did not have to clean up their act, just get back to work. In my days of working in a union shop, if this were to happen, the unions would strike and close the places down. Not now, Trump has bullied them to be quiet. His friends who own business make out again, and the working man gets screwed. I hope these people remember in Nov. when it is time to vote, who did not take care of them and their families and vote the Republicans out. We will see, people seem to have short memories.

Also scary is that states are staring to throw open the business even while their covid deaths are going up. Seems mostly the Rep. states. Can you imagine opening tattoo parlors, hair salons, gyms, massage parlors and shopping malls with social distancing of 6'? How does that work? And men with no masks and long guns marching in crowds and taking over state buildings because they have a right and were not arrested. Really?

Hopefully, natural selection will happen. You can't cure stupid, unfortunately they will get sick and take the beds and care away from those of us who followed the rules.

We will stay well and safe.

NBC News Headlines May 1, 2020

'Just impossible': Small Southern city struggles without testing but forced to reopen

Trump says U.S. is ready to contain the virus with contact tracing. Experts disagree.

Counter protesters try to mute message of stay-at-home opponents

While Trump minimizes the death toll, government orders 100,000 new body bags

Trump's Twitter outburst proves he can sympathize - just not with COVI D-19 victims

Target, Walmart workers and others plan 'sickout' protests over corona virus safety

Farmworkers sue Washington state over coronavirus protections

Is your state reopening today? See the breakdown of each state's stay- at-home order

CDC: Coronavirus a leading cause of death in some states

Joe Biden denies sexual assault allegation, calls for release of any records

Nearly 900 workers at a Tyson plant in Indiana test positive for coronavirus

Justin Trudeau announces Canada is banning assault-style weapons

Senate Democrats criticize McConnell's plan to bring lawmakers back to Washington

Reversing course, House won't return to D.C. because of coronavirus threat

A rare, dangerous complication is now being seen in some kids with coronavirus

If elections are canceled by the coronavirus, you'll wish you had vote by mail

Trump's defense of Michael Flynn insults America's COVID-19 victims. Here's why.

The U.K. bought 250 ventilators from China. Doctors warn they could kill.

Armed protesters storm Michigan Capitol as lawmakers debate governor's emergency powers

While Trump minimizes the toll, government orders 100,000 new body bags

NYC to suspend subway overnight

Appeals court strikes down Kansas law requiring proof of citizenship to vote

More than 200 countries and territories have confirmed coronavirus cases

Shopping Angels: Volunteer program brings supplies to those stuck inside during pandemic

CNN News

US makes big bet on company with unproven technology

This biotech firm received $483 million from the US to make a coronavirus vaccine. It has never brought a product to market before.

US Updates More than 4,900 workers in US meat and poultry facilities have Covid-19, CDC reports

Trump tweets support for Michigan protesters, some of whom were armed

Trump erupts at campaign manager over sliding poll numbers

It may be a year before sports return to normalcy in the US, Fauci warns

With families banned from nursing homes, are their loved ones safe?

FDA approves NASA ventilator for coronavirus patients

NBC News Headlines May 27, 2020

An American tragedy: As we mourn 100,000, U.S. reckons with its flaws and promise

Amid the memorials, the touching tributes, millions rushing to do their part and the political chaos that overshadows it all - America has emerged with new clarity.

George Floyd was 'very loving' and a 'gentle giant,' friends and family say

SpaceX launch postponed by weather, rescheduled for Saturday

Asymptomatic COVID-19 cases may be more common than suspected

Blood test nears for COVID-linked syndrome in children

Twitter is now fact-checking Trump. That won't stop him from tweeting.

As Trump rails against mail-in voting, his campaign tries to make it easier for Pennsylvania supporters

Two prominent Republicans call out Trump for repeating baseless conspiracy theory about MSNBC host

Hong Kong no longer has autonomy under China, Pompeo says

Hundreds arrested in Hong Kong as tensions rise over Chinese control

Far-right extremists blamed for surge in anti-Semitic crimes in Germany

How Trump is demolishing Cold War safety nets - and hastening a superpower crisis

China warns U.S. taking world to brink of 'new Cold War'

Boeing to lay off almost 7,000 workers this week

Senators sound alarm over coronavirus in juvenile detention facilities

Trump opposition throws surveillance legislation in doubt

'An ego trip': Pelosi blasts Trump's insistence that Republican convention occur

Missouri health officials call for self-quarantine of partiers at Lake of the Ozarks

Trump's scapegoating of Asian Americans is an affront to all Americans

Traders sign death waivers as Wall Street reopens, with a few differences

Massive coronavirus vaccine testing planned in U.S. to meet year-end goals

NBC News Headlines June 3, 2020

Minneapolis officers charged 3 more officers charged in George Floyd' s death, Derek Chauvin charges elevated

Nationwide protests over George Floyd's death

NAACP has urged Minneapolis police to ban fatal neck restraint technique for years

Bucking Trump, Pentagon chief Esper says no need for military response to protests

Esper revises account of what he knew about Trump's church photo-op

Mass protests continue across the U.S.

Senate Republicans struggle to respond to Trump's actions on protests

What is this, a banana republic? Pelosi unloads on Trump over teargassing of protesters outside White House

No way I was staying home': Trump's response leads more protesters to White House

They wanted to protest peacefully. Police responded with force. On the ground in Minneapolis.

Mass protests show no sign of fading more than a week after George Floyd's death

China, Russia and Iran attack U.S. over Floyd killing

Snapchat to stop promoting Trump's content

U.K. PM tells China that Britain will admit 3 Million from Hong Kong

Trump says he is postponing G7 summit

Thousands storm Paris streets as George Floyd's death helps reignite anger over racism

Trump risks potential backlash from evangelicals with 'tone-deaf' Bible photo-op

June 3, 2020

So, how is my family doing now?

Well, I must say, it is an interesting time. What with the Covid-19 pandemic, the tanked economy and now a week of rioting in the streets with George Floyd's murder by police in Minneapolis. Yes, in Portland a s well as tens of other cities across the US and now the world.

First, the covid crises. March 24 Oregon was closed, and we were told to stay home, May 15, most of Oregon opened to a phase 1 plan our county Washington opened June 1. Basically, no gatherings over 25 people, masks and social distancing in shops, restaurants and bars 25% occupancy. After 3 weeks we can go into phase 2 of 3.

Nancy and I wear our masks when we go where people are, we have found we need to protect ourselves. Still we walk 1.5 miles a day on the paved path near us and yes, almost all of the people we pass do not social distance still, nor wear masks. The President has made it clear that even though you are supposed to wear masks and he won't because it is a sign of weakness and not manly. So, we now have those who drink his Kool-Aid and don't wear masks, and those of us who are responsible and care about our health and others will wear masks. Again, the tribal mentality and the division of the country by Trump.

Our daughters and their families are hanging in. Heather who works for Portland State University has been working from home since the shutdown. She now has been put on furlough 20% or one day and has filed for unemployment through the school to get paid by the gov't for her time off. No telling how long it will be before she goes back full time. However, she will probably continue to work from home until the end of the year. Phillip works for Oracle and has been working from home, no telling for how long, at least until the fall.

Katie works for the Beaverton School District and will be furloughed come June 16 until when school starts in the fall. She has also filed for unemployment through her school district to be paid by the gov't until she goes back full time. Sam is a mortgage broker and works from the office and home as business is brisk with mortgage rates around 3%. We are in the middle of refinancing our home through him at 3.125%.

The grandkids are still schooling from home for a few more weeks, then off for the summer. It has been tough for them to be away from their normal school routine and friends and stuck at home with family. It has loosened up a bit for them, but now that most summer camps are closed this summer, it becomes interesting to have them find something to do. Trying to find out what the new normal for school will be in the fall. No doubt the virus will tell us, especially if it comes back then.

Our trip back east in July has been cancelled as the SAR National Congress in Richmond, VA has been cancelled. So now we will also not be going back to see Washington DC for a few days, Williamsburg, Jamestown and Yorktown. Oh well. Next year in the spring maybe. All SAR meetings from the chapter, state and national level are all on Zoom. All parades and gatherings cancelled for us from Memorial Day through end of August. Our Color Guard is now inactive until then. July 4th will be very different without the parades, fairs and large gatherings.

Our friends who spend a lot of time eating out in restaurants and bars more than eating at home are chomping at the bit to get back in them. Nancy and I don't do much of that, four or five times a year, not four times a week. So their closing has not been a problem for us.

Again, glad we are retired, if not and still had our art gallery in Cannon Beach, we would be out of business and wondering where we were going to get our next meal. Like most small businesses in a destination town we lived close to the line from month to month. Two of the restaurants we know there closed, one owner friend is 76 and has had his rest. In town for 13 years. Closed and now working as chef in a rest. In Astoria when it opens again.

Several weeks ago, CB opened the town and the beach for visitors but you had to wear masks and social distance in all of the shops. If you didn't they tossed you out. Knowing most of the shop owners, they would not hesitate. But they said on the streets most people did not follow the rules. They felt entitled and the rules do not apply to them. It will be a long summer.

Speaking of a long summer, now we have the protests, marches and riots because a week ago four police officers killed an unarmed black man in Minneapolis for passing a fake $20 bill. They held him down on the ground as one of them choked him with his knee on the throat … for almost 10 min. All filmed by people standing by. The people there, of all races marched in protest that the officers were not charged.

Now a week later more than 20 cities across the US have had daily and nightly protest marches that have unfortunately turned into riots. Including Portland. It is again time to stand up and protest the way people are treated and killed for not being the same color as you. In the late 60's and early 70's I was part of that crowd. Protesting the lack of Women's rights, and Black's rights and the war in Nam. I walked those streets, shoulder to shoulder with my fellow humans. Carried those signs, chanted the chants but always left when it started to go from protest to riot. Most of the marches I was in had we had our own security or marshals to make sure we were peaceful and respectful of the property and businesses around us. I still cannot understand why you would burn and loot your own. The few anarchist in the crowds then and today change the message of the crowd from peaceful protest to violence and that unfortunately is all that is remembered.

And we now have a President who incites the violence and division among the people. Look at the headlines in this journal. Last night he said he would command the U.S. military to take over the streets from the protesters, us the citizens. He says, "Screw the 1st Amendment", he is all powerful, he is our new dictator or king. Or so he thinks. I will go back out into the streets if need be to make sure that does not happen, and VOTE to get him and his lackies out. To get my country back from those who try to divide us and destroy the Constitution and all it stands for. Not in my lifetime. My ancestors fought for freedom and peace since before the Revolutionary War and I will not let them down. Freedom is not Free and can be destroyed in less than one generation. The Anarchist and Fascists will not take over this country. We the People have something to say about that.

NBC News Headlines June 30, 2020

Trump has lost his senior advantage. And that could cost him in November.

Trump's growing re-election threat: Republican skeptics

Biden says Trump has 'waved the white flag' on pandemic, promises bigger role for Fauci

U.S. virus cases could swell to 100,000 a day if current trends do not turn around, Fauci warns

U.S. becoming further isolated by COVID-19 crisis

Americans not welcome: E.U. bars U.S. travelers over coronavirus

Mississippi governor signs bill into law removing Confederate symbol from state flag

'The world's been taken': Unprecedented unemployment devastates America across generations

COVID-19 helped this small syringe business boom. Then came the taxpay er-backed windfall.

Six months into the pandemic, health experts confront a new fear: Two virus outbreaks

As states halt reopening of bars and indoor dining, public health experts urge more caution

Senate Republicans distance themselves from Trump on coronavirus masks

In contrast to Trump, Pence encourages wearing masks to prevent corona virus spread

Bounties or not, Russia has worked to expand its clout in Afghanistan as the U.S. eyes an exit

White House learned of Russian bounty intelligence in early 2019

Pompeo asks UN to extend an international arms embargo on Iran

Iran issues arrest warrant for Trump, requests Interpol's help

Comedy legend Carl Reiner, of 'The Dick Van Dyke Show' and 'The Jerk, ' dies at

98

NBC News Headlines Sept 1, 2020

The President used inflammatory language to discuss demonstrations and also spoke out about the media on his way to Wisconsin

Amid high tensions, Trump visits Kenosha in the wake of Jacob Blake shooting

Where protesters go, armed militias, vigilantes likely to follow

Why Kenosha's criminal justice advocates saw this coming

Trump's 'plane loaded with thugs' conspiracy theory matches months-old rumor

Trump claims without evidence that Biden controlled by people in 'the dark shadows'

Out of the 'basement,' Biden pummels Trump

Russian internet trolls hired U.S. journalists to push their news website, Facebook says

Critics want Twitter to halt its trending lists. Instead, Twitter will make tweaks.

Court temporarily blocks New York prosecutor from obtaining Trump tax returns

Black man is killed by Los Angeles sheriff's deputies, sparking protest

Breonna Taylor's boyfriend files civil complaint against Louisville police and city

Congressional investigation finds over $1 billion in PPP fraud

NYC delays return to classrooms due to COVID-19 safety concerns

As Hong Kong reports 12 new cases, it launches effort to test millions. That's raising eyebrows.

'This elevates it to angry': Doctors say CDC, FDA missteps cross the line into politics

Large trials for anticipated Oxford COVID-19 vaccine begin in the U.S.

Far-right group says fatal shooting victim in Portland was a supporter

Oregon governor announces additional police resources one day after fatal shooting

Workers deserved protection from COVID-19. The agency in charge didn't care.

Liberty University to investigate 'all facets' of Jerry Falwell Jr.' s presidency

'Do you believe in life after Trump?' Cher raises $2M for Biden at LGB TQ fundraiser

Trump raises eyebrows with tweet declaring he did not have 'a series of mini-strokes'

Meals on heels: San Francisco drag queens deliver amid pandemics

Maryland official fired after sharing Facebook posts supporting Kenosh a shooting suspect

Black jogger mistaken for suspect in Texas has all charges dismissed after arrest

Philadelphia mayor apologizes for dining indoors at Maryland restaurant

Barr orders more changes in FBI surveillance under FISA

New questions about Trump inauguration money raised in book 'Melania and Me'

Trump administration finalizes coal plant pollution rollback

White House to resume public tours on September 12, masks and social distancing required

Venezuela's Maduro pardons dozens of political opponents

Trump promised a health care plan in 'weeks,' but a month later, it hasn't come

52 former franchisees sue McDonald's for racial discrimination

Justice Ginsburg officiates in-person at friends' wedding weeks after cancer hospitalization

Saudi king fires two senior royals under defense corruption probe

Latino students live in fear of deportation, even when immigration enforcement is low

75 years later, Japanese man recalls bitter internment in U.S.

Tributes for Chadwick Boseman continue to pour in

Noted events in his life were:

Mayflower Descendant.

Physical Description: White Male, Blue Eyes, Brown Hair.

Religion: Methodist.

Education: Grad. North High School, 20 Jun 1968, Columbus, Franklin, Ohio, USA.

Occupation: Ohio/British Columbia/Washington, Between 1969 and 2012, Oregon.

Graduation: BFA, Columbus College of Art & Design, 20 Jun 1972, Columbus, Franklin, Ohio, USA.

Emigration: 14 Jan 1974, Vancouver, British Columbia, Canada.

Immigration: 20 Aug 1986, Portland, Multnomah, Oregon, USA.

Retirement: 1 Jan 2014, Cannon Beach, Clatsop, Oregon, USA.

Membership: Sons of the American Revolution Became National Member #196909, 1 Dec 2015, Lewis & Clark Chapter, Beaverton, Washington, OR, USA.

Children from this marriage were:

+ 144 F   i.   **Heather Anne TIEMAN [920]**[112,113,195,196,197] was born on 17 May 1976 in North Vancouver, British Columbia, Canada[195] and was christened in 1976 in North Vancouver, British Columbia, Canada.

Heather married **Phillip ERWIN [921]**[113,197,198] [MRIN: 326] (b. 30 May 1971) on 22 Jun 1996 in Lake Oswego, Clackamas, Oregon, USA.

+ 145 F   ii.   **Katherine Jane TIEMAN [919]**[112,113,196,199,200,201,202] was born on 25 Jun 1979 in North Vancouver, British Columbia, Canada.

Katherine married **Samuel Patrick WOODWARD** [3089][112,113,200,201,203] [MRIN: 1078] (b. 16 Sep 1975) on 25 Jul 2009 in Portland, Multnomah, Oregon, USA.[200]

Katherine next married **Shawn SCHULBERG** [3015][204] [MRIN: 325] on 4 Nov 2000 in Portland, Multnomah, Oregon, USA.

117. James Gordon MARSHALL [2515][88,112,113,141] (*Janet Alma ORMANDY [2224]* [85], *James Alma [2337]* [57], *William Lewithwaite [2339]* [44], *Thomas [2341]* [36], *John (Rev.) [2343]* [29], *Thomas (Rev) [2619]* [17], *Thomas [3123]* [7], *William [3324]* [5], *Richard [3923]* [1]) was born on 10 Jun 1954 in Vancouver, British Columbia, Canada.

General Notes: Born in Vancouver General Hospital
Occupation: Endodontist and taught at Oregon Health & Sciences University: Portland, Multnomah, Oregon, USA.

James married **Karla FRIEDE** [2614][112,113,142] [MRIN: 929], daughter of **William FRIEDE** [2615] and **Rhoda McGRAW** [2616], on 22 Apr 1994 in Hawaii, USA. Karla was born on 14 Jan 1961.

Children from this marriage were:

+ 146 F i. **Bailey Marie MARSHALL [2617]**[112,113] was born on 12 Mar 1998 in Portland, Multnomah, Oregon, USA.

+ 147 F ii. **Rowan Christine MARSHALL [2618]**[112,113] was born on 12 Mar 1998 in Portland, Multnomah, Oregon, USA.

118. Stephen Watt MARSHALL [2490][88,112,113,114,141,167] (*Janet Alma ORMANDY [2224]* [85], *James Alma [2337]* [57], *William Lewithwaite [2339]* [44], *Thomas [2341]* [36], *John (Rev.) [2343]* [29], *Thomas (Rev) [2619]* [17], *Thomas [3123]* [7], *William [3324]* [5], *Richard [3923]* [1]) was born on 6 Sep 1955 in Vancouver, British Columbia, Canada.

General Notes: Born in Vancouver General Hospital
Occupation: Trauma Doctor.

Stephen married **Connie Sue BRAUN** [2491][112,113,114] [MRIN: 922], daughter of **John Paul BRAUN** [2492][114,167,205] and **Nancy Lee WISECARVER** [2493],[114,167,206] on 4 Aug 1978 in Columbus, Franklin, Ohio, USA. Connie was born on 5 Apr 1955 in Columbus, Franklin, Ohio, USA.

General Notes: Ohio Marriage Index, 1970, 1972-2007

Name: Connie S Braun Age: 23 Birth Year: abt 1955 Residence County: Ou t of State Spouse's Name: Stephen W Marshall Spouse's Age: 22 Spouse' s Birth Year: abt 1956 Spouse's Residence County: Out Of State Marriage Date: 4 Aug 1978 Marriage License County: Franklin Certificate Number : 55093 Volume Number: 9532

Occupation: Dental Hygienist.
EDUC: RDH, BS, MBA.

Children from this marriage were:

+ 148 F   i.   **Emily Gene MARSHALL [2514]**[112,113,114,142] was born on 27 Apr 1984 in Evanston, Cook, Illinois, USA.

                 Emily had a relationship with **Lazaro CARRIÓN** [3810][112] [MRIN: 1357].

+ 149 M   ii.   **Luke Gordon MARSHALL [2513]**[112,113,114,142] was born on 2 Dec 1985 in Evanston, Cook, Illinois, USA.

                 Luke married **Hillary LATHROP** [3809][112] [MRIN: 1356] in 2016.

+ 150 M   iii.   **Carver Ormandy MARSHALL [2512]**[112,113,114,142] was born on 23 Sep 1990 in Bellevue, King, Washington, USA.

119. Richard Francis SAUSE Jr. [2596][85] (*Richard Francis SAUSE [2591]* [91], *Richard Victor SAUSE [2580]* [61], *Victoria ORMANDY [2352]* [46], *Thomas [2341]* [36], *John (Rev.) [2343]* [29], *Thomas (Rev) [2619]* [17], *Thomas [3123]* [7], *William [3324]* [5], *Richard [3923]* [1]) was born on 18 May 1926 in Staten Island, Richmond, New York, USA.

120. William James SAUSE [2597][85] (*Richard Francis SAUSE [2591]* [91], *Richard Victor SAUSE [2580]* [61], *Victoria ORMANDY [2352]* [46], *Thomas [2341]* [36], *John (Rev.) [2343]* [29], *Thomas (Rev) [2619]* [17], *Thomas [3123]* [7], *William [3324]* [5], *Richard [3923]* [1]) was born on 2 Jul 1929 in Staten Island, Richmond, New York, USA.

121. James Michael SAUSE [2598][85] (*Richard Francis SAUSE [2591]* [91], *Richard Victor SAUSE [2580]* [61], *Victoria ORMANDY [2352]* [46], *Thomas [2341]* [36], *John (Rev.) [2343]* [29], *Thomas (Rev) [2619]* [17], *Thomas [3123]* [7], *William [3324]* [5], *Richard [3923]* [1]) was born on 2 Nov 1935 in Staten Island, Richmond, New York, USA.

James married **Elaine RIVETT** [2599][85] [MRIN: 960], daughter of **RIVETT** [5206], in 1959.

Children from this marriage were:

+ 151 F i. **Kathleen Elaine SAUSE [2600]**[85] was born on 7 Jul 1960.

Kathleen had a relationship with **Rodger SADLER** [3866][85] [MRIN: 1373].

+ 152 F ii. **Patricia Mary SAUSE [2601]**[85] was born on 8 Sep 1961.

Patricia had a relationship with **William TAYLOR** [3869][85] [MRIN: 1374].

+ 153 F iii. **Jeanne Michelle SAUSE [2602]**[85] was born on 15 Dec 1967.

Jeanne had a relationship with **Geoff GRAHAM** [3872][85] [MRIN: 1375].

+ 154 F iv. **Christine Anne SAUSE [2603]**[85] was born on 23 Feb 1970.

Christine had a relationship with **Scott SMITH** [3873][85] [MRIN: 1376].

122. David L. LAMPHRON [2610] (*Ruth Mae ORMANDY [2608]* [93], *G. Edward [2605]* [75], *John Cliffborne [2345]* [53], *Thomas [2341]* [36], *John (Rev.) [2343]* [29], *Thomas (Rev) [2619]* [17], *Thomas [3123]* [7], *William [3324]* [5], *Richard [3923]* [1]).

11th Generation

123. Michael ORMANDY [2782][86] (*Ray [2779]*[94], *James Griswold [2375]*[76], *William Lewithwaite [2360]*[56], *William Lewithwaite [2339]*[44], *Thomas [2341]*[36], *John (Rev.) [2343]*[29], *Thomas (Rev) [2619]*[17], *Thomas [3123]*[7], *William [3324]*[5], *Richard [3923]*[1]).

124. Melise ORMANDY [2784][86] (*Ray [2779]*[94], *James Griswold [2375]*[76], *William Lewithwaite [2360]*[56], *William Lewithwaite [2339]*[44], *Thomas [2341]*[36], *John (Rev.) [2343]*[29], *Thomas (Rev) [2619]*[17], *Thomas [3123]*[7], *William [3324]*[5], *Richard [3923]*[1]).

125. Vanessa ORMANDY [2785][86] (*Ray [2779]*[94], *James Griswold [2375]*[76], *William Lewithwaite [2360]*[56], *William Lewithwaite [2339]*[44], *Thomas [2341]*[36], *John (Rev.) [2343]*[29], *Thomas (Rev) [2619]*[17], *Thomas [3123]*[7], *William [3324]*[5], *Richard [3923]*[1]).

126. Robert Mosier ORMANDY [2786][86] (*Ray [2779]*[94], *James Griswold [2375]*[76], *William Lewithwaite [2360]*[56], *William Lewithwaite [2339]*[44], *Thomas [2341]*[36], *John (Rev.) [2343]*[29], *Thomas (Rev) [2619]*[17], *Thomas [3123]*[7], *William [3324]*[5], *Richard [3923]*[1]).

127. Troy Albert BERBERICK [2770][86] (*Norman Albert BERBERICK [2768]*[104], *Esther Grace ORMANDY [2362]*[81], *William Lewithwaite [2360]*[56], *William Lewithwaite [2339]*[44], *Thomas [2341]*[36], *John (Rev.) [2343]*[29], *Thomas (Rev) [2619]*[17], *Thomas [3123]*[7], *William [3324]*[5], *Richard [3923]*[1]) was born on 19 Jun 1967.

Troy had a relationship with **Cathi KNUTSON** [2771][86] [MRIN: 994], daughter of **KNUTSON** [5208]. No evidence this couple married.

Their child was:

+ 155 F i. **Meghan Elizabeth BERBERICK [2772]**[86] was born on 28 Jul 1985.

Troy married **Katherine TULLY** [2773][86] [MRIN: 995], daughter of **TULLY** [5209], on 9 Mar 1990.

Children from this marriage were:

+ 156 F i. **Erinn Laura BERBERICK [2774]**[86] was born on 20 May 1990.
+ 157 M ii. **Joshua Roger BERBERICK [2775]**[86] was born on 18 Jul 1991.

128. Elizabeth Kristine LINGO [2796][86] (*Bridget Kayne NEAL [2371]*[105], *Ruth Naomi ORMANDY [2365]*[83], *William Lewithwaite [2360]*[56], *William Lewithwaite [2339]*[44], *Thomas [2341]*[36], *John (Rev.)*

[2343][29], *Thomas (Rev) [2619]*[17], *Thomas [3123]*[7], *William [3324]*[5], *Richard [3923]*[1]) was born on 24 Sep 1972.

129. Devin Courtney (?) LINGO [2797][86] (*Bridget Kayne NEAL [2371]*[105], *Ruth Naomi ORMANDY [2365]*[83], *William Lewithwaite [2360]*[56], *William Lewithwaite [2339]*[44], *Thomas [2341]*[36], *John (Rev.) [2343]*[29], *Thomas (Rev) [2619]*[17], *Thomas [3123]*[7], *William [3324]*[5], *Richard [3923]*[1]) was born on 11 Jul 1975.

130. Kacy Garrith NEAL [2800][86] (*Garreth Allan NEAL [2370]*[106], *Ruth Naomi ORMANDY [2365]*[83], *William Lewithwaite [2360]*[56], *William Lewithwaite [2339]*[44], *Thomas [2341]*[36], *John (Rev.) [2343]*[29], *Thomas (Rev) [2619]*[17], *Thomas [3123]*[7], *William [3324]*[5], *Richard [3923]*[1]).

131. Kriston NEAL [2799][86] (*Garreth Allan NEAL [2370]*[106], *Ruth Naomi ORMANDY [2365]*[83], *William Lewithwaite [2360]*[56], *William Lewithwaite [2339]*[44], *Thomas [2341]*[36], *John (Rev.) [2343]*[29], *Thomas (Rev) [2619]*[17], *Thomas [3123]*[7], *William [3324]*[5], *Richard [3923]*[1]) was born in Nov 1985.

132. Emily Katlyn NEAL [2803][86] (*Camdon Keith NEAL [2367]*[109], *Ruth Naomi ORMANDY [2365]*[83], *William Lewithwaite [2360]*[56], *William Lewithwaite [2339]*[44], *Thomas [2341]*[36], *John (Rev.) [2343]*[29], *Thomas (Rev) [2619]*[17], *Thomas [3123]*[7], *William [3324]*[5], *Richard [3923]*[1]) was born on 7 Jun 1988.

133. Benjamin Joseph NEAL [2804][86] (*Camdon Keith NEAL [2367]*[109], *Ruth Naomi ORMANDY [2365]*[83], *William Lewithwaite [2360]*[56], *William Lewithwaite [2339]*[44], *Thomas [2341]*[36], *John (Rev.) [2343]*[29], *Thomas (Rev) [2619]*[17], *Thomas [3123]*[7], *William [3324]*[5], *Richard [3923]*[1]) was born on 15 Jun 1990.

134. Gavin Keith NEAL [2807][86] (*Graden Patrick NEAL [2366]*[110], *Ruth Naomi ORMANDY [2365]*[83], *William Lewithwaite [2360]*[56], *William Lewithwaite [2339]*[44], *Thomas [2341]*[36], *John (Rev.) [2343]*[29], *Thomas (Rev) [2619]*[17], *Thomas [3123]*[7], *William [3324]*[5], *Richard [3923]*[1]) was born on 22 Apr 1986.

135. Jack BLAKESLEE [2481] (*Sandra Lee COFFIELD [2480]*[112], *Francis Ann ORMANDY [2470]*[84], *James Alma [2337]*[57], *William Lewithwaite [2339]*[44], *Thomas [2341]*[36], *John (Rev.) [2343]*[29], *Thomas (Rev) [2619]*[17], *Thomas [3123]*[7], *William [3324]*[5], *Richard [3923]*[1]).

136. Craig BLAKESLEE [2487] (*Sandra Lee COFFIELD [2480]*[112], *Francis Ann ORMANDY [2470]*[84], *James Alma [2337]*[57], *William Lewithwaite [2339]*[44], *Thomas [2341]*[36], *John (Rev.) [2343]*[29], *Thomas (Rev) [2619]*[17], *Thomas [3123]*[7], *William [3324]*[5], *Richard [3923]*[1]) was born on 27 Feb 1972.

137. Andrea BLAKESLEE [2486] (*Sandra Lee COFFIELD [2480]* [112]*, Francis Ann ORMANDY [2470]* [84]*, James Alma [2337]* [57]*, William Lewithwaite [2339]* [44]*, Thomas [2341]* [36]*, John (Rev.) [2343]* [29]*, Thomas (Rev) [2619]* [17]*, Thomas [3123]* [7]*, William [3324]* [5]*, Richard [3923]* [1]) was born on 13 Feb 1975.

138. Chris KALTENBACHER [2478] (*Susan COFFIELD [2477]* [113]*, Francis Ann ORMANDY [2470]* [84]*, James Alma [2337]* [57]*, William Lewithwaite [2339]* [44]*, Thomas [2341]* [36]*, John (Rev.) [2343]* [29]*, Thomas (Rev) [2619]* [17]*, Thomas [3123]* [7]*, William [3324]* [5]*, Richard [3923]* [1]).

139. Grace COFFIELD [2473] (*Ronald William COFFIELD [2471]* [114]*, Francis Ann ORMANDY [2470]* [84]*, James Alma [2337]* [57]*, William Lewithwaite [2339]* [44]*, Thomas [2341]* [36]*, John (Rev.) [2343]* [29]*, Thomas (Rev) [2619]* [17]*, Thomas [3123]* [7]*, William [3324]* [5]*, Richard [3923]* [1]).

140. Christine COFFIELD [2474] (*Ronald William COFFIELD [2471]* [114]*, Francis Ann ORMANDY [2470]* [84]*, James Alma [2337]* [57]*, William Lewithwaite [2339]* [44]*, Thomas [2341]* [36]*, John (Rev.) [2343]* [29]*, Thomas (Rev) [2619]* [17]*, Thomas [3123]* [7]*, William [3324]* [5]*, Richard [3923]* [1]) was born in Feb 1976.

141. Johnathan COFFIELD [2475] (*Ronald William COFFIELD [2471]* [114]*, Francis Ann ORMANDY [2470]* [84]*, James Alma [2337]* [57]*, William Lewithwaite [2339]* [44]*, Thomas [2341]* [36]*, John (Rev.) [2343]* [29]*, Thomas (Rev) [2619]* [17]*, Thomas [3123]* [7]*, William [3324]* [5]*, Richard [3923]* [1]) was born in Feb 1977.

142. Leslie Suzanne McINTYRE [2522] [113,142,144] (*Barbara Jean MARSHALL [2517]* [115]*, Janet Alma ORMANDY [2224]* [85]*, James Alma [2337]* [57]*, William Lewithwaite [2339]* [44]*, Thomas [2341]* [36]*, John (Rev.) [2343]* [29]*, Thomas (Rev) [2619]* [17]*, Thomas [3123]* [7]*, William [3324]* [5]*, Richard [3923]* [1]) was born on 22 Aug 1972 in Meyersdale, Somerset, Pennsylvania, USA.

Leslie married **Craig VAN KLEEK** [2621][113] [MRIN: 1097], son of **VAN KLEEK** [5162], on 13 Mar 1999. The marriage ended in divorce in 2016.

Children from this marriage were:

+   158   M   i.   **Rian James VAN KLEEK [5163]** died as an infant and was buried in Portland, Multnomah, Oregon, USA.

+   159   F   ii.   **Isabel Ya Ling VAN KLEEK [2663]**[113,144] was born on 22 Apr 2004.

143.   Erin Wynn ROADY [2576][112,113,142,144] (*Barbara Jean MARSHALL [2517]*[115], *Janet Alma ORMANDY [2224]*[85], *James Alma [2337]*[57], *William Lewithwaite [2339]*[44], *Thomas [2341]*[36], *John (Rev.) [2343]*[29], *Thomas (Rev) [2619]*[17], *Thomas [3123]*[7], *William [3324]*[5], *Richard [3923]*[1]) was born on 1 Aug 1976 in Portland, Multnomah, Oregon, USA.

Erin married **Aaron BLEDY** [2809][113,144] [MRIN: 10], son of **BLEDY** [5161], on 19 Feb 2000 in Las Vegas, Clark, Nevada, USA.

Occupation: CPA.

Children from this marriage were:

+   160   M   i.   **Eli Arthur BLEDY [17]**[113,144] was born on 7 Aug 2001 in Los Angeles, Los Angeles, California, USA.

+   161   M   ii.   **Maximus Julius BLEDY [3092]**[113,144] was born on 10 Sep 2003.

+   162   M   iii.   **Knox Robert BLEDY [3815]**[144] was born on 14 Jul 2011 in Portland, Multnomah, Oregon, USA.

144.   Heather Anne TIEMAN [920][112,113,195,196,197] *(Nancy Lee MARSHALL [2]* [116]*, Janet Alma ORMANDY [2224]* [85]*, James Alma [2337]* [57]*, William Lewithwaite [2339]* [44]*, Thomas [2341]* [36]*, John (Rev.) [2343]* [29]*, Thomas (Rev) [2619]* [17]*, Thomas [3123]* [7]*, William [3324]* [5]*, Richard [3923]* [1]*)* was born on 17 May 1976 in North Vancouver, British Columbia, Canada[195] and was christened in 1976 in North Vancouver, British Columbia, Canada.

General Notes: Grandkids call her Muzzy3.

Immigration: 20 Aug 1986, Portland, Multnomah, Oregon, USA.

Education: Lake Oswego High School, 1994, Lake Oswego, Clackamas, Oregon, USA.

Graduation: University of Idaho, BSEd, 1998, Moscow, Latah, Idaho, USA.

Naturalization: 2010, Portland, Multnomah, Oregon, USA.

Heather married **Phillip ERWIN** [921][113,197,198] [MRIN: 326], son of **Sidney Fred ERWIN** [1024][197] and **Judith Lee BENSCOTER** [1023],[197] on 22 Jun 1996 in Lake Oswego, Clackamas, Oregon, USA. Phillip was born on 30 May 1971 in Boise, Ada, Idaho, USA.

Noted events in his life were:

Religion: Lutheran.

EDUC: University of Idaho, BCS.

Occupation: Oracle, Computer Software Engineer: Portland, Multnomah, Oregon, USA.

Graduation: BS: Moscow, Latah, Idaho, USA.

Baptism: 1972, Bruneau, Owyhee, Idaho, USA.

Children from this marriage were:

+ 163 M i.   **Riley James ERWIN [1197]**[113,197,198] was born on 27 Sep 1999 in Portland, Multnomah, Oregon, USA and was christened in 2000 in Portland, Multnomah, Oregon, USA.

Riley had a relationship with **Ash SEBERS** [5482] [MRIN: 2118]. (b. 1996)

+ 164 M ii.   **Jackson Davis ERWIN [3091]**[113,198] was born on 26 Jul 2005 in Portland, Multnomah, Oregon, USA and was christened in Oct 2005 in Portland, Multnomah, Oregon, USA.

145. Katherine Jane TIEMAN [919][112,113,196,199,200,201,202] *(Nancy Lee MARSHALL [2]* [116]*, Janet Alma ORMANDY [2224]* [85]*, James Alma [2337]* [57]*, William Lewithwaite [2339]* [44]*, Thomas [2341]* [36]*, John (Rev.) [2343]* [29]*, Thomas (Rev) [2619]* [17]*, Thomas [3123]* [7]*, William [3324]* [5]*, Richard [3923]* [1]*)* was born on 25 Jun 1979 in North Vancouver, British Columbia, Canada.

    Baptism: 7 Oct 1979, Lake Oswego, Clackamas, Oregon, USA.

    Immigration: 20 Aug 1986, Portland, Multnomah, Oregon, USA.

    Education: Lake Oswego, Clackamas, Oregon, USA, Jun 1997, Lake Oswego High School.

    Occupation: Also Teacher, KinderCare Daycare, Cordon Bleu Pastry Chef, 2004, Portland, Multnomah, Oregon, USA.

    EDUC: Portland State University & Washington State University, 2004, Portland, Multnomah, Oregon, USA. Culinary Institute

    Graduation: Western Culinary Institute - Cordon Bleu, 2004, Portland, Multnomah, Oregon, USA.

    Katherine married **Samuel Patrick WOODWARD** [3089][112,113,200,201,203] [MRIN: 1078], son of **Gary Milton WOODWARD** [3189][201,203,207] and **(Rosa) Yung-Mei KAU** [3190],[201,203] on 25 Jul 2009 in Portland, Multnomah, Oregon, USA.[200] Samuel was born on 16 Sep 1975 in T'ai-Pei, Taiwan, Rep. of China.

    Children from this marriage were:

+   165   F   i.   **Alexis Jean TIEMAN-WOODWARD [3090]**[113,204] was born on 12 Nov 2006 in Portland, Multnomah, Oregon, USA.

+   166   M   ii.   **Owen Richard TIEMAN-WOODWARD [3268]**[204] was born on 18 Feb 2010 in Portland, Multnomah, Oregon, USA.[204]

    Katherine next married **Shawn SCHULBERG** [3015][204] [MRIN: 325], son of **SCHULBERG** [4624], on 4 Nov 2000 in Portland, Multnomah, Oregon, USA. The marriage ended in divorce.

    The child from this marriage was:

+   167   M   i.   **Connor Shamas TIEMAN-WOODWARD [3086]**[113,204] was born on 28 Oct 2002 in Portland, Multnomah, Oregon, USA.

146. Bailey Marie MARSHALL [2617][112,113] (*James Gordon MARSHALL [2515]* [117]*, Janet Alma ORMANDY [2224]* [85]*, James Alma [2337]* [57]*, William Lewithwaite [2339]* [44]*, Thomas [2341]* [36]*, John (Rev.) [2343]* [29]*, Thomas (Rev) [2619]* [17]*, Thomas [3123]* [7]*, William [3324]* [5]*, Richard [3923]* [1]) was born on 12 Mar 1998 in Portland, Multnomah, Oregon, USA.

147. Rowan Christine MARSHALL [2618][112,113] (*James Gordon MARSHALL [2515]* [117]*, Janet Alma ORMANDY [2224]* [85]*, James Alma [2337]* [57]*, William Lewithwaite [2339]* [44]*, Thomas [2341]* [36]*, John (Rev.) [2343]* [29]*, Thomas (Rev) [2619]* [17]*, Thomas [3123]* [7]*, William [3324]* [5]*, Richard [3923]* [1]) was born on 12 Mar 1998 in Portland, Multnomah, Oregon, USA.

148. Emily Gene MARSHALL [2514][112,113,114,142] (*Stephen Watt MARSHALL [2490]* [118]*, Janet Alma ORMANDY [2224]* [85]*, James Alma [2337]* [57]*, William Lewithwaite [2339]* [44]*, Thomas [2341]* [36]*, John (Rev.) [2343]* [29]*, Thomas (Rev) [2619]* [17]*, Thomas [3123]* [7]*, William [3324]* [5]*, Richard [3923]* [1]) was born on 27 Apr 1984 in Evanston, Cook, Illinois, USA.

Emily had a relationship with **Lazaro CARRIÓN** [3810][112] [MRIN: 1357], son of **CARRIÓN** [5164]. No evidence this couple married.

Their child was:

+ 168 M i. **Joaquín Marshall CARRIÓN [5258]** was born on 30 Mar 2019 in Seattle, King, Washington, USA.

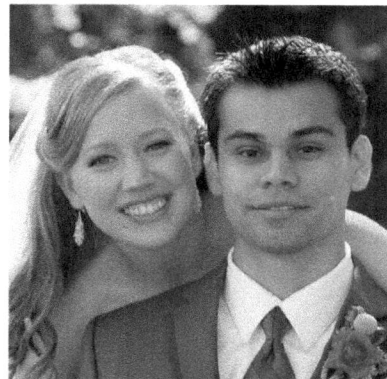
Lazaro & Emily Carrion wedding photo 2012?

149. Luke Gordon MARSHALL [2513][112,113,114,142] (*Stephen Watt MARSHALL [2490]* [118], *Janet Alma ORMANDY [2224]* [85], *James Alma [2337]* [57], *William Lewithwaite [2339]* [44], *Thomas [2341]* [36], *John (Rev.) [2343]* [29], *Thomas (Rev) [2619]* [17], *Thomas [3123]* [7], *William [3324]* [5], *Richard [3923]* [1]) was born on 2 Dec 1985 in Evanston, Cook, Illinois, USA.

General Notes: Education
Ph.D. in Materials Science & Engineering (2013): The University of Texas at Austin
B.A. in Physics & Philosophy (2008): Whitman College, cum laude

Research
As a Research Associate with the Nanomagnetism Research Group at Northeastern University, I am currently focused on reducing the amount of critical materials (such as rare-earth elements) needed for high performance magnets. Through our collaboration with an industrial partner, Rogers Corporation, we hope to bring our results from the lab bench to the real world.

While getting my Ph.D. in Materials Science & Engineering at the University of Texas at Austin, I worked with John B. Goodenough, inventor of the Li-ion battery cathode, in one of the top university-based high- pressure condensed matter physics laboratories. Here I focused on materials design and defined some of the intrinsic relationships between the structural, electronic and magnetic properties of several classes of functional oxide materials.

I have been privileged to collaborate with some the top scientists in the world, not only here in the U.S. at several of the National Laboratories, but also abroad including several weeks of work at the Insituto de Ciencia de Materiales de Madrid in Spain.

About

I have a passion for exploring the intersection of science, technology and business, particularly in the alternative energy sector. My motivation comes from imagining the ways in which my research may one day make a difference in the lives of real people. When I'm not in the lab you'll probably find me running with my dog, Eddy, on a bike ride with some friends, or cooking a tasty meal with my wife, Hillary.

Luke married **Hillary LATHROP** [3809][112] [MRIN: 1356], daughter of **Greg LATHROP** [5165] and **MARIE** [5594], in 2016.

150. Carver Ormandy MARSHALL [2512][112,113,114,142] (*Stephen Watt MARSHALL [2490]* [118]*, Janet Alma ORMANDY [2224]* [85]*, James Alma [2337]* [57]*, William Lewithwaite [2339]* [44]*, Thomas [2341]* [36]*, John (Rev.) [2343]* [29]*, Thomas (Rev) [2619]* [17]*, Thomas [3123]* [7]*, William [3324]* [5]*, Richard [3923]* [1]) was born on 23 Sep 1990 in Bellevue, King, Washington, USA.

151. Kathleen Elaine SAUSE [2600][85] (*James Michael SAUSE [2598]* [121]*, Richard Francis SAUSE [2591]* [91]*, Richard Victor SAUSE [2580]* [61]*, Victoria ORMANDY [2352]* [46]*, Thomas [2341]* [36]*, John (Rev.) [2343]* [29]*, Thomas (Rev) [2619]* [17]*, Thomas [3123]* [7]*, William [3324]* [5]*, Richard [3923]* [1]) was born on 7 Jul 1960.

Kathleen had a relationship with **Rodger SADLER** [3866][85] [MRIN: 1373], son of **SADLER** [5210]. No evidence this couple married.

Their children were:

+ 169 M   i.   **James SADLER [3867]**.[85]
+ 170 M   ii.   **Christopher SADLER [3868]**.[85]

152. Patricia Mary SAUSE [2601][85] (*James Michael SAUSE [2598]* [121], *Richard Francis SAUSE [2591]* [91], *Richard Victor SAUSE [2580]* [61], *Victoria ORMANDY [2352]* [46], *Thomas [2341]* [36], *John (Rev.) [2343]* [29], *Thomas (Rev) [2619]* [17], *Thomas [3123]* [7], *William [3324]* [5], *Richard [3923]* [1]) was born on 8 Sep 1961.

Patricia had a relationship with **William TAYLOR** [3869][85] [MRIN: 1374], son of **TAYLOR** [5211]. No evidence this couple married.

Their children were:

+ 171 M   i.   **Daniel TAYLOR [3870]**.[85]
+ 172 F   ii.   **Sandra TAYLOR [3871]**.[85]

153. Jeanne Michelle SAUSE [2602][85] (*James Michael SAUSE [2598]* [121], *Richard Francis SAUSE [2591]* [91], *Richard Victor SAUSE [2580]* [61], *Victoria ORMANDY [2352]* [46], *Thomas [2341]* [36], *John (Rev.) [2343]* [29], *Thomas (Rev) [2619]* [17], *Thomas [3123]* [7], *William [3324]* [5], *Richard [3923]* [1]) was born on 15 Dec 1967.

Jeanne had a relationship with **Geoff GRAHAM** [3872][85] [MRIN: 1375], son of **GRAHAM** [5212]. No evidence this couple married.

154. Christine Anne SAUSE [2603][85] (*James Michael SAUSE [2598]* [121], *Richard Francis SAUSE [2591]* [91], *Richard Victor SAUSE [2580]* [61], *Victoria ORMANDY [2352]* [46], *Thomas [2341]* [36], *John (Rev.) [2343]* [29], *Thomas (Rev) [2619]* [17], *Thomas [3123]* [7], *William [3324]* [5], *Richard [3923]* [1]) was born on 23 Feb 1970.

Christine had a relationship with **Scott SMITH** [3873][85] [MRIN: 1376], son of **SMITH** [5213]. No evidence this couple married.

12th Generation

155. Meghan Elizabeth BERBERICK [2772][86] (*Troy Albert BERBERICK [2770]* [127]*, Norman Albert BERBERICK [2768]* [104]*, Esther Grace ORMANDY [2362]* [81]*, William Lewithwaite [2360]* [56]*, William Lewithwaite [2339]* [44]*, Thomas [2341]* [36]*, John (Rev.) [2343]* [29]*, Thomas (Rev) [2619]* [17]*, Thomas [3123]* [7]*, William [3324]* [5]*, Richard [3923]* [1]) was born on 28 Jul 1985.

156. Erinn Laura BERBERICK [2774][86] (*Troy Albert BERBERICK [2770]* [127]*, Norman Albert BERBERICK [2768]* [104]*, Esther Grace ORMANDY [2362]* [81]*, William Lewithwaite [2360]* [56]*, William Lewithwaite [2339]* [44]*, Thomas [2341]* [36]*, John (Rev.) [2343]* [29]*, Thomas (Rev) [2619]* [17]*, Thomas [3123]* [7]*, William [3324]* [5]*, Richard [3923]* [1]) was born on 20 May 1990.

157. Joshua Roger BERBERICK [2775][86] (*Troy Albert BERBERICK [2770]* [127]*, Norman Albert BERBERICK [2768]* [104]*, Esther Grace ORMANDY [2362]* [81]*, William Lewithwaite [2360]* [56]*, William Lewithwaite [2339]* [44]*, Thomas [2341]* [36]*, John (Rev.) [2343]* [29]*, Thomas (Rev) [2619]* [17]*, Thomas [3123]* [7]*, William [3324]* [5]*, Richard [3923]* [1]) was born on 18 Jul 1991.

158. Rian James VAN KLEEK [5163] (*Leslie Suzanne McINTYRE [2522]* [142]*, Barbara Jean MARSHALL [2517]* [115]*, Janet Alma ORMANDY [2224]* [85]*, James Alma [2337]* [57]*, William Lewithwaite [2339]* [44]*, Thomas [2341]* [36]*, John (Rev.) [2343]* [29]*, Thomas (Rev) [2619]* [17]*, Thomas [3123]* [7]*, William [3324]* [5]*, Richard [3923]* [1]) died as an infant and was buried in Portland, Multnomah, Oregon, USA.

159. Isabel Ya Ling VAN KLEEK [2663][113,144] (*Leslie Suzanne McINTYRE [2522]* [142]*, Barbara Jean MARSHALL [2517]* [115]*, Janet Alma ORMANDY [2224]* [85]*, James Alma [2337]* [57]*, William Lewithwaite [2339]* [44]*, Thomas [2341]* [36]*, John (Rev.) [2343]* [29]*, Thomas (Rev) [2619]* [17]*, Thomas [3123]* [7]*, William [3324]* [5]*, Richard [3923]* [1]) was born on 22 Apr 2004.

General Notes: Adopted from China

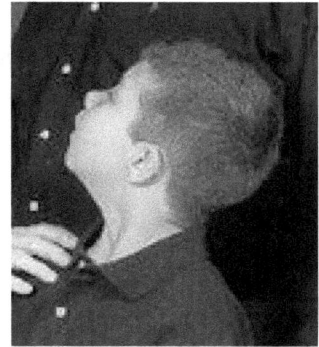

160. Eli Arthur BLEDY [17][113,144] (*Erin Wynn ROADY [2576]* [143], *Barbara Jean MARSHALL [2517]* [115], *Janet Alma ORMANDY [2224]* [85], *James Alma [2337]* [57], *William Lewithwaite [2339]* [44], *Thomas [2341]* [36], *John (Rev.) [2343]* [29], *Thomas (Rev) [2619]* [17], *Thomas [3123]* [7], *William [3324]* [5], *Richard [3923]* [1]) was born on 7 Aug 2001 in Los Angeles, Los Angeles, California, USA.

161. Maximus Julius BLEDY [3092][113,144] (*Erin Wynn ROADY [2576]* [143], *Barbara Jean MARSHALL [2517]* [115], *Janet Alma ORMANDY [2224]* [85], *James Alma [2337]* [57], *William Lewithwaite [2339]* [44], *Thomas [2341]* [36], *John (Rev.) [2343]* [29], *Thomas (Rev) [2619]* [17], *Thomas [3123]* [7], *William [3324]* [5], *Richard [3923]* [1]) was born on 10 Sep 2003.

162. Knox Robert BLEDY [3815][144] (*Erin Wynn ROADY [2576]* [143], *Barbara Jean MARSHALL [2517]* [115], *Janet Alma ORMANDY [2224]* [85], *James Alma [2337]* [57], *William Lewithwaite [2339]* [44], *Thomas [2341]* [36], *John (Rev.) [2343]* [29], *Thomas (Rev) [2619]* [17], *Thomas [3123]* [7], *William [3324]* [5], *Richard [3923]* [1]) was born on 14 Jul 2011 in Portland, Multnomah, Oregon, USA.

163. Riley James ERWIN [1197][113,197,198] (*Heather Anne TIEMAN [920]* [144], *Nancy Lee MARSHALL [2]* [116], *Janet Alma ORMANDY [2224]* [85], *James Alma [2337]* [57], *William Lewithwaite [2339]* [44], *Thomas [2341]* [36], *John (Rev.) [2343]* [29], *Thomas (Rev) [2619]* [17], *Thomas [3123]* [7], *William [3324]* [5], *Richard [3923]* [1]) was born on 27 Sep 1999 in Portland, Multnomah, Oregon, USA and was christened in 2000 in Portland, Multnomah, Oregon, USA.

Riley had a relationship with **Ash SEBERS** [5482] [MRIN: 2118]. No evidence this couple married. Ash was born in 1996.

Their child was:

+ 173 M i. **Justin Arthur SEBERS-ERWIN [5507]** was born on 30 Aug 2020 in Stanwood, Washington, USA.

164. Jackson Davis ERWIN [3091][113,198] (*Heather Anne TIEMAN [920]*[144], *Nancy Lee MARSHALL [2]*[116], *Janet Alma ORMANDY [2224]*[85], *James Alma [2337]*[57], *William Lewithwaite [2339]*[44], *Thomas [2341]*[36], *John (Rev.) [2343]*[29], *Thomas (Rev) [2619]*[17], *Thomas [3123]*[7], *William [3324]*[5], *Richard [3923]*[1]) was born on 26 Jul 2005 in Portland, Multnomah, Oregon, USA and was christened in Oct 2005 in Portland, Multnomah, Oregon, USA.

165. Alexis Jean TIEMAN-WOODWARD [3090][113,204] (*Katherine Jane TIEMAN [919]*[145], *Nancy Lee MARSHALL [2]*[116], *Janet Alma ORMANDY [2224]*[85], *James Alma [2337]*[57], *William Lewithwaite [2339]*[44], *Thomas [2341]*[36], *John (Rev.) [2343]*[29], *Thomas (Rev) [2619]*[17], *Thomas [3123]*[7], *William [3324]*[5], *Richard [3923]*[1]) was born on 12 Nov 2006 in Portland, Multnomah, Oregon, USA.

166. Owen Richard TIEMAN-WOODWARD [3268][204] (*Katherine Jane TIEMAN [919]* [145], *Nancy Lee MARSHALL [2]* [116], *Janet Alma ORMANDY [2224]* [85], *James Alma [2337]* [57], *William Lewithwaite [2339]* [44], *Thomas [2341]* [36], *John (Rev.) [2343]* [29], *Thomas (Rev) [2619]* [17], *Thomas [3123]* [7], *William [3324]* [5], *Richard [3923]* [1]) was born on 18 Feb 2010 in Portland, Multnomah, Oregon, USA.[204]

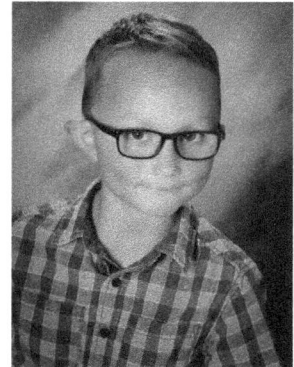

167. Connor Shamas TIEMAN-WOODWARD [3086][113,204] (*Katherine Jane TIEMAN [919]* [145], *Nancy Lee MARSHALL [2]* [116], *Janet Alma ORMANDY [2224]* [85], *James Alma [2337]* [57], *William Lewithwaite [2339]* [44], *Thomas [2341]* [36], *John (Rev.) [2343]* [29], *Thomas (Rev) [2619]* [17], *Thomas [3123]* [7], *William [3324]* [5], *Richard [3923]* [1]) was born on 28 Oct 2002 in Portland, Multnomah, Oregon, USA.

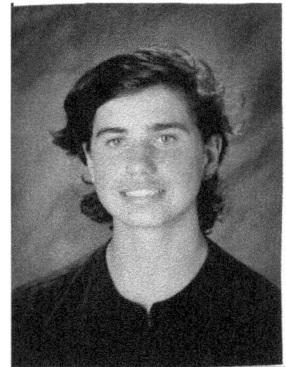

168. Joaquín Marshall CARRIÓN [5258] (*Emily Gene MARSHALL [2514]* [148], *Stephen Watt MARSHALL [2490]* [118], *Janet Alma ORMANDY [2224]* [85], *James Alma [2337]* [57], *William Lewithwaite [2339]* [44], *Thomas [2341]* [36], *John (Rev.) [2343]* [29], *Thomas (Rev) [2619]* [17], *Thomas [3123]* [7], *William [3324]* [5], *Richard [3923]* [1]) was born on 30 Mar 2019 in Seattle, King, Washington, USA.

169. James SADLER [3867][85] (*Kathleen Elaine SAUSE [2600]* [151], *James Michael SAUSE [2598]* [121], *Richard Francis SAUSE [2591]* [91], *Richard Victor SAUSE [2580]* [61], *Victoria ORMANDY [2352]* [46], *Thomas [2341]* [36], *John (Rev.) [2343]* [29], *Thomas (Rev) [2619]* [17], *Thomas [3123]* [7], *William [3324]* [5], *Richard [3923]* [1]).

170. Christopher SADLER [3868][85] (*Kathleen Elaine SAUSE [2600]* [151], *James Michael SAUSE [2598]* [121], *Richard Francis SAUSE [2591]* [91], *Richard Victor SAUSE [2580]* [61], *Victoria ORMANDY [2352]* [46], *Thomas [2341]* [36], *John (Rev.) [2343]* [29], *Thomas (Rev) [2619]* [17], *Thomas [3123]* [7], *William [3324]* [5], *Richard [3923]* [1]).

171. Daniel TAYLOR [3870][85] (*Patricia Mary SAUSE [2601]* [152], *James Michael SAUSE [2598]* [121], *Richard Francis SAUSE [2591]* [91], *Richard Victor SAUSE [2580]* [61], *Victoria ORMANDY [2352]* [46],

Thomas [2341] [36]*, John (Rev.) [2343]* [29]*, Thomas (Rev) [2619]* [17]*, Thomas [3123]* [7]*, William [3324]* [5]*, Richard [3923]* [1]*).*

172. Sandra TAYLOR [3871] [85] *(Patricia Mary SAUSE [2601]* [152]*, James Michael SAUSE [2598]* [121]*, Richard Francis SAUSE [2591]* [91]*, Richard Victor SAUSE [2580]* [61]*, Victoria ORMANDY [2352]* [46]*, Thomas [2341]* [36]*, John (Rev.) [2343]* [29]*, Thomas (Rev) [2619]* [17]*, Thomas [3123]* [7]*, William [3324]* [5]*, Richard [3923]* [1]*).*

13th Generation

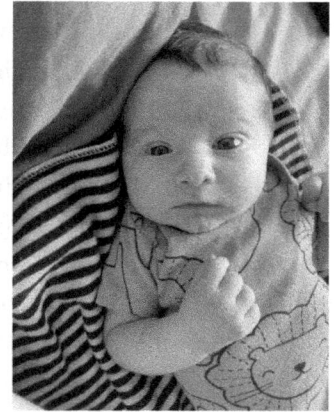

173. Justin Arthur SEBERS-ERWIN [5507] (*Riley James ERWIN [1197]* [163], *Heather Anne TIEMAN [920]* [144], *Nancy Lee MARSHALL [2]* [116], *Janet Alma ORMANDY [2224]* [85], *James Alma [2337]* [57], *William Lewithwaite [2339]* [44], *Thomas [2341]* [36], *John (Rev.) [2343]* [29], *Thomas (Rev) [2619]* [17], *Thomas [3123]* [7], *William [3324]* [5], *Richard [3923]* [1]) was born on 30 Aug 2020 in Stanwood, Washington, USA.

Source Citations

1. O653-29 Ormandy/Miliss Tree.
2. O653-47 Richard Ormandy 1635 - Marriage - Parish Records.
3. HY-0001 Brighton in Furness, Lancashire, England - History.
4. MP-0001 Millom, England 1805 - Map.
5. MP-0009 Cumberland, England 1646 - Map.
6. MP-0010 England 1598 - Map.
7. MP-0011 Cumberland, England 1607 - Map.
8. O653-88 Lancashire, England, Extracted Church of England Parish Records Richard Ormandy died 1706.
9. O653-86 Church of England Baptisms, Marriages and Burials, 1538-1812, Elizabeth Ormandy d.1699.
10. O653-8 Hauptman's Family Tree (Name: Name: Michael A. Hauptman;;).
11. O653-44 Thomas Ormandy 1717 - Baptism - Parish Records.
12. HY-0002 Millom, Cumberland, England - History.
13. "O653-89 Lancashire: Broughton-in-Furness (Kirksby Ireleth) - Parish Register, Birth 1634-1812 William Ormandy 1680."
14. O653-43 Bridget Ormandy - Burial - Parish Records.
15. O653-87 England & Wales, Christening Index, 1530-1980, Elizabeth Ormandy 1774.
16. O653-6 Corres. of Ormandy/Wilkinson Line. Jim M. Sause
17. O653-31 T. Ormandy 1749- England Select Births & Christenings 1538-197 5, FHL Film Number: 0844819IT2.
18. O653-45 Thomas Ormandy/Jane Stanley Marriage - Parish Records.
19. O653-46 Thomas Ormandy 1717 - Burial - Parish Records.
20. O653-48 Thomas Ormandy/Stanley Lancashire, England, Extracted Parish Records.
21. O653- 77 England, Select Births & Christenings, 1538-1975 (Name: N.p.: n.p., n.d;).
22. O653-65 England Select Births & Christenings 1538-1975 Anne Ormand y b1745 (Name: N.p.: n.p., n.d;).
23. O653-33 T. Ormandy/Boulton 1785 Marriage Register.
24. O653-32 T. Ormandy 1749- England Select Death & Burials 1538-1991, FHL Film Number: 1040315.
25. O653-30 T. Ormandy 1749- Lancashire England Extracted Parish Records, Parish Register, 1634-1812.
26. O635-40 John Ormandy 1792- Baptism - Parish Records.
27. O635-41 Thomas Ormandy/Dorothy Bolton - Marriage - Parish Records.
28. "O653-50 Tombstone - Thomas & Dorothy Ormandy," database.
29. "O653-51 Land Deed - Thomas Ormandy," database.
30. O653-42 Dorothy Ormandy - Burial - Parish Records.
31. O653-66 England Select Births & Christenings, 1538-1975, William A . Ormandy (Name: N.p.: n.p., n.d;).
32. O653-56 Burials 1750 - 1800 from the Bishop's Transcripts, Page 66 , Entry 11 Ormandy William

A (Name: N.p.: n.p., n.d;).

33. O653-54 Baptisms 1673 - 1796, Page 69, Entry 8 William A Ormandy b17 51 (Name: N.p.: n.p., n.d;).

34. O653-61 England & Wales Marriages 1538-1988 James Ormandy (Name: N.p., n.p., n.d;).

35. O653-58 Burials 1827 - 1831 from the Bishop's Transcripts, Entry 108 0 James Ormandy (Name: N.p.: n.p., n.d;).

36. Marriages 1750-1780 from the Bishop's Transcripts, Page 31, Entry 1 9 James Ormandy (Name: N.p.: n.p., n.d;).

37. O653-55 Baptisms 1673 - 1796, Page 71, Entry 7 James Ormandy b1753 (Name: N.p.: n.p., n.d;).

38. O653-60 England & Wales Marriage Records 1538-1988, Ormandy, Joseph Marriage Record (Name: N.p.: n.p., n.d;).

39. O653-68 England Select Deaths & Burials 1538-1991 Jane Ormandy d1753 (Name: N.p.: n.p., n.d;).

40. O653-69 England Select Deaths & Burials 1538-1991 Richard Ormandy d1 817 (Name: N.p.: n.p., n.d;).

41. O653-82 Ormandy, Joseph 1834 Burial Record (Name: N.p.: n.p., n.d;).

42. O653-10 England & Wales Census, 1841, John Ormandy.

43. Marriages 1813 - 1825 from the Bishop's Transcripts, Page 32, Entr y 95 Ormandy, William 1788 (Name: N.p.: n.p., n.d;).

44. O653-57 Burials 1821 - 1877 from the Bishop's Transcripts, Page 5 7 & 58, Entry 459 William Ormand (Name: N.p.: n.p., n.d;).

45. England, O653-51 - 1851 census of England Ormandy, William b1788. PRO HO 107. The National Archives of the UK, London.

46. UK & Ireland Find A Grave 1300's - Current William Ormandy d1856.

47. O653- 76 English & Wales National Probate Calendar, 1858-1995, Joseph Ormandy 1860 (Name: N.p.: n.p., n.d;).

48. England, O653-50 - 1841 census of England Ormandy_Joseph. PRO HO 107. The National Archives of the UK, London.

49. O653-9 England & Wales Census 1851, John Ormandy.

50. O653-11 England Births & Christenings, 1538-1975, Thomas Ormandy, Indexing Project #- C05832-1 System Orgin - England-ODM Film #-90668.

51. O653-5 Corres. of Sir John Ormandy. Unknown

52. O653-18 Rev. John Ormandy Death Certificate Index.

53. O653-19 Bulmer's History and Directory Of Cumberland 1901.

54. O653-35 Juliana Ormandy - Baptism - Parish Records.

55. O653-36 John Ormandy 1828 - Baptism- Parish Records.

56. O653-38 Rev. John Ormandy - Burial - Parish Records.

57. O653- 75 England, Select Marriages, 1538-1973 John Ormandy m1819 (Name: N.p.: n.p., n.d;).

58. O635-39 Mary Ormandy - Burial - Parish Records.

59. O653-67 England Select Births & Christening 1538-1975 James Ormandy 1 778 (Name: N.p.: n.p., n.d;).

60. O653-64 England Select Births $ Christenings, 1538-1975 Thomas Ormandy 1796 (Name: N.p.: n.p., n.d;).

61. England, O653-84 Ormandy_George_1851Census. PRO HO 107. The National Archives of the UK, London.

62. England, O653-49 - 1841 census of England Ormandy, Isaac. PRO HO 107. The National Archives of the UK, London.

63. O653-80 Ormandy, Isaac Marriage Record, O653-80 Ormandy, Isaac Marriage Record.

64. England, O653-83 Ormandy Isaac 1851 census of England. PRO HO 107. The National Archives of the UK, London.

65. O653-78 Liverpool, England, Church of England Marriages and Banns, 1754-1932 Ormandy, Dorothy (Name: N.p.: n.p., n.d;).

66. O653-73 England, Select Births and Christenings, 1538-1975 Dorothy Ormandy (Name: N.p.: n.p., n.d;).

67. O653-63 England & Wales, Civil Registration Death Index, 1837-1915 Dorothy Ormandy (Name: N.p.: n.p., n.d;).

68. O653-71 England Select Marriages 1538-1973 Mary Anne Ormandy (Name: N.p.: n.p., n.d;).

69. O653-62 England & Wales National Probate Calendar Mary Anne Ormandy (Name: N.p.: n.p., n.d;).

70. O653-74 England, Select Births and Christenings, 1538-1975 Ormandy, Mary Ann (Name: N.p.: n.p., n.d;).

71. O653-1 William Lewthwaite Ormandy Family Bible - Original (Name: Name: Original 1872;;). MEDI: Bible

72. M624-8 Marshall Ancestry Charts.

73. O653-16 T. Ormandy War Pensions Records.

74. O653-12 Indenture - Thomas Ormandy.

75. O653-14 Civil War Enlistment Papers - T. Ormandy, Headquarters, 491, Broadway (?); First Regiment; Seymour Light Infantry; N.Y.S.V; New York, April 29th, 1863.

76. O653-15 Civil War Military Records Thomas Ormandy, Ormandy, Thomas pg1581.

77. O653-49 UK Census 1861, Thomas Ormandy, Civil Parish; Ulverston; Town; Ulverston; County; Lancashire; Country: England; Ecclesiastical Parish: Holy Trinity; Registration District: Ulverston; Sub-registration District: Ulverston; Piece; 3168; Folio:71; Pages 2-3 Household Schedule #: 7.

78. O653-34 T. Ormandy 1823- Civil War Records & Profiles 1861-1865.

79. O653-70 England Select Marriages 1538-1973 Julia Ormandy (Name: N.p.: n.p., n.d;).

80. O653-37 John Ormandy 1828 - Burial - Parish Records.

81. O653-72 England Select Marriages 1538-1973 Ormandy, Harrison W b1832 (Name: N.p.: n.p., n.d;).

82. UK, Apprentices Indentured in Merchant Navy, 1824-1910 Ormandy, Harrison b1832 (Name: N.p.: n.p., n.d;).

83. O653-59 England & Wales Civil Registration Death Index 1837-1915 Ormandy, Harrison b1832 (Name: N.p.: n.p., n.d;).

84. O653-13 Marriage Certificate - Ormandy & Huston.

85. O653-17 Ormandy/Sause Line Email.

86. O653-7 Corres. of Ormandy/Griswold Line. Ruth Neal

87. O653-52 -1930 US Census Ormandy William L, b 1909, 1930 U.S. census, Digital images (Name: National Archives and Records Administration, n.d;), T626.

88. M624-3 Corres. Marshall Line (Name: Name: Janet (Ormandy) Marshall;).

89. S530-1 Corres. Smoot Ancestry (Name: Name: unknown;;).

90. O653-3 Obit-James A. Ormandy (Name: Name: Newspaper;;).

91. O653-81, 1940 U.S. census, Digital images (Name: National Archives and Records Administration, n.d;), T627.

92. O653-85 James A. Ormandy WWII Registration Card.

93. O653-93 Marriage Announcement to Ormandy.

94. O653-91 Confirmation Edith and James Ormandy.

95. S315-1 Birth Certificate Edith Francis Stephenson (Name: Name: Original;;).

96. S315-2 Obit Edith Stephenson Essex (Name: Name: Newspaper;;).

97. S530-2 Smoot Ancestor Chart.

98. S315-4 Corres. of Stephenson Family (Name: Name: Gerald Stephenson; Date: 1990;;).

99. O653-94 Newspaper article on Edith and her new show (Name: N.p.: n.p., n.d;).

100. O653-92 Marriage Record Freeman Essex to Edith Ormandy.

101. O653-2 In Memory - Esther Alice Ormandy.

102. O653-4 Obit-Esther A. Ormandy (Name: Name: Newspaper;;).

103. O653-53 -1930 US Census Ormandy William L, b 1909 1940 US Census Ormandy, Walter b1888, 1940 U.S. census, Digital images (Name: National Archives and Records Administration, n.d;), T627.

104. O653-83 Oregon Death Index 1898-2008 Ormandy, Walter S (Name: N.p.: n.p., n.d;).

105. U.S. WWII Draft Cards Young Men, 1940-1947 Ormandy, William L b1908 (Name: N.p.: n.p., n.d;).

106. S315-5 Bureau of Pensions, Wash. D.C., Marian Stephenson Patmore (Name: Name: photocopy;;).

107. S315-3 Military Records - revolutionary Descent from Lt. Casparus Pruyn.

108. F432-1 Bureau of Pensions Report - James Fletcher - A certified copy of the Bureau of Pensions National No. 86360 (Name: Name: Bureau of Pensions; Location: Washington, D.C; Date: 1777 ;;).

109. S315-20 1880 US Census Dr. AC Stephenson (Name: N.p.: n.p., n.d;).

110. S530-3 Smoot Pedigree Chart - Family Search Ancestral Files, A collection of genealogical information taken from Pedigree Charts and Family Group Records submitted to the Family History Dept. since 1978. Submitters: J.E. Daniel, C.E. Bauer, S.L. Smoot, Z.H. White.

111. S530-5 Humphrey Smoot Family Bible Records 1857. Privately held by M. Tieman (Name: N.p., 1857;).

112. From Individual.

113. M624-10 Marshall Family Chart (Name: Name: Bob Marshall; Date: 2008;;).

114. B600-1 Braun Family Line - 2008, Database online. Connie Braun

115. M624-38 Source from Geraldine Beverly (Nesbit) Marshall.

116. M624-43 Janet (Ormandy) Marshall Death Certif. (Name: Intercranial Hemorrhage;). MEDI: Death Certificate

117. M624-42 F James and Janet Marshall Marriage Certif. MEDI: Certificate

118. M624-9 Obit - F. James Marshall (Name: Oregonian Newspaper; Portland, Oregon; 2008;;). MEDI: Newspaper

119. M624-21 Baptism Certificate - Frederick James Marshall (Name: Name: St. George's Church, Vancouver, British Columbia, Easter Day 1925;;). MEDI: Certificate

120. M624-22, My Glengarry Dr. F. James Marshall (Name: Cannon Beach, OR, Michael Tieman

Publishing, 2007;). MEDI: Book

121. M624-23 Interview with F. James Marshall 1998.

122. M624-39 F. James Marshall US Naturalization Papers (Name: Columbus, OH;). MEDI: Naturalization Certificate DATE: 13 May 1969

123. M624-40 F James Marshall Death Certificate - Orig. MEDI: Death Certificate

124. M624-41 F James Marshall Cert. of Birth. MEDI: Birth Certificate

125. M624-44 F James Marshall WWII Discharge Papers. MEDI: Military

126. W300-1 Obit Bertha Watt Marshall (Name: Name: Newspaper;;). MEDI: Newspaper

127. M624-4 British Columbia Canada Birth Index 1872-1903 Leslie Marshall (Name: Name: British Columbia, Vital Statistics Agency; Location: British Columbia, Canada;;), Registration #: 1899-09-198639 BCA #: B13815 GSU#: 2134885.

128. M624-12 1901 Canada Census - Leslie Marshall. MEDI: Census/Tax

129. M624-14 1919 Passenger List - Les Marshall (Name: Name: Seattle Passenger and Crew Lists 1882-1957 - Name: Lesli e F. Marshall Arrival Date: Oct 1919 Age:20 Estimated Birth Year: 1 899 Birthplace: Canada Last Residence: CAN Gender: Male Race/Nationality: English Port of Arrival: Seattle, Washington Port of Departure : Vancouver, British Columbia Line# 11 Microfilm Roll# M1383_42; Location: Seattle Washington;;).

130. M624-13 1911 Canada Census - Les Marshall (Name: Name: Census of Canada 1911, Page # 29; Family# 296, Name: Lesli e Marshall, Marital Status: Single, Age: 11, Birth Date: Aug 1899, Birthplace: British Columbia, Relationship to Head of House: Son, Father's Name: Fred J. Marshall, Mother's Name: Fanny Marshall; Location: Tribal: English, Province: British Columbia, District: Vancouver, District #: 12, Sub-District: Vancouver City, Sub-District #: 41, Place of Habitation: 2335 Lanel; Date: Vancouver, British Columbia, Canada1911;;). MEDI: Census/Tax

131. M624-15 British Columbia Death Index 1872-1990 - Leslie Marshall (Name: Name: British Columbia, Canada, Death Index 1872-1990; Location : Birth Year: about 1900, Death Age: 71, Date Death: 30 Nov 1971, Death Location: Vancouver, Registration #: 1971-09-016851, BCA#: B13314, G SU#: 2034297;;).

132. M624-45 Leslie Frederick Marshall Birth Certificate.

133. M624-46 Leslie Frederick Marshall Death Certificate.

134. M624-52 1921 Canada Census Marshall, Leslie.

135. W300-8 1920 census Bertha Watt. MEDI: Census/Tax

136. W300-16 1901 Scotland Census Bertha Watt. MEDI: Census/Tax

137. W300-6 Encyclopedia Titanic, Bertha Watt. MEDI: Interview

138. W300-22 Titanic Passenger List - Robertha Watt. MEDI: Passenger List

139. W300-23 Titanic Story written by Robertha Watt. MEDI: Personal

140. M624-47 Robertha (Watt) Marshall Death Certificate. MEDI: Death Certificate

141. M624-1 Marriage Notice Barbara Marshall/McIntyre (Name: Name: Newspaper; Location: Columbus, Ohio;;).

142. Source From Janet O. Marshall.

143. R300-16 Arthur Roady Marriage Index.

144. Source from Barbara Jean (Marshall) Roady.

145. M624-5 Copy of Canadian Birth Certificate - Nancy Lee Marshall (Name: Name: British Columbia Division of Vital Statistics; Location: Vancouver, British Columbia, Canada; Date: March 13, 1952;;).

146. M624-6 Christening Papers - Nancy Lee Marshall.
147. M624-7 U.S. Passport - Nancy L. (Marshall) Tieman (Name: Date: Issued 25 APR 2008;;).
148. T500-16 Marriage Certificate Michael Tieman & Nancy Marshall (Name: Name: State of Ohio;;).
149. M624-20 US Certificate of Citizenship -Nancy Marshall (Name: Name: Application # A19 583 620, Certificate # 35294; Date: Issued on 13 FEB 1974, but became a U.S. citizen on date of birth5 MAR 195 2;;).
150. M624-17 Nancy Marshall Wedding Announcement (Name: Name: Newspaper; Location: Columbus, Ohio; Date: 1972;;). MEDI: Newspaper
151. M624-18 Nancy Marshall Engagement Announcement. MEDI: Newspaper
152. M624-19 Registration of Live Birth - Nancy Marshall (Name: Name: Dept. of Health & Welfare Division of Vital Statistics Victoria, BC- Certified A True Photographic Print of the Original Registration #52-09-004896; Date: 18 Mar 1952;;).
153. M624-16 Certificate of Canadian Citizenship - Nancy Marshall (Name: Name: Nancy Lee Tieman;;).
154. M624-24 Nancy Marshall Ohio State Admission.
155. T500-51 Nancy (Marshall) Tieman Portland State Admittance.
156. "DNA Story for Nancy Marshall Tieman - Ancestry DNA test results," database.
157. T500-13 Copy of State of Iowa Birth Certificate, - Michael L. Tieman (Name: Name: State of Iowa;;).
158. T500-14 U.S. Passport - Michael Tieman (Name: Name: US Government;;). MEDI: Vital
159. T500-6 Marquis Who's Who In The West 1989- Michael Tieman (Name: Name: 23rd Edition;;).
160. T500-20 Verne Tieman life History (Name: Name: Verne Tieman;;).
161. T500-21 Michael Tieman Bio (Name: Name: Michael Tieman;;).
162. T500-34 Birth Registration, Michael Tieman.
163. T500-35 Canada Immigration, Michael Tieman.
164. HY-0016 Keokuk, Lee Co., Iowa - History.
165. T500-63 Michael L. Tieman Birth Announcement, Daily Gate City Newspaper, Keokuk, Iowa. MEDI: Newspaper
166. "DNA Story for Michael Tieman - Ancestry DNA results," database.
167. B600-6 1940 Federal Census, C. Braun.
168. R300-11 1920 U.S. Census Harvey A Roady.
169. R300-12 1930 U.S. Census - Arthur W. Roady.
170. R300-14 1940 U.S. Census - Arthur W. Roady.
171. T500-23 US WWII Army Enlistment Records 1938-1946, LaVerne Tieman.
172. T500-24 1930 US Census, LaVerne Tieman.
173. T500-27 Iowa Births & Christenings Index 1857-1947 - Malcolm Tieman.
174. T500-15 1930 US Census - Malcolm Tieman, April 10, 1930 - Sheet #14B, Enumeration Dist. #56-17, Supervisor's Dist. #15, Keokuk Township, Lee Co. Iowa.
175. T500-37 WWII Separation Papers, LaVerne Tieman.
176. T500-42 LaVerne Tieman Marriage Announcement.
177. S360-2 Ancestor Chart - Starr (Name: Name: Amy Starr; Date: 1992;;).
178. T500-46 LaVerne Tieman National Thespian Certif.
179. T500-44 1940 U.S. Census Malcolm Tieman, April 12, 1940, Sheet #12B, S.D.#1, E.D. 56-17,

Keokuk, Lee Co. Iowa.3rd Ward.

180. T500-53 LaVerne Tieman WWII Honoree.

181. T500-50 LaVerne & Doris Tieman Marriage License.

182. T500-58 Birth Certificate (Orig) M. LaVerne Tieman, Dept of Vital Statistics, State of Iowa, County of Lee, City of Keokuk, Index # 05C-1451, Registered # 1725.

183. T500-59 Death Certificate (Orig), M. LaVerne Tieman, Ohio Dept. of Heath, Vital Statistics, Certificate of Death, Reg. Dist. # 77, Primary Reg. Dist. #7705.

184. T500-60 Military Papers, WWII, M. LaVerne Tieman, Greetings letter (Orig), Report for Induction letter (orig), Special Orders #162 (Orig), Honorable Discharge Certif.(Orig).

185. M640-20 Copy of Newspaper Death Notice - Doris E. (Morrill) Tieman (Name: Date: 2003;;).

186. T500-3 Tieman/Morrill 1989 (Name: Name: Unknown;;).

187. M640-40 Doris Morrill Birth Registration.

188. M640-41 Doris Morrill Birth Certificate.

189. M640-47 1930 United States Federal Census, Don Morrill (Name: Name: Ancestry.com Operations Inc; Location: Provo, UT, USA; Date: 2002;;). United States of America, Bureau of the Census. Fifteenth Census of the United States, 1930. Washington, D.C.: National Archives and Records Administration, 1930. T626, 2,667 rolls.

190. M640-48 1940 United States Federal Census, Don Morrill (Name: Name: Ancestry.com Operations, Inc; Location: Provo, UT, USA; D ate: 2012;;). United States of America, Bureau of the Census. Sixteenth Census of the United States, 1940. Washington, D.C.: National Archives and Records Administration, 1940. T627, 4,643 rolls.

191. M640-46 Iowa, State Census Collection, 1836-1925, Don Morrill (Name: Name: Ancestry.com Operations Inc; Location: Provo, UT, USA; Date: 2007;;). Microfilm of Iowa State Censuses, 1856, 1885, 1895, 1905, 1915, 1925 as well various special censuses from 1836-1897 obtained from the State Historical Society of Iowa via Heritage Quest.

192. M640-16 Corresp. Doris (Morrill) Tieman (Name: Name: Letter;;).

193. T500-67 Doris (Morrill) Tieman Orig Death Certif.

194. M640-143 U.S., World War II Cadet Nursing Corps Card Files, 1942-194 8 Doris Morrill (Name: Name: Ancestry.com Operations, Inc; Location: Provo, UT, USA; Date: 2011;;), National Archives and Records Administration; Washington, D.C; Cadet Nurse Corps Files, compiled 1943 - 1948, documenting the period 1942 -1948; Box #: 204.

195. T500-17 Copy of Canadian Birth Abroad Certificate - Heather A. Tieman.

196. Source From Nancy L. (Marshall) Tieman.

197. E300-1 Source From Book from Judy Erwin.

198. Source From Heather A. (Tieman) Erwin.

199. T500-18 Copy of Canadian Birth Abroad Certificate - Katherine J. Tieman.

200. W500-2 Marriage Certificate Sam Woodward/ Katie Tieman.

201. W500-1 Sam Woodward's family tree - Mother's side (Name: Name: Sam's Mother, Rosa; Date: 2008;;). Rosa's Chinese family history

202. T500-45 Katie Tieman Baptism Papers.

203. W500-12 Birth Cert. Sam Woodward.

204. Source From Katherine J. Tieman.

205. B600-5 1930 Federal Census, C. Braun.

206. W600-1 1930 US Census, Nancy L. Wisecarver.

207. "W500-3 Find a Grave - Gary Woodward Family," databas

Name Index

ORMANDY, Harrison Wilkinson [2376], 121, 127

ORMANDY, Harrison Wilkinson [2824], 109, 118

ORMANDY, Irwin Scott [2358], 131, 147

ORMANDY, Isaac (Dr.) [3334], 102, 111

ORMANDY, James [3331], 102, 109

ORMANDY, James [3931], 97, 104

ORMANDY, James [5401], 94, 99

ORMANDY, James Alma [2337], 121, 128

ORMANDY, James Alma [2348], 117, 125

ORMANDY, James Griswold [2375], 127, 136

ORMANDY, Jane [3930], 97, 104

ORMANDY, Janet Alma [2224], 130, 140

ORMANDY, John (Rev.) [2343], 102, 107

ORMANDY, John [2952], 109, 118

ORMANDY, John [3927], 97, 105

ORMANDY, John [5394], 91, 92

ORMANDY, John [5397], 94, 98

ORMANDY, John Cliffborne [2345], 117, 125

ORMANDY, Johnathan Harrison [2350], 117, 124

ORMANDY, Joseph [3330], 102, 107

ORMANDY, Joseph [3928], 97, 105

ORMANDY, Julia [2354], 116, 120

ORMANDY, Juliann [2823], 109, 118

ORMANDY, Margaret [5390], 111, 119

ORMANDY, Margaret Claribel [2612], 135, 148

ORMANDY, Margaret Mary [2373], 127, 136

ORMANDY, Mary Ann [2822], 108, 112

ORMANDY, Mary Francis [2357], 131, 147

ORMANDY, Mary Wilkinson [2353], 117, 122

ORMANDY, Melise [2784], 149, 202

ORMANDY, Michael [2782], 149, 202

ORMANDY, Phyllis Patricia [2372], 128, 136

ORMANDY, Ray [2779], 136, 149

ORMANDY, Richard [3923], 90

ORMANDY, Richard [3929], 97, 104

ORMANDY, Richard [5398], 94, 98

ORMANDY, Robert Mosier [2363], 128, 137

ORMANDY, Robert Mosier [2786], 149, 202

ORMANDY, Ruth [2346], 117, 125

ORMANDY, Ruth Mae [2608], 135, 148

ORMANDY, Ruth Naomi [2365], 128, 139

ORMANDY, Sarah [5395], 91, 93

ORMANDY, Sarah J. [3341], 124, 135

ORMANDY, Thomas (Rev) [2619], 97, 101

ORMANDY, Thomas (Rev.) [3332], 102, 110

ORMANDY, Thomas [2341], 109, 113

ORMANDY, Thomas [3123], 94, 96

ORMANDY, Vanessa [2785], 149, 202

ORMANDY, Victoria [2352], 117, 122

ORMANDY, Walter Scott [2355], 122, 131

ORMANDY, William [3324], 91, 93

ORMANDY, William [3327], 97, 103

ORMANDY, William [3329], 102, 106

ORMANDY, William [5391], 111, 119

ORMANDY, William Addison [3932], 97, 103

ORMANDY, William Lewithwaite [2339], 117, 120

ORMANDY, William Lewithwaite [2360], 121, 127

ORMANDY, William Lewithwaite [2374], 128, 138

PEARSON, [5189], 136

PEARSON, Candace [2788], 136, 150

PEARSON, Duke Christian [2787], 136, 149

PEARSON, Walter [2766], 128, 136

POOLE, [5181], 124

POOLE, Matilda Winifred [3340], 117, 124

RIVETT, [5206], 201

RIVETT, Elaine [2599], 148, 201

ROADY, Arthur William [2526], 154

ROADY, Arthur William Jr. [2523], 146, 154

ROADY, Erin Wynn [2576], 155, 205

SADLER, [5210], 211

SADLER, Christopher [3868], 211, 215

SADLER, James [3867], 211, 215

SADLER, Rodger [3866], 201, 211

SAUSE, [5179], 123

SAUSE, Christine Anne [2603], 201, 211

SAUSE, Clifton John [2585], 123, 133

SAUSE, Edward [2587], 123, 134

SAUSE, Edward [2594], 132, 147

SAUSE, Everline [2593], 132, 147

SAUSE, Florence [2588], 123, 134

SAUSE, Frank [2581], 123, 132

SAUSE, Genevieve [2582], 123, 132

SAUSE, George G. [2584], 123, 133

SAUSE, Grace [2586], 123, 134

Appendix A – Pedigree Charts
Pedigree Chart for Janet Alma ORMANDY
[2224]

Chart no. 1

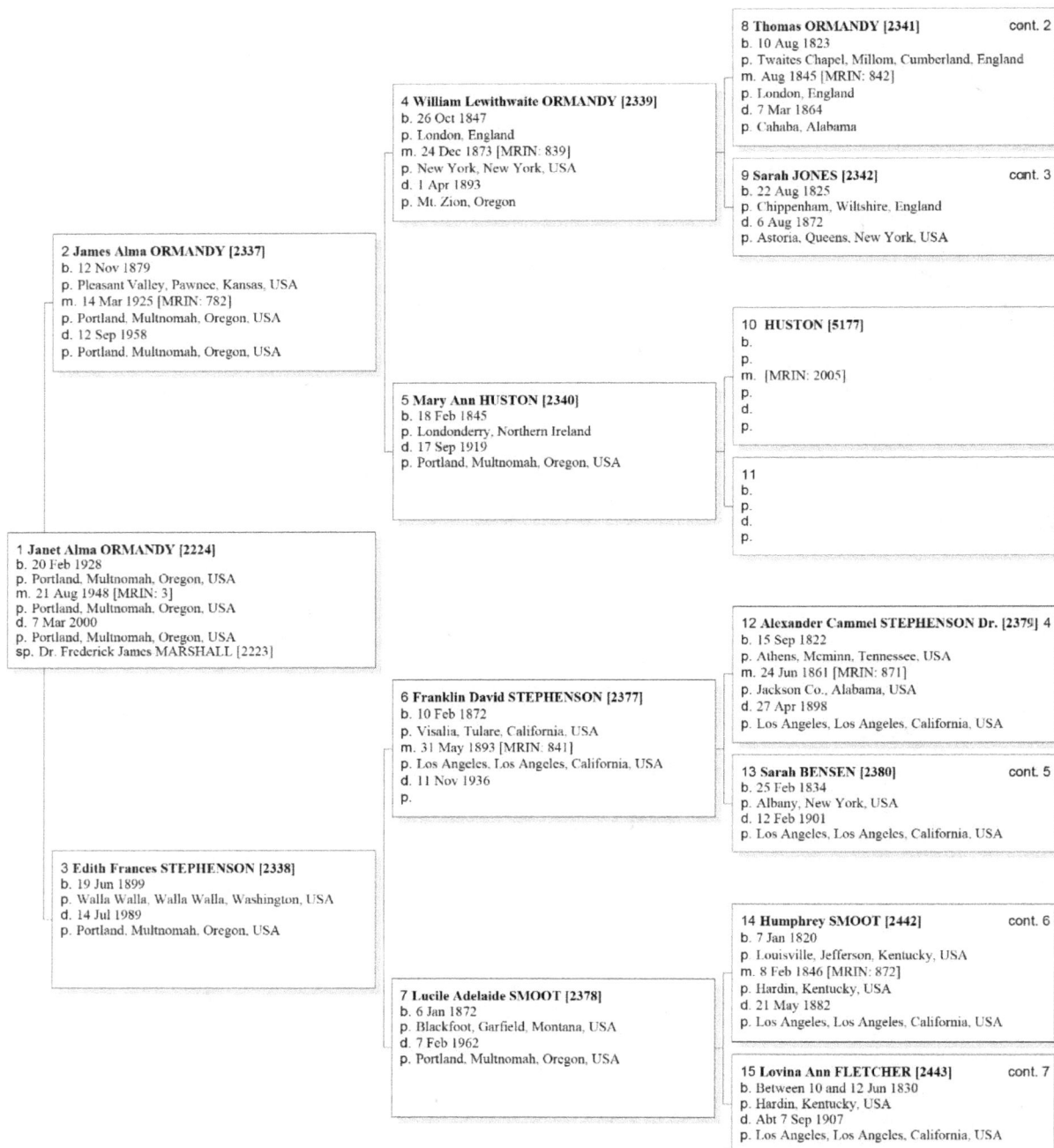

8 Thomas ORMANDY [2341] cont. 2
b. 10 Aug 1823
p. Twaites Chapel, Millom, Cumberland, England
m. Aug 1845 [MRIN: 842]
p. London, England
d. 7 Mar 1864
p. Cahaba, Alabama

9 Sarah JONES [2342] cont. 3
b. 22 Aug 1825
p. Chippenham, Wiltshire, England
d. 6 Aug 1872
p. Astoria, Queens, New York, USA

4 William Lewithwaite ORMANDY [2339]
b. 26 Oct 1847
p. London, England
m. 24 Dec 1873 [MRIN: 839]
p. New York, New York, USA
d. 1 Apr 1893
p. Mt. Zion, Oregon

10 HUSTON [5177]
b.
p.
m. [MRIN: 2005]
p.
d.
p.

11
b.
p.
d.
p.

5 Mary Ann HUSTON [2340]
b. 18 Feb 1845
p. Londonderry, Northern Ireland
d. 17 Sep 1919
p. Portland, Multnomah, Oregon, USA

2 James Alma ORMANDY [2337]
b. 12 Nov 1879
p. Pleasant Valley, Pawnee, Kansas, USA
m. 14 Mar 1925 [MRIN: 782]
p. Portland, Multnomah, Oregon, USA
d. 12 Sep 1958
p. Portland, Multnomah, Oregon, USA

1 Janet Alma ORMANDY [2224]
b. 20 Feb 1928
p. Portland, Multnomah, Oregon, USA
m. 21 Aug 1948 [MRIN: 3]
p. Portland, Multnomah, Oregon, USA
d. 7 Mar 2000
p. Portland, Multnomah, Oregon, USA
sp. Dr. Frederick James MARSHALL [2223]

12 Alexander Cammel STEPHENSON Dr. [2379] 4
b. 15 Sep 1822
p. Athens, Mcminn, Tennessee, USA
m. 24 Jun 1861 [MRIN: 871]
p. Jackson Co., Alabama, USA
d. 27 Apr 1898
p. Los Angeles, Los Angeles, California, USA

13 Sarah BENSEN [2380] cont. 5
b. 25 Feb 1834
p. Albany, New York, USA
d. 12 Feb 1901
p. Los Angeles, Los Angeles, California, USA

6 Franklin David STEPHENSON [2377]
b. 10 Feb 1872
p. Visalia, Tulare, California, USA
m. 31 May 1893 [MRIN: 841]
p. Los Angeles, Los Angeles, California, USA
d. 11 Nov 1936
p.

3 Edith Frances STEPHENSON [2338]
b. 19 Jun 1899
p. Walla Walla, Walla Walla, Washington, USA
d. 14 Jul 1989
p. Portland, Multnomah, Oregon, USA

14 Humphrey SMOOT [2442] cont. 6
b. 7 Jan 1820
p. Louisville, Jefferson, Kentucky, USA
m. 8 Feb 1846 [MRIN: 872]
p. Hardin, Kentucky, USA
d. 21 May 1882
p. Los Angeles, Los Angeles, California, USA

15 Lovina Ann FLETCHER [2443] cont. 7
b. Between 10 and 12 Jun 1830
p. Hardin, Kentucky, USA
d. Abt 7 Sep 1907
p. Los Angeles, Los Angeles, California, USA

7 Lucile Adelaide SMOOT [2378]
b. 6 Jan 1872
p. Blackfoot, Garfield, Montana, USA
d. 7 Feb 1962
p. Portland, Multnomah, Oregon, USA

Pedigree Chart for Thomas ORMANDY
[2341]

Chart no. 2

No. 1 on this chart is the same as no. 8 on chart no. 1

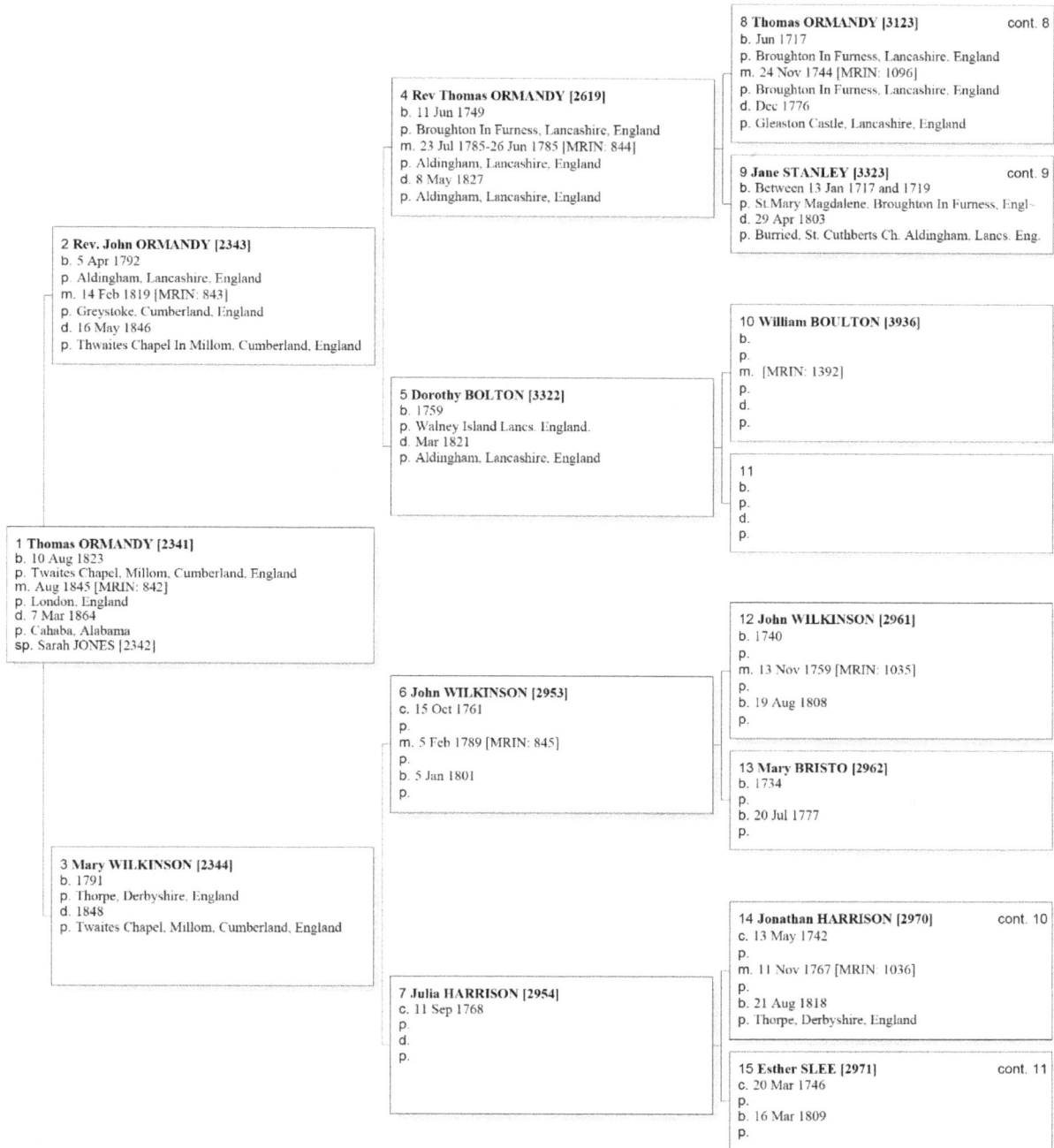

8 Thomas ORMANDY [3123]   cont. 8
b. Jun 1717
p. Broughton In Furness, Lancashire, England
m. 24 Nov 1744 [MRIN: 1096]
p. Broughton In Furness, Lancashire, England
d. Dec 1776
p. Gleaston Castle, Lancashire, England

4 Rev Thomas ORMANDY [2619]
b. 11 Jun 1749
p. Broughton In Furness, Lancashire, England
m. 23 Jul 1785-26 Jun 1785 [MRIN: 844]
p. Aldingham, Lancashire, England
d. 8 May 1827
p. Aldingham, Lancashire, England

9 Jane STANLEY [3323]   cont. 9
b. Between 13 Jan 1717 and 1719
p. St.Mary Magdalene, Broughton In Furness, Engl~
d. 29 Apr 1803
p. Burried, St. Cuthberts Ch. Aldingham, Lancs. Eng.

2 Rev. John ORMANDY [2343]
b. 5 Apr 1792
p. Aldingham, Lancashire, England
m. 14 Feb 1819 [MRIN: 843]
p. Greystoke, Cumberland, England
d. 16 May 1846
p. Thwaites Chapel In Millom, Cumberland, England

10 William BOULTON [3936]
b.
p.
m. [MRIN: 1392]
p.
d.
p.

5 Dorothy BOLTON [3322]
b. 1759
p. Walney Island Lancs. England.
d. Mar 1821
p. Aldingham, Lancashire, England

11
b.
p.
d.
p.

1 Thomas ORMANDY [2341]
b. 10 Aug 1823
p. Twaites Chapel, Millom, Cumberland, England
m. Aug 1845 [MRIN: 842]
p. London, England
d. 7 Mar 1864
p. Cahaba, Alabama
sp. Sarah JONES [2342]

12 John WILKINSON [2961]
b. 1740
p.
m. 13 Nov 1759 [MRIN: 1035]
p.
b. 19 Aug 1808
p.

6 John WILKINSON [2953]
c. 15 Oct 1761
p.
m. 5 Feb 1789 [MRIN: 845]
p.
b. 5 Jan 1801
p.

13 Mary BRISTO [2962]
b. 1734
p.
b. 20 Jul 1777
p.

3 Mary WILKINSON [2344]
b. 1791
p. Thorpe, Derbyshire, England
d. 1848
p. Twaites Chapel, Millom, Cumberland, England

14 Jonathan HARRISON [2970]   cont. 10
c. 13 May 1742
p.
m. 11 Nov 1767 [MRIN: 1036]
p.
b. 21 Aug 1818
p. Thorpe, Derbyshire, England

7 Julia HARRISON [2954]
c. 11 Sep 1768
p.
d.
p.

15 Esther SLEE [2971]   cont. 11
c. 20 Mar 1746
p.
b. 16 Mar 1809
p.

Pedigree Chart for Sarah JONES [2342]

Chart no. 3

No. 1 on this chart is the same as no. 9 on chart no. 1

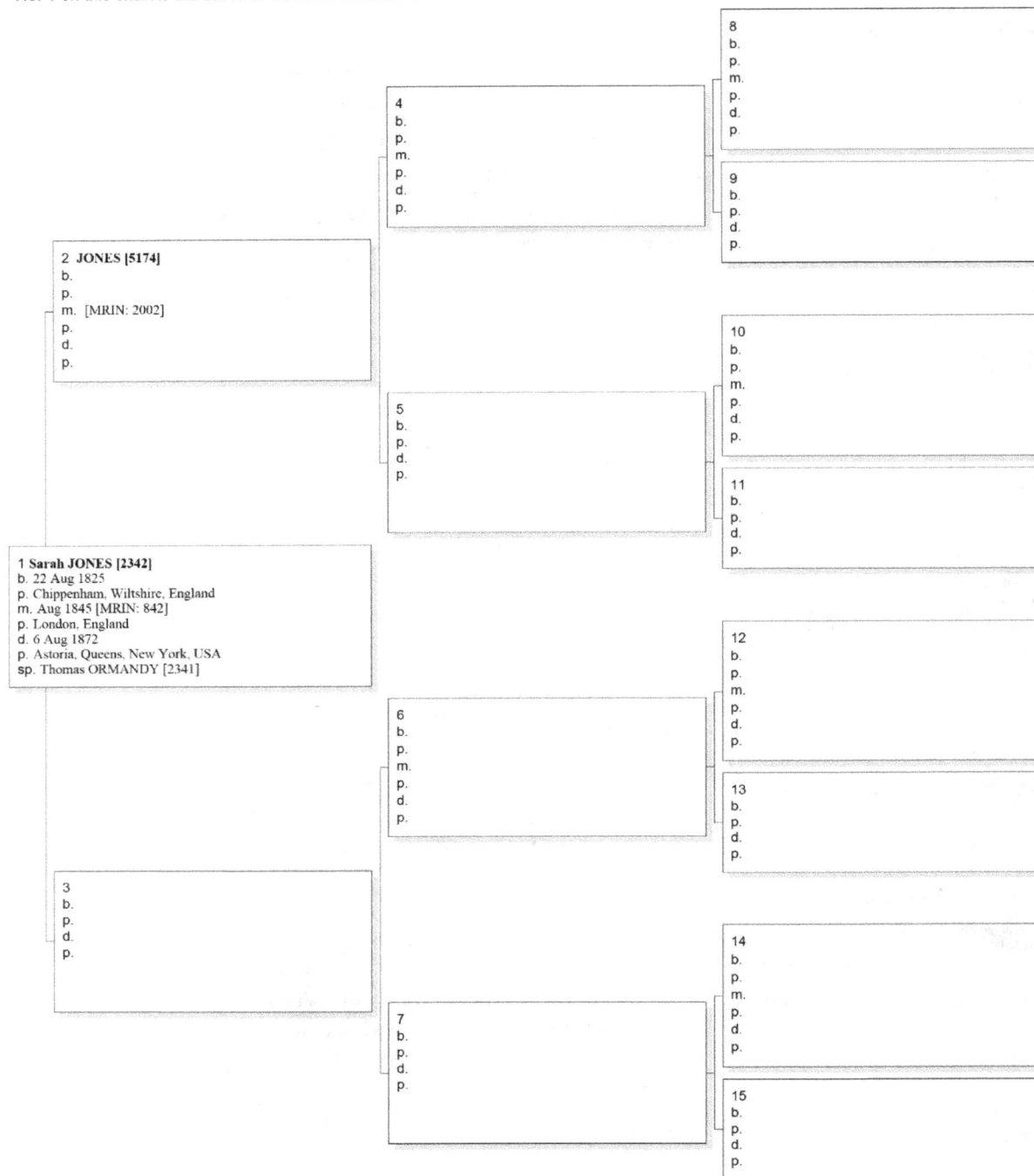

```
                                                              8
                                                              b.
                                                              p.
                                                              m.
                                        4                     p.
                                        b.                    d.
                                        p.                    p.
                                        m.
                                        p.                    9
                                        d.                    b.
                                        p.                    p.
                                                              d.
        2  JONES [5174]                                       p.
        b.
        p.
        m.  [MRIN: 2002]                                      10
        p.                                                    b.
        d.                                                    p.
        p.                                                    m.
                                        5                     p.
                                        b.                    d.
                                        p.                    p.
                                        d.
                                        p.                    11
                                                              b.
                                                              p.
                                                              d.
        1 Sarah JONES [2342]                                  p.
        b. 22 Aug 1825
        p. Chippenham, Wiltshire, England
        m. Aug 1845 [MRIN: 842]
        p. London, England                                   12
        d. 6 Aug 1872                                        b.
        p. Astoria, Queens, New York, USA                    p.
        sp. Thomas ORMANDY [2341]                            m.
                                        6                     p.
                                        b.                    d.
                                        p.                    p.
                                        m.
                                        p.                    13
                                        d.                    b.
                                        p.                    p.
                                                              d.
                                                              p.

        3                                                    14
        b.                                                   b.
        p.                                                   p.
        d.                                                   m.
        p.                                                   p.
                                        7                     d.
                                        b.                    p.
                                        p.
                                        d.                    15
                                        p.                    b.
                                                              p.
                                                              d.
                                                              p.
```

Pedigree Chart for Alexander Cammel
STEPHENSON Dr. [2379]

Chart no. 4

No. 1 on this chart is the same as no. 12 on chart no. 1

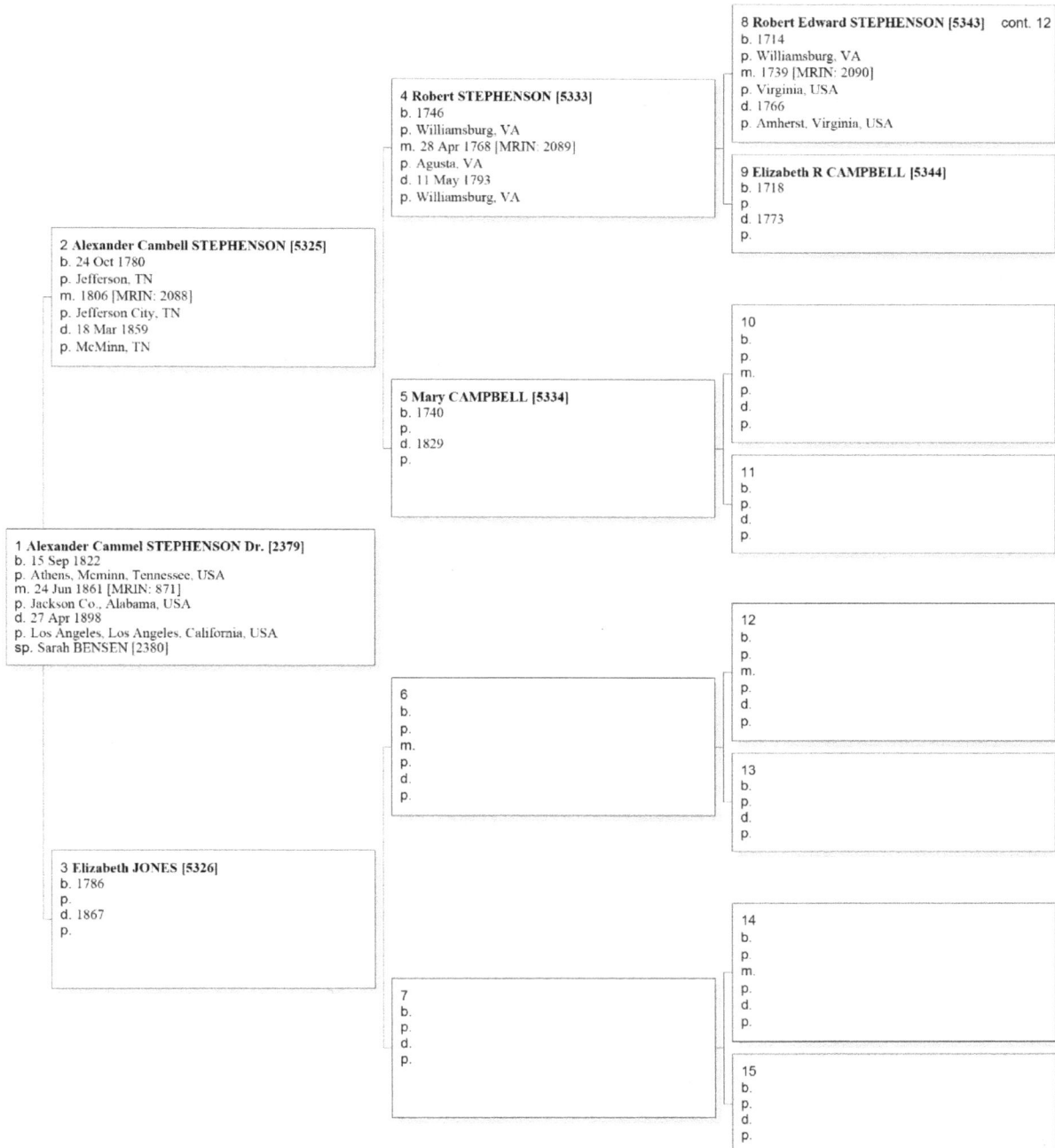

8 Robert Edward STEPHENSON [5343]   cont. 12
b. 1714
p. Williamsburg, VA
m. 1739 [MRIN: 2090]
p. Virginia, USA
d. 1766
p. Amherst, Virginia, USA

4 Robert STEPHENSON [5333]
b. 1746
p. Williamsburg, VA
m. 28 Apr 1768 [MRIN: 2089]
p. Agusta, VA
d. 11 May 1793
p. Williamsburg, VA

9 Elizabeth R CAMPBELL [5344]
b. 1718
p
d. 1773
p.

2 Alexander Cambell STEPHENSON [5325]
b. 24 Oct 1780
p. Jefferson, TN
m. 1806 [MRIN: 2088]
p. Jefferson City, TN
d. 18 Mar 1859
p. McMinn, TN

10
b.
p.
m.
p.
d.
p.

5 Mary CAMPBELL [5334]
b. 1740
p.
d. 1829
p.

11
b.
p.
d.
p.

1 Alexander Cammel STEPHENSON Dr. [2379]
b. 15 Sep 1822
p. Athens, Mcminn, Tennessee, USA
m. 24 Jun 1861 [MRIN: 871]
p. Jackson Co., Alabama, USA
d. 27 Apr 1898
p. Los Angeles, Los Angeles, California, USA
sp. Sarah BENSEN [2380]

12
b.
p.
m.
p.
d.
p.

6
b.
p.
m.
p.
d.
p.

13
b.
p.
d.
p.

3 Elizabeth JONES [5326]
b. 1786
p.
d. 1867
p.

14
b.
p.
m.
p.
d.
p.

7
b.
p.
d.
p.

15
b.
p.
d.
p.

Pedigree Chart for Sarah BENSEN [2380]

Chart no. 5

No. 1 on this chart is the same as no. 13 on chart no. 1

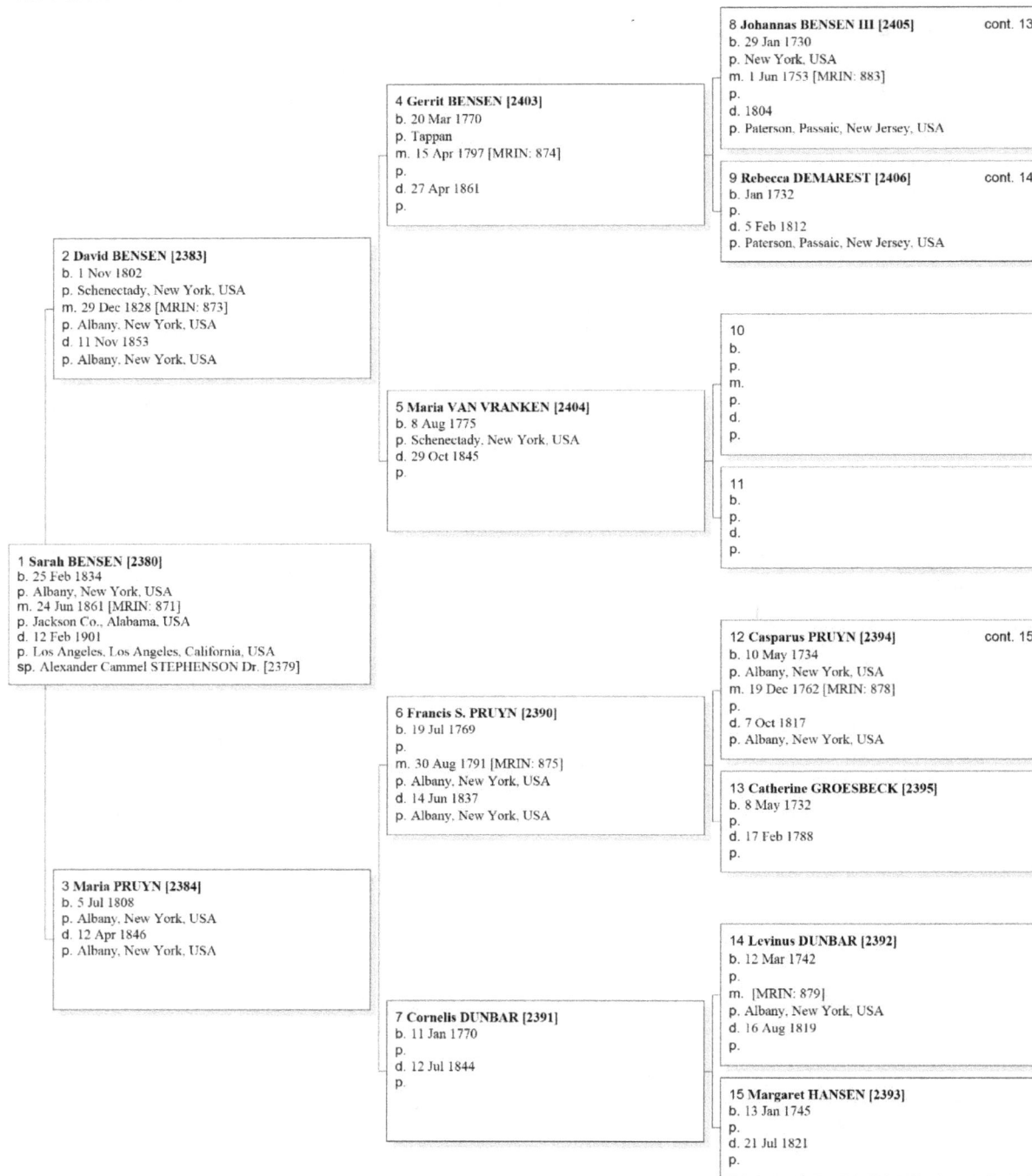

8 Johannas BENSEN III [2405]   cont. 13
b. 29 Jan 1730
p. New York, USA
m. 1 Jun 1753 [MRIN: 883]
p.
d. 1804
p. Paterson, Passaic, New Jersey, USA

4 Gerrit BENSEN [2403]
b. 20 Mar 1770
p. Tappan
m. 15 Apr 1797 [MRIN: 874]
p.
d. 27 Apr 1861
p.

9 Rebecca DEMAREST [2406]   cont. 14
b. Jan 1732
p.
d. 5 Feb 1812
p. Paterson, Passaic, New Jersey, USA

2 David BENSEN [2383]
b. 1 Nov 1802
p. Schenectady, New York, USA
m. 29 Dec 1828 [MRIN: 873]
p. Albany, New York, USA
d. 11 Nov 1853
p. Albany, New York, USA

10
b.
p.
m.
p.
d.
p.

5 Maria VAN VRANKEN [2404]
b. 8 Aug 1775
p. Schenectady, New York, USA
d. 29 Oct 1845
p.

11
b.
p.
d.
p.

1 Sarah BENSEN [2380]
b. 25 Feb 1834
p. Albany, New York, USA
m. 24 Jun 1861 [MRIN: 871]
p. Jackson Co., Alabama, USA
d. 12 Feb 1901
p. Los Angeles, Los Angeles, California, USA
sp. Alexander Cammel STEPHENSON Dr. [2379]

12 Casparus PRUYN [2394]   cont. 15
b. 10 May 1734
p. Albany, New York, USA
m. 19 Dec 1762 [MRIN: 878]
p.
d. 7 Oct 1817
p. Albany, New York, USA

6 Francis S. PRUYN [2390]
b. 19 Jul 1769
p.
m. 30 Aug 1791 [MRIN: 875]
p. Albany, New York, USA
d. 14 Jun 1837
p. Albany, New York, USA

13 Catherine GROESBECK [2395]
b. 8 May 1732
p.
d. 17 Feb 1788
p.

3 Maria PRUYN [2384]
b. 5 Jul 1808
p. Albany, New York, USA
d. 12 Apr 1846
p. Albany, New York, USA

14 Levinus DUNBAR [2392]
b. 12 Mar 1742
p.
m. [MRIN: 879]
p. Albany, New York, USA
d. 16 Aug 1819
p.

7 Cornelis DUNBAR [2391]
b. 11 Jan 1770
p.
d. 12 Jul 1844
p.

15 Margaret HANSEN [2393]
b. 13 Jan 1745
p.
d. 21 Jul 1821
p.

Pedigree Chart for Humphrey SMOOT
[2442]

No. 1 on this chart is the same as no. 14 on chart no. 1

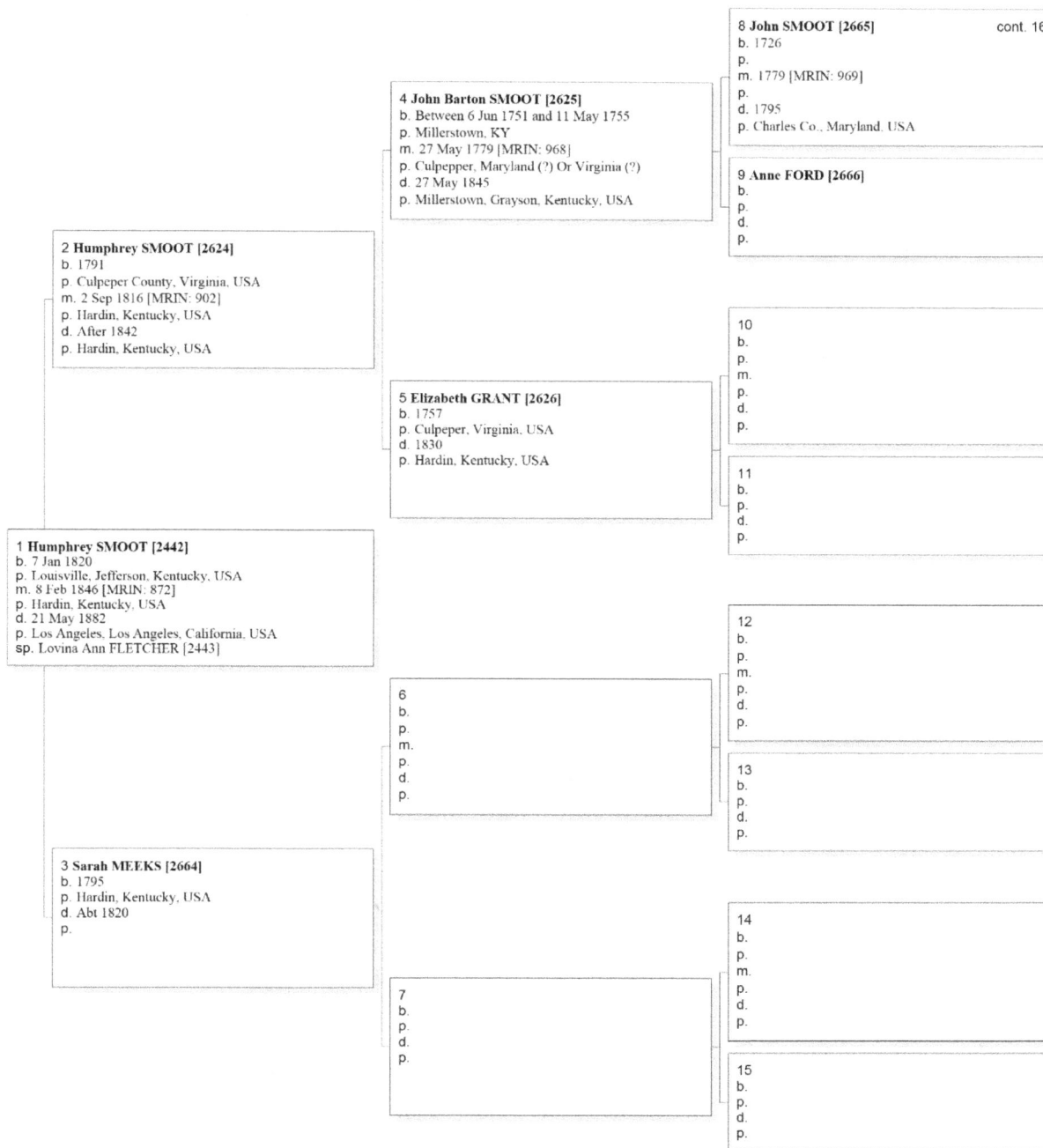

8 John SMOOT [2665]   cont. 16
b. 1726
p.
m. 1779 [MRIN: 969]
p.
d. 1795
p. Charles Co., Maryland, USA

4 John Barton SMOOT [2625]
b. Between 6 Jun 1751 and 11 May 1755
p. Millerstown, KY
m. 27 May 1779 [MRIN: 968]
p. Culpepper, Maryland (?) Or Virginia (?)
d. 27 May 1845
p. Millerstown, Grayson, Kentucky, USA

9 Anne FORD [2666]
b.
p.
d.
p.

2 Humphrey SMOOT [2624]
b. 1791
p. Culpeper County, Virginia, USA
m. 2 Sep 1816 [MRIN: 902]
p. Hardin, Kentucky, USA
d. After 1842
p. Hardin, Kentucky, USA

10
b.
p.
m.
p.
d.
p.

5 Elizabeth GRANT [2626]
b. 1757
p. Culpeper, Virginia, USA
d. 1830
p. Hardin, Kentucky, USA

11
b.
p.
d.
p.

1 Humphrey SMOOT [2442]
b. 7 Jan 1820
p. Louisville, Jefferson, Kentucky, USA
m. 8 Feb 1846 [MRIN: 872]
p. Hardin, Kentucky, USA
d. 21 May 1882
p. Los Angeles, Los Angeles, California, USA
sp. Lovina Ann FLETCHER [2443]

12
b.
p.
m.
p.
d.
p.

6
b.
p.
m.
p.
d.
p.

13
b.
p.
d.
p.

3 Sarah MEEKS [2664]
b. 1795
p. Hardin, Kentucky, USA
d. Abt 1820
p.

14
b.
p.
m.
p.
d.
p.

7
b.
p.
d.
p.

15
b.
p.
d.
p.

Pedigree Chart for Lovina Ann FLETCHER
[2443]

Chart no. 7

No. 1 on this chart is the same as no. 15 on chart no. 1

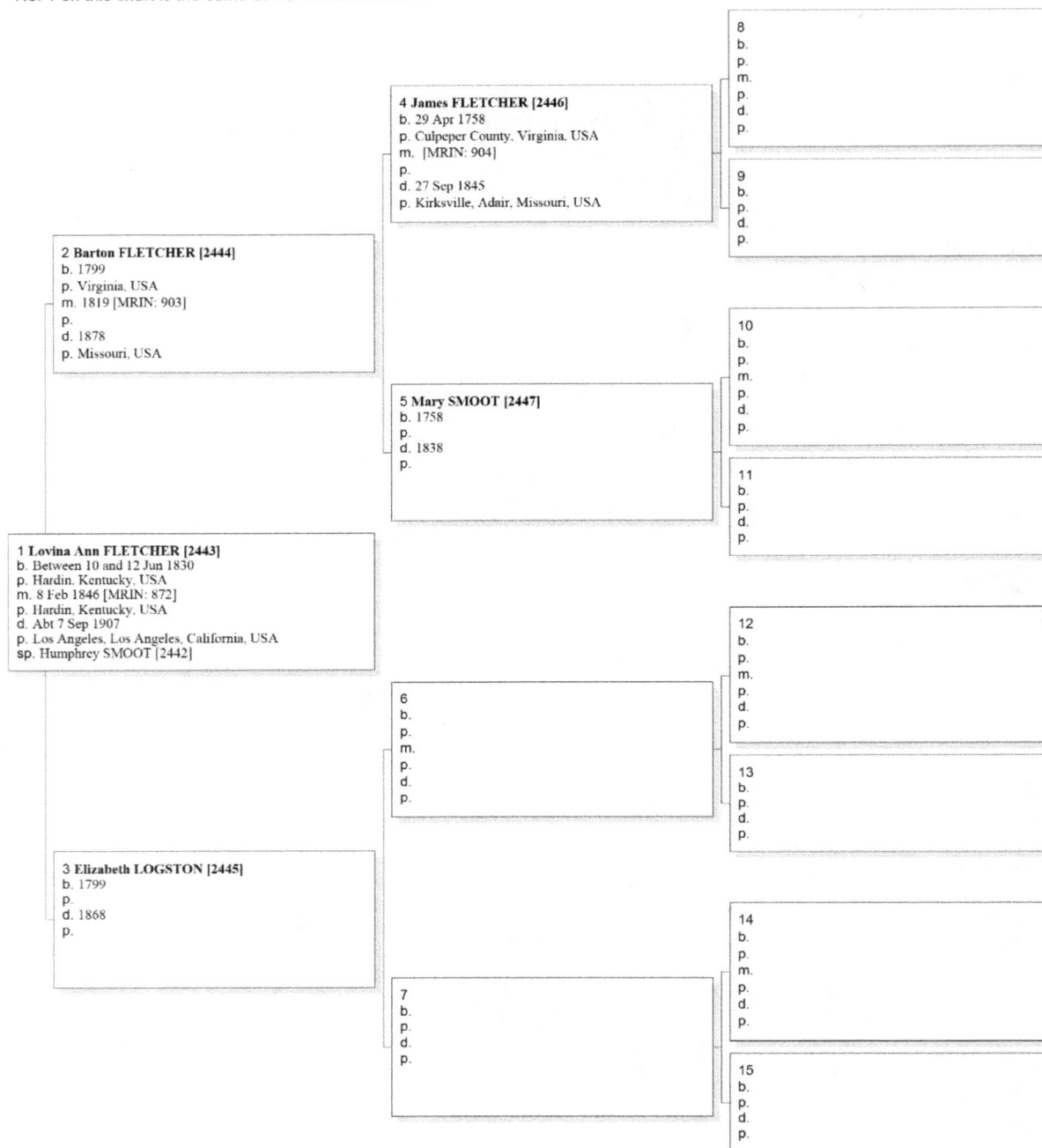

4 James FLETCHER [2446] b. 29 Apr 1758 p. Culpeper County, Virginia, USA m. [MRIN: 904] p. d. 27 Sep 1845 p. Kirksville, Adair, Missouri, USA	8 b. p. m. p. d. p.
	9 b. p. d. p.

2 Barton FLETCHER [2444]
b. 1799
p. Virginia, USA
m. 1819 [MRIN: 903]
p.
d. 1878
p. Missouri, USA

5 Mary SMOOT [2447] b. 1758 p. d. 1838 p.	10 b. p. m. p. d. p.
	11 b. p. d. p.

1 Lovina Ann FLETCHER [2443]
b. Between 10 and 12 Jun 1830
p. Hardin, Kentucky, USA
m. 8 Feb 1846 [MRIN: 872]
p. Hardin, Kentucky, USA
d. Abt 7 Sep 1907
p. Los Angeles, Los Angeles, California, USA
sp. Humphrey SMOOT [2442]

6 b. p. m. p. d. p.	12 b. p. m. p. d. p.
	13 b. p. d. p.

3 Elizabeth LOGSTON [2445]
b. 1799
p.
d. 1868
p.

7 b. p. d. p.	14 b. p. m. p. d. p.
	15 b. p. d. p.

Pedigree Chart for Thomas ORMANDY
[3123]

Chart no. 8

No. 1 on this chart is the same as no. 8 on chart no. 2

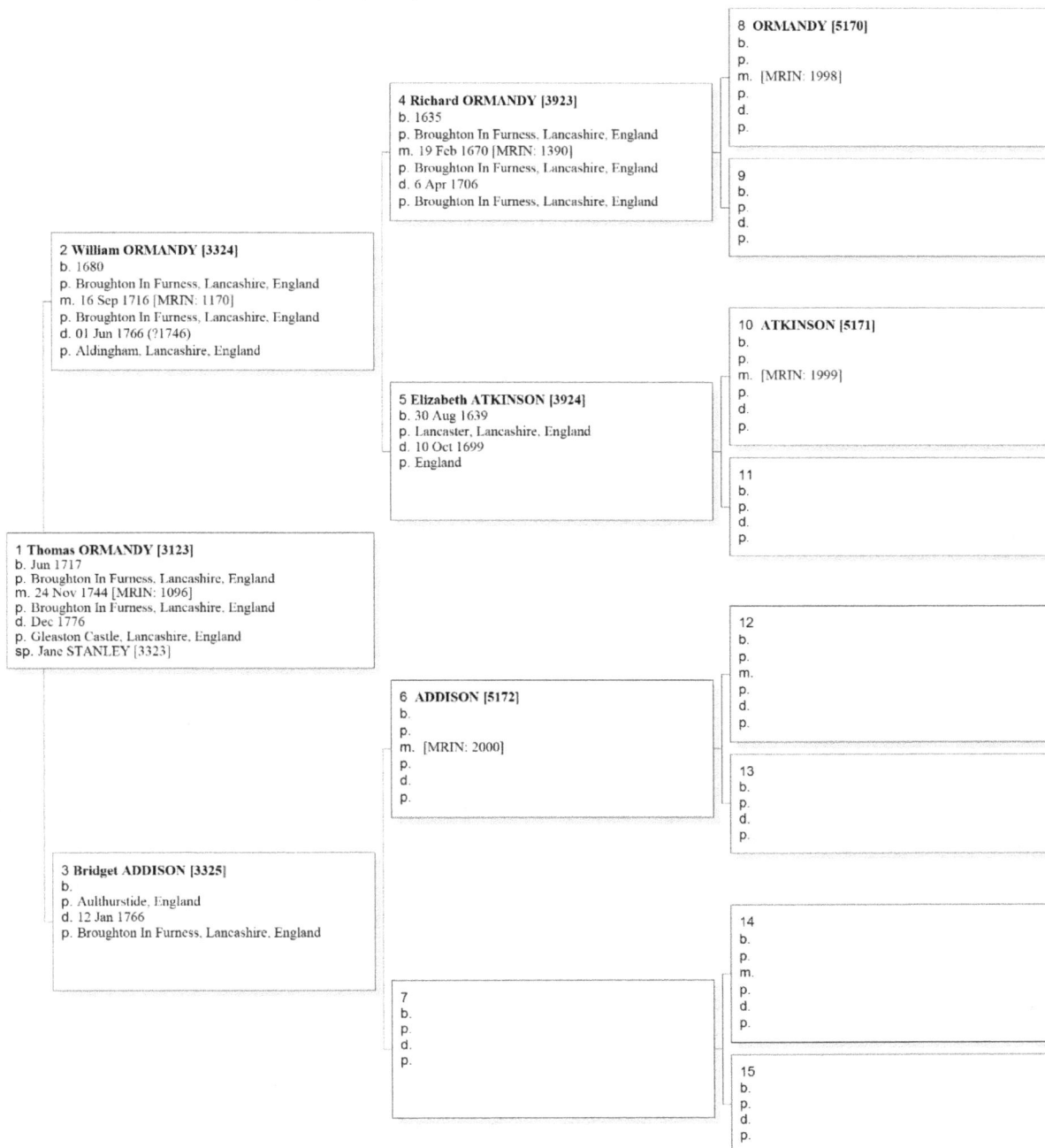

8 ORMANDY [5170]
b.
p.
m. [MRIN: 1998]
p.
d.
p.

4 Richard ORMANDY [3923]
b. 1635
p. Broughton In Furness, Lancashire, England
m. 19 Feb 1670 [MRIN: 1390]
p. Broughton In Furness, Lancashire, England
d. 6 Apr 1706
p. Broughton In Furness, Lancashire, England

9
b.
p.
d.
p.

2 William ORMANDY [3324]
b. 1680
p. Broughton In Furness, Lancashire, England
m. 16 Sep 1716 [MRIN: 1170]
p. Broughton In Furness, Lancashire, England
d. 01 Jun 1766 (?1746)
p. Aldingham, Lancashire, England

10 ATKINSON [5171]
b.
p.
m. [MRIN: 1999]
p.
d.
p.

5 Elizabeth ATKINSON [3924]
b. 30 Aug 1639
p. Lancaster, Lancashire, England
d. 10 Oct 1699
p. England

11
b.
p.
d.
p.

1 Thomas ORMANDY [3123]
b. Jun 1717
p. Broughton In Furness, Lancashire, England
m. 24 Nov 1744 [MRIN: 1096]
p. Broughton In Furness, Lancashire, England
d. Dec 1776
p. Gleaston Castle, Lancashire, England
sp. Jane STANLEY [3323]

12
b.
p.
m.
p.
d.
p.

6 ADDISON [5172]
b.
p.
m. [MRIN: 2000]
p.
d.
p.

13
b.
p.
d.
p.

3 Bridget ADDISON [3325]
b.
p. Aulthurstide, England
d. 12 Jan 1766
p. Broughton In Furness, Lancashire, England

14
b.
p.
m.
p.
d.
p.

7
b.
p.
d.
p.

15
b.
p.
d.
p.

Pedigree Chart for Jane STANLEY [3323]

No. 1 on this chart is the same as no. 9 on chart no. 2

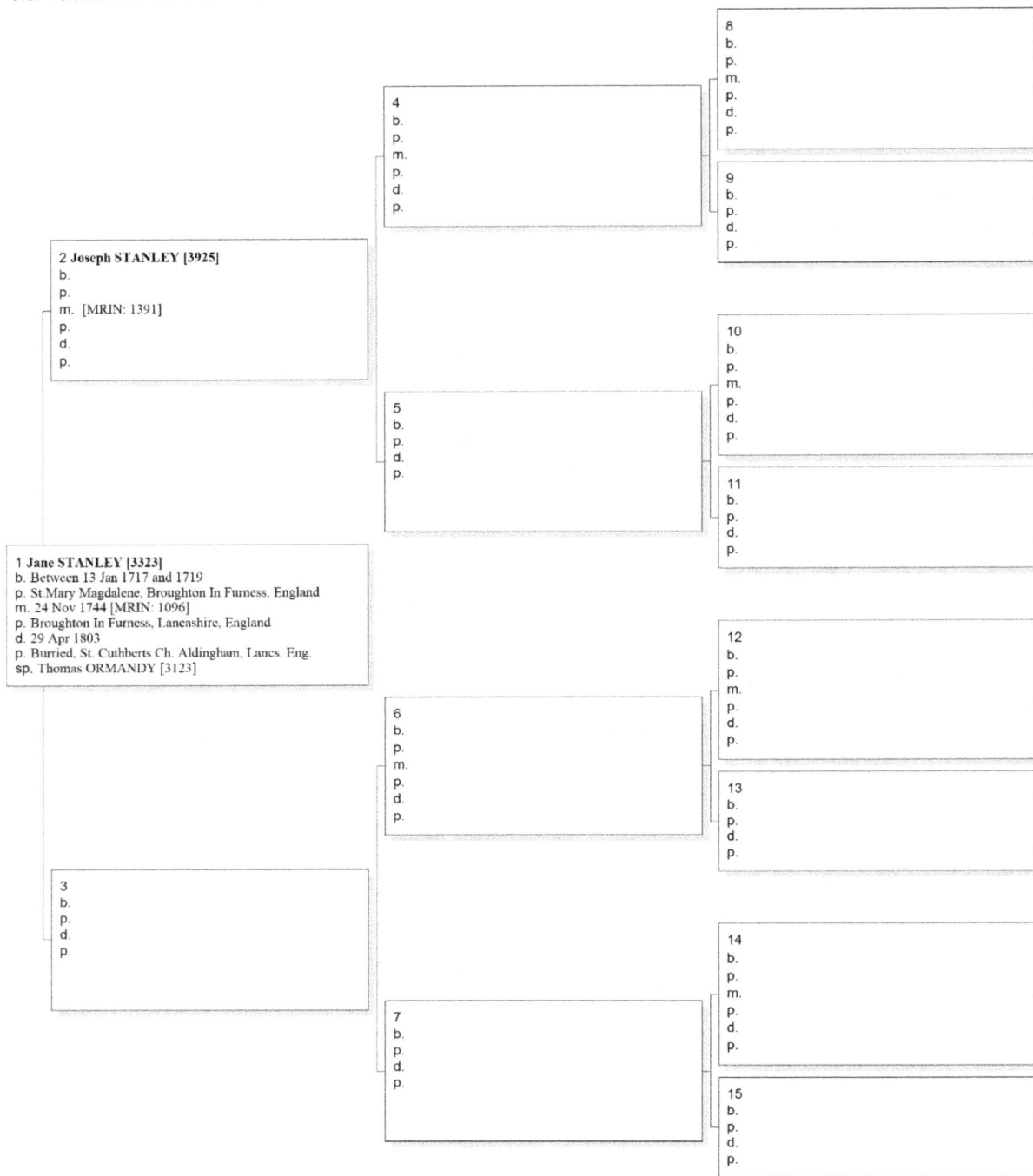

```
                                                                    8
                                                                    b.
                                                                    p.
                                                                    m.
                                          4                         p.
                                          b.                        d.
                                          p.                        p.
                                          p.
                                          m.
                                          p.                        9
                                          d.                        b.
                                          p.                        p.
                                                                    d.
                                                                    p.
      2 Joseph STANLEY [3925]
      b.
      p.                                                            10
      m. [MRIN: 1391]                                               b.
      p.                                                            p.
      d.                                                            m.
      p.                                      5                     p.
                                              b.                    d.
                                              p.                    p.
                                              d.
                                              p.                    11
                                                                    b.
                                                                    p.
                                                                    d.
      1 Jane STANLEY [3323]                                         p.
      b. Between 13 Jan 1717 and 1719
      p. St.Mary Magdalene, Broughton In Furness, England
      m. 24 Nov 1744 [MRIN: 1096]
      p. Broughton In Furness, Lancashire, England                 12
      d. 29 Apr 1803                                                b.
      p. Burried, St. Cuthberts Ch. Aldingham, Lancs. Eng.          p.
      sp. Thomas ORMANDY [3123]                                     m.
                                              6                     p.
                                              b.                    d.
                                              p.                    p.
                                              m.
                                              p.                    13
                                              d.                    b.
                                              p.                    p.
                                                                    d.
                                                                    p.
      3
      b.
      p.                                                            14
      d.                                                            b.
      p.                                                            p.
                                                                    m.
                                              7                     p.
                                              b.                    d.
                                              p.                    p.
                                              d.
                                              p.                    15
                                                                    b.
                                                                    p.
                                                                    d.
                                                                    p.
```

Pedigree Chart for Jonathan HARRISON
[2970]

No. 1 on this chart is the same as no. 14 on chart no. 2

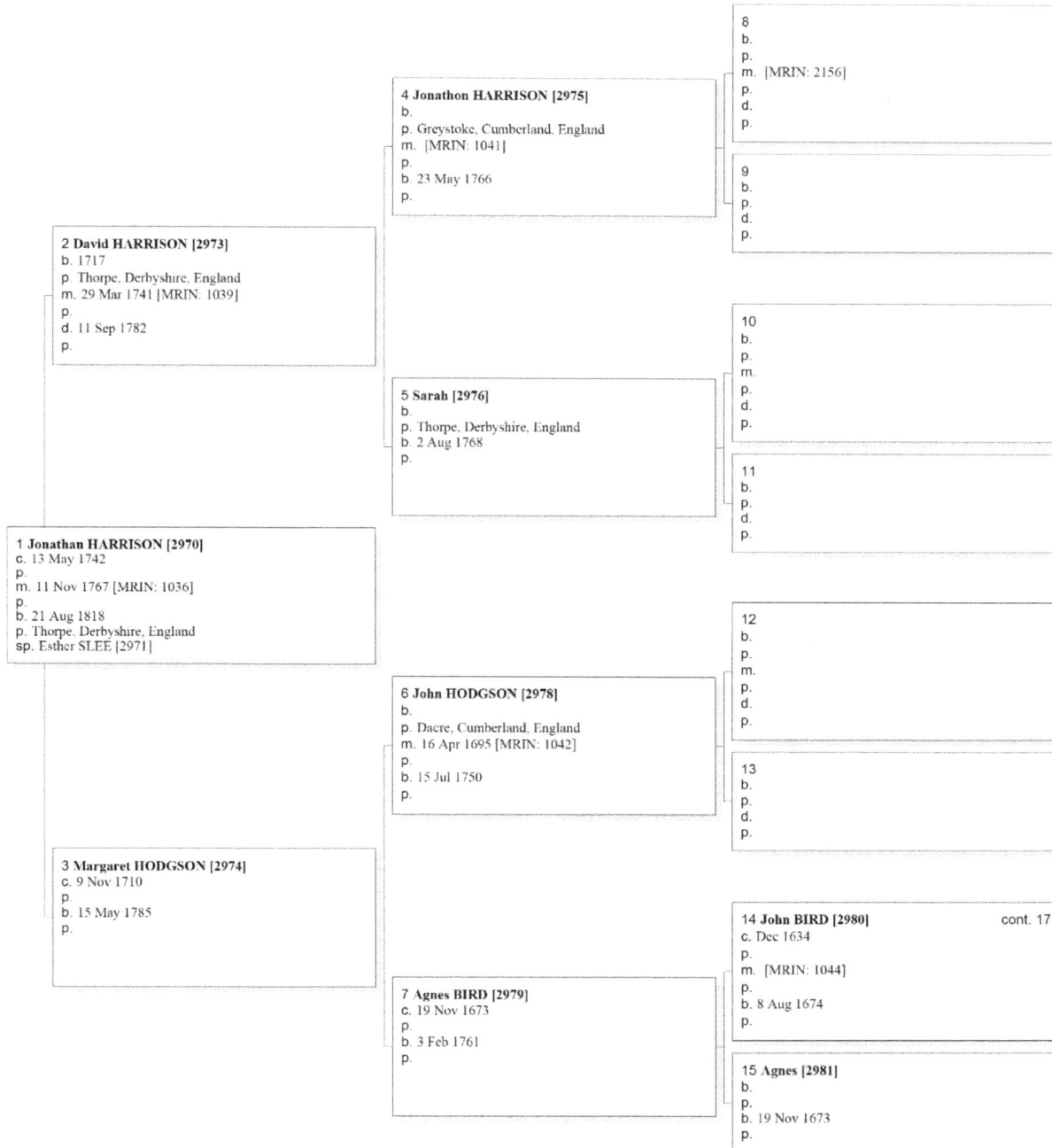

Chart no. 10

4 Jonathon HARRISON [2975]
b.
p. Greystoke, Cumberland, England
m. [MRIN: 1041]
p.
b. 23 May 1766
p.

2 David HARRISON [2973]
b. 1717
p. Thorpe, Derbyshire, England
m. 29 Mar 1741 [MRIN: 1039]
p.
d. 11 Sep 1782
p.

5 Sarah [2976]
b.
p. Thorpe, Derbyshire, England
b. 2 Aug 1768
p.

1 Jonathan HARRISON [2970]
c. 13 May 1742
p.
m. 11 Nov 1767 [MRIN: 1036]
p.
b. 21 Aug 1818
p. Thorpe, Derbyshire, England
sp. Esther SLEE [2971]

6 John HODGSON [2978]
b.
p. Dacre, Cumberland, England
m. 16 Apr 1695 [MRIN: 1042]
p.
b. 15 Jul 1750
p.

3 Margaret HODGSON [2974]
c. 9 Nov 1710
p.
b. 15 May 1785
p.

7 Agnes BIRD [2979]
c. 19 Nov 1673
p.
b. 3 Feb 1761
p.

8
b.
p.
m. [MRIN: 2156]
p.
d.
p.

9
b.
p.
d.
p.

10
b.
p.
m.
p.
d.
p.

11
b.
p.
d.
p.

12
b.
p.
m.
p.
d.
p.

13
b.
p.
d.
p.

14 John BIRD [2980]   cont. 17
c. Dec 1634
p.
m. [MRIN: 1044]
p.
b. 8 Aug 1674
p.

15 Agnes [2981]
b.
p.
b. 19 Nov 1673
p.

Pedigree Chart for Esther SLEE [2971]

Chart no. 11

No. 1 on this chart is the same as no. 15 on chart no. 2

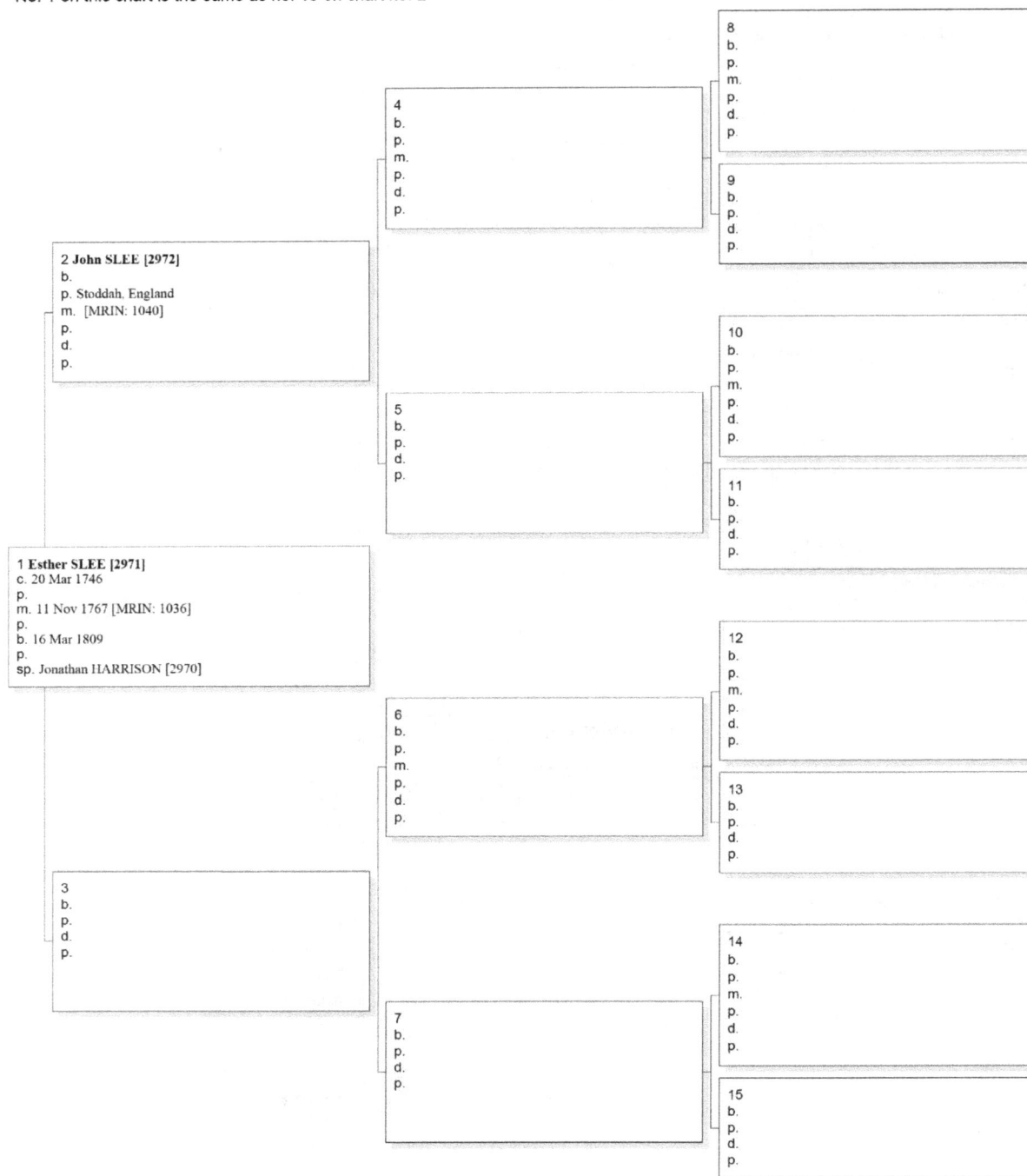

```
                                                          8
                                                          b.
                                                          p.
                                                          m.
                                    4                     p.
                                    b.                    d.
                                    p.                    p.
                                    m.
                                    p.                    9
                                    d.                    b.
                                    p.                    p.
                                                          d.
     2 John SLEE [2972]                                   p.
     b.
     p. Stoddah, England
     m.  [MRIN: 1040]                                     10
     p.                                                   b.
     d.                                                   p.
     p.                                                   m.
                                    5                     p.
                                    b.                    d.
                                    p.                    p.
                                    d.
                                    p.                    11
                                                          b.
     1 Esther SLEE [2971]                                 p.
     c. 20 Mar 1746                                       d.
     p.                                                   p.
     m. 11 Nov 1767 [MRIN: 1036]
     p.                                                   12
     b. 16 Mar 1809                                       b.
     p.                                                   p.
     sp. Jonathan HARRISON [2970]                         m.
                                    6                     p.
                                    b.                    d.
                                    p.                    p.
                                    m.
                                    p.                    13
                                    d.                    b.
                                    p.                    p.
                                                          d.
                                                          p.
     3
     b.                                                   14
     p.                                                   b.
     d.                                                   p.
     p.                                                   m.
                                                          p.
                                                          d.
                                    7                     p.
                                    b.
                                    p.                    15
                                    d.                    b.
                                    p.                    p.
                                                          d.
                                                          p.
```

Pedigree Chart for Robert Edward
STEPHENSON [5343]

Chart no. 12

No. 1 on this chart is the same as no. 8 on chart no. 4

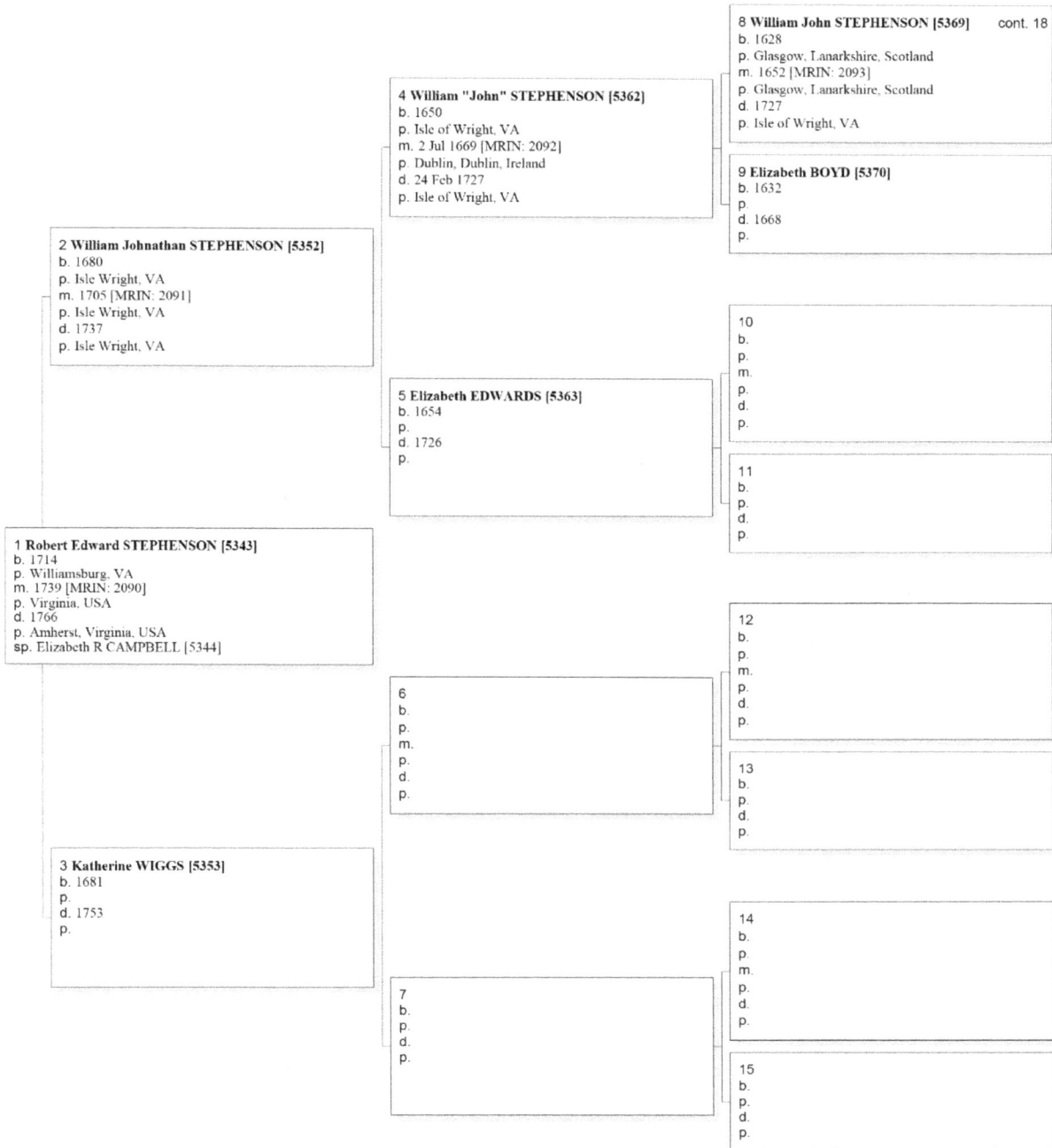

8 William John STEPHENSON [5369]   cont. 18
b. 1628
p. Glasgow, Lanarkshire, Scotland
m. 1652 [MRIN: 2093]
p. Glasgow, Lanarkshire, Scotland
d. 1727
p. Isle of Wight, VA

4 William "John" STEPHENSON [5362]
b. 1650
p. Isle of Wright, VA
m. 2 Jul 1669 [MRIN: 2092]
p. Dublin, Dublin, Ireland
d. 24 Feb 1727
p. Isle of Wright, VA

9 Elizabeth BOYD [5370]
b. 1632
p.
d. 1668
p.

2 William Johnathan STEPHENSON [5352]
b. 1680
p. Isle Wright, VA
m. 1705 [MRIN: 2091]
p. Isle Wright, VA
d. 1737
p. Isle Wright, VA

10
b.
p.
m.
p.
d.
p.

5 Elizabeth EDWARDS [5363]
b. 1654
p.
d. 1726
p.

11
b.
p.
d.
p.

1 Robert Edward STEPHENSON [5343]
b. 1714
p. Williamsburg, VA
m. 1739 [MRIN: 2090]
p. Virginia, USA
d. 1766
p. Amherst, Virginia, USA
sp. Elizabeth R CAMPBELL [5344]

12
b.
p.
m.
p.
d.
p.

6
b.
p.
m.
p.
d.
p.

13
b.
p.
d.
p.

3 Katherine WIGGS [5353]
b. 1681
p.
d. 1753
p.

14
b.
p.
m.
p.
d.
p.

7
b.
p.
d.
p.

15
b.
p.
d.
p.

Pedigree Chart for Johannas BENSEN III
[2405]

Chart no. 13

No. 1 on this chart is the same as no. 8 on chart no. 5

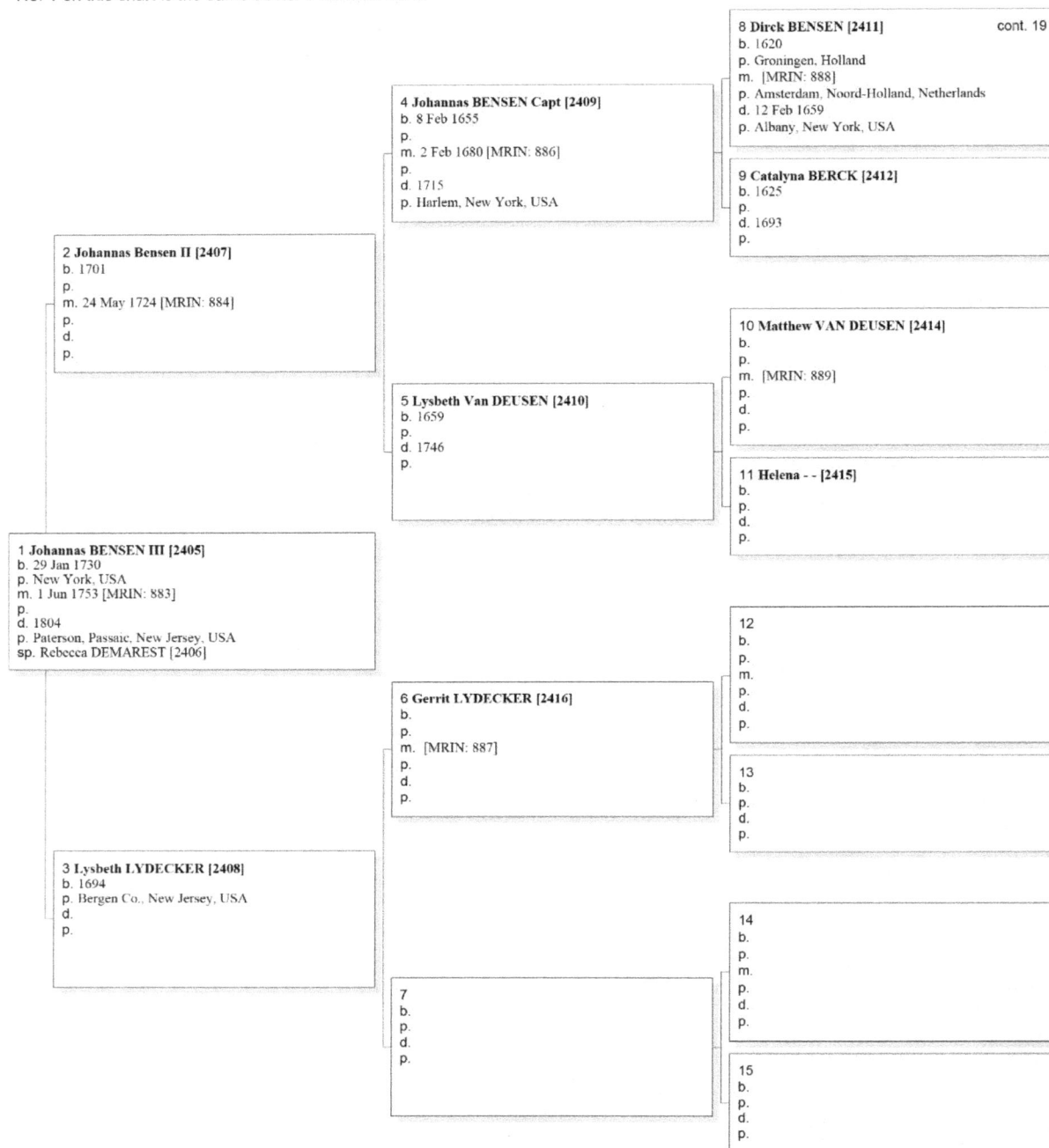

8 Dirck BENSEN [2411]   cont. 19
b. 1620
p. Groningen, Holland
m. [MRIN: 888]
p. Amsterdam, Noord-Holland, Netherlands
d. 12 Feb 1659
p. Albany, New York, USA

4 Johannas BENSEN Capt [2409]
b. 8 Feb 1655
p.
m. 2 Feb 1680 [MRIN: 886]
p.
d. 1715
p. Harlem, New York, USA

9 Catalyna BERCK [2412]
b. 1625
p.
d. 1693
p.

2 Johannas Bensen II [2407]
b. 1701
p.
m. 24 May 1724 [MRIN: 884]
p.
d.
p.

10 Matthew VAN DEUSEN [2414]
b.
p.
m. [MRIN: 889]
p.
d.
p.

5 Lysbeth Van DEUSEN [2410]
b. 1659
p.
d. 1746
p.

11 Helena - - [2415]
b.
p.
d.
p.

1 Johannas BENSEN III [2405]
b. 29 Jan 1730
p. New York, USA
m. 1 Jun 1753 [MRIN: 883]
p.
d. 1804
p. Paterson, Passaic, New Jersey, USA
sp. Rebecca DEMAREST [2406]

12
b.
p.
m.
p.
d.
p.

6 Gerrit LYDECKER [2416]
b.
p.
m. [MRIN: 887]
p.
d.
p.

13
b.
p.
d.
p.

3 Lysbeth LYDECKER [2408]
b. 1694
p. Bergen Co., New Jersey, USA
d.
p.

14
b.
p.
m.
p.
d.
p.

7
b.
p.
d.
p.

15
b.
p.
d.
p.

Pedigree Chart for Rebecca DEMAREST
[2406]

Chart no. 14

No. 1 on this chart is the same as no. 9 on chart no. 5

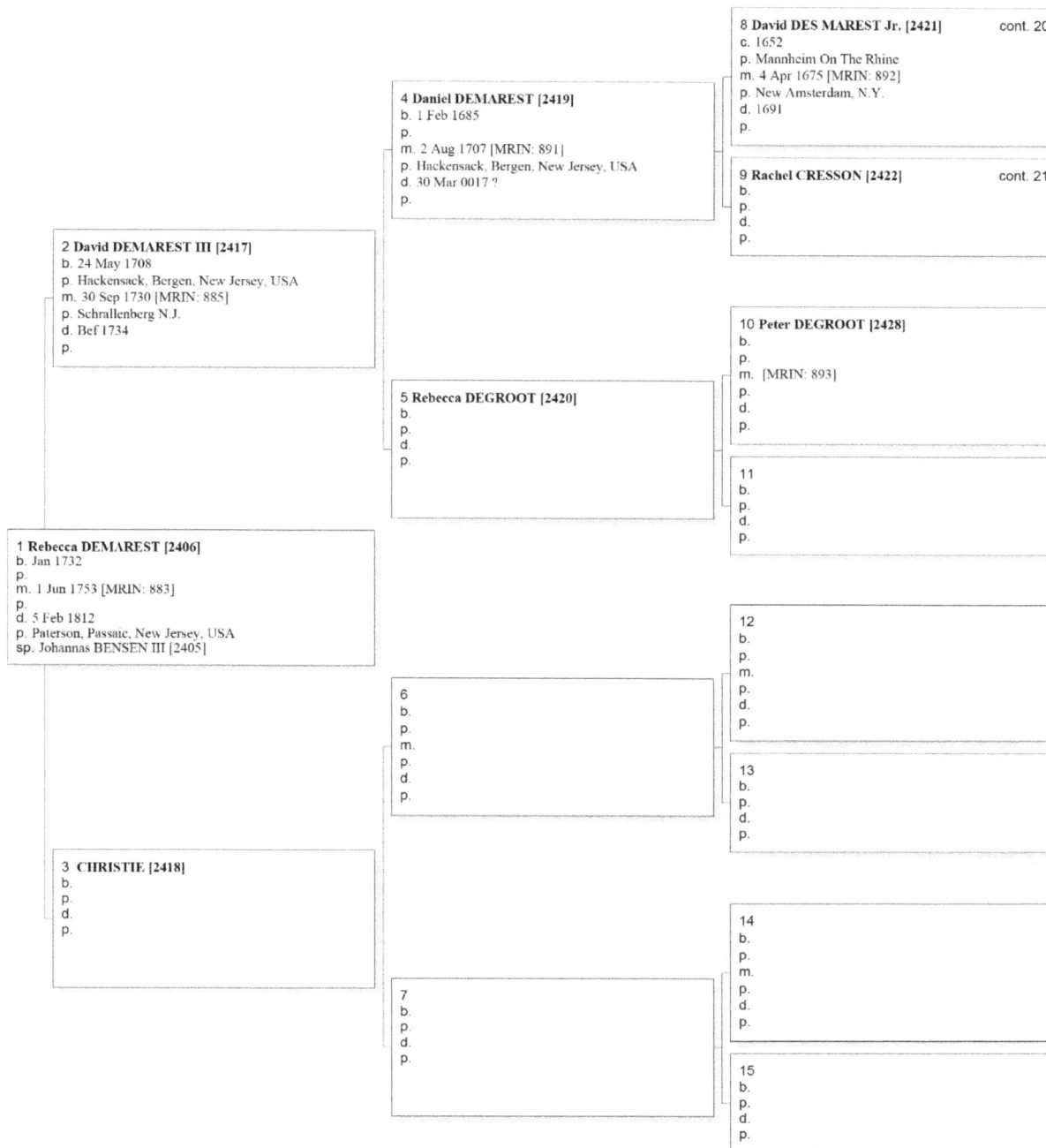

8 David DES MAREST Jr. [2421] cont. 20
c. 1652
p. Mannheim On The Rhine
m. 4 Apr 1675 [MRIN: 892]
p. New Amsterdam, N.Y.
d. 1691
p.

4 Daniel DEMAREST [2419]
b. 1 Feb 1685
p.
m. 2 Aug 1707 [MRIN: 891]
p. Hackensack, Bergen, New Jersey, USA
d. 30 Mar 0017 ?
p.

9 Rachel CRESSON [2422] cont. 21
b.
p.
d.
p.

2 David DEMAREST III [2417]
b. 24 May 1708
p. Hackensack, Bergen, New Jersey, USA
m. 30 Sep 1730 [MRIN: 885]
p. Schrallenberg N.J.
d. Bef 1734
p.

10 Peter DEGROOT [2428]
b.
p.
m. [MRIN: 893]
p.
d.
p.

5 Rebecca DEGROOT [2420]
b.
p.
d.
p.

11
b.
p.
d.
p.

1 Rebecca DEMAREST [2406]
b. Jan 1732
p.
m. 1 Jun 1753 [MRIN: 883]
p.
d. 5 Feb 1812
p. Paterson, Passaic, New Jersey, USA
sp. Johannas BENSEN III [2405]

12
b.
p.
m.
p.
d.
p.

6
b.
p.
m.
p.
d.
p.

13
b.
p.
d.
p.

3 CHRISTIE [2418]
b.
p.
d.
p.

14
b.
p.
m.
p.
d.
p.

7
b.
p.
d.
p.

15
b.
p.
d.
p.

Pedigree Chart for Casparus PRUYN [2394]

Chart no. 15

No. 1 on this chart is the same as no. 12 on chart no. 5

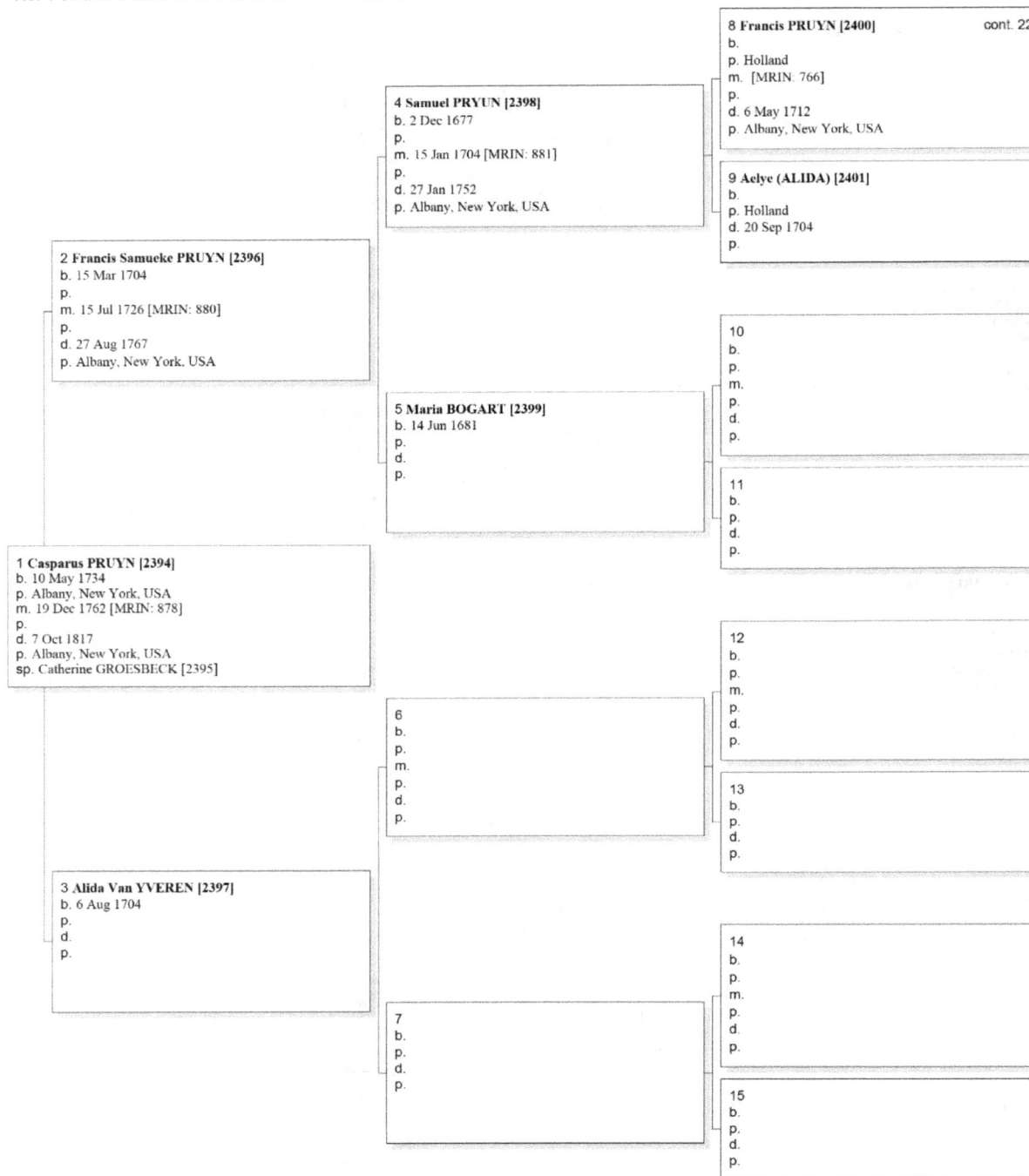

8 Francis PRUYN [2400]   cont. 22
b.
p. Holland
m. [MRIN: 766]
p.
d. 6 May 1712
p. Albany, New York, USA

9 Aelye (ALIDA) [2401]
b.
p. Holland
d. 20 Sep 1704
p.

4 Samuel PRYUN [2398]
b. 2 Dec 1677
p.
m. 15 Jan 1704 [MRIN: 881]
p.
d. 27 Jan 1752
p. Albany, New York, USA

2 Francis Samueke PRUYN [2396]
b. 15 Mar 1704
p.
m. 15 Jul 1726 [MRIN: 880]
p.
d. 27 Aug 1767
p. Albany, New York, USA

10
b.
p.
m.
p.
d.
p.

11
b.
p.
d.
p.

5 Maria BOGART [2399]
b. 14 Jun 1681
p.
d.
p.

1 Casparus PRUYN [2394]
b. 10 May 1734
p. Albany, New York, USA
m. 19 Dec 1762 [MRIN: 878]
p.
d. 7 Oct 1817
p. Albany, New York, USA
sp. Catherine GROESBECK [2395]

12
b.
p.
m.
p.
d.
p.

6
b.
p.
m.
p.
d.
p.

13
b.
p.
d.
p.

3 Alida Van YVEREN [2397]
b. 6 Aug 1704
p.
d.
p.

14
b.
p.
m.
p.
d.
p.

7
b.
p.
d.
p.

15
b.
p.
d.
p.

Pedigree Chart for John SMOOT [2665]

No. 1 on this chart is the same as no. 8 on chart no. 6

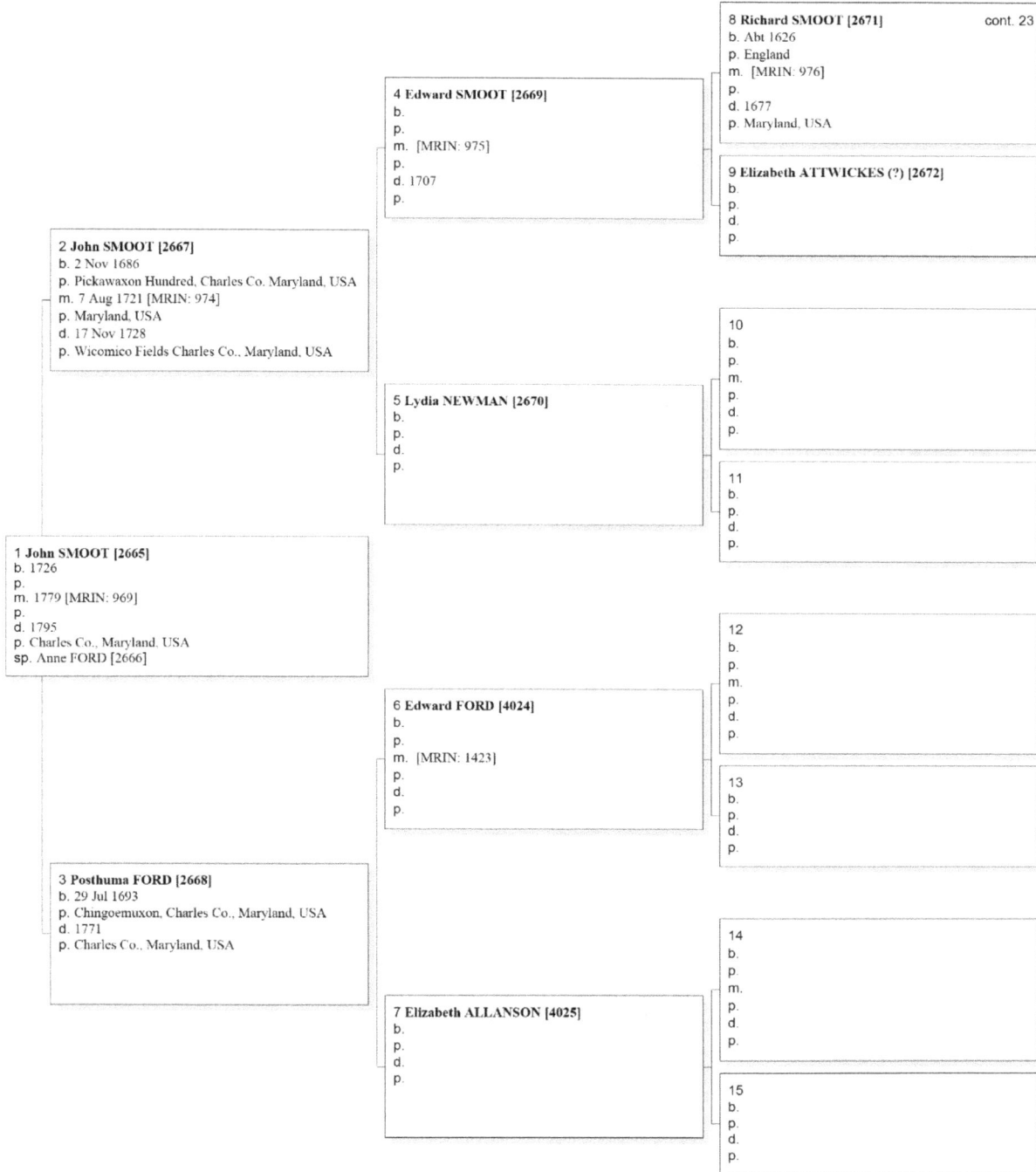

8 Richard SMOOT [2671]   cont. 23
b. Abt 1626
p. England
m. [MRIN: 976]
p.
d. 1677
p. Maryland, USA

4 Edward SMOOT [2669]
b.
p.
m. [MRIN: 975]
p.
d. 1707
p.

9 Elizabeth ATTWICKES (?) [2672]
b.
p.
d.
p.

2 John SMOOT [2667]
b. 2 Nov 1686
p. Pickawaxon Hundred, Charles Co. Maryland, USA
m. 7 Aug 1721 [MRIN: 974]
p. Maryland, USA
d. 17 Nov 1728
p. Wicomico Fields Charles Co., Maryland, USA

10
b.
p.
m.
p.
d.
p.

5 Lydia NEWMAN [2670]
b.
p.
d.
p.

11
b.
p.
d.
p.

1 John SMOOT [2665]
b. 1726
p.
m. 1779 [MRIN: 969]
p.
d. 1795
p. Charles Co., Maryland, USA
sp. Anne FORD [2666]

12
b.
p.
m.
p.
d.
p.

6 Edward FORD [4024]
b.
p.
m. [MRIN: 1423]
p.
d.
p.

13
b.
p.
d.
p.

3 Posthuma FORD [2668]
b. 29 Jul 1693
p. Chingoemuxon, Charles Co., Maryland, USA
d. 1771
p. Charles Co., Maryland, USA

14
b.
p.
m.
p.
d.
p.

7 Elizabeth ALLANSON [4025]
b.
p.
d.
p.

15
b.
p.
d.
p.

Pedigree Chart for John BIRD [2980]

No. 1 on this chart is the same as no. 14 on chart no. 10

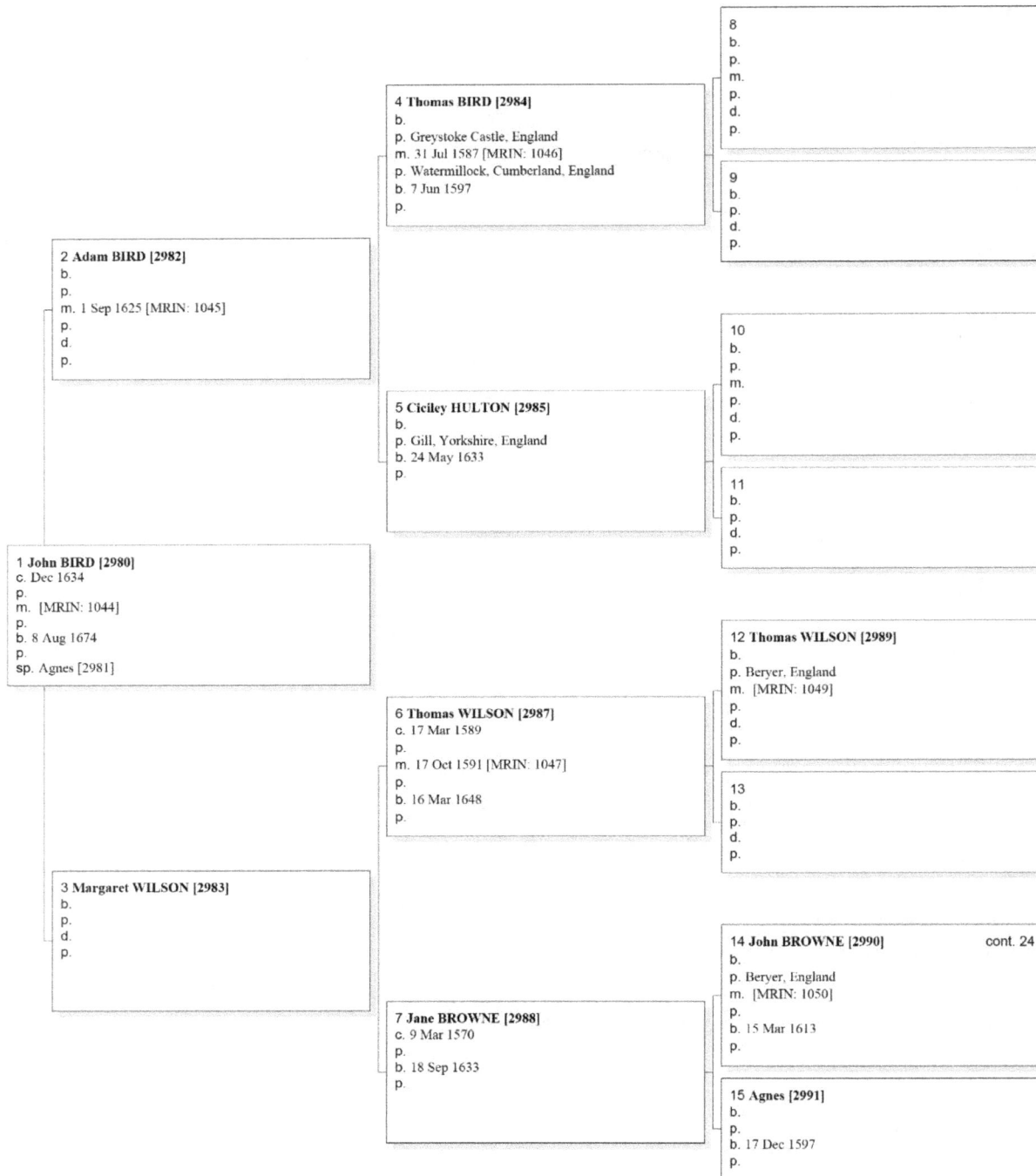

```
                                                                          8
                                                                          b.
                                                                          p.
                                                                          m.
                                           4 Thomas BIRD [2984]           p.
                                           b.                             d.
                                           p. Greystoke Castle, England   p.
                                           m. 31 Jul 1587 [MRIN: 1046]
                                           p. Watermillock, Cumberland, England
                                           b. 7 Jun 1597                  9
                                           p.                             b.
                                                                          p.
                                                                          d.
        2 Adam BIRD [2982]                                                p.
        b.
        p.
        m. 1 Sep 1625 [MRIN: 1045]
        p.                                                                10
        d.                                                                b.
        p.                                                                p.
                                                                          m.
                                           5 Ciciley HULTON [2985]        p.
                                           b.                             d.
                                           p. Gill, Yorkshire, England    p.
                                           b. 24 May 1633
                                           p.                             11
                                                                          b.
                                                                          p.
  1 John BIRD [2980]                                                      d.
  c. Dec 1634                                                             p.
  p.
  m.  [MRIN: 1044]
  p.
  b. 8 Aug 1674                                                           12 Thomas WILSON [2989]
  p.                                                                      b.
  sp. Agnes [2981]                                                        p. Beryer, England
                                                                          m.  [MRIN: 1049]
                                                                          p.
                                           6 Thomas WILSON [2987]         d.
                                           c. 17 Mar 1589                 p.
                                           p.
                                           m. 17 Oct 1591 [MRIN: 1047]
                                           p.                             13
                                           b. 16 Mar 1648                 b.
                                           p.                             p.
                                                                          d.
                                                                          p.

        3 Margaret WILSON [2983]
        b.
        p.                                                                14 John BROWNE [2990]        cont. 24
        d.                                                                b.
        p.                                                                p. Beryer, England
                                                                          m.  [MRIN: 1050]
                                                                          p.
                                           7 Jane BROWNE [2988]           b. 15 Mar 1613
                                           c. 9 Mar 1570                  p.
                                           p.
                                           b. 18 Sep 1633                 15 Agnes [2991]
                                           p.                             b.
                                                                          p.
                                                                          b. 17 Dec 1597
                                                                          p.
```

Pedigree Chart for William John
STEPHENSON [5369]

No. 1 on this chart is the same as no. 8 on chart no. 12

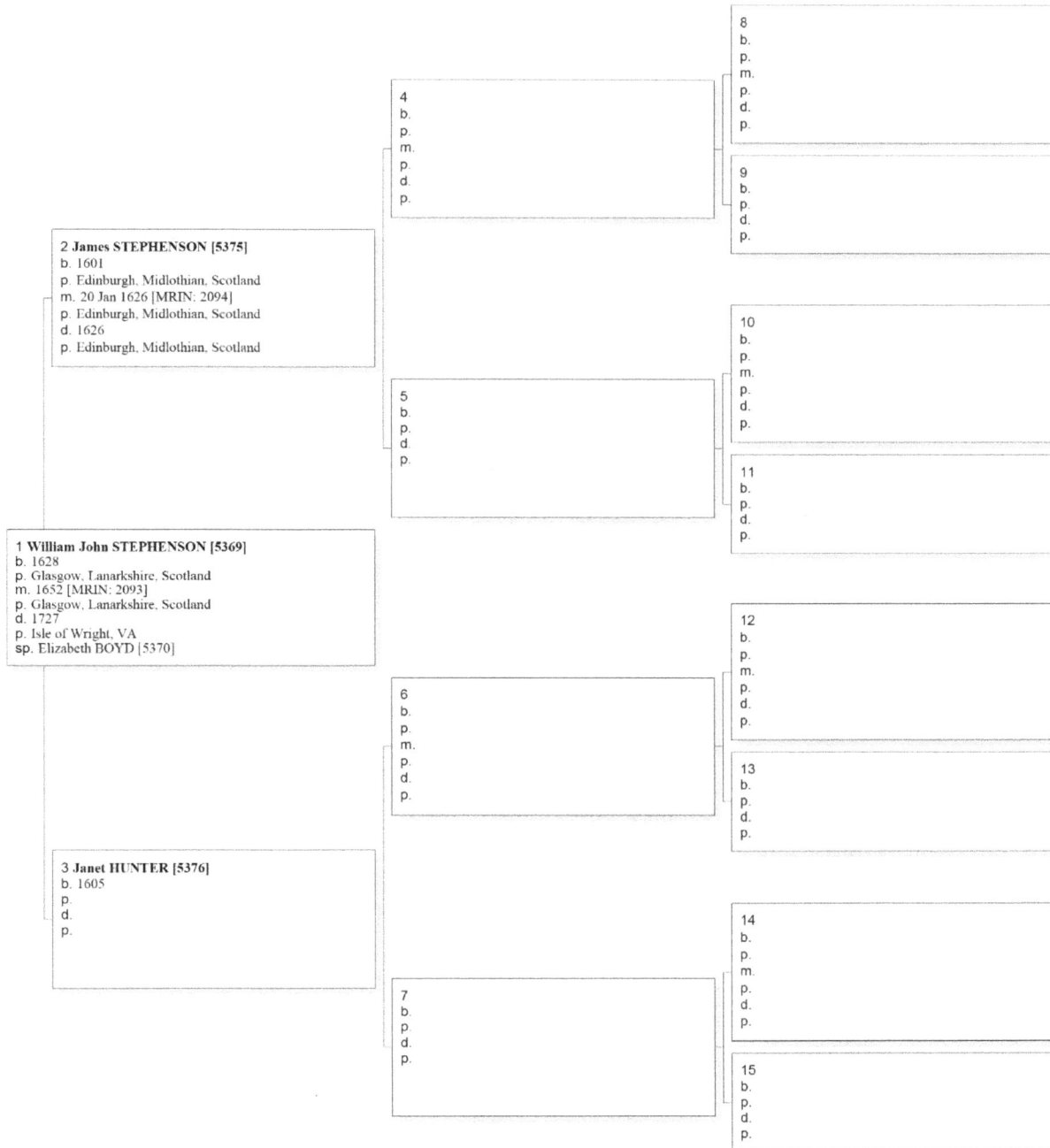

```
                                                              ┌──────────────────────┐
                                                              │ 8                    │
                                                              │ b.                   │
                                                              │ p.                   │
                                          ┌─────────────────┐ │ m.                   │
                                          │ 4               │ │ p.                   │
                                          │ b.              │ │ d.                   │
                                          │ p.              │ │ p.                   │
                                          │ m.              ├─┤                      │
                                          │ p.              │ └──────────────────────┘
                                          │ d.              │ ┌──────────────────────┐
                                          │ p.              │ │ 9                    │
           ┌──────────────────────────┐   │                 │ │ b.                   │
           │ 2 James STEPHENSON [5375]│   │                 │ │ p.                   │
           │ b. 1601                  │   │                 └─┤ d.                   │
           │ p. Edinburgh, Midlothian,│   │                   │ p.                   │
           │    Scotland              ├───┤                   └──────────────────────┘
           │ m. 20 Jan 1626 [MRIN: 2094]                       ┌──────────────────────┐
           │ p. Edinburgh, Midlothian,│   │                   │ 10                   │
           │    Scotland              │   │                   │ b.                   │
           │ d. 1626                  │   │ ┌─────────────────┐│ p.                   │
           │ p. Edinburgh, Midlothian,│   │ │ 5               ││ m.                   │
           │    Scotland              │   │ │ b.              ││ p.                   │
           └──────────────────────────┘   │ │ p.              ├┤ d.                   │
                                          └─┤ d.              ││ p.                   │
                                            │ p.              │└──────────────────────┘
                                            │                 │┌──────────────────────┐
                                            │                 ││ 11                   │
                                            │                 ││ b.                   │
                                            │                 └┤ p.                   │
                                            └─────────────────┘│ d.                   │
                                                               │ p.                   │
                                                               └──────────────────────┘
```

1 William John STEPHENSON [5369]
b. 1628
p. Glasgow, Lanarkshire, Scotland
m. 1652 [MRIN: 2093]
p. Glasgow, Lanarkshire, Scotland
d. 1727
p. Isle of Wright, VA
sp. Elizabeth BOYD [5370]

```
                                          ┌─────────────────┐ ┌──────────────────────┐
                                          │ 6               │ │ 12                   │
                                          │ b.              │ │ b.                   │
                                          │ p.              │ │ p.                   │
                                          │ m.              │ │ m.                   │
                                          │ p.              ├─┤ p.                   │
                                          │ d.              │ │ d.                   │
                                          │ p.              │ │ p.                   │
                                          │                 │ └──────────────────────┘
                                          │                 │ ┌──────────────────────┐
                                          │                 │ │ 13                   │
                                          │                 │ │ b.                   │
                                          │                 └─┤ p.                   │
           ┌──────────────────────────┐   │                   │ d.                   │
           │ 3 Janet HUNTER [5376]    │   │                   │ p.                   │
           │ b. 1605                  │   │                   └──────────────────────┘
           │ p.                       ├───┤
           │ d.                       │   │
           │ p.                       │   │                   ┌──────────────────────┐
           └──────────────────────────┘   │                   │ 14                   │
                                          │                   │ b.                   │
                                          │                   │ p.                   │
                                          │ ┌─────────────────┐│ m.                   │
                                          │ │ 7               ││ p.                   │
                                          │ │ b.              ├┤ d.                   │
                                          └─┤ p.              ││ p.                   │
                                            │ d.              │└──────────────────────┘
                                            │ p.              │┌──────────────────────┐
                                            │                 ││ 15                   │
                                            │                 ││ b.                   │
                                            │                 └┤ p.                   │
                                            └─────────────────┘│ d.                   │
                                                               │ p.                   │
                                                               └──────────────────────┘
```

Pedigree Chart for Dirck BENSEN [2411]

Chart no. 19

No. 1 on this chart is the same as no. 8 on chart no. 13

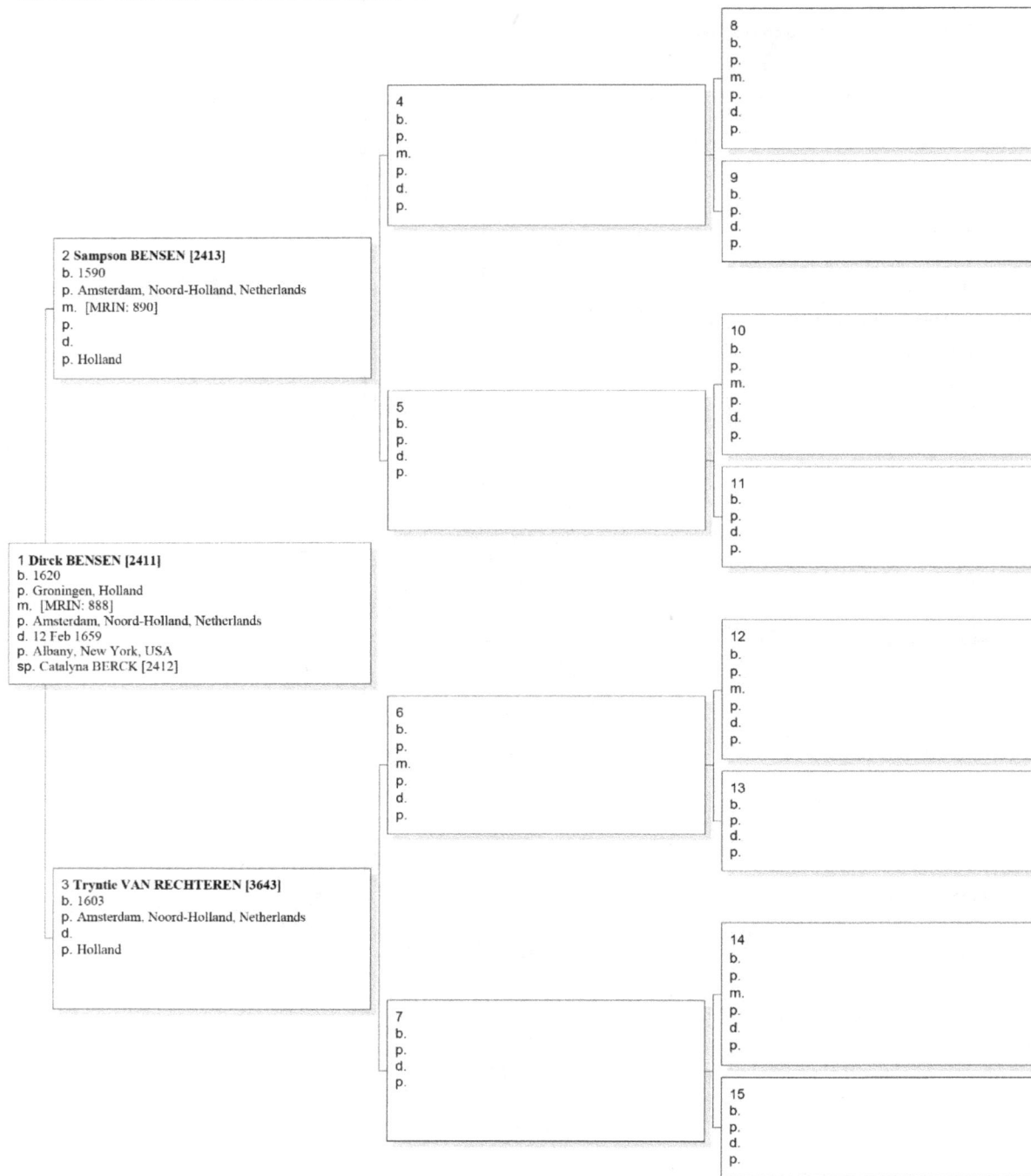

```
                                                          8
                                                          b.
                                                          p.
                                         4                m.
                                         b.               p.
                                         p.               d.
                                         m.               p.
                                         p.
            2 Sampson BENSEN [2413]      d.               9
            b. 1590                       p.              b.
            p. Amsterdam, Noord-Holland, Netherlands      p.
            m.  [MRIN: 890]                               d.
            p.                                            p.
            d.
            p. Holland                                    10
                                                          b.
                                                          p.
                                         5                m.
                                         b.               p.
                                         p.               d.
                                         d.               p.
                                         p.
                                                          11
1 Dirck BENSEN [2411]                                     b.
b. 1620                                                   p.
p. Groningen, Holland                                     d.
m.  [MRIN: 888]                                           p.
p. Amsterdam, Noord-Holland, Netherlands
d. 12 Feb 1659                                            12
p. Albany, New York, USA                                  b.
sp. Catalyna BERCK [2412]                                 p.
                                         6                m.
                                         b.               p.
                                         p.               d.
                                         m.               p.
                                         p.
                                         d.               13
                                         p.               b.
                                                          p.
                                                          d.
            3 Tryntie VAN RECHTEREN [3643]                p.
            b. 1603
            p. Amsterdam, Noord-Holland, Netherlands      14
            d.                                            b.
            p. Holland                                    p.
                                                          m.
                                         7                p.
                                         b.               d.
                                         p.               p.
                                         d.
                                         p.               15
                                                          b.
                                                          p.
                                                          d.
                                                          p.
```

Pedigree Chart for David DES MAREST Jr.
[2421]

No. 1 on this chart is the same as no. 8 on chart no. 14

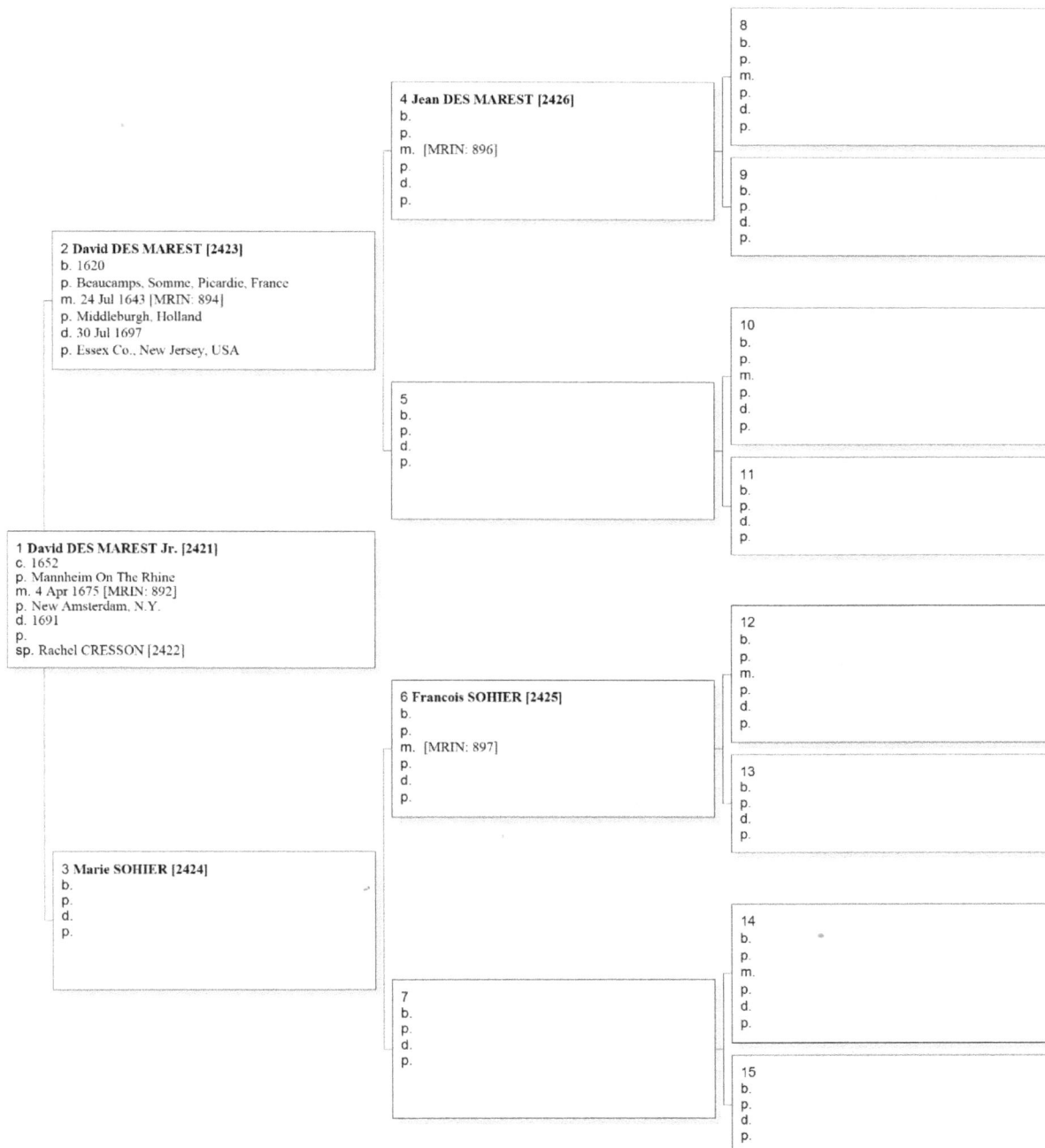

Chart no. 20

2 David DES MAREST [2423]
b. 1620
p. Beaucamps, Somme, Picardie, France
m. 24 Jul 1643 [MRIN: 894]
p. Middleburgh, Holland
d. 30 Jul 1697
p. Essex Co., New Jersey, USA

1 David DES MAREST Jr. [2421]
c. 1652
p. Mannheim On The Rhine
m. 4 Apr 1675 [MRIN: 892]
p. New Amsterdam, N.Y.
d. 1691
p.
sp. Rachel CRESSON [2422]

3 Marie SOHIER [2424]
b.
p.
d.
p.

4 Jean DES MAREST [2426]
b.
p.
m. [MRIN: 896]
p.
d.
p.

5
b.
p.
d.
p.

6 Francois SOHIER [2425]
b.
p.
m. [MRIN: 897]
p.
d.
p.

7
b.
p.
d.
p.

8
b.
p.
m.
p.
d.
p.

9
b.
p.
d.
p.

10
b.
p.
m.
p.
d.
p.

11
b.
p.
d.
p.

12
b.
p.
m.
p.
d.
p.

13
b.
p.
d.
p.

14
b.
p.
m.
p.
d.
p.

15
b.
p.
d.
p.

Pedigree Chart for Rachel CRESSON [2422]

No. 1 on this chart is the same as no. 9 on chart no. 14

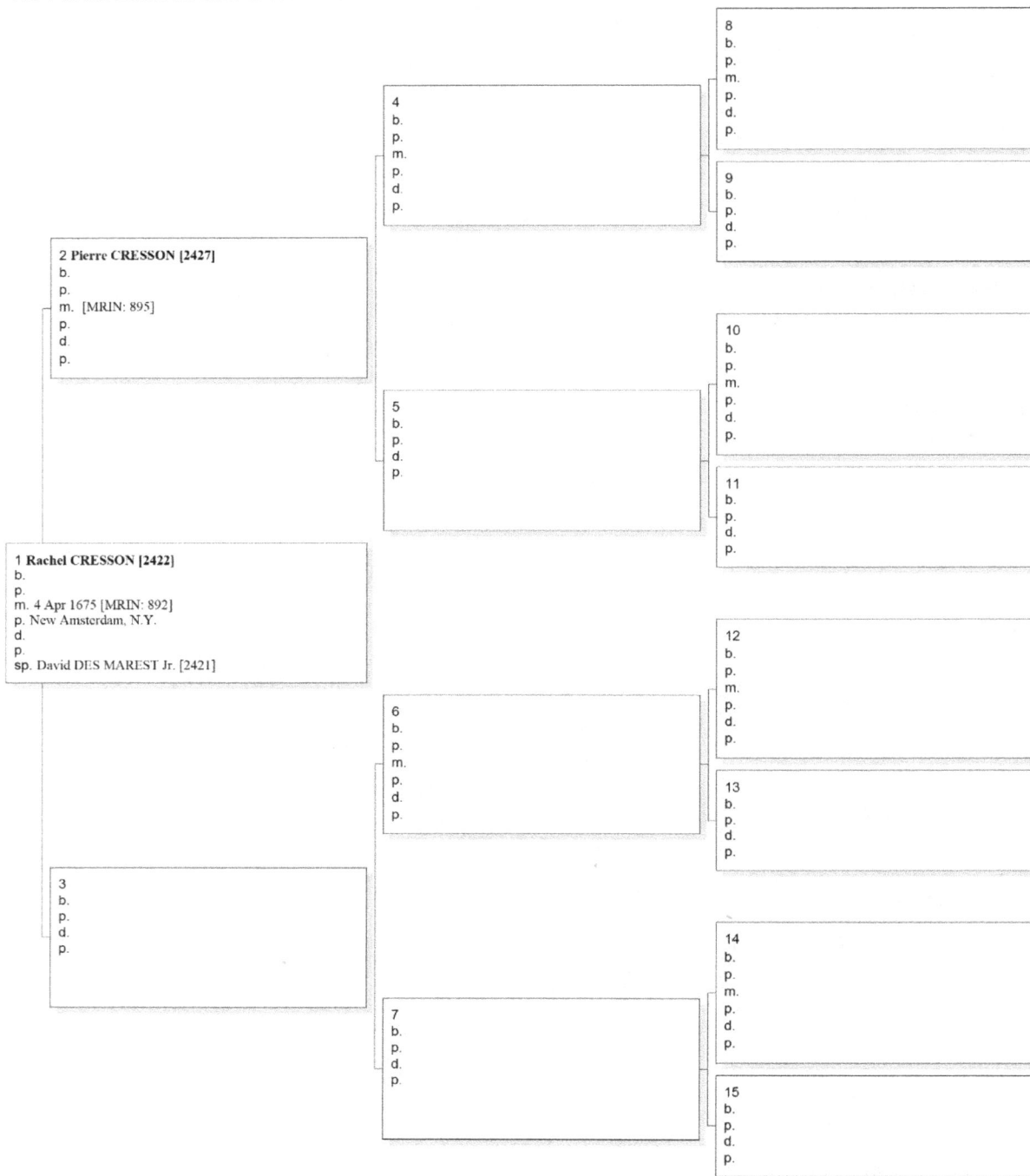

```
                                                              8
                                                              b.
                                                              p.
                                                              m.
                                          4                   p.
                                          b.                  d.
                                          p.                  p.
                                          m.
                                          p.                  9
                                          d.                  b.
                                          p.                  p.
                                                              d.
         2 Pierre CRESSON [2427]                              p.
         b.
         p.
         m.  [MRIN: 895]                                      10
         p.                                                   b.
         d.                                                   p.
         p.                                                   m.
                                          5                   p.
                                          b.                  d.
                                          p.                  p.
                                          d.
                                          p.                  11
                                                              b.
                                                              p.
                                                              d.
 1 Rachel CRESSON [2422]                                      p.
 b.
 p.
 m. 4 Apr 1675 [MRIN: 892]
 p. New Amsterdam, N.Y.
 d.                                                           12
 p.                                                           b.
 sp. David DES MAREST Jr. [2421]                              p.
                                                              m.
                                          6                   p.
                                          b.                  d.
                                          p.                  p.
                                          m.
                                          p.                  13
                                          d.                  b.
                                          p.                  p.
                                                              d.
                                                              p.
         3
         b.
         p.
         d.                                                   14
         p.                                                   b.
                                                              p.
                                                              m.
                                          7                   p.
                                          b.                  d.
                                          p.                  p.
                                          d.
                                          p.                  15
                                                              b.
                                                              p.
                                                              d.
                                                              p.
```

Pedigree Chart for Francis PRUYN [2400]

No. 1 on this chart is the same as no. 8 on chart no. 15

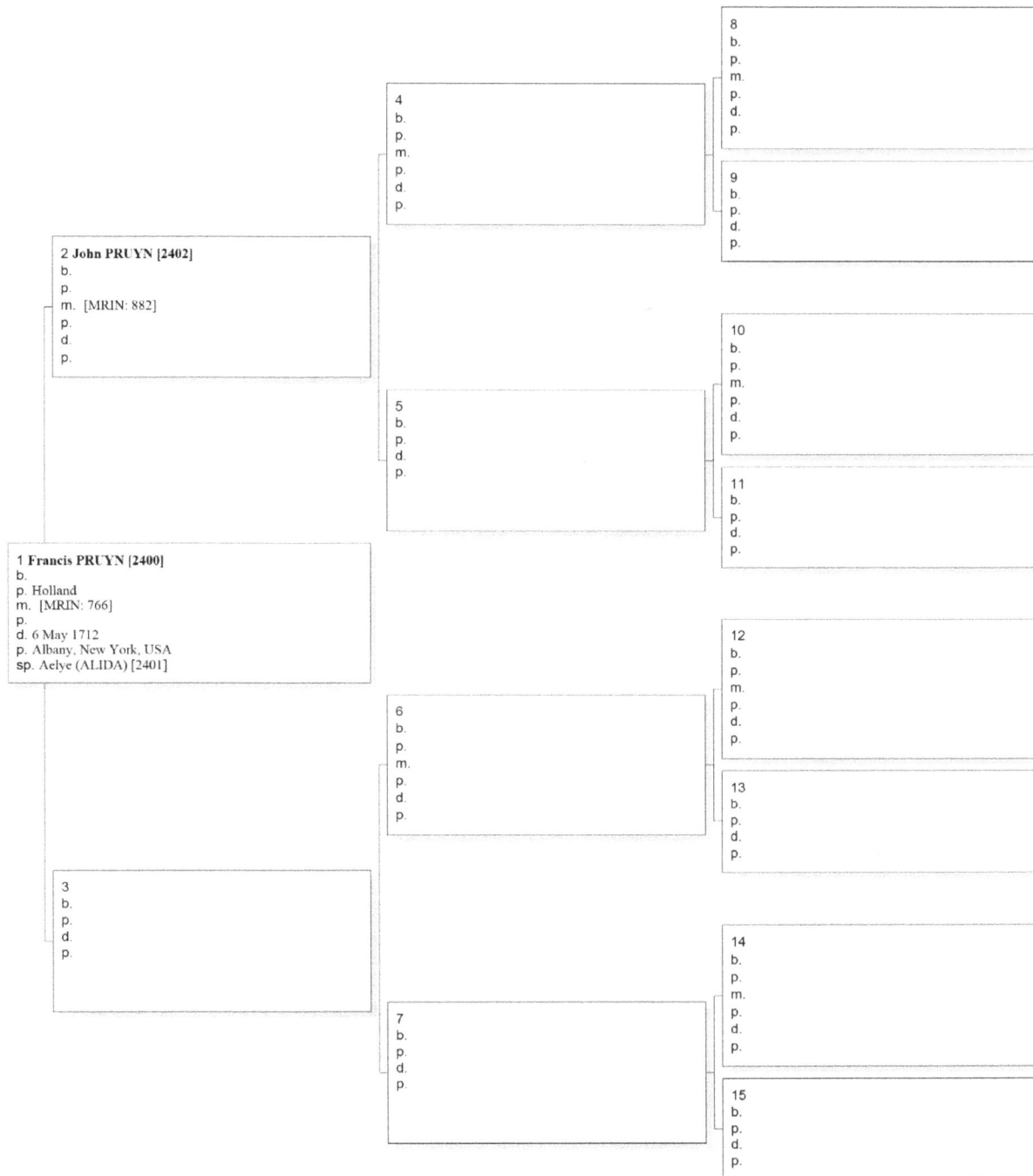

```
                                                                    8
                                                                    b.
                                                                    p.
                                                                    m.
                                            4                       p.
                                            b.                      d.
                                            p.                      p.
                                            m.
                                            p.                      9
                                            d.                      b.
                                            p.                      p.
                                                                    d.
                                                                    p.
        2 John PRUYN [2402]
        b.
        p.
        m. [MRIN: 882]                                              10
        p.                                                          b.
        d.                                                          p.
        p.                                                          m.
                                            5                       p.
                                            b.                      d.
                                            p.                      p.
                                            d.
                                            p.                      11
                                                                    b.
                                                                    p.
                                                                    d.
    1 Francis PRUYN [2400]                                          p.
    b.
    p. Holland
    m. [MRIN: 766]                                                  12
    p.                                                              b.
    d. 6 May 1712                                                   p.
    p. Albany, New York, USA                                       m.
    sp. Aelye (ALIDA) [2401]                                        p.
                                            6                       d.
                                            b.                      p.
                                            p.
                                            m.                      13
                                            p.                      b.
                                            d.                      p.
                                            p.                      d.
                                                                    p.
        3
        b.
        p.
        d.                                                          14
        p.                                                          b.
                                                                    p.
                                                                    m.
                                            7                       p.
                                            b.                      d.
                                            p.                      p.
                                            d.
                                            p.                      15
                                                                    b.
                                                                    p.
                                                                    d.
                                                                    p.
```

Pedigree Chart for Richard SMOOT [2671]

Chart no. 23

No. 1 on this chart is the same as no. 8 on chart no. 16

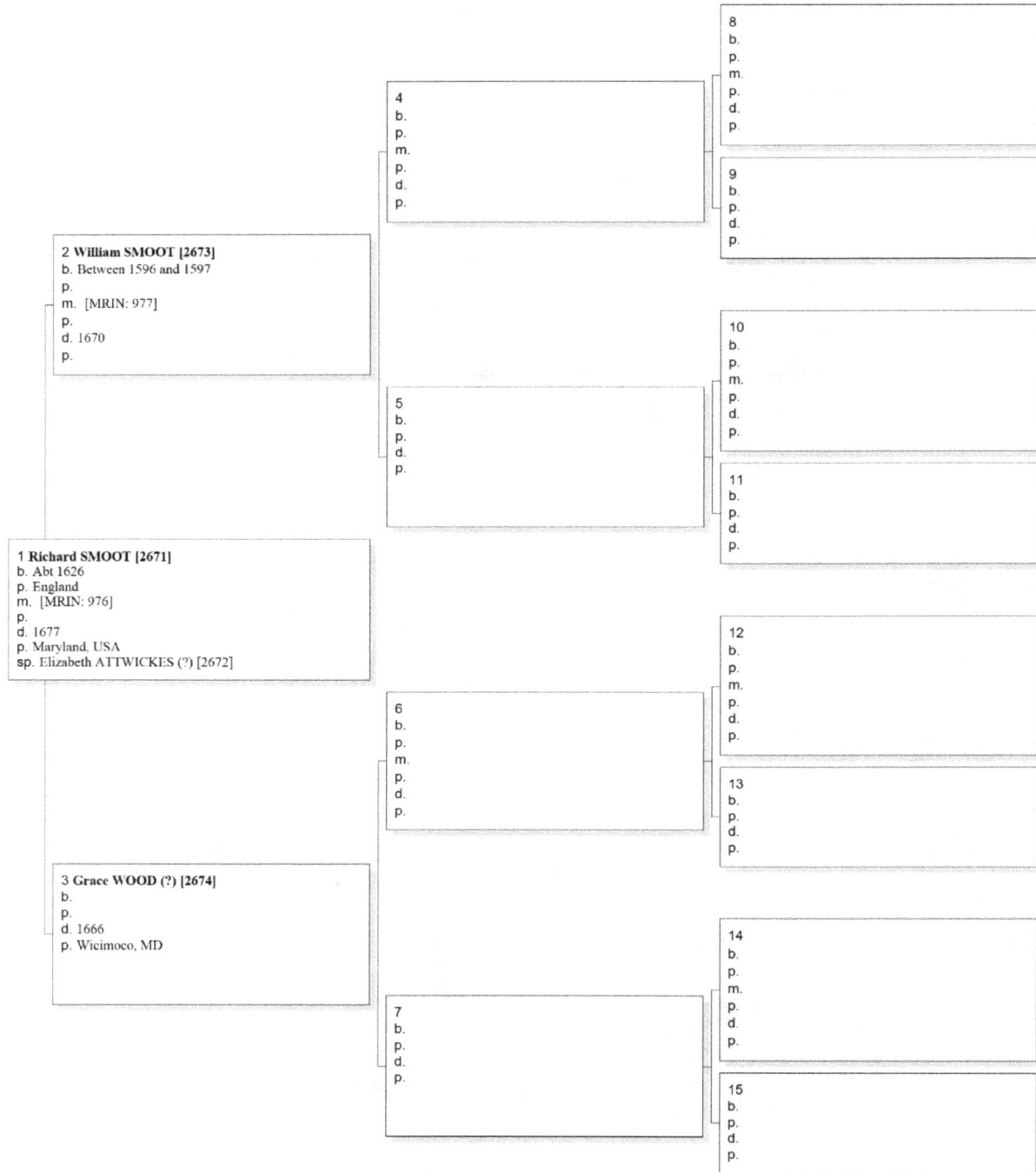

```
8
b.
p.
m.
p.
d.
p.

9
b.
p.
d.
p.
```

```
4
b.
p.
m.
p.
d.
p.
```

```
10
b.
p.
m.
p.
d.
p.

11
b.
p.
d.
p.
```

```
5
b.
p.
d.
p.
```

2 William SMOOT [2673]
b. Between 1596 and 1597
p.
m. [MRIN: 977]
p.
d. 1670
p.

1 Richard SMOOT [2671]
b. Abt 1626
p. England
m. [MRIN: 976]
p.
d. 1677
p. Maryland, USA
sp. Elizabeth ATTWICKES (?) [2672]

```
12
b.
p.
m.
p.
d.
p.

13
b.
p.
d.
p.
```

```
6
b.
p.
m.
p.
d.
p.
```

3 Grace WOOD (?) [2674]
b.
p.
d. 1666
p. Wicimoco, MD

```
14
b.
p.
m.
p.
d.
p.

15
b.
p.
d.
p.
```

```
7
b.
p.
d.
p.
```

Pedigree Chart for John BROWNE [2990]

No. 1 on this chart is the same as no. 14 on chart no. 17

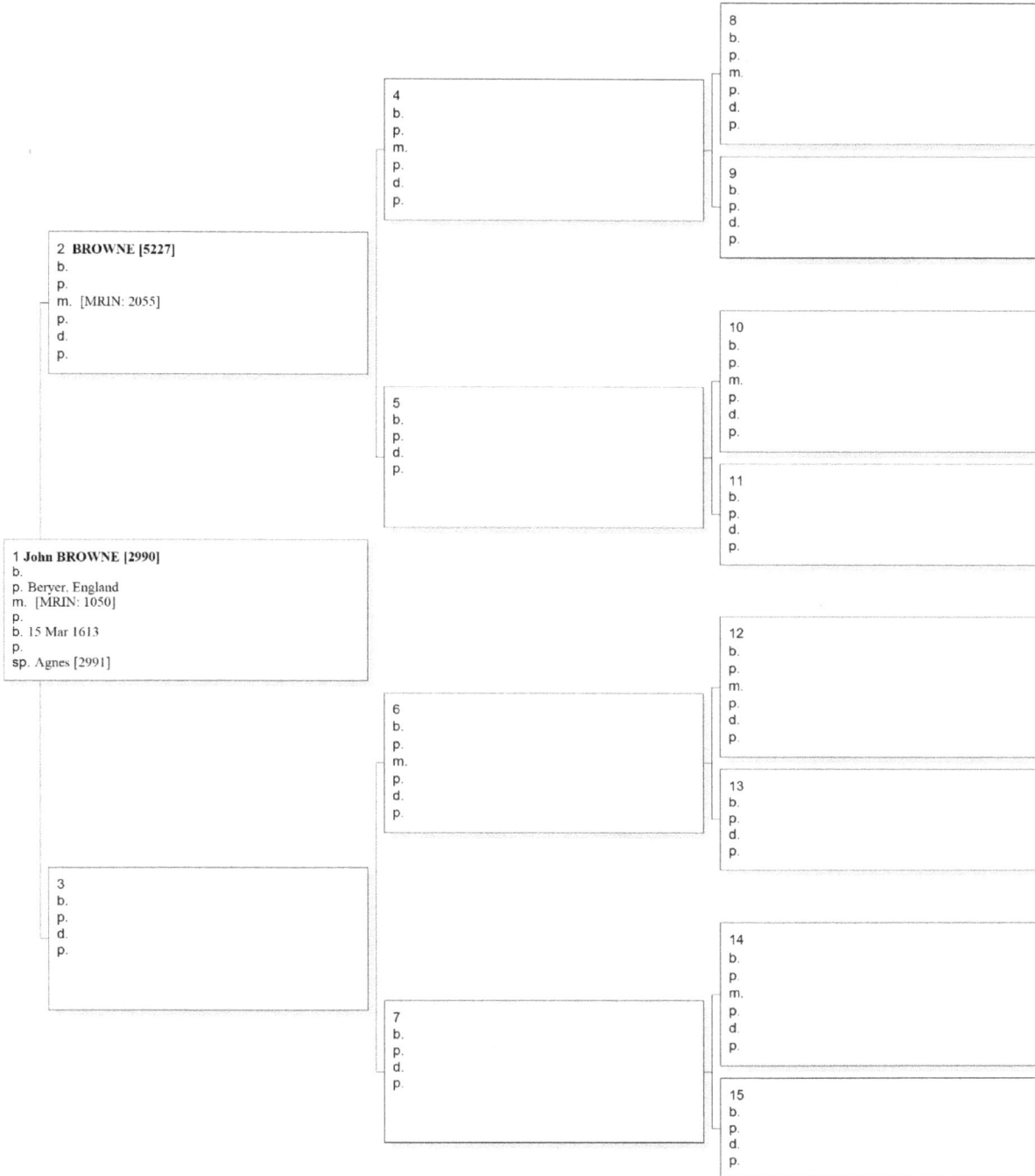

Chart no. 24

```
                                                    ┌──────────────────
                                                    │ 8
                                                    │ b.
                                                    │ p.
                                                    │ m.
                            ┌──────────────┐         │ p.
                            │ 4            │         │ d.
                            │ b.           │         │ p.
                            │ p.           │         └──────────────────
                            │ m.           │
                            │ p.           │         ┌──────────────────
                            │ d.           │         │ 9
                            │ p.           │         │ b.
          ┌──────────────┐  └──────────────┘         │ p.
          │ 2  BROWNE    │                           │ d.
          │   [5227]     │                           │ p.
          │ b.           │                           └──────────────────
          │ p.           │
          │ m. [MRIN:2055]│                          ┌──────────────────
          │ p.           │                           │ 10
          │ d.           │                           │ b.
          │ p.           │                           │ p.
          └──────────────┘  ┌──────────────┐         │ m.
                            │ 5            │         │ p.
                            │ b.           │         │ d.
                            │ p.           │         │ p.
                            │ d.           │         └──────────────────
                            │ p.           │
                            └──────────────┘         ┌──────────────────
                                                    │ 11
                                                    │ b.
                                                    │ p.
                                                    │ d.
                                                    │ p.
                                                    └──────────────────
```

1 John BROWNE [2990]
b.
p. Beryer, England
m. [MRIN: 1050]
p.
b. 15 Mar 1613
p.
sp. Agnes [2991]

```
                            ┌──────────────┐         ┌──────────────────
                            │ 6            │         │ 12
                            │ b.           │         │ b.
                            │ p.           │         │ p.
                            │ m.           │         │ m.
                            │ p.           │         │ p.
                            │ d.           │         │ d.
                            │ p.           │         │ p.
          ┌──────────────┐  └──────────────┘         └──────────────────
          │ 3            │                           ┌──────────────────
          │ b.           │                           │ 13
          │ p.           │                           │ b.
          │ d.           │                           │ p.
          │ p.           │                           │ d.
          └──────────────┘                           │ p.
                                                    └──────────────────
                            ┌──────────────┐         ┌──────────────────
                            │ 7            │         │ 14
                            │ b.           │         │ b.
                            │ p.           │         │ p.
                            │ d.           │         │ m.
                            │ p.           │         │ p.
                            └──────────────┘         │ d.
                                                    │ p.
                                                    └──────────────────
                                                    ┌──────────────────
                                                    │ 15
                                                    │ b.
                                                    │ p.
                                                    │ d.
                                                    │ p.
                                                    └──────────────────
```

Appendix B – Maps

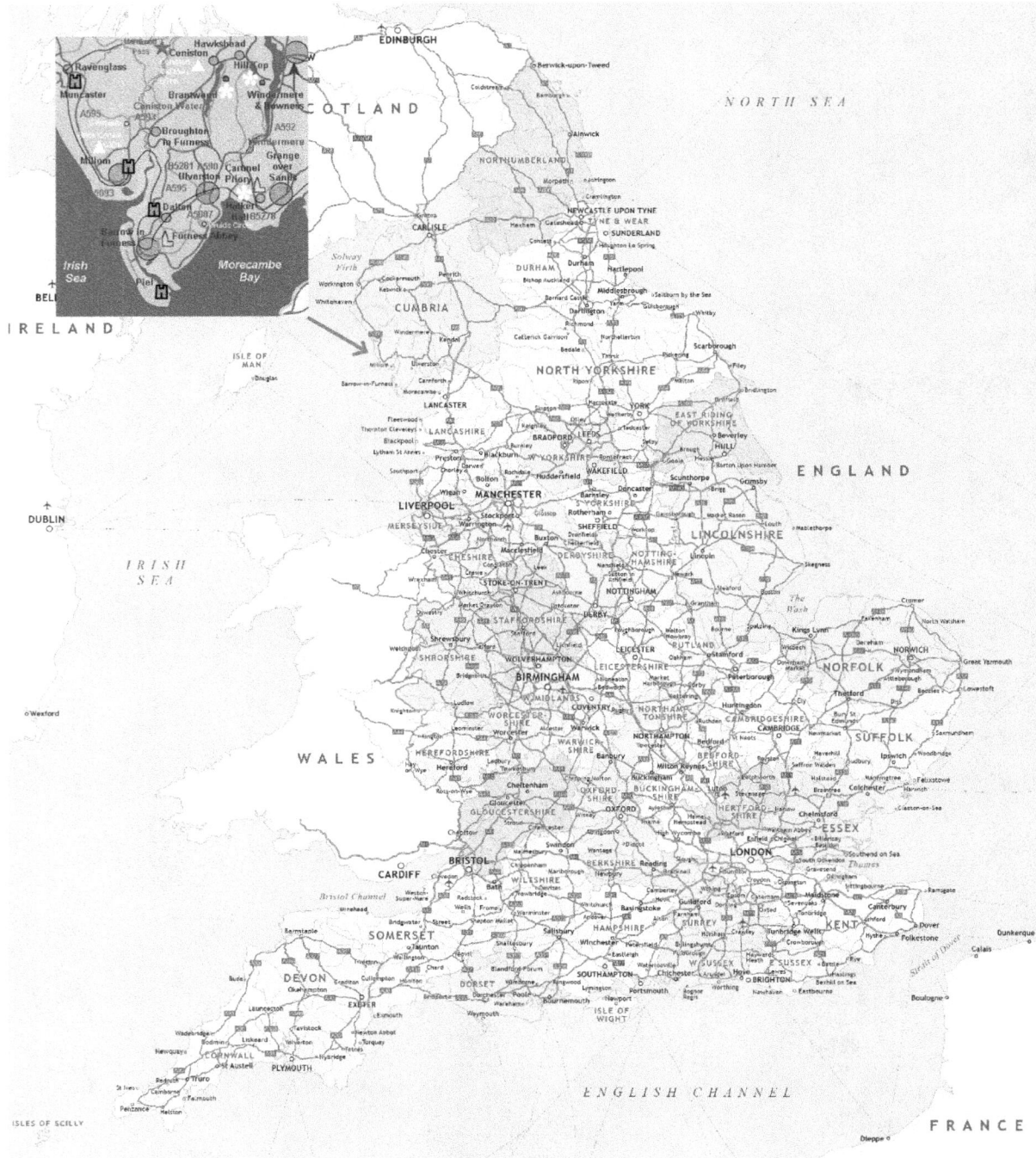

England and Cumbria County City Detail

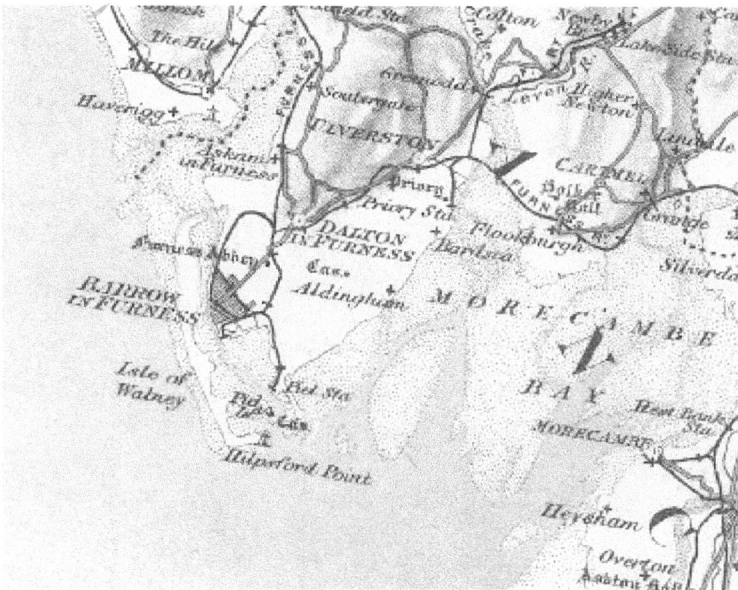

Broughton In Furness, Millom

Cumbria County

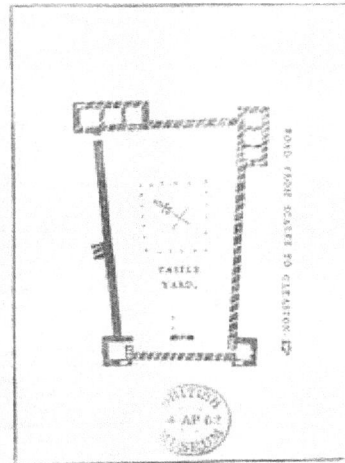

Aldingham, Gleaston Castle and map of Gleaston Castle

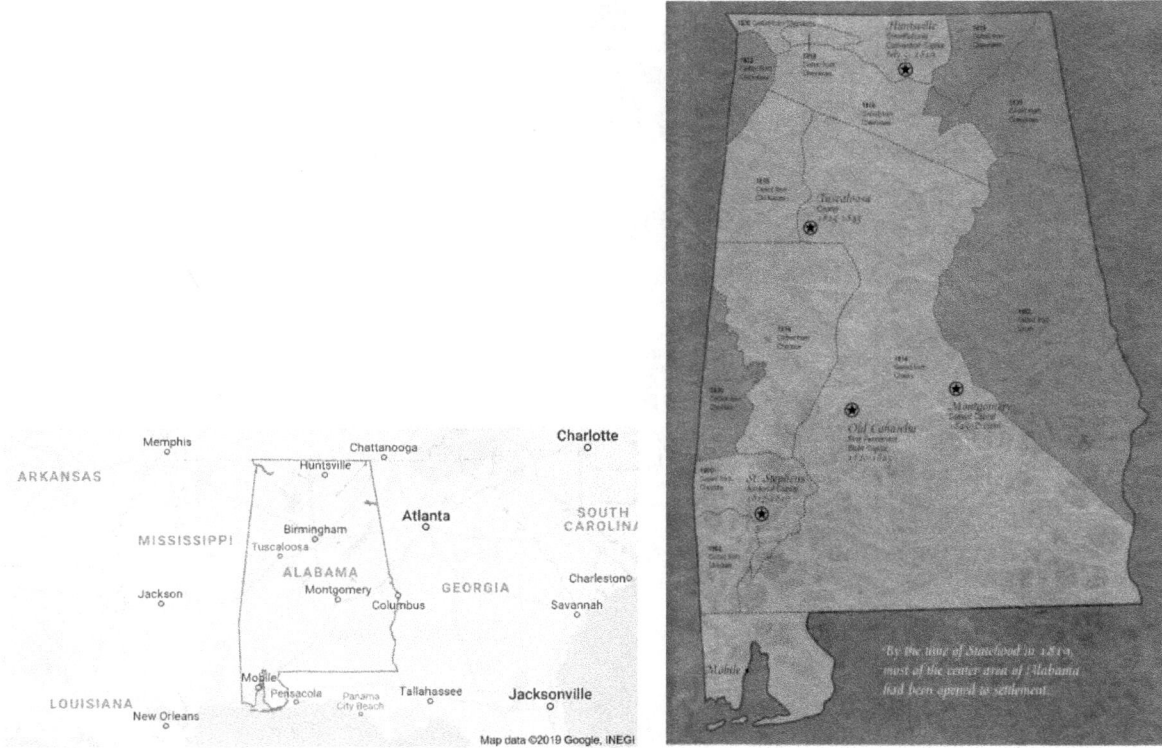

Alabama and Detail Map with Old Cahawba

Map of United States

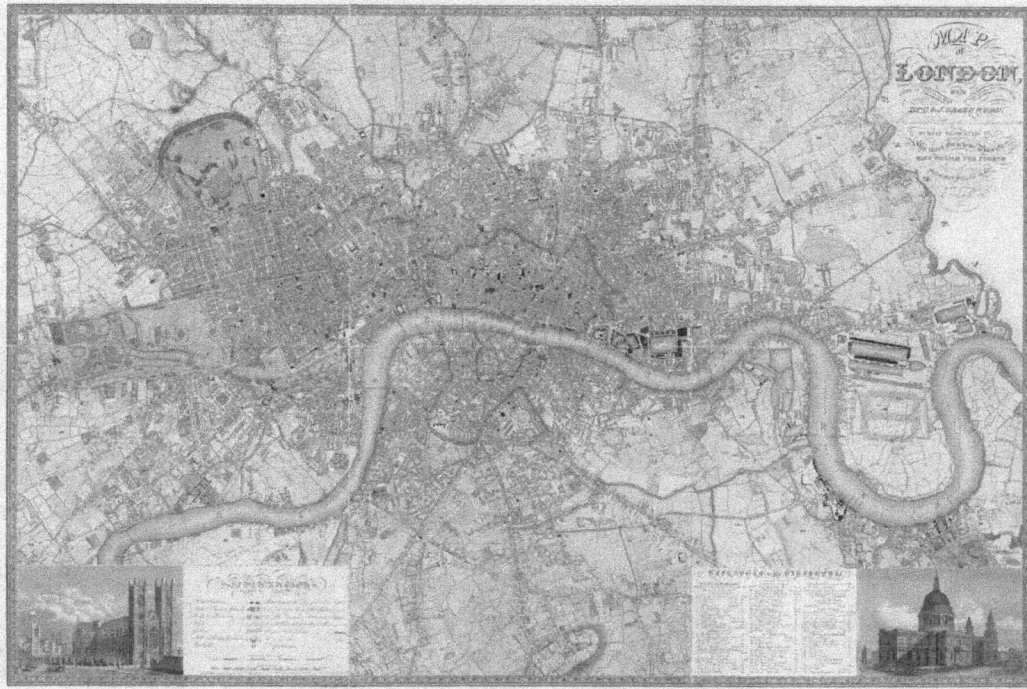

London England Map from King William IV

New York State Map

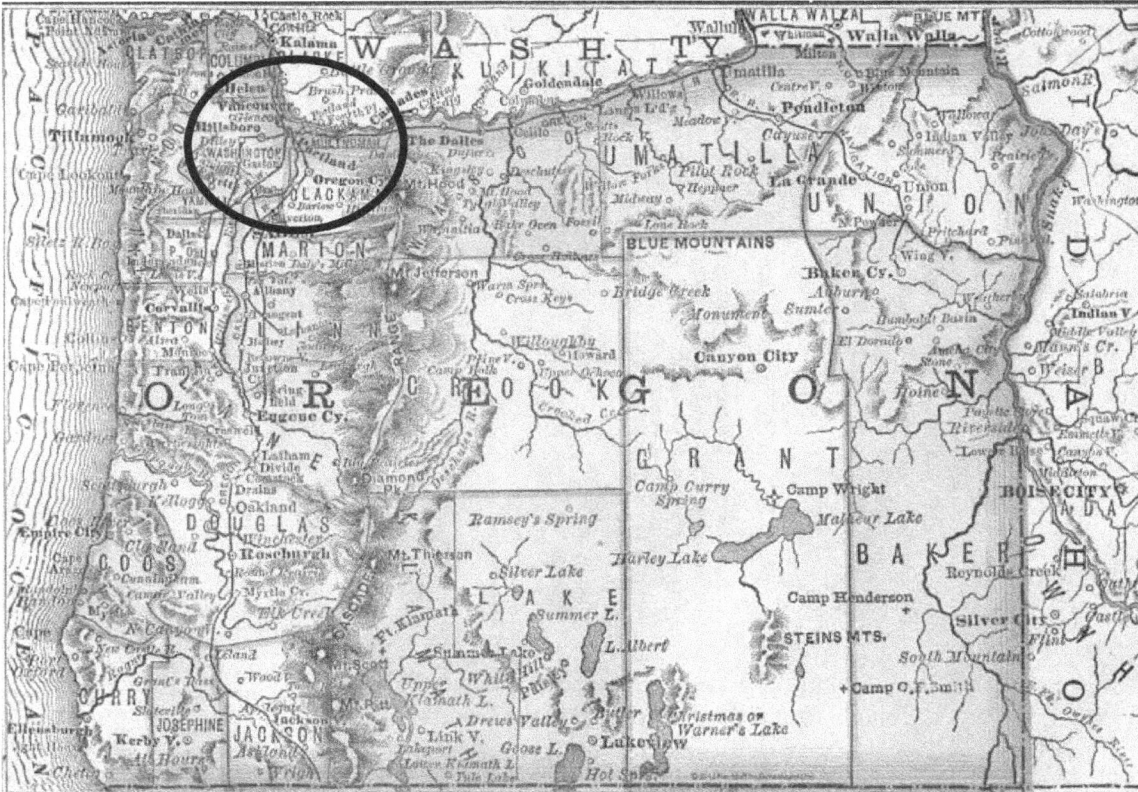

Oregon State Map

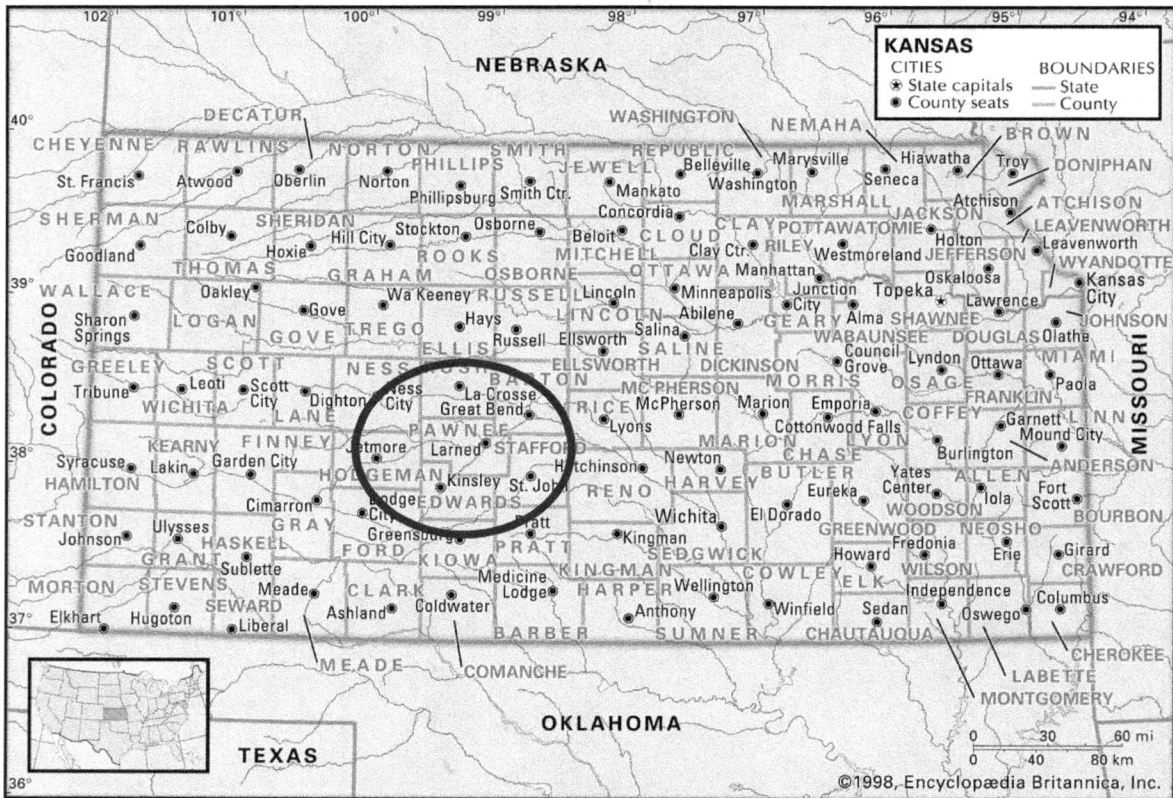

Kansas Counties

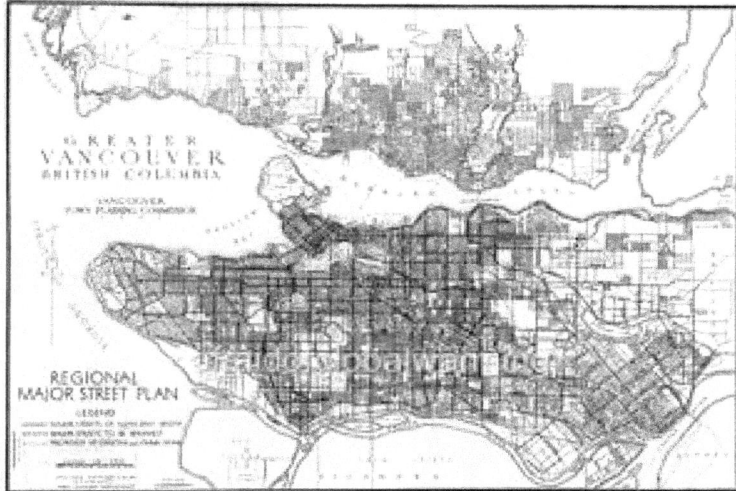

Vancouver British Columbia Canada Map

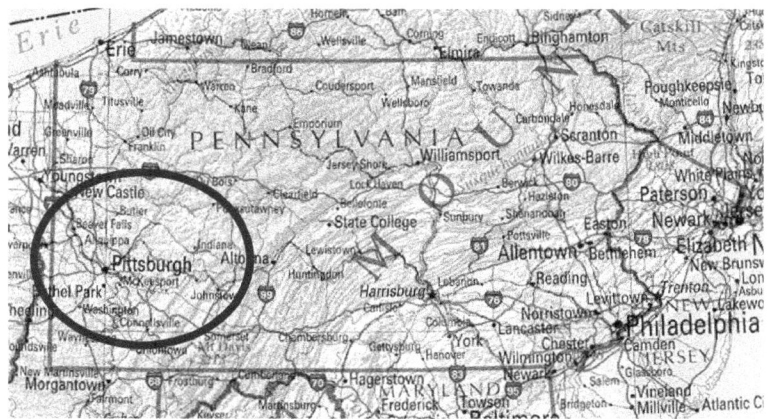

Illinois State Map

Pennsylvania State Map

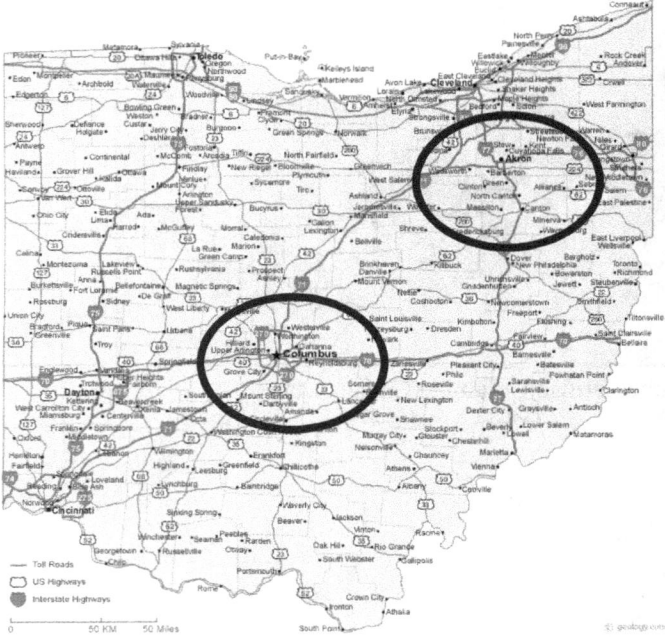

Ohio State Map

Londonderry, Northern Ireland

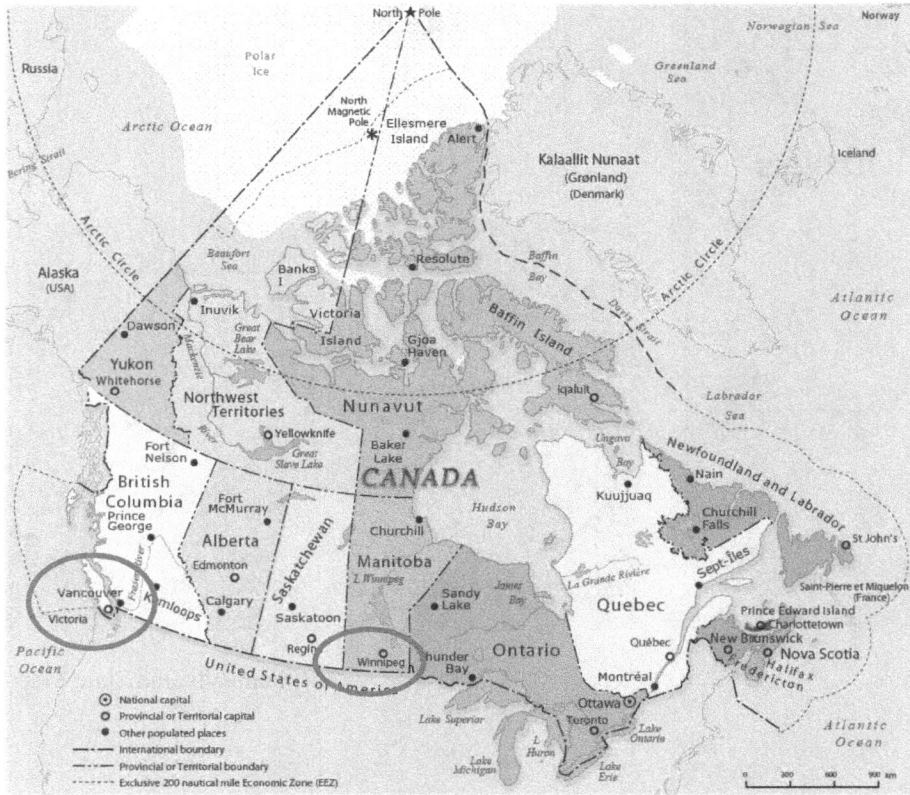

Canada Map

Appendix C- History England/Ireland

Life in 17th Century England

At the beginning of the seventeenth century, when permanent English settlements were begun in America, the people of Great Britain had just passed from the reign of an age of Faith into that of an age of Reason. In the realm of the former, there was such absolute intellectual laziness, and indifference to the exercise of reason in speculative matters, that men accepted tenets in religion and politics, however absurd, as truths, and bestowed no thought upon them.

Theology was like a cast-iron machine, utterly inflexible. It fashioned social life in its most minute details. The people were simply passive portions of that machine obedient to its ecclesiastic movers. The monastery governed the throne and its subjects as a rigid master, and for centuries there had been very little improvement in the condition of the inhabitants. At length, the glare of the moral volcano which had suddenly burst out in Germany shot across Western Europe and the English Channel and awoke the British mind from its sluggish repose. Faith gave way to Reason. A secular revolt assumed formidable proportions, and at the close of the same year, when the right of private judgment was proclaimed at Spires, the English House of Commons-the representatives of the people-presented a petition to King Henry the Eighth, which contained the germs of the English reformation. It accused the clergy of disloyalty and immorality and attributed the disorders which affected the realm to the malign influence of the ecclesiastics. The king presented this petition to the bishops for an answer. That answer was arrogant, and offensive to the House of Commons. The latter stood firm in the position of accuser and champion for the laity and waged a bitter war with the clergy. Henry, stimulated by his love for Anne Boleyn and angered by the opposition of the church to his unholy scheme of divorcement from his queen, united with the Commons, and employed the resolute Thomas Cromwell to lead a movement for the disseverance of the civil government of England from the controlling spiritual power of Rome. Cromwell did so, with a high hand, sanctioned and assisted by the Parliament, for already the rule of the people through representatives was recognized. That body, by law, suppressed all the monasteries in the kingdom, confiscated their property, and compelled the ecclesiastics to work for their own sustenance. "Go spin, jades; go spin!" was the unfeeling remark of Cromwell to some aged nuns. By law, henry was made the supreme head of the church in England-a pontiff of a church in rebellion-and so was established the principle that canon or ecclesiastical laws must be subservient to the civil laws. It was a new thing under the sun.

England was now partially freed from a long political bondage, and the age of Reason dawned. The English mind was thoroughly aroused to action. Wonderful social changes followed; and during the reign of the adroit trimmer Queen Elizabeth, all classes had more freedom than ever before. Yet the laity were not wholly free. Henry had not specially changed the theology or the rituals of the church in England, and there appeared three powerful and antagonistic parties in the realm. These were the English party, or Churchmen, who adhered to and enforced the doctrines and rituals of the Church of Rome, but who gave their allegiance to the English monarch, and not to the Pope; the papal party or supporters of the authority of the Roman hierarchy, and the doctrinal Protestants who were disliked by the others. When Parliament established a liturgy for the Church of England, the latter refused conformity to it, for they acknowledged no authority but the Bible in matters of religion. They were more austere in manners, simpler in their worship, and demanded greater purity of life, and so they acquired the name of Puritans. It was given in derision, but soon became an honorable title. Each class was intolerant, and for more than a century and a half, there was a chronic triangular contest between the English Churchmen, the Roman Catholics, and the Puritans, which caused many of each class to seek peace in the forests of America. But Reason swayed the age with a potent scepter and stamped its insignia of authority upon the movements of society. Individuals and associations found new and promising fields of action, the most attractive of which was the virgin soil of America. As we have seen, it's worth was known and fairly estimated at the beginning of the seventeenth century; and then dawned the Era of Settlements within the domain of our Republic, now at the noontide of success, and turning the wilderness, everywhere, into a blooming garden.

The condition of the rural population of England had greatly improved under the new order of things. Down to the time of Henry the Eighth, there had been very little improvement since the Romans left the island. There was not much tillage, and that little was unskillfully done. Vast forests and fens covered the land, and malaria (unwholesome exhalations) was a perpetual scourge. The population was sparse and increased very slowly. It did not exceed five million in the whole island of Great Britain, when Henry the Eighth ascended the throne. The food of the common people was not equal in its nutrition and variety, nor their clothing in comfort, to that of our Indians when Europeans first came to America. Our Indians lived in better habitations than did their British contemporaries. Pestilence and famine kept the rural population sparse. The ecclesiastics rioted in coarse luxuries, and the morals of the towns were beastly in the extreme.

At the beginning of the seventeenth century, or a hundred years later, all this had materially changed. The methods of agriculture had been greatly improved, and its bounds immensely enlarged. Implements were better and tillage was far more productive. The farmers, generally, had an abundance of good food; lived in better houses; pewter dishes had taken the place of wooden ones; feather beds, those of straw and coarse wool, and the yeoman was fond of entertaining his neighbors. Clover had been introduced from the Netherlands and increased the food for sheep and cattle. Gardens had begun to be cultivated. From the Netherlands had come the hop; also, the cabbage, lettuce, apricot, gooseberry, muskmelon and apple. Cherries had come from France; currants from Greece, and plums from Italy; and from Flanders the Flemmings had brought the rose and other fragrant plants, natives of the East. Rural feasts were common among the yeomanry, and the materials for good cheer are enumerated in the following lines:

"Good bread and good drink, a good fire in the hall; Braun, pudding and sauce, and good mustard withal; Beef, mutton and pork, shred pies of the best; Pig, veal, goose and capon, and turkey well drest; Cheese, apples and nuts; jolly carols to hear; All these in the country are counted good cheer."

In cities and among the nobility rapidly increasing wealth had fostered a taste for luxuries. Dwellings, furniture, and dress felt its influence. Elegant and substantial houses were built. Furniture was elaborately carved and inlaid; glass mirrors had been introduced from France early in the reign of Elizabeth, and carpets from Turkey, which English weavers soon imitated, took the place on floors of rushes and mats on which royalty had before trodden. Chairs were cushioned with velvet coverings, and costly beds and bedsteads were seen. In many houses were ornamental French clocks, and knives were seen on English dinner-tables; but forks were not used whilst Elizabeth lived.

An old chronicler tells us of a merry scene in the palace of Henry the Eighth. On the morning after the supple-kneed Archbishop Cranmer pronounced the marriage of his king with Anne Boleyn lawful, the new queen received visits of congratulation from the whole court and the archbishop and several prelates in full canonicals. Henry was delighted with the honors paid to his beautiful wife, and whilst they were pressing about her, and both ladies and gentlemen were giving her tokens of their regard, the king went to a small cabinet, unlocked it, and taking from it a French clock which he had bought in France while he was there with Anne when she was a marchioness, he brought it and put it in her hands as a public pledge of his love and constancy whilst time should endure. It was of "silver gilt, richly chased, engraved and ornamented with fleur-de-lys, little heads, etc. On the top sits a lion holding the arms of England, which are also on their sides." It was about sixteen inches in height.

The costume of this period we are considering was a little less extravagant in mode and richness of materials than it had been when Elizabeth was in her prime, for Puritan simplicity better suited good taste. Crimson and blue velvets embroidered with gold were still worn by the rich and noble; and the ruff was yet seen around the necks of both men and women, but somewhat diminished in volume. Jewelry was yet used to excess, and perfumed gloves bordered with silver were common among the rich. Headdresses were of every variety of pattern, but generally were not offensive to good taste. The pastimes of the common people were ball-playing, bowling, archery and rude theatrical exhibitions, whilst the gentry engaged in bullbaiting and horse-racing out of doors, and chess and backgammon amused them in hall and castle. Learning, until late in Elizabeth's reign, had been much neglected. Nobles and clergy were ignorant; but now a mighty impulse had been given to literature in England, for it was the age of Spenser and Shakespeare. Yet not one in ten of the gentry could write his or her name. The father of Shakespeare could only make his mark with a pen. The fine arts were very little encouraged. Henry the Eighth, who possessed good taste, caused some very fine buildings to be erected, and invited to his court painters and sculptors from abroad. Holbein the painter came from Switzerland, and Torregiano the sculptor came from Florence. But Elizabeth had no artistic taste, and we find only one eminent English painter during her reign-Nicolas Hilliard-to whom she sat for her miniature several times. She encouraged art so far as it ministered to the gratification of her vanity.

Such, in brief outline, is a picture of the social condition of England when the inhabitants of that realm began to make permanent settlements in America, at the beginning of the seventeenth century. The Tudor dynasty had ended with Elizabeth, and that of the Stuarts had begun. James the Sixth of Scotland, the only son of Mary Queen of Scots, had ascended the throne as James the First of England in 1603. He was in private and public an unwashed, ill-mannered, vulgar and contemptible man; fond of gross shows on which he wasted the treasures of the kingdom; and so great was his egotism that he considered himself wiser and more learned than any man in his realm in church or state. He was a bigoted believer in the royal prerogative or exclusive privileges exercised by divine right; and he was a fickle tyrant who gave continual uneasiness to his subjects. This was the monarch who granted charters to the London and Plymouth Companies, authorizing them to make settlements in America.

The roots of the Church of England go back to the time of the Roman Empire when a Christian church came into existence in what was then the Roman province of Britain. The early Christian writers Tertullian and Origen mention the existence of a British church in the third century AD and in the fourth century British bishops attended a number of the great councils of the Church such as the Council of Arles in 314 and the Council of Rimini in 359. The first member of the British church whom we know by name is St Alban, who, tradition tells us, was martyred for his faith on the spot where St Albans Abbey now stands.

The British church was a missionary church with figures such as St. Illtud, St. Ninian and St. Patrick evangelizing in Wales, Scotland and Ireland, but the invasions by the pagan Angles, Saxons and Jutes in the fifth century seem to have destroyed the organization of the church in much of what is now England. In 597 a mission sent by Pope Gregory the Great and led by St Augustine of Canterbury landed in Kent to begin the work of converting these pagan peoples. What eventually became known as the Church of England (the *Ecclesia Anglicana* - or the English Church) was the result of a combination of three streams of Christianity, the Roman tradition of St Augustine and his successors, the remnants of the old Romano-British church and the Celtic tradition coming down from Scotland and associated with people like St Aidan and St Cuthbert.

An English Church

These three streams came together as a result of increasing contact and a number of local synods, of which the Synod of Whitby in 664 has traditionally been seen as the most important. The result was an English Church, led by the two Archbishops of Canterbury and York, that was fully brought into the Christian Church of the west. This meant that it was influenced by the wider development of the Western Christian tradition in areas such as theology, liturgy, church architecture, and the development of monasticism. It also meant that until the Reformation in the 16th century the Church of England accepted the authority of the Pope.

A reformed Church

At the Reformation, the Western Church became divided between those who continued to accept Papal authority and the various Protestant churches that did not. The Church of England was among the churches that broke with Rome. The catalyst for this decision was the refusal of the Pope to annul the marriage of Henry VIII and Catherine of Aragon, but also a Tudor nationalist belief that authority over the English Church properly belonged to the English monarchy. In the reign of Henry's son Edward VI the Church of England underwent further reformation, driven by the conviction that the theology being developed by the theologians of the Protestant Reformation was more faithful to the teaching of the Bible and the Early Church than the teaching of those who continued to support the Pope.

In the reign of Mary Tudor, the Church of England once again submitted to Papal authority. However, this policy was reversed when Elizabeth I became Queen in 1558.

The religious settlement that eventually emerged in the reign of Elizabeth gave the Church of England the distinctive identity that it still has today. It resulted in a Church that consciously retained a large amount of continuity with the Church of the Patristic and Medieval periods in terms of its use of the catholic creeds, its pattern of ministry, its buildings and aspects of its liturgy, but which also embodied Protestant insights in its theology and in the overall shape of its liturgical practice. The way that this is often expressed is by saying that the Church of England is both 'catholic and reformed.'

At the end of the 16th century Richard Hooker produced the classic defense of the Elizabethan settlement in his *Of the Laws of Ecclesiastical Polity*, a work which sought to defend the Church of England against its Puritan critics who wanted further changes to make the Church of England more like the churches of Geneva or Scotland.

An established Church

In the 17th century continuing tensions within the Church of England over theological and liturgical issues were among the reasons that led to the English Civil War. The Church was associated with the losing Royalist side and during the period of the Commonwealth from 1649-1660 its bishops were abolished and its prayer book, the *Book of Common Prayer*, was banned. With the restoration of the monarchy in 1660 this situation was reversed and in 1662 those clergy who could not accept this were forced to leave their posts. These clergy and their congregations were then persecuted until 1689 when the Toleration Act gave legal existence to those Protestant groups outside the Church of England who accepted the doctrine of the Trinity.

The settlement of 1689 has remained the basis of the constitutional position of the Church of England ever since, a constitutional position in which the Church of England has remained the established Church with a range of legal privileges and responsibilities, but with ever increasing religious and civil rights being granted to other Christians, those of other faiths and those of no faith at all.

As well as being the established Church in England, the Church of England has also become the mother church of the Anglican Communion, a group of separate churches that are in communion with the Archbishop of Canterbury and for whom he is the focus of unity.

London

The Victorian city of London was a city of startling contrasts. New building and affluent development went hand in hand with horribly overcrowded slums where people lived in the worst conditions imaginable. The population surged during the 19th century, from about 1 million in 1800 to over 6 million a century later. This growth far exceeded London's ability to look after the basic needs of its citizens.

A combination of coal-fired stoves and poor sanitation made the air heavy and foul-smelling. Immense amounts of raw sewage was dumped straight into the Thames River. Even royals were not immune from the stench of London - when Queen Victoria occupied Buckingham Palace her apartments were ventilated through the common sewers, a fact that was not disclosed until some 40 years later.

Upon this scene entered an unlikely hero, an engineer named Joseph Bazalgette. Bazalgette was responsible for the building of over 2100 km of tunnels and pipes to divert sewage outside the city. This made a drastic impact on the death rate, and outbreaks of cholera dropped dramatically after Bazlgette's work was finished. For an encore, Bazalgette also was responsible for the design of the Embankment, and the Battersea, Hammersmith, and Albert Bridges.

Before the engineering triumphs of Bazalgette came the architectural triumphs of George IV's favorite designer, John Nash. Nash designed the broad avenues of Regent Street, Piccadilly Circus, Carlton House Terrace, and Oxford Circus, as well as the ongoing creation of Buckingham transformation of Buckingham House into a palace worthy of a monarch.

In 1829 Sir Robert Peel founded the Metropolitan Police to handle law and order in areas outside the City proper. These police became known as "Bobbies" after their founder.

Just behind Buckingham Palace the Grosvenor family developed the aristocratic Belgrave Square. In 1830 land just east of the palace was cleared of the royal stables to create Trafalgar Square, and the new National Gallery sprang up there just two years later.

The early part of the 19th century was the golden age of steam. The first railway in London was built from London Bridge to Greenwich in 1836, and a great railway boom followed. Major stations were built at Euston (1837), Paddington (1838), Fenchurch Street (1841), Waterloo (1848), and King's Cross (1850).

In 1834 the Houses of Parliament at Westminster Palace burned down. They were gradually replaced by the triumphant mock-Gothic Houses of Parliament designed by Charles Barry and A.W. Pugin.

The clock tower of the Houses of Parliament, known erroneously as Big Ben, was built in 1859. The origin of the name Big Ben is in some dispute, but there is no argument that the moniker refers to the bells of the tower, NOT to the large clock itself.

In 1848 the great Potato Famine struck Ireland. What has this to do with the history of London? Plenty. Over 100,000 impoverished Irish fled their native land and settled in London, making at one time up to 20% of the total population of the city.

Prince Albert, consort of Queen Victoria was largely responsible for one of the defining moments of the era that bears his wife's name; the Great Exhibition of 1851. This was the first great world's fair, a showcase of technology and manufacturing from countries all over the world. The Exhibition was held in Hyde Park, and the centerpiece was Joseph Paxton's revolutionary iron and glass hall, dubbed the "Crystal Palace".

The exhibition was an immense success, with over 200,000 attendees. After the event, the Crystal Palace was moved to Sydenham, in South London, where it stayed until it burned to the ground in 1936. The proceeds from the Great Exhibition went towards the founding of two new permanent displays, which became the Science Museum and the Victoria and Albert Museum.

The year 1863 saw the completion of the very first underground railway in London, from Paddington to Farringdon Road. The project was so successful that other lines soon followed.

But the expansion of transport was not limited to dry land. As the hub of the British Empire, the Thames was clogged with ships from all over the world, and London had more shipyards than anyplace on the globe.

For all the economic expansion of the Industrial Revolution, living conditions among London's poor were appalling. Children as young as 5 were often set to work begging or sweeping chimneys. Campaigners like

Charles Dickens did much to make the plight of the poor in London known to the literate classes with his novels, notably Oliver Twist. In 1870 those efforts bore some fruit with the passage of laws providing compulsory education for children between the ages of 5 and 12.

https://www.britainexpress.com/London/victorian-london.htm

Broughton in Furness is mentioned in the Domesday Book as one of the townships forming the Manor of Hougun held by Tostig Godwinson, Earl of North Umbria. Dating from around the eleventh century, the original settlement grew to become the local market town for both fishing and agriculture. Wool was particularly important for the town's development. The town was given a charter in 1575.

Market Square was formally laid out in 1760 by John Gilpin Sawrey, the Lord of the Manor, who lived at Broughton Tower, a large mansion just a short distance from the Square. In the 1990s the A595 road was diverted in an attempt to improve the environment of the town and help it retain its rural feel.

Aldingham parish, composed of a single township of the same name, occupies a pleasant position on the southeast side of Low Furness overlooking Morecambe Bay. The surface is undulating, being highest in the north, where 400 ft. above sea level is attained on the border of Birkrigg; in the northern half also at the coast it rises steeply from the sea, 200 ft. being attained a quarter to half a mile from the shore. The southern end is flat and low near the shore, but to the north-west, on the border of Dalton, rises to 214 ft. above sea level at Scarbarrow. The two portions are known as Upper and Lower Aldingham.

Gleaston Castle is a medieval building in a valley about 1 kilometer (0.62 mi) north-east of the village of Gleaston. The village lies between the towns of Ulverston and Barrow-in-Furness in the Furness peninsula, Cumbria, England. Gleaston Castle has a quadrilateral plan, with a tower at each corner. The largest of these, the north-west tower, probably housed a hall.

The castle was most likely built for John Harington, 1st Baron Harington in the 14th century, replacing nearby Aldingham Motte. Gleaston Castle descended through the Harrington family until 1458 when it passed to William Bonville through marriage and was subsequently abandoned. The castle passed to the Grey family until Henry Grey, 1st Duke of Suffolk was executed for treason in 1554. As a result, Gleaston Castle became royal property before it was bought by the Preston family in the 17th century, and then passed to the Cavendish family.

As the castle was disused from the mid-15th century it fell into dilapidation, and antiquarian depictions from the 18th century show Gleaston in a state of ruin. Though it is not open to the public, it has been the subject of historical and archaeological investigation in the 20th and 21st centuries.

"**THWAITES**, a chapelry in the parish of Millom, ward of Allerdale-above-Derwent, county Cumberland, 4 miles from Broughton, in Lancashire, its post town, and 10 S.E. of Ravenglass. The chapelry includes the hamlets of Duddon Bridge, Hall Thwaites, and Lady Hall. The living is a perpetual curacy in the diocese of Carlisle, value £115, in the patronage of landowners. The church is dedicated to St. Anne. There is a Druidical temple at Swineside, about 2 miles from the church." [Description(s) from *The National Gazetteer of Great Britain and Ireland* (1868) - Transcribed by Colin Hinson ©2003]

Northern Ireland

EARLY Londonderry Derry is an ancient settlement. Its name is believed to be derived from the Gaelic word doire meaning a grove of oak trees.

From the 6th AD onwards century there was a monastery in Derry. (Tradition says St Columba founded it). In time a settlement grew up by the monastery. However, for centuries, Derry was a rather small settlement. It did not become truly important until the 17th century.

In 1566 Derry was captured by the English. However, they did not hold it for long. In 1567 a gunpowder store exploded, and the English departed. The English captured Derry again in 1600.

A new town was founded at Derry in 1603. King James gave a charter founding the new town and a large number of merchants and tradesmen settled there. However, this first new town was destroyed by Cahir O'Doherty and his men in 1608.

Nevertheless, a second new town was created soon afterwards. King James confiscated large amounts of land from the Irish. He then settled large numbers of Scots and English people in Ulster to try and create a loyal population in the area. As part of the Ulster Plantation, several new towns were created.

King James invited the merchants of London to help him settle English Protestants in Northern Ireland. They agreed to build a new town at Derry. It was to have 200 houses and a population of about 1,000. The new town was called Londonderry. It was given a charter in 1613 and had a mayor and corporation. In 1617 it gained a grammar school.

By 1630 the population of Londonderry was probably about 1,000. Streets in the new town were laid out in a rectangular pattern. In the years 1613-1618 walls were built around Londonderry and St. Columb's Cathedral was built in 1633.

During the Irish rebellion of 1641 Derry was besieged but the Irish were unable to capture it. In 1649 during the civil wars between the king and parliament Derry was besieged by royalists for 20 weeks but again the city did not fall.

The most famous siege of Londonderry took place in 1689. In 1688 the Catholic king James II was deposed. However, the Lord Deputy of Ireland, The Earl of Tyrconnell stayed loyal to James so did most of Ireland. Londonderry was one of the few places that remained loyal to William. A Catholic army attempted to enter Londonderry. On December 7, 1688, 13 apprentice boys shut the Ferryquay Gate against them. As a result, Protestants fled to the town, swelling its population.

In March 1689 James landed at Kinsale in an attempt to regain his throne. The siege of Londonderry began in April 1689. Since they were not strong enough to take the town by storm the besiegers tried to starve the defenders into submission. Conditions inside the city grew worse and worse. There was a terrible shortage of food and the defenders were reduced to eating horse meat and tallow. Disease also broke out. Nevertheless, the defenders held firm.

In June three ships arrived from England, carrying supplies However for several weeks they were unable to reach the city as James's men had erected a wooden boom across the Foyle. Eventually, on 28 July, one of the ships, The Mountjoy, broke the boom and the city was relieved. Three days later the besiegers realized the game was up and they left.

18th Century

In 1704 an Act of Parliament stated that only Anglicans could hold office in Ireland. Presbyterians were excluded. Partly as a result of this measure many Presbyterians emigrated from Derry to North America in the early 18th century.

Despite this Derry grew larger in the 18th century and suburbs appeared outside the walls. Boom Hall was built in the 1770s at the point where the boom crossed the river during the siege.

A number of new buildings were erected in Derry in the 18th century. The Irish Society House was built in 1764. Long Tower Church was built in 1784-86. Bishopgate was rebuilt in 1789.

From about 1750 a linen industry grew up in Derry.

Until the end of the 18th century there was only a ferry across the River Foyle. In 1789-91 a wooden bridge was built. This greatly boosted trade and industry in Derry. Meanwhile The Derry Journal began in 1772.

19th Century

In 1821, at the time of the first Irish census, Derry had a population of 9,313. It grew rapidly during the 19th century and had reached a population of 40,000 by its end. In the early 19th century large numbers of Catholics came to Derry from the countryside looking for work.

The Courthouse was built in 1813. Derry workhouse opened in 1840 and the railway reached Derry in 1845.

Magee College was founded in 1865 to train men for the Presbyterian ministry. St. Columb's College was founded in 1879.

In 1863 another bridge, this one of steel, was erected across the Foyle. Carlisle Bridge, as it was called, was demolished in 1933.

St. Augustines Church was built in 1872. St Eugene's Cathedral was built in 1873. Its spire was added in 1902.

Derry Guildhall opened in 1890. It burned in 1908 and was rebuilt. It was bombed in 1972 then refurbished.

Meanwhile in 1831 a man named William Scott began making shirts in Derry. From the 1850s the shirt making trade in Derry boomed. By the 1870s shirt making was the main industry in the town. There was also a shipbuilding industry in 19th century Derry. Meanwhile the port of Derry prospered.

During the 19th century many emigrants from Ireland to North America left from Derry. Today they are remembered by an 'emigrants' sculpture.

http://www.localhistories.org/derry.html

Appendix C – History America

Iowa State

IOWA OFFICIAL REGISTER **HISTORY OF IOWA** *By Dorothy Schwieder, professor of history, Iowa State University*

Marquette and Joliet Find Iowa Lush and Green

In the summer of 1673, French explorers Louis Joliet and Father Jacques Marquette traveled down the Mississippi River past the land that was to become the state of Iowa. The two explorers, along with their five crewmen, stepped ashore near where the Iowa river flowed into the Mississippi. It is believed that the 1673 voyage marked the first time that white people visited the region of Iowa. After surveying the surrounding area, the Frenchmen recorded in their journals that Iowa appeared lush, green, and fertile. For the next 300 years, thousands of white settlers would agree with these early visitors: Iowa was indeed lush and green; moreover, its soil was highly productive. In fact, much of the history of the Hawkeye State is inseparably intertwined with its agricultural productivity. Iowa stands today as one of the leading agricultural states in the nation, a fact foreshadowed by the observation of the early French explorers.

The Indians

Before 1673, however, the region had long been home to many Native Americans. Approximately 17 different Indian tribes had resided here at various times including the Ioway, Sauk, Mesquaki, Sioux, Potawatomi, Oto, and Missouri. The Potawatomi, Oto, and Missouri Indians had sold their land to the federal government by 1830 while the Sauk and Mesquaki remained in the Iowa region until 1845. The Santee Band of the Sioux was the last to negotiate a treaty with the federal government in 1851.

The Sauk and Mesquaki constituted the largest and most powerful tribes in the Upper Mississippi Valley. They had earlier moved from the Michigan region into Wisconsin and by the 1730s, they had relocated in western Illinois. There they established their villages along the Rock and Mississippi Rivers. They lived in their main villages only for a few months each year. At other times, they traveled throughout western Illinois and eastern Iowa hunting, fishing, and gathering food and materials with which to make domestic articles. Every spring, the two tribes traveled northward into Minnesota where they tapped maple trees and made syrup.

In 1829, the federal government informed the two tribes that they must leave their villages in western Illinois and move across the Mississippi River into the Iowa region. The federal government claimed ownership of the Illinois land as a result of the Treaty of 1804. The move was made but not without violence. Chief Black hawk, a highly respected Sauk leader, protested the move and in 1832 returned to reclaim the Illinois village of Saukenauk. For the next three months, the Illinois militia pursued Black Hawk and his band of approximately 400 Indians northward along the eastern side of the Mississippi River. The Indians surrendered at the Bad Axe River in Wisconsin; their numbers having dwindled to about 200. This encounter is known as the Black Hawk War. As punishment for their resistance, the federal government required the Sauk and Mesquaki to relinquish some of their land in eastern Iowa. This land, known as the Black Hawk Purchase, constituted a strip 50 miles wide lying along the Mississippi River, stretching from the Missouri border to approximately Fayette and Clayton Counties in Northeastern Iowa.

Today, Iowa is still home to one Indian group, the Mesquaki, who reside on the Mesquaki Settlement in Tama County. After most Sauk and Mesquaki members had been removed from the state, some Mesquaki tribal members, along with a few Sauk, returned to hunt and fish in eastern Iowa. The Indians then approached

Governor James Grimes with the request that they be allowed to purchase back some of their original land. They collected $735 for their first land purchase and eventually they bought back approximately 3,200 acres.

Iowa's First White Settlers

The first official white settlement in Iowa began in June 1833, in the Black Hawk Purchase. Most of Iowa's first white settlers came from Ohio, Pennsylvania, New York, Indiana, Kentucky, and Virginia. The great majority of newcomers came in family units. Most families had resided in at least one additional state between the time they left their state of birth and the time they arrived in Iowa. Sometimes families had relocated three or four times before they reached Iowa. At the same time, not all settlers remained here; many soon moved on to the Dakotas or other areas in the Great Plains.

Iowa's earliest white settlers soon discovered an environment different from that which they had known back East. Most northeastern and southeastern states were heavily timbered; settlers there had material for building homes, outbuildings, and fences. Moreover, wood also provided ample fuel. Once past the extreme eastern portion of Iowa, settlers quickly discovered that the state was primarily a prairie or tall grass region. Trees grew abundantly in the extreme eastern and southeastern portions, and along rivers and streams, but elsewhere timber was limited.

In most portions of eastern and central Iowa, settlers could find sufficient timber for construction of log cabins, but substitute materials had to be found for fuel and fencing. For fuel, they turned to dried prairie hay, corn cobs, and dried animal droppings. In southern Iowa, early settlers found coal outcroppings along rivers and streams. People moving into northwest Iowa, an area also devoid of trees, constructed sod houses. Some of the early sod house residents wrote in glowing terms about their new quarters, insisting that "soddies" were not only cheap to build but were warm in the winter and cool in the summer. Settlers experimented endlessly with substitute fencing materials. Some residents built stone fences; some constructed dirt ridges; others dug ditches. The most successful fencing material was the osage orange hedge until the 1870s when the invention of barbed wire provided farmers with satisfactory fencing material.

Early settlers recognized other disadvantages of prairie living. Many people complained that the prairie looked bleak and desolate. One woman, newly arrived from New York State, told her husband that she thought she would die without any trees. Emigrants from Europe, particularly the Scandinavian countries, reacted in similar fashion. These newcomers also discovered that the prairies held another disadvantage - one that could be deadly. Prairie fires were common in the tall grass country, often occurring yearly. Diaries of pioneer families provide dramatic accounts of the reactions of early Iowans to prairie fires, often a mixture of fear and awe. When a prairie fire approached, all family members were called out to help keep the flames away. One nineteenth century Iowan wrote that in the fall, people slept "with one eye open" until the first snow fell, indicating that the threat of fire had passed.

Pioneer families faced additional hardships in their early years in Iowa. Constructing a farmstead was hard work in itself. Families not only had to build their homes, but often they had to construct the furniture used. Newcomers were often lonely for friends and relatives. Pioneers frequently contracted communicable diseases such as scarlet fever. Fever and ague, which consisted of alternating fevers and chills, was a constant complaint. Later generations would learn that fever and ague was a form of malaria, but pioneers thought that it was caused by gas emitted from the newly turned sod. Moreover, pioneers had few ways to relieve even common colds or toothaches.

Early life on the Iowa prairie was sometimes made more difficult by the death of family members. Some pioneer women wrote of the heartache caused by the death of a child. One woman, Kitturah Belknap, had lost one baby to lung fever. When a second child died, she confided in her diary:

"I have had to pass thru another season of sorrow. Death has again entered our home. This time it claimed our dear little John for its victim. It was hard for me to give him up but dropsy on the brain ended its work in four short days... We are left again with one baby and I feel that my health is giving way."

But for the pioneers who remained on the land, and most did, the rewards were substantial. These early settlers soon discovered that prairie land, although requiring some adjustments, was some of the richest land to be found anywhere in the world. Moreover, by the late 1860s, most of the state had been settled and the isolation and loneliness associated with pioneer living had quickly vanished.

Transportation: Railroad Fever

As thousands of settlers poured into Iowa in the mid-1800s, all shared a common concern for the development of adequate transportation. The earliest settlers shipped their agricultural goods down the Mississippi River to New Orleans, but by the 1850s, Iowans had caught the nation's railroad fever. The nation's first railroad had been built near Baltimore in 1831, and by 1860, Chicago was served by almost a dozen lines. Iowans, like other Midwesterners, were anxious to start railroad building in their state.

In the early 1850s, city officials in the river communities of Dubuque, Clinton, Davenport, and Burlington began to organize local railroad companies. City officials knew that railroads building west from Chicago would soon reach the Mississippi River opposite the four Iowa cities. With the 1850s, railroad planning took place which eventually resulted in the development of the Illinois Central, the Chicago and North Western, reaching Council Bluffs in 1867. Council Bluffs had been designated as the eastern terminus for the Union Pacific, the railroad that would eventually extend across the western half of the nation and along with the Central Pacific, provide the nation's first transcontinental railroad. A short time later a fifth railroad, the Chicago, Milwaukee, St. Paul, and Pacific, also completed its line across the state.

The completion of five railroads across Iowa brought major economic changes. Of primary importance, Iowans could travel every month of the year. During the latter ninetieth and early twentieth centuries, even small Iowa towns had six passenger trains a day. Steamboats and stagecoaches had previously provided transportation, but both were highly dependent on the weather, and steamboats could not travel at all once the rivers had frozen over. Railroads also provided year-round transportation for Iowa's farmers. With Chicago's pre-eminence as a railroad center, the corn, wheat, beef, and pork raised by Iowa's farmers could be shipped through Chicago, across the nation to eastern seaports, and from there, anywhere in the world.

Railroads also brought major changes in Iowa's industrial sector. Before 1870, Iowa contained some manufacturing firms in the eastern portion of the state, particularly all made possible by year-around railroad transportation. Many of the new industries were related to agriculture. In Cedar Rapid, John and Robert Stuart, along with their cousin, George Douglas, started an oats processing plant. In time, this firm took the name Quaker Oats. Meat packing plants also appeared in the 1870s in different parts of the state: Sinclair Meat Packing opened in Cedar Rapids and John Morrell and Company set up operations in Ottumwa.

Education and Religion

As Iowa's population and economy continued to grow, education and religious institutions also began to take shape. Americans had long considered education important and Iowans did not deviate from that belief. Early in any neighborhood, residents began to organize schools. The first step was to set up township elementary schools, aided financially by the sale or lease of section 16 in each of the state's many townships. The first high school was established in the 1850s, but in general, high schools did not become widespread until after 1900. Private and public colleges also soon appeared. By 1900, the Congregationalists had established Grinnell College. The Catholics and Methodists were most visible in private higher education, however. As of 1900, they had each created five colleges: Iowa Wesleyan, Simpson, Cornell, Morningside, and Upper Iowa University by the Methodists; and Marycrest, St. Ambrose, Briar Cliff, Loras, and Clarke by the Catholics. Other church colleges present in Iowa by 1900 were Coe and Dubuque (Presbyterian); Wartburg and Luther (Lutheran); Central (Baptist); and Drake (Disciples of Christ).

The establishment of private colleges coincided with the establishment of state educational institutions. In the mid-1800s, state officials organized three state institutions of higher learning, each with a different mission. The University of Iowa, established in 1855, was to provide classical and professional education for Iowa's young people; Iowa State College of Science and Technology (now Iowa State University), established in 1858; was to offer agricultural and technical training. Iowa State Teachers' College (now University of Northern Iowa) founded in 1876 was to train teachers for the state's public schools.

Iowans were also quick to organize churches. Beginning in the 1840s, the Methodist Church sent out circuit riders to travel throughout the settled portion of the state. Each circuit rider typically had a two-week circuit in which he visited individual families and conducted sermons for local Methodist congregations. Because the circuit riders' sermons tended to be emotional and simply stated, Iowa's frontiers-people could readily identify with them. The Methodists profited greatly from their "floating ministry," attracting hundreds of converts in Iowa's early years. As more settled communities appeared, the Methodist Church assigned ministers to these stationary charges.

Catholics also moved into Iowa soon after white settlement began. Dubuque served as the center for Iowa Catholicism as Catholics established their first diocese in that city. The leading Catholic figure was Bishop Mathias Loras, a Frenchman, who came to Dubuque in the late 1830s. Bishop Loras helped establish Catholic churches in the area and worked hard to attract priests and nuns from foreign countries. Before the Civil War, most of Iowa's Catholic clergy were from France, Ireland, and Germany. After the Civil War, more and more of that group tended to be native-born. Bishop Loras also helped establish two Catholic educational institutions in Dubuque, Clarke College and Loras College.

Congregationalists were the third group to play an important role in Iowa before the Civil War. The first group of Congregationalist ministers here were known as the Iowa Band. This was a group of 11 ministers, all trained at Andover Theological Seminary, who agreed to carry the gospel into a frontier region. The group arrived in 1843, and each minister selected a different town in which to establish a congregation. The Iowa Band's motto was "each a church; all a college." After a number of years when each minister worked independently, the ministers collectively helped to establish Iowa College in Davenport. Later church officials move the college to Grinnell and changed its name to Grinnell College.

Throughout the nineteenth century, many other denominations also established churches within the state. Quakers established meeting houses in the communities of West Branch, Springdale, and Salem. Presbyterians were also well represented in Iowa communities. Baptists often followed the practice of hiring local farmers to preach on Sunday mornings. And as early as the 1840s, Mennonite Churches began to appear in eastern Iowa. The work of the different denominations meant that during the first three decades of settlement, Iowans had quickly established their basic religious institutions.

The Civil War

By 1860, Iowa had achieved statehood (December 28, 1846), and the state continued to attract many settlers, both native and foreign-born. Only the extreme northwestern part of the state remained a frontier area. But after almost 30 years of peaceful development, Iowans found their lives greatly altered with the outbreak of the Civil War in 1861. While Iowans had no battles fought on their soil, the state paid dearly through the contributions of its fighting men. Iowa males responded enthusiastically to the call for Union volunteers and more than 75,000 Iowa men served with distinction in campaigns fought in the East and in the South. Of that number,

13,001 died in the war, many of disease rather than from battle wounds. Some men died in the Confederate prison camps, particularly Andersonville, Georgia. A total of 8,500 Iowa men were wounded.

Many Iowans served with distinction in the Union Army. Probably the best known was Grenville Dodge, who became a general during the war. Dodge fulfilled two important functions: he supervised the rebuilding of many southern railroad lines to enable Union troops to move more quickly through the South; and he directed the counter intelligence operation for the union Army, locating Northern sympathizers in the South who, in turn, would relay information on Southern troop movements and military plans to military men in the North.

Another Iowan, Cyrus Carpenter, was 31 years old when he entered the army in 1861. Living in Ft. Dodge, Carpenter requested a commission from the army rather than enlisting. He was given the rank of captain and was installed as quartermaster. Carpenter had never served in that capacity before, but with the aid of an army clerk, he proceeded to carry out his duties. Most of the time, Carpenter was responsible for feeding 40,000 men. Not only was it difficult to have sufficient food for the men, but Carpenter constantly had to keep his supplies and staff on the move. Carpenter found it an immensely frustrating task, but most of the time, he managed to have the food and other necessities at the right place at the right time.

Iowa women also served their nation during the war. Hundreds of women knitted sweaters, sewed uniforms, rolled bandages, and collected money for military supplies. Women formed soldiers' relief societies throughout the state. Annie Wittenmyer particularly distinguished herself through volunteer work. She spent much time during the war raising money and needed supplies for Iowa soldiers. At one point, Mrs. Wittenmyer visited her brother in a Union army hospital. She objected to the food served to the patients, contending that no one could get well on greasy bacon and cold coffee. She suggested to hospital authorities that they establish diet kitchens so that the patients would receive proper nutrition. Eventually, some diet kitchens were established in military hospitals. Mrs. Wittenmyer also was responsible for the establishment of several homes for soldiers' orphans.

The Political Arena

The Civil War era brought considerable change to Iowa and perhaps one of the most visible changes came in the political arena. During the 1840's, most Iowans voted Democratic although the state also contained some Whigs. Iowa's first two United States Senators were Democrats as were most state officials. During the 1850s, however, the state's Democratic Party developed serious internal problems as well as being unsuccessful in getting the national Democratic Party to respond to their needs. Iowans soon turned to the newly emerging Republican Party; the political career of James Grimes illustrates this change. In 1854, Iowans elected Grimes governor on the Whig ticket. Two years later, Iowans elected Grimes governor on the Republican ticket. Grimes would later serve as a Republican United States Senator from Iowa. Republicans took over state politics in the 1850s and quickly instigated several changes. They moved the state capital from Iowa City to Des Moines, they established the University of Iowa and they wrote a new state constitution. From the late 1850s until well into the twentieth century, Iowans remained strongly Republican. Iowans sent many highly capable Republicans to Washington, particularly William Boyd Allison of Dubuque, Jonathan P. Dolliver of Ft. Dodge, and Albert Baird Cummins of Des Moines. These men served their state and their nation with distinction.

Another political issue facing Iowans in the 1860s was the issue of women's suffrage. From the 1860s on, Iowa contained a large number of women, and some men, who strongly supported the measure and who worked endlessly for its adoption. In keeping with the general reform mood of the latter 1860s and 1870s, the issue first received serious consideration when both houses of the General Assembly passed a women's suffrage amendment in 1870. Two years later, however, when the legislature had to consider the amendment again before it could be submitted to the general electorate, interest had waned, opposition had developed, and the amendment was defeated.

For the next 47 years, Iowa women worked continually to secure passage of a women's suffrage amendment to Iowa's state constitution. During that time, the issue was considered in almost every session of the state legislature, but an amendment was offered (having passed both houses of the state legislature in two consecutive sessions) to the general electorate only once, in 1916. In that election, voters defeated the amendment by about 10,000 votes.

The arguments against women's suffrage ranged from the charge that women were not interested in the vote to the charge that women's suffrage would bring the downfall of the family and would cause delinquency in children. Regarding the defeat of the 1916 state referendum on the female vote, Iowa-born Carrie Chapman Catt, a leader for the women's suffrage cause, argued that the liquor interests in the state should accept responsibility as they had worked hard to defeat the measure. During the long campaign to secure the vote, however, the women themselves were not always in agreement as to the best approach to secure a victory. Catt herself led the final victorious assault in 1918 and 1919 in Washington with her "winning plan." This called for women to work for both state (state constitutions) and national (national constitution) amendments. Finally, in 1920, after both houses of the United States Congress passed the measure and it had been approved by the proper number of states, woman's suffrage became a reality for American women everywhere.

Iowa: Home for Immigrants

While Iowans were debating the issues of women's suffrage in the post-Civil War period, the state itself was attracting many more people. Following the Civil War, Iowa's population continued to grow dramatically, from 674,913 people in 1860 to 1,194,020 in 1870. Moreover, the ethnic composition of Iowa's population also changed substantially. Before the Civil War, Iowa had attracted some foreign-born settlers, but the number remained small. After the Civil War, the number of immigrants increased. In 1869, the state encouraged immigration by printing a 96-page booklet entitled Iowa: The Home of Immigrants. The publication gave physical, social, educational, and political descriptions of Iowa. The legislature instructed that the booklet be published in English, German, Dutch, Swedish, and Danish.

Iowans were not alone in their efforts to attract more northern and western Europeans. Throughout the nation, Americans regarded these newcomers as "good stock" and welcomed them enthusiastically. Most immigrants from these countries came in family units. Germans constituted the largest group, settling in every county within the state. The great majority became farmers, but many also became craftsmen and shopkeepers. Moreover, many German Americans edited newspapers, taught school, and headed banking establishments. In Iowa, Germans exhibited the greatest diversity in occupations, religion, and geographical settlement.

The Marx Goettsch family of Davenport serves well as an example of German immigrants. At the time of his emigration in 1871, Goettsch was 24 years old, married and the father of a young son. During a two-year term in the German Army, Goettsch had learned the trade of shoemaking. Goettsch and his family chose to settle in Davenport, among Germans from the Schleswig-Holstein area. By working hard as a shoemaker, Goettsch managed not only to purchase a building for his home and shop, but also to purchased five additional town lots. Later, Goettsch had homes built on the lots which he rented out. He had then become both a small businessman and a landlord.

During the next 25 years, Goettsch and his wife, Anna, raised six children and enjoyed considerable prosperity. For Marx and Anna, life in America, surrounded by fellow German Americans, did not differ greatly from life in the old country. For their children, however, life was quite different. The lives of the Goettsch children - or the second generation - best illustrate the social and economic opportunities available to immigrants in the United States. If the family had remained in Germany, probably all five sons would have followed their father's occupation of shoemaker. In the United States, all five pursued higher education. Two sons received Ph.D.'s, two sons received M.D.s, and one son became a professional engineer. With the third generation, education was also a crucial factor. Of seven grandchildren, all became professionals. Moreover, five of the seven were female. As the Goettsch experience indicates, opportunities abounded for immigrants settling in Iowa in the nineteenth and twentieth centuries. The newcomers and their children could take up land, go into business, or pursue higher education. For most immigrants, these areas offered a better, more prosperous life than their parents had known in the old country.

Iowa also attracted many other people from Europe, including Swedes, Norwegians, Danes, Hollanders, and many emigrants from the British Isles as shown by the following table. After 1900, people also emigrated from southern and eastern Europe. In many instances, immigrant groups were identified with particular occupations. The Scandinavians, including Norwegians, who settled in Winneshiek and Story Counties; Swedes, who settled in Boone County; and Danes, who settled in southwestern Iowa; were largely associated with farming. Many Swedes also became coal miners. The Hollanders made two major settlements in Iowa, the first in Marion County, and the second in northwest Iowa.

Proportionately far more southern and eastern immigrants, particularly Italians and Croatians, went into coal mining than did western and northern Europeans. Arriving in Iowa with little money and few skills, these groups gravitated toward work that required little or no training and provided them with immediate employment. In Iowa around the turn of the century, that work happened to be coal mining.

Coal Miners

Italian emigration differed from earlier emigration in that it tended to be male dominated. Typically, the Italian male emigrated with financial support of family or friends. Once in Iowa, he worked in the mines to pay back his sponsors; then he began to save to bring his wife and family from Italy. For two generations, Italian males worked in coal mines scattered throughout central and southern Iowa. Beginning around 1925, however, the Iowa coal industry began to decline. By the mid-1950s only a few underground mines remained in the state.

Life in a coal camp differed greatly from life in more settled Iowa communities. Most residents described the camps as bleak and dismal. The typical coal camp contained a company store, a tavern and pool hall, a miners' union hall, and an elementary school. Only rarely did coal camps contain churches or high schools. Coal camp residents had few social or economic opportunities. Most sons followed their fathers into the mines, and daughters tended to marry miners and continued to live in the camps.

The majority of blacks who migrated to Iowa during the late nineteenth and early twentieth centuries also worked as coal miners. Before the Civil War, Iowa had only a small black population, but in the 1880s that number increased considerably. Unfortunately, many of the early blacks were hired as strike breakers by Iowa coal operators. In later decades, however, coal companies hired blacks as regular miners.

The most notable coal community in Iowa was Buxton. Located in northern Monroe County, Buxton contained almost 5,000 people. By contrast, most coal camps averaged around 200 residents. Consolidation Coal Company owned and operated Buxton and instigated many progressive policies. Perhaps most unusual, Buxton had a high black population, at one time almost 54 percent. Most social and economic institutions were racially integrated, and the town contained many black professionals. Buxton existed from 1900 to 1922 when coal seams around the area were depleted. Black families then moved on to Des Moines, Waterloo, Cedar Rapids and to communities outside the state.

The Family Farm

After the Civil War, Iowa's agriculture also underwent considerable change. By the 1870s, farms and small towns blanketed the entire state. Also, in that decade, Iowa farmers established definite production patterns, which led to considerable prosperity. During the Civil War, Iowa farmers had raised considerable wheat. After the war, however, prominent Iowa farmers like "Tama Jim" Wilson, later to be national secretary of agriculture for 16 years, urged farmers to diversify their production, raise corn rather than wheat, and convert that corn into pork, beef, and wool whenever possible. For many generations, Iowa farmers have followed Wilson's advice.

Even though farmers changed their agricultural production, farm work continued to be dictated by the seasons. Wintertime meant butchering, fence mending, ice cutting, and wood chopping. In the spring, farmers prepared and planted their fields. Summertime brought sheep shearing, haying, and threshing. In the fall, farmers picked corn, the most difficult farm task of all.

Farm women's work also progressed according to the seasons. During the winter, women did their sewing and mending, and helped with butchering. Spring brought the greatest activity. Then women had to hatch and care for chickens, plant gardens, and do spring housekeeping. During the summer, women canned large amounts of vegetables and fruit. Canning often extended into the fall. Foods like apples and potatoes were stored for winter use. Throughout all the seasons, there were many constants in farm women's routines. Everyday meals had to be prepared, children cared for, and housekeeping done. With gardens to tend and chickens to feed and water, farm women had both indoor and outdoor work. Through their activities however, women produced most of their families' food supply.

During the late 1800s and early 1900s, social activities for farm families were limited. Most families made few trips to town. Some Iowans remember that even in the 1920s, they went to town only on Saturday night. Family members looked to each other for companionship and socializing. Moreover, the country church and the country school were important social centers. Families gathered at neighborhood schools several times each year for Christmas programs, spelling bees, and annual end-of-the-year picnics.

Many rural neighborhoods had distinct ethnic identifications, often merged into religion. Throughout the Iowa countryside, churches abounded with designations such as German Lutheran, German Catholic, German Methodist, Swedish Lutheran, Swedish Methodist, and Swedish Baptist.

Vast Changes

In 1917, the United States entered World War I and farmers as well as all Iowans experienced a wartime economy. For farmers, the change was significant. Since the beginning of the war in 1914, Iowa farmers had experienced economic prosperity. Along with farmers everywhere, they were urged to be patriotic by increasing their production. Farmers purchased more land and raised more corn, beef, and pork for the war effort. It seemed that no one could lose as farmers expanded their operations, made more money, and at the same time, helped the Allied war effort.

After the war, however, Iowa farmers soon saw wartime farm subsidies eliminated. Beginning in 1920, many farmers had difficulty making the payment for debts they had incurred during the war. The 1920s were a time of hardship for Iowa's farm families and for many families, these hardships carried over into the 1930s.

As economic difficulties worsened, Iowa farmers sought to find local solutions. Faced with extremely low farm prices, including corn at 10 cents a bushel and pork at three cents a pound, some Iowa farmers joined the Farm Holiday Association. This group, which had its greatest strength in the area around Sioux City, tried to withhold farm products from markets. They believed this practice would force up farm prices. The Farm Holiday Association had only limited success as many farmers did not cooperate and the withholding itself did little to raise prices. Farmers experienced little relief until 1933 when the federal government, as part of Franklin Roosevelt's New Deal, created a federal farm program.

In 1933, native Iowan Henry A. Wallace went to Washington as secretary of agriculture and served as principle architect for the new farm program. Wallace, former editor of the Midwest's leading farm journal, Wallace's Farmer, believed that prosperity would return to the agricultural sector only if agricultural production was curtailed. Further, he believed that farmers would be monetarily compensated for withholding agricultural land from production. These two principals were incorporated into the Agricultural Adjustment Act passed in 1933. Iowa farmers experienced some recovery as a result of the legislation but like all Iowans, they did not experience total recovery until the 1940s.

Since World War II, Iowans have continued to undergo considerable economic, political, and social change. In the political area, Iowan experienced a major change in the 1960s when liquor by the drink came into effect. During both the nineteenth and early twentieth centuries, Iowans had strongly supported prohibition, but in 1933 with the repeal of national prohibition, Iowans established a state liquor commission. This group was charged with control and regulation of Iowa's liquor sales. From 1933 until the early 1960s, Iowans could purchase packaged liquor only. In the 1970s, Iowans witnessed a reapportionment of the General Assembly, achieved only after a long struggle for an equitably apportioned state legislature. Another major political change was in regard to voting. By the mid-1950s, Iowa had developed a fairly competitive two-party structure, ending almost 100 years of Republican domination within the state.

In the economic sector, Iowa also has undergone considerable change. Beginning with the first farm-related industries developed in the 1870s, Iowa has experienced a gradual increase in the number of business and manufacturing operations. The period since World War II has witnessed a particular increase in manufacturing operations. While agriculture continues to be the state's dominant industry, Iowans also produce a wide variety of products including refrigerators, washing machines, fountain pens, farm implements, and food products that are shipped around the world.

Strong Traditions

At the same time, some traditions remain unchanged. Iowans are still widely known for their strong educational systems, both in secondary as well as in higher education. Today, Iowa State University and the University of Iowa continue to be recognized nationally and internationally as outstanding educational institutions. Iowa remains a state composed mostly of farms and small towns, with a limited number of larger cities. Moreover, Iowa is still a place where most people live stable, comfortable lives, where family relationships are strong and where the quality of life is high. In many peoples' minds, Iowa is "middle America." Throughout the years, Iowans have profited from their environment and the result is a progressive people and a bountiful land.

Quoted in Glenda Riley's, Frontiers woman: The Iowa Experience (Ames: Iowa State University Press, 1981), p. 81.

Quoted in Joseph Wall's, Iowa: A History (New York: W.W. Norton & Company Inc., 1978), p. 70.

Des Moines County is a county located in the U.S. state of Iowa. As of the 2010 census, the population was 40,325. The county seat is Burlington. It is one of Iowa's two original counties along with Dubuque County; both were organized by the Michigan Territorial legislature in 1834.

Des Moines County should not be confused with the city of Des Moines, which is the capital of Iowa. Des Moines County sits on Iowa's eastern border alongside the Mississippi River. The city of Des Moines is in Polk County in south-central Iowa. Both places derive their name from the Des Moines River, which flows through the city of Des Moines and originally flowed through the county. When the county was divided early in Iowa's history, the river ended up further west, forming the border between Lee County, Iowa and the state of Missouri.

At an extra session of the Sixth Legislative Assembly of Michigan Territory held in September 1834, the Iowa District was divided into two counties by running a line due west from the lower end of Rock Island in the Mississippi River. The territory north of this line (which started just south of the present-day Davenport) was named Dubuque County, and all south of it was Demoine County. It was named after the Des Moines River. From July 3, 1836 until July 3, 1838, Des Moines County was part of Wisconsin Territory. The county underwent various border changes during this time. July 4, 1838, the named county became part of Iowa Territory (later the state of Iowa).

Lee County, Iowa, was established in 1836. As of the 2010 census, the population was 35,862. It has two county seats — Fort Madison and Keokuk.

Fort Madison dates to the War of 1812. Lee County was the location of the Half-Breed Tract, established by treaty in 1824. Allocations of land were made to American Indian descendants of European fathers and Indian mothers at this tract. Originally the land was to be held in common. Some who had an allocation lived in cities, where they hoped to make better livings.

Lee County as a named entity was formed on December 7, 1836, under the jurisdiction of Wisconsin Territory. It would become a part of Iowa Territory when it was formed on July 4, 1838. Large-scale European-American settlement in the area began in 1839, after Congress allowed owners to sell land individually. Members of the Church of Christ (Latter Day Saints) fled persecutions in Missouri to settle in Illinois and Iowa. Nauvoo, across the border in Hancock County, Illinois, became the main center of Latter-day Saints settlement, but there was also a Latter Day Saints stake organized in Lee County under the direction of John Smith, the uncle of Joseph Smith, land that was sold to them by Isaac Galland in 1839.

Lee has two county seats — Fort Madison and Keokuk. The latter was established in 1847 when disagreements led to a second court jurisdiction.

Lee County's population grew to about 19,000 in 1850, the first US census, to 37,000 per the 3rd census in 1870, peaking at 44,000 people in 1960. It has continuously decreased since and as of 2010, 35,862 people lived there, comparable to the years between 1860-1870.

The City of **Keokuk** is named for Chief Keokuk, a chief of the Sac and Fox Indians. His bones were brought here in 1883 from Franklin County, Kansas, and reinterred in Rand Park beneath a massive stone pedestal which is surrounded by a life-sized statue of an Indian chieftain. On the east side of this monument is embedded the marble slab taken from the grave in Kansas which is lettered as follows: "Sacred to the memory of Keokuk, a distinguished Sac chief born at Rock Island in 1788. Died in April 1848" Keokuk, "The Watchful Fox", was not a hereditary chief, but raised himself to the dignity by the force of talent and enterprise. He was a man of extraordinary eloquence in council and never at a loss in an emergency. He was a noble looking man about six feet tall, portly and weighing over 200 pounds. He had an eagle eye, dignified bearing, and a manly, intelligent expression of countenance.

On November 23, 1985 a new Keokuk Hamilton (IL) bridge was opened. This bridge which is 3,340 feet long and 64 feet wide eliminates the tie up of traffic from the former swing span bridge, allowing both automobile and barge traffic to move more efficiently.

http://www.cityofkeokuk.org/community/history-of-keokuk/

Illinois State

Before Illinois became a State, it was known as the *Illinois Territory*. In early 1818, the General Assembly of the Illinois Territory sent a petition to the United States Congress asking to be admitted into the Union. Part of the process for being admitted as a State was for Illinois to adopt its own constitution.

The word Illinois comes from the French word meaning Illini or Land of Illini. It is an Algonquin word meaning Men or Warriors. Illinois was discovered in 1673, settled in 1720 and entered the Union on December 3, 1818. Illinois is surrounded by bodies of water on nearly every border: the Mississippi River on the west; the Ohio and Wabash Rivers in the south, and Lake Michigan in the North. The States that border Illinois are Kentucky, Iowa, Wisconsin, Missouri, and Indiana. The first Railroad train crossed the Mississippi River on the river's first bridge in Rock Island, Illinois on April 21, 1856. The highest point in Illinois is Charles Mound in JoDaviess County, elevation, 1,235 feet, and the lowest point is in Cairo, Alexander county at the Mississippi River, elevation 279 feet.

Thousands of years before the French reached Illinois, Paleo-Indians, a nomadic people, and their descendants, archaic Indians, had explored Illinois. The culture of these hunters, dated before 5000 BC, can be studied at the Modoc Rock Shelter in Randolph County. Woodland Indians were their descendants. By 900 AD, Middle Mississippi Indians, who succeeded the Woodland Indians, built large earthen mounds and developed complex urban areas. These cities disappeared possibly because of overpopulation, disease, and exhaustion of resources. The descendants of the Mississippians were the Illiniwek tribes of the 17th, 18th, and 19th centuries. After years of losing land and wars to other Indian groups and European colonists, the Illiniweks were moved to a Kansas reservation.

The French controlled areas along the Mississippi River valley in the American Bottoms between Cahokia and Kaskaskia. Their occupation, from about 1675 to 1763, left few lasting marks, as did the ineffective British rule. European control was ended by the U.S. militia of George Rogers Clark in 1778, whereupon Virginia claimed Illinois as within its territory.

The Northwest Ordinance of 1787 charted this region and organized counties, and in 1809 the Territory of Illinois was created. During the early years of settlement by fur trappers, southern Illinois was the focus of migration to the area, especially along the Mississippi River valley and the Wabash and Ohio rivers. Granting of statehood in 1818 was controversial. The population numbered less than the required 60,000. Moreover, in order to include the Chicago port area, territorial representatives induced the U.S. Congress to draw the Illinois border 51 miles to the north of the original boundary as delimited by the Northwest Ordinance. The first capital was Kaskaskia, followed by Vandalia, along the Kaskaskia River, which held the position for 20 years. After strong pressure from Abraham Lincoln, the capital was moved to Springfield by an 1837 legislative vote.

Early statehood problems engulfed Illinois.

The state population in 1830 was 157,445. By then the state was near bankruptcy because of government financing of canals and railroad construction. The Black Hawk War in 1832 was fought by the Indians and newly arrived settlers over possession of Illinois land.

In 1833 Chicago was founded, and the final Indian treaty pertaining to Illinois land, the Treaty of Chicago, was concluded with the Potawatomi, Chippewa, and Ottawa tribes. Also, the first higher education institution for women in Illinois, the Jacksonville Female Seminary, was opened.

In 1839, the state capital was moved to Springfield, while the population in Illinois had grown to nearly 500,000. The first railroad, The Northern Cross, started running from the Illinois River to Springfield. Later in 1844, the Mormon prophet Joseph Smith and his brother Hyrum were killed by a mob at Carthage, prompting the Mormons to move out of Illinois by 1848. The Illinois and Michigan Canal opened the same year. By that time, the population was nearly one million.

By 1860, debates were held in seven Illinois communities. The state's population was 1,711,951. In 1861, Abraham Lincoln of Springfield is inaugurated as president. The Civil War caused mixed loyalties among Illinoisans, many of whom were first- or second-generation Southerners; however, many took pride in the fact that the Union was led by a native son, Lincoln, and the state provided 250,000 soldiers to the Union army. Illinois also was the weapons manufacturer, supplier of iron products, and major grain and meat supplier for the North. The Civil War ended in 1865, and Lincoln was assassinated.

In 1867, the Illinois Industrial University (later the University of Illinois) was established. In 1868, a new statehouse was authorized, and construction began, but would not be completed for 20 years. By 1870, the state's population is 2,539,891.

By 1880, Illinois had become the fourth most populous state. It was a leader in grain production and manufacturing. Large-scale European immigration provided labor to mine coal, run steel mills, and enhance the economy and culture of the state. Its leadership was achieved despite the economic slumps of the 1880s, 1890s, and early 1900s; the labor disputes in coal mining and railroading; the Chicago fire of 1871. By 1890, the state's population was 3,836,352, and Chicago became a metropolis of 1,099,850.

By 1910, the state's population was 5,638,591. In 1911, Starved Rock State park became the first state park in Illinois. In 1912, Poetry magazine was founded in Chicago by Harriet Monroe, and it helped to launch the careers of Vachel Lindsay, Carl Sandburg, and other notable poets. In 1913, the Women's Suffrage Act was passed, extending voting rights for Illinois women. In 1917, the United States entered World War I, in which 314,504 Illinois men participated. In 1918, Illinois celebrated its centennial. Also, an influenza epidemic killed thousands of Illinois residents and more than 600,000 people nationwide.

By 1920, Illinois was counted among the foremost states in nearly every significant growth variable—coal mining, industry, farming, urbanization, transportation, and wholesaling. WWII saw Illinois send thousands of its residents to fight in Europe and the Pacific.

The post-World War II era was a time of industrial modification for the production of consumer goods. Even though meat-packing companies began to move away from Chicago and East Saint Louis, in part because of obsolete physical plants, Illinois farms were being mechanized and upgraded for increased output. The use of hybrid seed, chemical fertilizer, herbicides, and insecticides resulted in larger crop yields. Post-World War II Illinois experienced rapid population growth. The rising number of school-age children brought public school reform, rural school consolidations, and huge suburban educational plants. Migration streams of blacks from the South, Hispanics from Mexico and Puerto Rico, and whites from Appalachia reshaped neighborhoods in Chicago, its suburbs, and other large Illinois cities.

As of the census of 2000, Illinois currently has the 6th largest population of the 50 U.S. states. Chicago, in terms of population, is the third largest city in the country.

http://www.illinoiscourts.gov/kids/IL_Hist/default.asp

Freeport is the county seat and largest city of Stephenson County, Illinois. The population was 25,638 at the 2010 census. Freeport is known for hosting the second Lincoln-Douglas debate of 1858, and as "Pretzel City, USA", named after the heritage of its Germanic settlers in the 1850s and the Billerbeck Bakery pretzel company that started as a result of their arrival.

The community was originally called **Winneshiek**. When it was incorporated, the new municipality took its name from the generosity of Tutty Baker, who was credited with running a "free port" on the Pecatonica River. The name "Winneshiek" was later adopted, and is preserved to this day, by the Freeport Community Theatre Group.

In 1837, Stephenson County was formed, and Freeport became its seat of government in 1838. Linked by a stagecoach with Chicago, the community grew rapidly. In 1840, a frame courthouse was erected, and the first school was founded. Within two years, Freeport had two newspapers and in 1853, the two were joined by a third which published in German. By then, the community had a population of 2,000.

On August 27, 1858, the second debate between Abraham Lincoln and Stephen A. Douglas took place in Freeport and gave the nation direction in the following years. Although Stephen Douglas won the election and retained his U.S. Senate seat, his reply to a question on slavery alienated the South, which called it the "Freeport Heresy", and split the Democratic Party. This enabled Abraham Lincoln to win the Presidency in 1860.

Freeport is known as the "Pretzel City", and its public high school's team is named the Pretzels. The nickname is a reminder of Freeport's ethnic heritage; in the late 1850s, many Germans, both from Pennsylvania and from their European homeland, resettled in Stephenson County bringing with them their love of pretzel snacks. In 1869, a German immigrant named John Billerbeck established the Billerbeck Bakery, which distributed so many pretzels to residents that the local newspaper later dubbed Freeport the "Pretzel City". The city later capitalized on this nickname in 2003 by starting Freeport's first Pretzel Festival.

Freeport is home to the oldest Carnegie Library in Illinois and one of the first Carnegie Libraries designed by the famous Chicago architectural firm of Patton and Miller.

The area of **Nauvoo** was first called **Quashquema**, named in honor of the Native American chief who headed a Sauk and Fox settlement numbering nearly 500 lodges. By 1827, white settlers had built cabins in the area. By 1829 this area of Hancock County had grown sufficiently so that a post office was needed and in 1832 the town, now called **Venus**, was one of the contenders for the new county seat. However, the honor was awarded to a nearby city, Carthage. In 1834 the name Venus was changed to **Commerce** because the settlers felt the new name better suited their plans.

In late 1839, arriving Mormons bought the small town of Commerce and in April 1840 it was renamed **Nauvoo** by Joseph Smith, who led the Latter-Day Saints to Nauvoo to escape conflict with the state government in Missouri. The name Nauvoo is derived from the traditional Hebrew language with an anglicized spelling. The word comes from Isaiah 52:7, "How beautiful upon the mountains..." It is notable that "by 1844 Nauvoo's population had swollen to 12,000, rivaling the size of Chicago" at the time.

1 Engraving of Nauvoo, ca. 1855

After Joseph Smith's death in 1844, continued violence from surrounding non-Mormons forced most Latter-Day Saints to leave Nauvoo. Most of these followers, led by Brigham Young, emigrated to the Great Salt Lake Valley. In 1849, Icarians moved to the Nauvoo area to implement a utopian socialist commune based on the ideals of French philosopher Étienne Cabet. The colony had over 500 members at its peak, but Cabet's death in 1856 led some members to leave this parent colony. In the early and mid-20th century Nauvoo was primarily a Roman Catholic town, and a plurality of the population today is Methodist or another Christian faith.

Elgin is a city in Cook and Kane counties in the northern part of the U.S. state of Illinois. Located roughly 35 mi (56 km) northwest of Chicago, it lies along the Fox River. As of 2013, the city had a total population of 110,145, making it the eighth-largest city in Illinois.

The Indian Removal Act of 1830 and the Black Hawk Indian War of 1832 led to the expulsion of the Native Americans who had settlements and burial mounds in the area and set the stage for the founding of Elgin. Thousands of militiamen and soldiers of Gen. Winfield Scott's army marched through the Fox River valley during the war, and accounts of the area's fertile soils and flowing springs soon filtered east.

In New York, James T. Gifford and his brother Hezekiah Gifford heard tales of this area ripe for settlement and travelled west. Looking for a site on the stagecoach route from Chicago to Galena, Illinois, they eventually settled on a spot where the Fox River could be bridged. In April 1835, they established the city, namingit after the Scottish tune "Elgin".

Early Elgin achieved fame for the butter and dairy goods it sold to the city of Chicago. Gail Borden established a condensed milk factory here in 1866, and the local library is named in his honor. The dairy industry became less important with the arrival of the Elgin Watch Company. The watch factory employed three generations of Elginites from the late 19th to the mid-20th century, when it was the largest producer of fine watches in the United States (the factory ceased production in 1965 and was torn down in the summer of 1966) and the operator of the largest watchmaking complex in the world. Today, the clocks at Chicago's Union Station still bear the Elgin name.

Elgin has a long tradition of education and invention. Elgin is home to the Elgin Academy, the oldest coeducational, non-sectarian college preparatory school west of the Allegheny Mountains. Elgin High School boasts five navy admirals, a Nobel Prize winner, a Pulitzer Prize winner, a Tony Award winner, two Academy Award–winning producers, Olympic athletes and a General Motors CEO among its alumni. Elgin resident John Murphy invented the motorized streetsweeper in 1914 and later formed the Elgin Sweeper Corporation. Pioneering African American chemist Lloyd Hall was an Elgin native, as was the legendary marketer and car stereo pioneer Earl "Madman" Muntz and Max Adler, founder of the Adler Planetarium in Chicago, America's first planetarium.

Ohio State

In prehistoric times Ohio was inhabited by the Mound Builders, many of whose mounds are preserved in state parks and in the Hopewell Culture National Historical Park (see National Parks and Monuments, table). Before the arrival of Europeans, E Ohio was the scene of warfare between the Iroquois and the Erie, which resulted in the extermination of the Erie. In addition to the Iroquois, other Native American tribes soon prominent in the region were the Miami, the Shawnee, and the Ottawa.

La Salle began his explorations of the Ohio valley in 1669 and claimed the entire area for France. The Ohio River became a magnet for fur traders and land seekers, and the British, attempting to move in (see Ohio Company), hotly contested the French claims. Rivalry for control of the forks of the Ohio River led to the outbreak (1754) of the last of the French and Indian Wars. The defeat of the French gave the land to the British, but British possession was disturbed by Pontiac's Rebellion. The British government issued a proclamation in 1763 forbidding settlement W of the Appalachian Mts. Then in 1774, with the Quebec Act, the British placed the region between the Ohio River and the Great Lakes within the boundaries of Canada. The colonists' resentment over these acts contributed to the discontent that led to the American Revolution, during which military operations were conducted in the Ohio country.

From the Settlement of the Old Northwest to Statehood

Ohio was part of the vast area ceded to the United States by the Treaty of Paris 1783. Conflicting claims to land in that area made by Connecticut, Massachusetts, and Virginia were settled by relinquishment of almost all of the claims and the organization of the Old Northwest by the Ordinance of 1787. Ohio was the first region developed under the provisions of that ordinance, with the activities of the Ohio Company of Associates promoted by Rufus Putnam and Manasseh Cutler. Marietta, founded in 1788, was the first permanent American settlement in the Old Northwest.

In the years that followed, various land companies were formed, and settlers poured in from the East, either down the Ohio on flatboats and barges, or across the mountains by wagon—their numbers varying with conditions but steadily expanding the area's population. The Native Americans, supported by the British, resisted American settlement. They successfully opposed campaigns led by Josiah Harmar and Arthur St. Clair but were decisively defeated by Anthony Wayne in the battle of Fallen Timbers (1794). The British thereafter (1796) withdrew their outposts from the Northwest under the terms of Jay's Treaty, and the area was pacified. Ohio became a territory in 1799. General St. Clair, as the first governor, ruled in an arbitrary fashion that made

Ohioans for many years afterward distrustful of all government. In 1802 a state convention drafted a constitution, and in 1803 Ohio entered the Union, with Chillicothe as its capital. Columbus became the permanent capital in 1816.

The War of 1812 and Further Settlement

In the War of 1812, the Americans lost many of the early battles of the war that took place in the Old Northwest, and their military frontier was pushed back to the Ohio River. Two British attacks on Ohio soil were successfully resisted: one against Fort Meigs at the mouth of the Maumee River and the other against Fort Stephenson on the Sandusky. The area was further secured by Oliver Hazard Perry's naval victory on Lake Erie near Put-in-Bay, Ohio, and William Henry Harrison's victory in the battle of the Thames on Canadian soil.

After the war Ohio's growth was spurred by the building of the Erie Canal, other canals, and toll roads. The National Road was a vital settlement and commercial artery. Settlement of the Western Reserve by New Englanders (especially those from Connecticut) gives NE Ohio a decidedly New England cultural landscape. Ohio's society of small farmers exported their produce down the Ohio and the Mississippi rivers to St. Louis and New Orleans. In 1837 Ohio won a territorial struggle with Michigan usually called the Toledo War. The Loan Law, adopted in the Panic of 1837, encouraged railroad and industrial development. Railroads gradually succeeded canals, preparing the way for the industrial expansion that followed the Civil War.

The Civil War, Industrialization, and Politics

Most Ohioans were sympathetic with the Union in the Civil War, and many Ohioans served in the Union army. Native sons such as Joshua R. Giddings, Salmon P. Chase, and Edwin M. Stanton had long been prominent opponents of slavery. Nevertheless, the Peace Democrats, the Knights of the Golden Circle, and the Copperheads were very active; Clement L. Vallandigham drew many votes in the gubernatorial election of 1863. Ohio was the scene of the northernmost penetration of Confederate forces in the war—the famous raid (1863) of John Hunt Morgan, which terrorized the people of the countryside until Morgan and most of his men were finally captured in the southeast corner of the state.

After the Civil War industrial development grew rapidly when shipments of ore from the upper Great Lakes region increased and the development of the petroleum industry in NE Ohio shifted the center of economic activity from the banks of the Ohio River to the shores of Lake Erie, particularly around Cleveland. Immigrants began to swell the population, and huge fortunes were made.

Ohio became very important politically. The state contributed seven American presidents: Ulysses S. Grant, Rutherford B. Hayes, James A. Garfield, Benjamin Harrison, William McKinley, William Howard Taft, and Warren G. Harding. Big business and politics became entwined as in the relations of Marcus A. Hanna and McKinley. City bosses such as Cincinnati's George B. Cox also followed this pattern. The state as a whole was for many years steadily Republican, despite the rise of organized labor in the late 19th cent. and considerable labor strife. In the 1890s the reform-minded mayor of Toledo, Samuel "Golden Rule" Jones, won national fame for his espousal of city ownership of municipal utilities

.

Twentieth-Century Developments

Floods in the many rivers flowing to the Ohio and in the Ohio River itself have long been a problem; a devastating flood in 1913 led to the establishment of the Miami valley conservation project. Continuing long-term state and federal projects have improved locks and dams along the entire length of the Ohio and its major tributaries, for navigation as well as flood control purposes.

Both farms and industries in Ohio were hard hit by the Great Depression that began in 1929. In the 1930s the state was wracked by major strikes such as the sit-down strikes in Akron (1935–36) and the so-called Little

Steel strike (1937). World War II brought great prosperity to Ohio, but labor strife later resumed, as in the steel strikes of 1949 and 1959. Political unrest also affected the state in the protests of the 1960s and most violently in 1970 when four students were killed by national guardsmen who fired on a group of Vietnam War protesters at Kent State Univ.

Ohio's economy went into massive decline in the 1970s and 80s as the automobile, steel, and coal industries virtually collapsed, causing unemployment to soar. Akron, once world famous as a rubber center, stopped manufacturing rubber products altogether by the mid-1980s. During this period, the state's northern industrial centers were especially hard hit and lost much of their population. Since then, Ohio has concentrated on diversifying its economy, largely through expansion of the service sector. The state became an important center for the health-care industry with the opening of the Cleveland Clinic. Industrial research is also important, with Nela Park near Cleveland and Battelle Memorial Institute in Columbus among the more notable research centers; there are also still important rubber research laboratories in Akron.

http://www.infoplease.com/encyclopedia/us/ohio-state-united-states-history.html

Akron is the fifth-largest city in the U.S. state of Ohio and is the county seat of Summit County, the fourth most populous county in the state. The city is located in northeastern Ohio on the western edge of the Glaciated Allegheny Plateau, approximately 39 miles (63 km) south of Lake Erie and was co-founded along the Little Cuyahoga River in 1825 by Simon Perkins and Paul Williams. The name derived from the Greek word "ἄκρον" signifying a summit or high point. Due to Eliakim Crosby founding "North Akron" (Cascade) in 1833, "South" was added to the city's name until the two merged into an incorporated village in 1836. Neighboring settlements Kenmore and Ellet were annexed in 1929. As of the 2015 Census Estimate, the city proper had a total population of 197,542, making Akron the 119th largest city in the United States, and the fifth largest city in Ohio. The Akron, OH Metropolitan Statistical Area (MSA) covers Summit and Portage counties, and in 2010 had a population of 703,200. Akron is also part of the larger Cleveland-Akron-Canton, OH Combined Statistical Area, which in 2013 had a population of 3,501,538, ranking 15th. Creating the first Joint Economic Development Districts, it did so with Springfield, Coventry, and Copley, also Bath in conjunction with Fairlawn. Residents of Akron are called "Akronites". Akron has had many nicknames, three of which are "Rubber City" "Cross Roads of the Deaf", and "City of Invention".

The city became a manufacturing center owing to its location on the Ohio and Erie Canal, as well as being connected to numerous others and railroad lines. With Goodyear, Gojo Industries, FirstEnergy, FirstMerit Corporation, and Time Warner Cable among employers, Akron's economy has diversified sectors that include manufacturing, education, healthcare, and biomedical. Akron is home to the All-American Soapbox Derby. It is also the former home of Goodrich, Firestone, General Tire. Listed by Newsweek as one of ten Information Age high tech havens, it was awarded by the National Civic League and National Arbor Day Foundation, plus named one of the world's most livable cities. Residents Frank and Charles Menches have a disputable claim of inventing the hamburger thus the annual national festival is hosted in the city. A creature often referred to as the Kenmore Grassman is reported through history.

Three major civil unrest events took place during the riot of 1900, rubber strike of 1936, and the Wooster Avenue riots of 1968. Dr. W.E.B. Du Bois (1920) and President Bill Clinton (1997) both gave speeches on race relations in the city. Headquartered on the north side, mobster Rosario Borgio ran black hand operations, Pretty Boy Floyd's Walker-Mitchell mob was also headquartered in the city. Though Akron was part of the Underground Railroad while active, the city also had many officials who were members of the Ku Klux Klan which Wendell Willkie suppressed, and abolitionist John Brown as a resident.

Despite the number of rubber workers decreasing by approximately half from 2000–07, Akron's research in polymers gained an international reputation. It now centers the Polymer Valley which consist of 400 polymer-related companies, of which 94 were located in the city itself. Because of its contributions to the Information Age, *Newsweek's* listed Akron fifth of ten high tech havens in 2001. In 2008 "City of Invention" was added to the seal when the All-America City Award was received for the third time.

Columbus is the capital and largest city of the U.S. state of Ohio. It is the 15th largest city in the United States, with a population of 850,106 (2015 estimate). It is the core city of the Columbus, OH Metropolitan Statistical Area (MSA), which encompasses a ten-county area. It is Ohio's third largest metropolitan area, behind Cleveland and Cincinnati.

It is also the fourth most populous state capital in the United States, and the third largest city in the Midwestern United States.

Columbus is the county seat of Franklin County. Named for explorer Christopher Columbus, the city was founded in 1812 at the confluence of the Scioto and Olentangy rivers and assumed the functions of state capital in 1816.

The city has a diverse economy based on education, government, insurance, banking, fashion, defense, aviation, food, clothes, logistics, steel, energy, medical research, health care, hospitality, retail, and technology. Columbus is home to the Battelle Memorial Institute, the world's largest private research and development foundation; Chemical Abstracts Service, the world's largest clearinghouse of chemical information; and The Ohio State University, one of the largest universities in the United States.

In 2012, Columbus was ranked in *BusinessWeek*'s 50 best cities in America. In 2007, *fDi Magazine* ranked the city no. 3 in the U.S. for cities of the future, and the Columbus Zoo and Aquarium was rated no. 1 in 2009 by *USA Travel Guide*.

The National Road reached Columbus from Baltimore in 1831, which complemented the city's new link to the Ohio and Erie Canal and facilitated a population boom. A wave of European immigrants led to the creation of two ethnic enclaves on the city's outskirts. A large Irish population settled in the north along Naghten Street (presently Nationwide Boulevard), while the Germans took advantage of the cheap land to the south, creating a community that came to be known as the *Das Alte Südende* (The Old South End).

Before the abolition of slavery in the South in 1863, the Underground Railroad was active in Columbus; led, in part, by James Preston Poindexter. Poindexter arrived in Columbus in the 1830s and became a Baptist Preacher and leader in the city's African American community until the turn of the century.

New York State

In 1811 a new fort called West Battery replaced Fort George. In 1815 it was renamed Castle Clinton after the mayor DeWitt Clinton.

At first New York City grew in a haphazard way. However, in 1807 the governor of the state of New York appointed a commission to draw up a plan for the city. The commission reported in 1811. The plan proposed that new streets should be laid out on a grid pattern. There would be 12 avenues running north to south and 155 streets running east to west. As New York City grew the grid pattern spread north across Manhattan.

By 1820 New York had become the USA's largest city with a population of 123,000. It continued to grow rapidly. By 1840 New York had a population of 312,000. By 1860 it had 813,000 inhabitants.

However, in 1835 fire destroyed much of the old district of New York but it was soon rebuilt. In 1837 Harlem was connected to New York by railway. As a result, it grew rapidly.

Meanwhile New York boomed as a port. In 1807 Robert Fulton launched a steamboat on the Hudson River. In 1818 ship owners in New York formed the Black Ball Line, the first shipping line between New York and Liverpool.

However, the port of New York really boomed when the Erie Canal was built. It allowed goods to be transported from the coast to the interior cheaply and quickly. The shipbuilding industry in New York flourished in the 19th century.

New York University was founded in 1831. New York City Police Force was founded in 1845.

The Astor Place Riot occurred in May 1849. On 10 May 1849 English actor William Macready played Macbeth at Astor Place Opera House. It was a time of anti-English feeling in New York and an angry crowd gathered outside. The crowd then began to riot. The National Guard was called and they fired on the rioters. Altogether at least 25 civilians were killed and many more were wounded. Afterwards 86 rioters were arrested.

On 12 July 1863 New York City was rocked by draft riots. Angry about a new law on conscription rioters roamed the streets until Lincoln sent troops to quell the disorder. Many lives were lost and a great deal of material damage was done.

Like other cities in the 19th century in Europe and North America, New York was an unhealthy place. As a result, cholera struck New York in 1832 and in 1849. it returned in 1866.

Nevertheless, amenities in New York City improved during the 19th century. Trinity Church was rebuilt in the 1840s. It was consecrated in 1846. The architect was Richard Upjohn (1802-1878). Macy's opened in 1858. Central Synagogue was built in 1870. Bloomingdales was founded in 1872. St Patrick's Cathedral was dedicated in 1879.

In 1832 the first horse drawn streetcars ran in New York. The first elevated railway in New York began carrying passengers in 1868. It was soon followed by many other elevated railways or 'els'. The first line of the New York subway opened in 1904.

The Croton Reservoir was built in 1842 to provide New York with piped drinking water. Madison Square opened in 1847. The New York Times began publication in 1851.

Washington Square Park was created in 1826. Then, in 1858 Frederick Law Olmsted and Calvert Vaux created Central Park. Prospect Park was laid out in 1867. Bryant Park was laid out in 1884. It was named after the poet William Cullen Bryant (1794-1878).

Meanwhile the first telephones were installed in New York City in 1878. New York gained an electricity supply in the 1880s.

Brooklyn Bridge opened in 1883. Unfortunately, on the opening day a crowd on the bridge panicked, thinking it was going to collapse. As a result, 12 people were trampled to death.

The Museum of Natural History in New York was founded in 1869. The Metropolitan Museum of Art was founded in 1870. Carnegie Hall opened in 1891. Bronx Zoo opened in 1899.

In 1883 Metropolitan Opera House was founded on Broadway. In the early 20th century Broadway became famous for its theaters.

Meanwhile the Statue of Liberty was dedicated by President Grover Cleveland on 28 October 1886. Then in 1888 New York City was struck by a terrible blizzard and 400 people froze to death.

The Statue of Liberty

In the mid-19th century many Germans and Irish went to live in New York. In the late 19th century many Italians arrived and in the 1890s many Eastern European Jews came to New York.

In 1892 the United States Immigration Station opened on Ellis Island. Between 1892 and its closure in 1954 almost 17 million immigrants passed through Ellis Island. However, restrictions were placed on Chinese immigration in 1882, on Japanese in 1907 and on illiterate people in 1917. At the end of the 19th century and the beginning of the 20th many African Americans went to live in Harlem.

At that time many poor New Yorkers lived in tenements. They were overcrowded, poorly ventilated and rooms often lacked windows.

In 1892 a notorious slum called Five Points was demolished and replaced by Columbus Park. Seward Park was created in 1901.

Furthermore, at the end of the 19th century the garment trade in New York boomed. However, working conditions were often appalling with people working very long hours for very low wages.

On 15 June disaster struck New York. A ship called the General Slocum was taking people on an excursion. It caught fire and 1,021 people were killed.

Furthermore, on 25 March 1911 a dreadful fire at the Triangle Shirtwaist Factory took the lives of 146 workers.

Meanwhile in 1898 the 5 boroughs were united under a single municipal government. The city of New York had a population of 3.4 million.

Washington State

Washington's early history is shared with that of the whole Oregon Territory. The perennial search for the Northwest Passage aroused initial interest in the area. Of the early explorers along the Pacific coast, Spanish expeditions under Juan Pérez (1774) and Bruno Heceta (1775) are the first known to have definitely skirted the coast of what is now Washington. Capt. James Cook's English expedition (1778) first opened up the area to the maritime fur trade with China, and British fur companies were soon exploring the West and encountering Russians pushing southward from posts in Alaska. In 1787, Charles William Barkley found the inland channel, which the following year John Meares named the Juan de Fuca Strait (after the sailor who is alleged to have discovered it). In 1792, the British explorer George Vancouver and the American fur trader Robert Gray crossed paths along the Washington coast. Vancouver sailed into Puget Sound and mapped the area; Gray, convinced of the existence of a great river that the other explorers rejected, found the entrance, crossed the dangerous bar, and sailed up the Columbia, establishing U.S. claims to the areas that it drained.

Early Settlement and Boundary Disputes

The Lewis and Clark expedition, which reached the area in 1805, and the establishment of John Jacob Astor's settlement, Astoria, both helped to further the American claim; but in 1807 the Canadian trader David Thompson traveled the length of the Columbia, mapping the region and establishing British counterclaims. After Astoria was sold to the North West Company in the War of 1812, British interests appeared paramount, although in 1818 a treaty provided for 10 years (later extended) of joint rights for the United States and Great Britain in the Columbia River country. The Hudson's Bay Company absorbed the North West Company in 1821 and, under the patriarchal guidance of Dr. John McLoughlin, dominated the region until challenged by the Americans in the 1840s.

Fort Vancouver, on the site of present-day Vancouver, sheltered American overland traders—particularly Jedediah Smith, Benjamin Bonneville, and Nathaniel Wyeth—and later the American missionaries, who were the first real settlers in the area north of the Columbia. Marcus Whitman established (1836) a mission at Waiilatpu (near present-day Walla Walla), which for a decade not only served Native Americans as a medical and religious center but also provided an indispensable rest stop for immigrants on the Oregon Trail. Meanwhile the British, although despairing of control over the area S of the Columbia, were still determined to retain the region to the north; the Americans, on the other hand, demanded the ouster of the British from the whole of the Columbia River country up to a lat. of 54°40−N. "Fifty-four forty or fight" became a slogan in the 1844 election campaign, and for a time war with Britain threatened. However, diplomacy prevailed, and in 1846 the boundary was set at lat. 49°N.

Native American Resistance and Territorial Status

Peace with the British did not, however, preclude Native American conflict. Partly as a protective measure, the Oregon Territory, embracing the Washington area, was created the following year; but in 1853 the region was divided, and Washington Territory (containing a part of what is now Idaho) was set up, with Isaac Stevens as the first governor. (The Idaho section was cut away when Idaho Territory was formed in 1863.) Meanwhile, some of the pioneers on the Oregon trail began to turn northward, and a small settlement sprang up at New Market, or Tumwater (near present-day Olympia).

After word of the needs of California gold-seekers for lumber and food spread northward, settlers recognized the commercial potential of the Puget Sound country and poured into the area in ever-increasing numbers. Lumber and fishing industries arose to satisfy the demand to the south, and new towns, including Seattle, were founded. Meanwhile Stevens, who also served as superintendent of Indian affairs, set about persuading the Native Americans to sell much of their lands and settle on reservations. Treaties with the coast tribes were quickly concluded, but the inland tribes revolted, and hostilities with the Cayuse, the Yakima, and the Nez Percé tribes continued for many years. Over the years, Native Americans remained a small but significant presence in the state; in the early 1990s their population was over 81,000.

Gold, Immigration, and Statehood

Gold was first discovered in Washington in 1852 by a Hudson's Bay Company agent at Fort Colville, but the Yakima War was then in progress and it hindered extensive mining activity. In 1860 the Orofino Creek and Clearwater River deposits were uncovered, bringing a rush of prospectors to the Walla Walla area. The major influx of settlers was delayed, however, until the 1880s, when transport by rail became possible (the first of three transcontinental railroads linked to Washington was completed in 1883).

The population almost quadrupled between 1880 and 1890; although the majority of the new settlers were from the East and Midwest, the territory also absorbed large numbers of foreign immigrants. Chinese laborers had been brought in during the 1860s to aid in placer mining; after 1870 they were followed by substantial groups of Germans, Scandinavians, Russians, Dutch, and Japanese immigrants. By the time Washington became a state in 1889, the wide sagebrush plains of E Washington had been given over to cattle and sheep, agriculture was flourishing in the fertile valleys, and the lumber industry had been founded.

Although some agrarian and labor dissatisfaction with the railroads and other big corporations existed, giving rise to the Granger movement and the Populist party, the discovery of gold in Alaska in 1897 brought renewed prosperity. Seattle, the primary departure point for the Klondike, became a boomtown. Labor and election reform laws were enacted, and the primary, the initiative, the referendum, and the recall were adopted.

The Early Twentieth Century

The turn of the century brought labor clashes that gave Washington a reputation as a radical state. The extreme policies of the Industrial Workers of the World (IWW; also known as the "Wobblies") proved appealing to the shipyard and dock workers and to the loggers, and in 1917 the U.S. War Dept. was forced to intervene in a lumber industry dispute. A general strike following World War I had a crippling effect on the state's economy; antilabor feeling increased, and the famous incident at Centralia resulted in bloody strife between the IWW and the American Legion. The alarmed and brutal reaction of management to radical labor policies produced a confrontational atmosphere that hindered the mediation until the onset of the lean days of the 1930s and the emergence of the New Deal.

Washington was an important center of the defense industry during World War II, particularly with the immense aircraft industry in Seattle and the Manhattan Project's Hanford Works at Richland. (Decades later it was discovered that the Hanford facility had leaked large amounts of hazardous radioactive waste in the 1940s and 50s.) During the war, the large Japanese American population in the state (more than 15,000 persons) was moved eastward to camps, where they suffered great physical and emotional hardship.

Postwar Change and New Industry

In the postwar period military spending continued to pour into such facilities as the Hanford nuclear reservation and the Bremerton naval shipyard, as well as into Boeing's bomber production. At the same time, trade with Asia boomed. Since the 1970s, Washington has attracted a large number of firms moving from California to a more favorable business climate. These include computer software manufacturers and other high-technology companies. The increased economic diversification and stepped-up activity in high-tech industries have cushioned the impact of job losses in the 1990s from post–cold war cutbacks, especially in aerospace orders for Boeing. At the same time, industrial and residential growth has brought the state face to face with environmental issues, among them the effects of continued massive logging and the impact of dams on fish populations.

http://www.infoplease.com/encyclopedia/us/washington-state-united-states-history.html

Camas is a city in Clark County, Washington, with a population of 19,355 at the 2010 census. Officially incorporated on June 18, 1906, the city is named after the camas lily, a plant with an onion-like bulb prized by Native Americans. At the west end of downtown Camas is a large Georgia-Pacific paper-mill from which the high school teams get their name "the Papermakers". Accordingly, the city is about 20 miles east (upwind) from Portland, Oregon. Historically, the commercial base of the city was almost solely the paper mill; however, the diversity of industries has been enhanced considerably in recent years by the influx of several white-collar, high-tech companies including Hewlett-Packard, Sharp Microelectronics, Linear Technology, WaferTech and Underwriters Labs.

Camas was founded as the LaCamas colony in 1883 by Henry Pittock who owned the Oregonian. The upriver location from Vancouver made it a good site for his new paper mill. The town was named after the Camas lilly which was used as food by the local chinook tribes. This agriculture town was incorporated in 1906 as an active Prohibition town. Its incorporation was done to control alcohol. Due to high-tech companies moving in the landscape of the town began to change.

Walla Walla

Recorded history in this state begins with the establishment of Fort Nez Perce in 1818 by the North West Company to trade with the Walla Walla people and other local Native American groups. At the time, the term "Nez Perce" was used more broadly than today and included the Walla Walla in its scope in English usage. Fort Nez Perce had its name shift to Fort Walla Walla. It was located significantly west of the present city.

On September 1, 1836, Marcus Whitman arrived with his wife Narcissa Whitman. Here they established the Whitman Mission in an unsuccessful attempt to convert the local Walla Walla tribe to Christianity. Following a disease epidemic, both were killed in 1847 by the Cayuse who believed that the missionaries were poisoning the native peoples. Whitman College was established in their honor.

On July 24, 1846, Pope Pius IX established the Diocese of Walla Walla and appointed Augustin-Magloire Blanchet to become the first Bishop of Walla Walla. The diocese was short-lived as Bishop Blanchet fled to St. Paul, Oregon, after the Whitman Massacre. In 1850, the Diocese of Nesqually was established in Vancouver and in 1853 the Diocese of Walla Walla was suppressed and absorbed into the Diocese of Nesqually. Today, the Diocese of Walla Walla is a titular see currently held by Witold Mroziewski, an auxiliary bishop of Brooklyn.

The original North West Company and later Hudson's Bay Company Fort Nez Percés fur trading outpost, became a major stopping point for migrants moving west to Oregon Country. The fort has been restored with many of the original buildings preserved. The current Fort Walla Walla contains these buildings, albeit in a different location from the original, as well as a museum about the early settlers' lives.

The origins of Walla Walla at its present site begin with the establishment of Fort Walla Walla by the United States Army here in 1856. The Walla Walla River, where it adjoins the Columbia River, was the starting point for the Mullan Road, constructed between 1859 and 1860 by US Army Lieut. John Mullan, connecting the head of navigation on the Columbia at Walla Walla (i.e., the west coast of the United States) with the head of navigation on the Missouri-Mississippi (that is, the east and gulf coasts of the U.S.) at Fort Benton, Montana.

Walla Walla was incorporated on January 11, 1862.As a result of a gold rush in Idaho, during this decade the city became the largest community in the territory of Washington, at one point slated to be the new state's capital. Following this period of rapid growth, agriculture became the city's primary industry. Baker Boyer Bank, the oldest bank in the state of Washington, was founded in Walla Walla in 1869. *https://en.wikipedia.org/wiki/Walla_Walla,_Washington*

Kansas State

When the Spanish explorer Francisco Vásquez de Coronado visited (1541) the Kansas area in his search for Quivira, a fabled kingdom of riches, the area was occupied by various Native American groups of the Plains descent, notably the Kansa, the Wichita and the Pawnee. Another Spanish explorer, Juan de Oñate, penetrated the region in 1601. A result of Spanish entry into the region was the introduction of the horse, which revolutionized the life of the Native Americans. While not actually exploring the Kansas area, Robert Cavelier, sieur de La Salle, claimed (c.1682) for France all territory drained by the Mississippi River, including Kansas.

French traders and Native Americans had a great deal of contact during most of the 18th cent. By the Treaty of Paris of 1763 ending the French and Indian Wars, France ceded the territory of W Louisiana (including Kansas) to Spain. In 1800, Spain secretly retroceded the territory to France, from whom the United States acquired it in the Louisiana Purchase in 1803. The region was little known, however, and subsequent explorations to include Kansas were the Lewis and Clark expedition (1803–6), the Arkansas River journey of Zebulon M. Pike in 1806, and the scientific expedition of Stephen H. Long in 1819.

Most of the territory that eventually became Kansas was in an area known as the Great American Desert, considered unsuitable for U.S. settlement because of its apparent barrenness. In the 1830s the region was designated a permanent home for Native Americans, and northern and eastern tribes were relocated there. Forts were constructed for frontier defense and for the protection of the growing trade along the Santa Fe Trail, which crossed Kansas. Fort Leavenworth was established in 1827, Fort Scott in 1842, and Fort Riley in 1853.

Kansas, at this time mainly a region to be crossed on the way to California and Oregon, was organized as a territory in 1854. Its settlement, however, was spurred not so much by natural westward expansion as by the determination of both proslavery and antislavery factions to achieve a majority population in the territory. The struggle between the factions was further complicated by conflict over the location of a transcontinental railroad, with proponents of a central route (rather than a southern route) eager to resolve the slavery issue in the area and promote settlement.

The Kansas-Nebraska Act (1854), an attempted compromise on the extension of slavery, repealed the Missouri Compromise and reopened the issue of extending slavery north of lat. 36°30′ by providing for popular sovereignty in Kansas and Nebraska, allowing settlers of territories to decide the matter themselves. Meanwhile, the Emigrant Aid Company was organized in Massachusetts to foster antislavery immigration to Kansas, and proslavery interests in Missouri and throughout the South took counteraction. Towns were established by each faction—Lawrence and Topeka by the free-staters and Leavenworth and Atchison by the proslavery settlers.

Soon all the problems attendant upon organizing a territory for statehood became subsidiary to the single issue of slavery. The first elections in 1854 and 1855 were won by the proslavery group; armed Missourians intimidated voters and election officials and stuffed the ballot boxes. Andrew H. Reeder was appointed the first territorial governor in 1854. The first territorial legislature ousted (1855) all free-state members, secured the removal of Gov. Reeder, established the capital in Lecompton, and adopted proslavery statutes. In retaliation the abolitionists set up a rival government at Topeka in Oct., 1855.

Violence soon came to the territory. The murder of a free-state man in Nov., 1855, led to the so-called Wakarusa War, a bloodless series of encounters along the Wakarusa River. The intervention of the new governor, Wilson Shannon, kept proslavery men from attacking Lawrence. However, civil war ultimately turned the territory into bleeding Kansas. On May 21, 1856, proslavery groups and armed Missourians known as Border Ruffians raided Lawrence. A few days later a band led by the abolitionist crusader John Brown murdered five proslavery men in the Pottawatamie massacre. Guerrilla warfare between free-state men called Jayhawkers and proslavery bands—both sides abetted by desperadoes and opportunists—terrorized the land. After a new governor, John W. Geary, persuaded a large group of Border Ruffians to return to Missouri, the violence subsided.

The Lecompton legislature met in 1857 to make preparations for convening a constitutional convention. Gov. Geary resigned after it became clear that free elections would not be held to approve a new constitution. Robert J. Walker was appointed governor, and a convention held at Lecompton drafted a constitution. Only that part of the resulting proslavery constitution dealing with slavery was submitted to the electorate, and the question was drafted to favor the proslavery group. Free-state men refused to participate in the election with the result that the constitution was overwhelmingly approved.

Despite the dubious validity of the Lecompton constitution, President James Buchanan recommended (1858) that Congress accept it and approve statehood for the territory. Instead, Congress returned it for another territorial vote. The proslavery group boycotted the election, and the constitution was rejected. Lawrence became de facto capital of the troubled territory until after the Wyandotte constitution (framed in 1859 and totally forbidding slavery) was accepted by Congress. The Kansas conflict and the question of statehood for the territory became a national issue and figured in the 1860 Republican party platform.

Kansas became a state in 1861, with the capital at Topeka. Charles Robinson was the first governor and James H. Lane, an active free stater during the 1850s, one of the U.S. Senators. In the Civil War, Kansas fought with the North and suffered the highest rate of fatal casualties of any state in the Union. Confederate William C. Quantrill and his guerrilla band burned Lawrence in 1863.

With peace came the development of the prairie lands. The construction of railroads made cow towns such as Abilene and Dodge City, with their cowboys, saloons, and frontier marshals, the shipping point for large herds of cattle driven overland from Texas. The buffalo herds disappeared (some buffalo still roam in state parks and game preserves), and cattle took their place. Pioneer homesteaders, adjusting to life on the timberless prairie and living in sod houses, suffered privation. In 1874, Mennonite emigrants from Russia brought the Turkey Red variety of winter wheat to Kansas. This wheat was instrumental in making Kansas the Wheat State as winter wheat replaced spring wheat on an ever-increasing scale. Corn, too, soon became a major cash crop.

Agricultural production was periodically disrupted by national depressions and natural disasters. Repeated and prolonged droughts accompanied by dust storms, occasional grasshopper invasions, and floods all caused severe economic dislocation. Mortgages often weighed heavily on farmers, and discontent was expressed in farmer support of radical farm organizations and third-party movements, such as the Granger movement, Greenback party, and Populist party. Tax relief, better regulation of interest rates, and curbs on the power of railroads were sought by these organizations. Twice in the 1890s, Populist-Democrats were elected to the governorship.

As conditions improved, Kansas returned largely to its allegiance to the Republican party and gained a reputation as a conservative stronghold with a bent for moral reform, indicated in the state's strong support of prohibition; laws against the sale of liquor remained on the books in Kansas from 1880 to 1949. Over the years the use of improved agricultural methods and machines increased crop yield. Irrigation proved practicable in some areas, and winter wheat and alfalfa could be cultivated in dry regions.

Wheat production greatly expanded during World War I, but the end of the war brought financial difficulties. During the 1920s and 30s, Kansas was faced with labor unrest and the economic hardships of the depression. As part of the Dust Bowl, Kansas sustained serious land erosion during the long drought of the 1930s. Erosion led to the implementation of conservation and reclamation projects, particularly in the northern and western parts of the state. In 1924 an effort of the Ku Klux Klan to gain political control was fought by William Allen White, editor of the Emporia *Gazette,* who supported many liberal causes. Alfred M. Landon, elected governor in 1932, was one of the few Republican candidates in the country to win election in the midst of the sweeping Democratic victory that year. He was nominated as the Republican presidential candidate in 1936.

During World War II agriculture thrived and industry expanded rapidly. The food-processing industry grew substantially, the cement industry enjoyed a major revival, and the aircraft industry boomed. After the war agricultural prosperity once again declined when the state was hit by a severe drought and grasshopper invasion in 1948. Prosperity returned briefly during the Korean War, but afterward farm surpluses and insufficient world markets combined to make the state's tremendous agricultural ability part of the national farm problem.

Kansas has become increasingly industrialized and urbanized, and industrial production has surpassed farm production in economic importance. Flood damage in the state, especially after a major flood in 1951, spurred the construction of dams (such as the Tuttle Creek, Milford, and Wilson dams) on major Kansas rivers, and their reservoirs have vastly increased water recreational facilities for Kansans. Since the 1970s, Kansas has become increasingly more urban and suburban. Accordingly, the economy has shifted its emphasis to finance and service industries located in and around the major urban centers.

www.infoplease.com/encyclopedia/places/north-america/us/kansas-state-united-states/history

Pawnee County was organized on November 4, 1872, by A. H. Boyd; Henry Booth; Timothy McCarthy; and George J. Cox. Containing the cities of Garfield, Burdett, Rozel and Larned, the county was named for the Pawnee Indians

The establishment of Fort Larned in 1859 on the Santa Fe Trail was significant not only for defense of the Trail, but also to assist settlers in the area. The Hancock-Custer expedition of 1867 arrived at Fort Larned on April 7, 1867, and the two men conducted meetings with two Cheyenne chiefs, Tall Bull, and White Horse in an attempt to satisfy Indian displeasure at white settlement in the area. This meeting temporarily halted any problems along the Santa Fe Trail.

The Larned Presbyterian Church was organized on July 15, 1873. The first county fair was held in 1876. Currently it is a 4-H fair. The first school district was Pawnee Number 1, formed in Larned on June 24, 1873.

Two notable Kansans hail from this county. Henry Booth (1838-1898) served in the Kansas Cavalry during the Civil War, and later became a businessman and politician. He was appointed Postmaster at Fort Larned in 1869 and later became the fort's sutler. He and associates formed the Larned Town Company. He served in the Kansas Legislature for many years and as Speaker of the House. Clyde W. Tombaugh (1906-1997), and family moved to Burdett in 1922, where he graduated from Burdett High School in 1925. Working at the Lowell Observatory in Flagstaff, Arizona, Burdett discovered the planet Pluto in February 1930.

A story is told that residents of Phillipsburg once were convinced that Plotner Creek carried a deposit of gold in its waters. The morning after the rumor began, businesses didn't open, county officers held their business elsewhere, and all worked away at slate out-cropping's trying to find the mother lode. A visiting Colorado miner confided in some that the creek was a salted mine, then left before the local citizens could find a rope.

Oregon State

Initial European interest in the region was aroused by the search for the Northwest Passage. Spanish seamen skirted the Pacific coast from the 16th to the 18th cent., hoping to claim the area. The English may first have arrived in the person of Sir Francis Drake, who sailed along the coast in 1579, possibly as far as Oregon.

Two centuries later, in 1778, Capt. James Cook, seeking the award of £20,000 for the discovery of the Northwest Passage, charted some of the coastline. By this time the Russians were pushing southward from posts in Alaska and the British fur companies were exploring the West. Oregon's furs promised to become an important factor in the rapidly expanding China trade, and the Oregon coast was soon active with the vessels of several nations engaged in fur trade with the Native Americans. British captains, among them John Meares and George Vancouver, made the coastal area known, but it was an American, Robert Gray, who first sailed up the Columbia River (1792), thus establishing U.S. claim to the areas that it drained.

Canadian traders of the North West Company were approaching the Columbia River country when the overland Lewis and Clark expedition arrived in 1805. David Thompson was already making his way to the lower river when John Jacob Astor's agents (in the Pacific Fur Company) founded Astoria, the first permanent settlement in the Oregon country. In the War of 1812, the post was sold (1813) to the North West Company, but in 1818 a treaty provided for 10 years of joint rights for the United States and Great Britain in Oregon (i.e., the whole Columbia River area). This agreement was later extended. The North West Company merged with the Hudson's Bay Company in 1821, and soon the region was dominated by John McLoughlin at Fort Vancouver.

Settlement and Statehood

In 1842 and 1843 enormous wagon trains began the "great migration" westward over the Oregon Trail. Trouble between the settlers and the British followed. The Americans set out to form their own government, and demanded the British be removed from the whole of the Columbia River country up to lat. 54°40–N; one of the slogans of the 1844 election was "Fifty-four forty or fight." War with Britain was a threat momentarily, but diplomacy prevailed. In 1846 the boundary was set at the line of lat. 49°N, but disagreements over the interpretation of the 1846 treaty were not successfully arbitrated until 1872.

Two years later the Oregon Territory was created, embracing the area W of the Rockies from the 42d to the 49th parallel. The area was reduced with the creation of the Washington Territory in 1853, and Oregon became a state in 1859 with a constitution that prohibited slaveholding but also forbade free blacks from entering the state. Although the California gold rush caused a temporary exodus of settlers, it also brought a new market for Oregon's goods, and the Oregon gold strike that followed attracted some permanent settlement to the eastern hills and valleys.

Wheat farming prospered and in 1867–68 a surplus crop was shipped to England—the beginning of Oregon's great wheat export trade. Cattle and sheep were driven up from California to graze on the tallgrass of the semiarid plateaus, and soon cattle barons, such as Henry Miller, acquired huge herds. They dominated the industry until the late 19th cent., when sheepmen and homesteaders succeeded in reducing the cattle range. The 1850s, 60s, and 70s were plagued by Native American uprisings, but by 1880 troubles with the Native American were over, and the next few decades brought increasing settlement and internal improvements.

Railroads and Industrialization

During the 1880s, and largely under the management of Henry Villard of the Northern Pacific RR, transcontinental rail lines were completed to the coast and down the Willamette Valley into California, bringing new trade and stimulating the beginnings of manufacture. Lumbering, which had long been important, became a leading industry. Seemingly overnight logging camps and sawmills were built in the western foothills. The huge stands of Douglas fir and cedar brought fortunes to the lumbering kings, but the threat to natural resources led ultimately to the creation of national forests.

By the time of the Lewis and Clark Centennial Exposition at Portland in 1905, less than 50 years after statehood had been gained, the frontier era had passed. Most of the feuding on the eastern plateaus was over, and cattle and sheep grazed peacefully on fenced-in ranges. In spring the Willamette Valley was abloom with fruit blossoms, and the river cities were busy with trade and industry.

Reform Movements and Environmental Issues

Oregon has been a leader in social, environmental, and political reforms. It was the first state, for example, to institute initiative, referendum, and recall; to ease the laws governing the use of marijuana; and to initiate a ban against nonrecyclable containers. Several issues have sharply divided conservatives and liberals; one of the most important has been the question of minority groups. In the 1880s the influx of Chinese threatened the labor market and brought violent anti-Chinese sentiment, and in the 20th cent. there was opposition to the Japanese. Feeling against minorities has never been statewide, however, and large groups have vigorously opposed it.

In the 1930s one of the most disputed issues was the question of whether the development of power should be public or private. Today, however, it is widely recognized that the federal power and irrigation projects have had a profoundly positive effect on the economy of the entire Pacific Northwest. Many acres have been opened to irrigated farming, and the tremendous industrial expansion of World War II was to a large extent dependent on Bonneville power.

Environmental issues have dominated Oregon politics since the 1970s. Controversy arose in the late 1980s over the spotted owl, which has become endangered as old-growth forest has been cut down. Restrictions on logging on public lands were initiated in 1991 and attempts to establish forest policies acceptable to both environmentalists and the timber industry bogged down as other species were also shown to be in danger. There also is concern that the state's numerous hydroelectric dams are disrupting the migratory cycle of Pacific salmon.

http://www.infoplease.com/encyclopedia/us/oregon-state-united-states-history.html

Beaverton is a city in Washington County, in the U.S. state of Oregon. The city center is 7 miles (11 km) west of downtown Portland in the Tualatin River Valley. As of the 2010 census, the population is 89,803.[1] This makes it the second-largest city in the county and Oregon's sixth-largest city. Fire protection and EMS services are provided through Tualatin Valley Fire and Rescue.

In 2010, Beaverton was named by *Money* magazine as one of the 100 "best places to live", among smaller cities in the country. Along with Hillsboro, Beaverton is one of the economic centers for Washington County, home to numerous corporations in a variety of industries.

According to *Oregon Geographic Names*, Beaverton got its name because of the settlement's proximity to a large body of water resulting from beaver dams.

The area of Tualatin Valley which became Beaverton was originally the home of a Native American tribe known as the *Atfalati*, which settlers mispronounced as *Tualatin*. The Atfalati population dwindled in the latter part of the 18th century, and the prosperous tribe was no longer dominant in the area by the 19th century when settlers arrived.

19th century

The natives had a village called *Chakeipi*, meaning *Place of the Beaver*, and early settlers referred to it as "Beaverdam". Early settlers include the Hall Family from Kentucky, the Denneys who lived on their claim near present-day Scholls Ferry Road and Hall Blvd, and Orin S. Allen, from western New York

Beginning of the town

After the American Civil War, numerous other settlers, including Joshua Welch, George Betts, Charles Angel, W. P. Watson, and John Henry, laid out what is now known as Beaverton hoping they could bring a railroad to an area once described as, "mostly swamps & marshes connected by beaver dams to create what looked like a huge lake." In 1872, Beaverton's first post office opened in a general store operated by Betts, who also served as the first postmaster of the community. Betts Street, where the current post office now stands, is named in honor of him. In 1893, Beaverton, which by that time had a population of 400, was officially incorporated. Alonzo Cady, a local businessman, served as the first mayor. Many major roads in Beaverton are named for these early settlers.

The city has tried to encourage transit-oriented development around the city's MAX Light Rail stations. The Round, a mixed-use development around Beaverton Central MAX Station on the site of a former sewer plant, was originally announced in 1996 It is only partially complete, due to the bankruptcy of one developer and the Great Recession. In 2014, the City of Beaverton moved its city hall into a vacant office building in The Round. Further development and an arts center have been proposed for the former site of the Westgate Theatre, adjacent to The Round.

Portland is the largest city in the U.S. state of Oregon and the seat of Multnomah County. It is located in the Willamette Valley region of the Pacific Northwest, at the confluence of the Willamette and Columbia Rivers. The city covers 145 square miles (380 square kilometers) and had an estimated population of 632,309 in 2015, making it the 26th most populous city in the United States. Approximately 2,389,228 people live in the Portland metropolitan statistical. Roughly 60% of Oregon's population resides within the Portland metropolitan area.

Named after the city on the coast of Maine, the Oregon settlement began to be populated in the 1830s near the end of the Oregon Trail. Its water access provided convenient transportation of goods, and the timber industry was a major force in the city's early economy. At the turn of the 20th century, the city had developed a reputation as one of the most dangerous port cities in the world, a hub for organized crime and racketeering. After the city's economy experienced an industrial boom during World War II, its hard-edged reputation began to dissipate. Beginning in the 1960s, Portland became noted for its growing liberal political values, and the city has earned a reputation as a bastion of counterculture, which proceeded into the 21st century. According to a 2009 Pew Research Center study, Portland ranks as the eighth most popular American city, based on where people want to live.

The city operates with a commission-based government guided by a mayor and four commissioners as well as Metro, the only directly elected metropolitan planning organization in the United States. The city government is notable for its land-use planning and investment in public transportation. Portland is frequently recognized as one of the most environmentally conscious cities in the world because of its high walkability, large community of bicyclists, farm-to-table dining, expansive network of public transportation options, and over 10,000 acres (4,000 hectares) of public parks. Its climate is marked by warm, dry summers and cold, rainy winters. This climate is ideal for growing roses, and Portland has been called the "City of Roses" for over a century. "Keep Portland Weird" is an unofficial slogan for the city.

During the prehistoric period, the land that would become Portland was flooded after the collapse of glacial dams from Lake Missoula, located in what would later become Montana. These massive floods occurred during the last ice age and filled the Willamette Valley with 300 to 400 feet (91 to 122 m) of water.

Before American pioneers began arriving in the 1800s, the land that eventually became Portland and surrounding Multnomah County was inhabited for many centuries by two bands of indigenous Chinook people— the Multnomah and the Clackamas peoples. The Chinook people occupying the land which would become Portland were first documented by Meriwether Lewis and William Clark in 1805. Before its European settlement, the Portland Basin of the lower Columbia River and Willamette River valleys had been one of the most densely populated regions on the Pacific Coast.

Settlement

Significant numbers of pioneer settlers began arriving in the Willamette Valley in the 1830s via the Oregon Trail, though life was originally centered in nearby Oregon City. In the early 1840s a new settlement began emerging ten miles from the mouth of the Willamette River, roughly halfway between Oregon City and Fort Vancouver. This community was initially referred to as "Stumptown" and "The Clearing" because of the many trees being cut down to allow for its growth. In 1843 William Overton saw potential in the new settlement but lacked the funds

At the time of its incorporation on February 8, 1851, Portland had over 800 inhabitants, a steam sawmill, a log cabin hotel, and a newspaper, the *Weekly Oregonian*. A major fire swept through downtown in August 1873, destroying twenty blocks on the west side of the Willamette along Yamhill and Morrison Streets, and causing $1.3 million in damage. By 1879, the population had grown to 17,500 and by 1890 it had grown to 46,385. In 1888, the city constructed the first steel bridge built on the West Coast.

Portland's access to the Pacific Ocean via the Willamette and the Columbia rivers, as well as its easy access to the agricultural Tualatin Valley via the "Great Plank Road" (the route of current-day U.S. Route 26), provided the pioneer city with an advantage over other nearby ports, and it grew very quickly. Portland remained the major port in the Pacific Northwest for much of the 19th century, until the 1890s, when Seattle's deep-water harbor was connected to the rest of the mainland by rail, affording an inland route without the treacherous navigation of the Columbia River.

Portland developed a reputation early on in its history as a hard-edged and gritty port town. In 1889, *The Oregonian* called Portland "the most filthy city in the Northern States," due to the unsanitary sewers and gutters, and, at the turn of the 20th century, it was considered one of the most dangerous port cities in the world. By the early 20th century, the city had lost its reputation as a "sober frontier city" and garnered a reputation for being violent and dangerous.-

Between 1900 and 1930, the population of the city tripled from nearly 100,000 to 301,815. Following this population boom, Portland became a notorious hub for underground criminal activity and organized crime between the 1940s and 1950s. In 1957, *LIFE* Magazine published an article detailing the city's history of government corruption and crime, specifically its gambling rackets and illegal nightclubs. In spite of the city's seedier undercurrent of criminal activity, Portland was experiencing an economic and industrial surge during World War II. Ship builder Henry J. Kaiser had been awarded contracts to construct Liberty ships and aircraft carrier escorts, and chose sites in Portland and Vancouver, Washington for work yards.- During this time, Portland's population rose by over 150,000, largely attributed to recruited laborers.-

During the 1960s, an influx of hippie subculture began to take root in the city in the wake of San Francisco's burgeoning countercultural scene. A large social activist presence evolved during this time as well, specifically concerning Native American rights, environmentalist causes, and gay rights. By the 1970s, Portland had well established itself as a progressive city, and experienced an economic boom for the majority of the decade; however, the slowing of the housing market in 1979 caused demand for the city and state timber industries to drop significantly.

In the 1990s, the technology industry began to emerge in Portland, specifically with the establishment of companies like Intel, which brought more than $10 billion in investments in 1995 alone. After the year 2000, Portland experienced significant growth, with a population rise of over 90,000 between the years 2000 and 2014. The city's increased presence within the cultural lexicon has established it a popular city for young people, and it was second only to Louisville, Kentucky as one of the cities to attract and retain the highest number of college-educated people in the United States. Between 2001 and 2012, Portland's gross domestic product per person grew fifty percent, more than any other city in the country.

The city has acquired a diverse range of nicknames throughout its history, though it is most frequently called "Rose City" or "The City of Roses", the latter of which being its unofficial nickname since 1888 and its official nickname since 2003. Another widely utilized nickname by local residents in everyday speech is "PDX", which is also the airport code for Portland International Airport. Other nicknames include Bridgetown, Stumptown, Rip City, Soccer City, P-Town, Portlandia, and the more antiquated Little Beirut.

Cannon Beach, Oregon

The first recorded journey by a European to what is now **Cannon Beach** was made by William Clark, one of the leaders of the Lewis and Clark Expedition in early 1805. The expedition was wintering at Fort Clatsop, roughly 20 miles (32 km) to the north near the mouth of the Columbia River. In December 1805, two members of the expedition returned to camp with blubber from a whale that had beached several miles south, near the mouth of Ecola Creek. Clark later explored the region himself. From a spot near the western cliffs of the headland he saw "...the grandest and most pleasing prospects which my eyes ever surveyed, in front of a boundless Ocean..." That viewpoint, later dubbed "Clark's Point of View," can be accessed by a hiking trail from Indian Beach in Ecola State Park.

Clark and several of his companions, including Sacagawea, completed a three-day journey on January 10, 1806, to the site of the beached whale. They encountered a group of Native Americans from the Tillamook tribe who were boiling blubber for storage. Clark and his party met with them and successfully bartered for 300 pounds (140 kg) of blubber and some whale oil before returning to Fort Clatsop. There is a wooden whale sculpture commemorating the encounter between Clark's group and the Tillamooks in a small park at the northern end of Hemlock Street.

Clark applied the name "*Ekoli*" to what is now Ecola Creek. *Ehkoli* is a Chinook word for "whale". Early settlers later renamed the creek "Elk Creek", and a community with the same name formed nearby.

In 1846, a cannon from the US Navy schooner Shark washed ashore just north of Arch Cape, a few miles south of the community. The schooner hit land while attempting to cross the Columbia Bar, also known as the "Graveyard of the Pacific." The cannon, rediscovered in 1898, eventually inspired a name change for the growing community. In 1922, Elk Creek was redubbed Cannon Beach (after the name of the beach that extends south of Ecola Creek for 8 miles (13 km), ending at Arch Cape) at the insistence of the Post Office Department because the name was frequently confused with Eola. Elk Creek itself was renamed Ecola Creek to honor William Clark's original name.

The cannon is now housed in the city's museum and a replica of it can be seen alongside U.S. Route 101. Two more cannons, also believed to have been from the *Shark*, were discovered on Arch Cape over the weekend of February 16, 2008.

U.S. Highway 101 formerly ran through Cannon Beach. In 1964, a tsunami generated by the Good Friday earthquake came ashore along the coast of the Pacific Northwest. The subsequent flooding inundated parts of Cannon Beach and washed away the highway bridge located on the north side of city. The city, now isolated from the highway, decided to attract visitors by holding a sandcastle contest, an event that still continues annually every June.

Cannon Beach is an affluent tourist resort destination. Because of its proximity to Portland, Oregon, it is particularly known as a weekend getaway spot for Portlanders.

Pennsylvania

At the time of European settlement, the Native American population was small and widely scattered. The Delaware, or Lenni Lenape, occupied the Delaware valley; the Susquehannock were in the lower Susquehanna River valley; the Erie and various groups of the Iroquois Confederacy—Seneca, Cayuga, Onondaga, and Oneida—were in northern Pennsylvania. Tribes of the Ohio River valley lived in the central and western parts of the state.

Swedes were the first European settlers in Pennsylvania. Traveling up the Delaware from a settlement at the present site of Wilmington, Del., Gov. Johan Printz of the colony of New Sweden established his capital on Tinicum Island (New Gothenborg) in 1643. Other Europeans, primarily the Dutch, established trading posts within Pennsylvania as early as 1647. A rivalry between the Dutch and the Swedes led Peter Stuyvesant, governor of New Netherland, to seize New Sweden in 1650. Dutch control of the region ended in 1664, when the English seized all of New Netherland in the name of the Duke of York (the future King James II).

The Quaker colony

In March 1681 Charles II of England signed a charter giving any unoccupied regions to William Penn in payment of a debt owed by the king to Penn's father, Adm. Sir William Penn. The charter, which was officially proclaimed on April 2, 1681, named the territory for Admiral Penn and included also the term *sylvania* ("woodlands"), at the son's request.

William Penn intended that the colony provide a home for his fellow Quakers (members of the Society of Friends). While still in England, he drew up the first of his "frames of government" and sent his cousin, William Markham, to establish a claim to the land and also to establish the boundaries of what became the city of Philadelphia. Penn arrived in 1682 and called a General Assembly to discuss the first Frame of Government and to adopt the Great Law, which guaranteed freedom of conscience in the colony. Under Penn's influence, fair treatment was accorded the Native Americans, who responded with friendship in return. When Penn returned to England in 1684, the new Quaker province had a firmly established government based on the people's will and religious tolerance.

Colonial growth

The century that followed was a period of great expansion and turmoil for Pennsylvania. Its interior included land that was claimed by the French, and, as time went on, the Indians became increasingly hostile to the expansion of settlements to the west and north. Much of the fighting during the French and Indian War (1754–63) took place in Pennsylvania. There the young George Washington began his journey into the Ohio valley to warn the French to leave; later, it was in Pennsylvania that the English general Edward Braddock suffered defeat at the hands of the French forces and their Native American allies.

For many Pennsylvanians, the period following these conflicts marked growing dissatisfaction with British rule. Limitations on westward expansion, especially as established by proclamation in 1763, were imposed to pacify the Indians, but Pennsylvanians pressed westward over the Allegheny Mountains. Outposts such as Fort Pitt (Fort Duquesne under the French; now Pittsburgh) became settlements vital to the flow of trade from the opening lands to the west.

By the eve of the American Revolution, Pennsylvania had become a centre of military, economic, and political activity. The first (1774) and second (1775–76) Continental Congresses met in Philadelphia; the Declaration of Independence was signed there; and after the war the city became the capital of the short-lived Confederation and of the fledgling U.S. government.

Early years as a state

In 1790 a new state constitution was adopted that replaced the unicameral legislature of the Revolutionary period with a bicameral one and a fairly strong governor. During the next 70 years, roads were improved and extended, canals were built, farm equipment was mechanized, and railroads spanned the state, all combining with the economic strength of the thrifty Philadelphians to make Pennsylvania a major commercial power. Beginning in 1820, important mining companies were formed to exploit Pennsylvania's deposits of hard and soft coal, and in 1859 Edwin L. Drake drilled the world's first successful oil well at Titusville. During this same period, the state became a leading producer of textiles, ships, lumber, tobacco, and, most important, iron and steel.

The Pennsylvania Emancipation Act of 1781 had pledged the gradual abolition of slavery in the state. The southern boundary of Pennsylvania, ratified in 1769, was the Mason and Dixon Line, which became the dividing line between the slave and the free states before the American Civil War. Once the war broke out, Pennsylvania once again became a centre of military and political activity. At Gettysburg, the Union army achieved one of the decisive victories of the war, against a Confederate force led by Gen. Robert E. Lee.

Emergence of the modern state

With the end of the Civil War came a period of great economic, industrial, and population expansion in Pennsylvania. Until well into the 20th century, Pennsylvania was the second most populous state in the country. In 1873 the state passed its fourth constitution; with amendments, that document survived until 1968, when it was so fundamentally reshaped that it became known as the constitution of 1968. In 1898, construction of a state capitol (replacing a structure that had burned the previous year) was begun at Harrisburg, the capital since 1812. The new building was completed in 1908.

In both world wars, Pennsylvania's heavy industries were major suppliers of iron and steel, arms, and machinery. After World War II, however, the many changes taking place in the global economy began to affect Pennsylvania's emphasis on heavy industry. A relative decline in the state's manufacturing occurred between the mid-1960s and the mid-1980s, and Pennsylvania came to be identified as part of a "rust belt" in which former industrial economies fell victim to strong competition from overseas. The state's economy relied increasingly on a variety of high-technology industries and on the service sector.

www.britannica.com/place/Pennsylvania-state/Emergence-of-the-modern-state

Pittsburgh, city, seat (1788) of Allegheny county, southwestern Pennsylvania, U.S. The city is located at the confluence of the Allegheny and Monongahela rivers, which unite at the point of the "Golden Triangle" (the business district) to form the Ohio River. A city of hills, parks, and valleys, it is the centre of an urban industrial complex that includes the surrounding cities of Aliquippa (northwest), New Kensington (northeast), McKeesport (southeast), and Washington (southwest) and the borough of Wilkinsburg (east). Inc. borough, 1794; city, 1816. Area city, 58 square miles (150 square km). Pop. (2000) 334,563; Pittsburgh Metro Area, 2,431,087; (2010) 305,704; Pittsburgh Metro Area, 2,356,285.

Algonquian- and Iroquoian-speaking peoples were early inhabitants of the region. The conflict between the British and French over territorial claims in the area was settled in 1758 when General John Forbes and his British and colonial army expelled the French from Fort Duquesne (built 1754). Forbes named the site for the British statesman William Pitt the Elder. The British built Fort Pitt (1761) to ensure their dominance at the source of the Ohio. Settlers began arriving after Native American forces led by Ottawa chief Pontiac were defeated in 1763; an agreement subsequently was made between Native American groups and the Penn family, and a boundary dispute was ended between Pennsylvania and Virginia. Pittsburgh was laid out (1764) by John Campbell in the area around the fort (now the Golden Triangle). Following the American Revolution, the town became an outfitting point for settlers traveling westward down the Ohio River.

Pittsburgh's strategic location and wealth of natural resources spurred its commercial and industrial growth in the 19th century. A blast furnace, erected by George Anschutz about 1792, was the forerunner of the iron and steel industry that for more than a century was the city's economic mainstay; by 1850 Pittsburgh was known as the "Iron City." The Pennsylvania Canal and the Portage Railroad, both completed in 1834, opened vital markets for trade and shipping. The city suffered a great loss in 1845 when some 24 blocks of businesses, homes, churches, and other buildings were destroyed by fire.

After the American Civil War, great numbers of European immigrants swelled Pittsburgh's population, and industrial magnates such as Andrew Carnegie, Henry Clay Frick, and Thomas Mellon built their steel empires there. The city became the focus of historic friction between labor and management, and the American Federation of Labor was born there in 1881.

By 1900 the city's population had reached 321,616. Growth continued nearly unabated through World War II, the war years bringing a particularly great boon for the economy. The population crested at more than 675,000 in 1950, after which it steadily declined; by the end of the century, it had returned almost to the 1900 level. Most citizens were still of European ancestry, but the growing African American proportion of the population exceeded one-fourth. During the period of economic and population growth, Pittsburgh had come to epitomize the grimy, polluted industrial city. After the war, however, the city undertook an extensive redevelopment program that emphasized smoke-pollution control, flood prevention, and sewage disposal. In 1957 it became the first American city to generate electricity by nuclear power.

By the late 1970s and early '80s, the steel industry had virtually disappeared—a result of foreign competition and decreased demand. Many of the surrounding mill towns were laid to waste by unemployment. Pittsburgh, however, successfully diversified its economy through more emphasis on light industries—though metalworking, chemicals, and plastics remained important—and on such high-technology industries as computer software, industrial automation (robotics), and biomedical and environmental technologies. Numerous industrial research laboratories were established in the area, and the service sector became increasingly important. Pittsburgh long has been one of the nation's largest inland ports, and it remains a leading transportation centre.

Much of the Golden Triangle has been rebuilt and includes the Mellon Arena, Point State Park (containing Fort Pitt Blockhouse and Fort Pitt Museum), the Gateway Center (site of several skyscrapers and a garden), and the David L. Lawrence Convention Center. The University of Pittsburgh was chartered in 1787. Other educational institutions include Carnegie Mellon (1900), Duquesne (1878), and Point Park (1960) universities, Chatham (1869) and Carlow (1929) colleges, and two campuses of the Community College of Allegheny County (1966).

Central to the city's cultural life is the Carnegie Museums of Pittsburgh (formerly Carnegie Institute), an umbrella organization consisting of a number of institutions. Its museums include those for the fine arts and natural history (both founded in 1895), the Carnegie Science Center (1991), which now also houses the Henry Buhl, Jr., Planetarium and Observatory (1939), and the Andy Warhol Museum (1994), which exhibits the works of the Pittsburgh-born artist and filmmaker. Other institutions affiliated with the organization are the Carnegie Library of Pittsburgh, which contains more than 3.3 million volumes, and the Carnegie Music Hall. The Pittsburgh Symphony Orchestra performs at Heinz Hall, a restored movie theatre.

www.britannica.com/place/Pittsburgh

United States of America

The **United States (U.S.)**, officially the **United States of America (USA)**, and commonly referred to as **America**, is a federal republic composed of 50 states, a federal district, five major self-governing territories, and various possessions.- Forty-eight of the fifty states and the federal district are contiguous and located in North America between Canada and Mexico. The state of Alaska is in the far northwestern corner of North America, with a land border to the east with Canada and separated by the Bering Strait from Russia. The state of Hawaii is an archipelago in the mid-Pacific. The territories are scattered about the Pacific Ocean and the Caribbean Sea.

At 3.8 million square miles (9.8 million km^2) and with over 324 million people, the United States is the world's fourth-largest country by total area (and fourth-largest by land area)- and the third-most populous. It is one of the world's most ethnically diverse and multicultural nations, the product of large-scale immigration from many other countries. Urbanization climbed to over 80% in 2010 and leads to growing megaregions. The country's capital is Washington, D.C. and its largest city is New York City; the other top metropolitan areas, all with around five million or more inhabitants, are Los Angeles, Chicago, Dallas, San Francisco, Boston, Philadelphia, Houston, Atlanta, and Miami.

Paleo-Indians migrated from Asia to the North American mainland at least 15,000 years ago.-European colonization began in the 16th century. The United States emerged from 13 British colonies along the East Coast. Numerous disputes between Great Britain and the colonies in the aftermath of the Seven Years' War led to the American Revolution, which began in 1775. On July 4, 1776, as the colonies were fighting Great Britain in the American Revolutionary War, delegates from the 13 colonies unanimously adopted the Declaration of Independence. The war ended in 1783 with recognition of the independence of the United States by Great Britain, and was the first successful war of independence against a European colonial empire.- The current constitution was adopted in 1788, after the Articles of Confederation, adopted in 1781, were felt to have provided inadequate federal powers. The first ten amendments, collectively named the Bill of Rights, were ratified in 1791 and designed to guarantee many fundamental civil liberties.

The United States embarked on a vigorous expansion across North America throughout the 19th century, displacing American Indian tribes, acquiring new territories, and gradually admitting new states until it spanned the continent by 1848. During the second half of the 19th century, the American Civil War led to the end of legal slavery in the country. By the end of that century, the United States extended into the Pacific Ocean, and its economy, driven in large part by the Industrial Revolution, began to soar.- The Spanish–American War and World War I confirmed the country's status as a global military power. The United States emerged from World War II as a global superpower, the first country to develop nuclear weapons, the only country to use them in warfare, and a permanent member of the United Nations Security Council. It is a founding member of the Organization of American States (UAS) and various other Pan-American and international organizations. The end of the Cold War and the dissolution of the Soviet Union in 1991 left the United States as the world's sole superpower.-

The United States is a highly developed country, with the world's largest economy by nominal GDP. It ranks highly in several measures of socioeconomic performance, including average wage, human development, per capita GDP, and productivity per person.- While the U.S. economy is considered post-industrial, characterized by the dominance of services and knowledge economy, the manufacturing sector remains the second-largest in the world. Though its population is only 4.4% of the world total, the United States accounts for nearly a quarter of world GDP and almost a third of global military spending, making it the world's foremost military and economic power. The United States is a prominent political and cultural force internationally, and a leader in scientific research and technological innovations.

Appendix C – History Canada

Canada is a country in the northern half of North America. Its ten provinces and three territories extend from the Atlantic to the Pacific and northward into the Arctic Ocean, covering 9.98 million square kilometres (3.85 million square miles), making it the world's second-largest country by total area and the fourth-largest country by land area. Canada's border with the United States is the world's longest land border. The majority of the country has a cold or severely cold winter climate, but southerly areas are warm in summer. Canada is sparsely populated; the majority of its land territory being dominated by forest and tundra and the Rocky Mountains. About four-fifths of the country's population of 36 million people is urbanized and live near the southern border. Its capital is Ottawa.

Canada has been inhabited for millennia by various Aboriginal peoples. Beginning in the 16th century, British and French claims were made on the area, with the colony of Canada first being established by the French in 1537. As a consequence of various conflicts, the United Kingdom gained and lost territories within British North America until it was left, in the late 18th century, with what mostly geographically comprises Canada today. Pursuant to the British North America Act, on July 1, 1867, the colonies of Canada, New Brunswick, and Nova Scotia joined to form the semi-autonomous federal Dominion of Canada. This began an accretion of provinces and territories to the mostly self-governing Dominion to the present ten provinces and three territories forming modern Canada.

In 1931, Canada achieved near total independence from the United Kingdom with the Statute of Westminster 1931, and full sovereignty was attained when the Canada Act 1982 removed the last remaining ties of legal dependence on the Parliament of the United Kingdom. Canada is a federal parliamentary democracy and a constitutional monarchy, with Queen Elizabeth II being the head of state. The country is officially bilingual at the federal level. It is one of the world's most ethnically diverse and multicultural nations, the product of large-scale immigration from many other countries. Its advanced economy is the eleventh largest in the world, relying chiefly upon its abundant natural resources and well-developed international trade networks. Canada's long and complex relationship with the United States has had a significant impact on its economy and culture.

Canada is a developed country and has the tenth highest nominal per capita income globally as well as the ninth highest ranking in the Human Development Index. It ranks among the highest in international measurements of government transparency, civil liberties, quality of life, economic freedom, and education. Canada is a Commonwealth realm member of the Commonwealth of Nations, a member of the Francophonie, and part of several major international and intergovernmental institutions or groupings including the United Nations, the North Atlantic Treaty Organization, the G8, the Group of Ten, the G20, the North American Free Trade Agreement and the Asia-Pacific Economic Cooperation forum.

British Columbia

The earliest known inhabitants of the province are indigenous peoples of the Pacific Northwest (widely known for their totem poles and potlatches); carbon dating has confirmed their occupation of some sites 6,000 to 8,000 years ago. Juan Peréz was probably the first European to sail (1774) along the coast, but he did not make a landing. In 1778, Capt. James Cook, on his last voyage, explored the coast in his search for the Pacific entrance to the elusive Northwest Passage and claimed the area for Great Britain.

Rival British and Spanish claims for the area were partly resolved by the Nootka Conventions of 1790–92, which gave both equal trading rights but did not resolve ownership. The British sent George Vancouver to take possession of the land, and in 1792–94 he explored and mapped the coast from Oregon to Alaska. In 1793, Sir

Alexander Mackenzie reached the Pacific overland; he was followed early in the 19th cent. by fur traders and explorers of the North West Company who crossed the mountains to establish posts in New Caledonia, as the region was then called.

The Hudson's Bay Company Era

After the Hudson's Bay Company (HBC) absorbed the North West Company in 1821, the region became a preserve of the new company. In 1843, Fort Victoria was established by James Douglas as an HBC trading post. Rival British and American claims to the area were settled three years later when the boundary was set at the 49th parallel, but further controversy led to the San Juan Boundary Dispute. Partly as protection against American expansion, Vancouver Island was ceded (1849) to Britain by the HBC and became a crown colony.

In 1858 gold was discovered in the sandbars and tributaries of the Fraser River. The gold rushes that resulted brought profound changes. Fort Victoria boomed as a supply base for miners, and a town sprang up around it. Officials of the crown were dispatched to keep order and to supervise government projects and the building of roads. Some 30,000 miners moved into what was then unorganized territory; this led to the creation (1858) of a new colony on the mainland, called British Columbia, and the end of the HBC's supremacy. In 1863 the newly settled territory about the Stikine River was added to British Columbia.

Confederation

In 1866, Vancouver Island and British Columbia were merged, and in 1871 the united British Columbia, lured by promises of financial aid and the building of a transcontinental railroad that would link it to the rest of Canada, voted to join the new Canadian confederation. The Canadian Pacific Railway finally reached the coast in 1885, and a new era began. By providing access to new markets, the railroad furthered agriculture, mining, and lumbering; steamship service with Asia was inaugurated, and Vancouver grew as a busy port, serving many provinces. The opening (1914) of the Panama Canal further boosted trade and commerce. A long dispute with the United States over the Alaska boundary was finally settled by the Alaska Boundary Commission in 1903.

The Twentieth Century

The Conservatives and Liberals alternated in power from 1903 (when the national parties were first introduced into local politics) until 1941, when a wartime coalition was formed. The Social Credit party came into power in 1952, under the leadership of W. A. C. Bennett, and retained control until 1972, when the New Democratic party, led by David Barrett, won a majority. The Social Credit party regained control in 1975 under Premier William Richards Bennett, who was succeeded in 1986 by William Vander Zalm and in 1991 by Rita Johnston, the province's first woman premier. The New Democratic party again took power in late 1991, with Michael Harcourt as premier, succeeded in 1996 by Glen Clark, in 1999 by Dan Miller, and in 2000 by Ujjal Dosanjh (Canada's first nonwhite provincial premier). In 2001, however, the Liberals, led by Gordon Campbell, won a landslide victory; they were returned to power in 2005 and 2009, albeit with narrower majorities. Liberal Christy Clark succeeded the retiring Campbell as premier in 2011; the Liberals remained in power after the 2013 elections.

This fastest growing of Canada's provinces increased its national political clout in 1995 when it was given its own veto power over constitutional amendments rather than being subsumed under the western regional vote. By the end of the 1990s, metropolitan Vancouver had become one of the Pacific Rim's most dynamic cities, with a population c.10% Chinese and c.7% Asian Indian. At the same time, land claims by indigenous peoples, claims that could return much of the province to aboriginal ownership, had become a significant political and economic issue in the province. British Columbia, unlike Canada's other provinces, largely did not have signed treaties with most indigenous peoples, despite a 1763 Crown directive requiring such treaties. As a result, the provincial and federal governments began negotiating with the native tribes in the 1990s to sign treaties with them.

British Columbia sends 6 senators and 32 representatives to the national parliament.
http://www.infoplease.com/encyclopedia/world/british-columbia-history-politics.html

BC's first people may have journeyed to the region from Asia via a land bridge across the Bering Sea. As the ice receded, forests advanced and fluctuating sea levels exposed the temporary land passage linking Asia to the New World.

It is thought that BC's coastal region became one of the most densely populated areas in North America. Prior to European contact, BC's First Nations populations may have numbered some 300,000. The Aboriginal way of life would continue undisturbed for thousands of years, until the arrival of the British in 1778.

European Arrival

When British naval explorer Captain James Cook reached the west coast of Vancouver Island in 1778, he was eager to trade with the Nuu-chah-nulth (Nootka) people. In his wake, waves of European settlers arrived, carrying smallpox and other diseases that decimated Aboriginal populations in the late 1700s.

Nearly a century later, British agent James Douglas was searching the Pacific Coast for a new Hudson's Bay Company headquarters. He was welcomed by the Lekwammen, whose villages dotted the shores of what is now Greater Victoria. Douglas settled in and selected a site called Camosack. A year later, in 1843, Fort Victoria was built in the area now known as Old Town, the heart of Victoria's downtown.

Gold Rush in BC

The discovery of gold in the Fraser River and the Cariboo brought a rapid influx of prospectors, merchants, pioneers and other colourful figures to BC in the 1860s. They came from around the world, arriving from as far away as China. It was a time of rapid economic expansion; sleepy hamlets became bustling cities, and new roads, railways and steamships were constructed to carry the extra load.

Boomtowns were born and legends made, but not all experienced good fortune. The Aboriginal peoples lost most of their ancestral lands and, in 1876, First Nations populations were made subject to the federal Indian Act, which regulated every aspect of their lives

Rapid Expansion in BC

Transportation and development marked another period of rapid economic expansion during the 1950s and 60s. Massive building projects changed the shape of the BC landscape. Expansive damming projects turned rivers into lakes; giant turbines powered dozens of new pulp mills and smelters; and the Trans-Canada Highway was completed, while new bridges, railways, and BC Ferries linked land, people and technological progress.

BC's Cultural Diversity

Today, BC's population is wonderfully diverse. More than 40 major Aboriginal cultural groups are represented in the region. The province's large Asian communities have made Chinese and Punjabi the most spoken languages after English. There are also sizeable German, Italian, Japanese and Russian communities – all creating a vibrant cultural mosaic in which distinct cuisine, architecture, language and arts thrive.

In 1986 the City of Vancouver celebrated its centennial, hosting the Expo '86 World Exposition. That same year, the Sechelt Indian Band was the first Aboriginal group in BC to gain a municipal style of self-government.

In 2000, the Nisga'a Treaty came into being. The Nisga'a Nation, who has lived in the Nass area since time immemorial, negotiated with the provincial and federal governments to achieve BC's first modern-day, constitutionally protected self-governance agreement. This marked a momentous achievement in the history of the relationship among British Columbia, Canada and First Nations.

In February and March 2010, Vancouver was the host city for the 2010 Olympic and Paralympic Winter Games.

http://www.hellobc.com/british-columbia/about-bc/culture-history.aspx

North Vancouver, British Columbia

The City of North Vancouver is a waterfront municipality on the north shore of Burrard Inlet, directly across from Vancouver, British Columbia. It is the smallest of the three North Shore municipalities, and the most urbanized as well. Although it has significant industry of its own, including shipping, chemical production, and film production, the city is usually considered to be a suburb of Vancouver. The city is served by the Royal Canadian Mounted Police.

Moodyville (at the south end of Moody Avenue, now Moodyville Park), is the oldest settlement on Burrard Inlet, predating Vancouver; only New Westminster is the older non-native settlement in the region. Logging came to the virgin forests of Douglas Fir in North Vancouver, as sailing ships called in to load. A water-powered sawmill was set up in the 1860s at Moodyville, by Sewell Moody. Subsequently, post offices, schools and a village sprang up. In time, the municipality of North Vancouver (which encompassed the entire North Shore from Deep Cove to Dundarave) was incorporated. In the 1880s, Arthur Heywood-Lonsdale and a relation James Pemberton Fell, made substantial investments in North Vancouver and in 1882 he financed the Moodyville investments. Several locations in the North Vancouver area are named after Lonsdale and his family. The financial collapses of the 1890s and 1907 aggrieved the young city into bankruptcy. As a result of this, the separate areas of West Vancouver, and District of North Vancouver came into being, with the city holding on to only a small portion of its former area.

Part of the reason was the cost of developing raw mountainous terrain. And originally the ocean foreshore was primarily swamp. The great distances, and large rivers to span, hindered development. Bridges were built, only to have them washed out in a few years from winter floods. The city and district-built Keith Road in 1912, which undulated from West Vancouver to Deep Cove amid the slashed sidehills, swamps, and burnt stumps.

Yet the city did gain a strong foothold, with Lonsdale Avenue. Serviced by the North Vancouver Ferries, it proved a popular area. Commuters used the ferries to work in Vancouver. Street cars and early land speculation, spurred interest in the area. Streets, city blocks and houses were slowly built around lower Lonsdale.

Manitoba

The area that became Manitoba is part of the traditional territory of the Assiniboine and Dakota who lived on the plains in the south, the Cree whose vast territory stretched from the plains to the Hudson Bay Lowland in the north, and the Dene who occupied the far north. The ancestors of these groups arrived in Manitoba between 10,000 and 13,000 BCE. The Anishinaabeg (*see* Ojibwa), today one of the largest Indigenous groups in Manitoba alongside the Cree, are much more recent arrivals, having lived in Manitoba for less than 300 years.

Prior to the arrival of Europeans, Indigenous people in Manitoba relied on hunting moose, caribou, bear and beaver, and to a lesser degree fishing. Those who lived in the Hudson Bay Lowland also hunted waterfowl such as geese, while the Indigenous people of the plains relied on buffalo as a source of food and material for clothing, shelter and tools. Items made of copper, pipestone, obsidian and shells found at archaeological sites in Manitoba indicate that prior to European contact, Indigenous people participated in long-distance trade networks that stretched as far as the Pacific Coast in the West and the Gulf of Mexico in the South.

Exploration: 1600s – 1700s

The history of European exploration in Manitoba did not begin in the south, but in the coldest and most remote area — the shores of Hudson Bay. In the early 1600s, a succession of navigators, including Thomas Button (1612), Jens Munk (1619–20), and Luke Fox and Thomas James (1631), searched the shoreline for the Northwest Passage.

The westward expansion of the fur trade encouraged further exploration in Manitoba. In 1670, two French Canadian explorers interested in the fur trade, Des Groseilliers and Radisson, persuaded Charles II of England to establish the Hudson's Bay Company and to grant it a huge territory (part of which is modern Manitoba), to be called Rupert's Land.

Trading posts were soon established along the shores of Hudson Bay: Fort Hayes in 1682 (replaced with Fort York in 1684); and Fort Churchill in 1717–18 (replaced with Prince of Wales Fort in 1731). In 1690–92, Henry Kelsey, an HBC employee, penetrated southwest across the prairies to the Saskatchewan River. The La Vérendrye family then travelled west via the Great Lakes, building Fort Maurepas on the Red River (1734), followed by four other posts within the present area of Manitoba. The subsequent invasion of lands granted to the HBC by independent traders stimulated an intense rivalry for pelts, which ended only with amalgamation of the HBC and the North West Company in 1821. Although about 20 forts existed at various times south of latitude 54° N, the early explorers left few permanent impressions on the landscape.

The arrival of the fur trade, however, had a lasting impact on Indigenous people in Manitoba. Participation in the trade altered their traditional social and economic patterns as well as their territorial distribution. The ability to trade furs meant hunters now killed a surplus of animals rather than simply hunting enough for their own needs. With the introduction of European-made goods, Indigenous people abandoned their traditional tools and clothing, and became reliant on the fur trade to provide the necessities of life. The Cree and the Anishinaabeg, whose traditional territory had been the north shores of Lakes Huron and Superior, both expanded their territories westward in search of fur-bearing animals in order to retain their position in the trade. The increased interaction between these two neighboring groups resulted in the creation of a hybrid Oji-Cree language and culture.

Interaction with European traders produced another more well-known culture: the Métis. Although intermarriage between explorers and fur traders and Indigenous women had occurred from the first arrival of Europeans in North America, in the early 19th century, the Red River Métis formed a distinctive culture which was a blend of Indigenous, French, English and Scottish influences. The Métis were renowned buffalo hunters and established a role for themselves as intermediaries in the fur trade, supplying North West Company traders with pemmican.

The arrival of Europeans also introduced diseases such as smallpox that devastated Indigenous populations. An outbreak of smallpox in 1781 is estimated to have killed nine-tenths of the Indigenous population around Churchill.

European Settlement: 1800s

Between 1682 and 1812, European settlement in Manitoba consisted of fur-trading posts established by the Hudson's Bay Company, the North West Company and numerous independent traders. Agricultural settlement began in 1812 when the HBC granted Lord Selkirk a large tract of land at the junction of the Red and Assiniboine rivers to establish a colony for displaced Scottish and Irish tenant farmers. Over the next 45 years, the Red River Colony at Assiniboia survived hail, frost, floods, grasshoppers and skirmishes with the

Nor'Westers and Métis over attempts by the colonists to restrict the sale of pemmican and the hunting of buffalo.

Further settlement was discouraged by the HBC monopoly as well as by the prevailing belief that the region was unsuited for agriculture. In 1857, the British government sponsored an expedition to assess the potential of Rupert's Land for agricultural settlement. That same year, the Canadian government, spurred by an expansionist movement in Upper Canada, sent Henry Youle Hind to do a similar assessment. The reports of these two expeditions encouraged settlement in the northwest, describing a fertile crescent of land suitable for agriculture extending northwest from the Red River Valley.

Red River Rebellion: 1869–70

In the 1860s, the Canadian and British governments wanted to expand westward, and began negotiating with the Hudson's Bay Company for the transfer of Rupert's Land to the Dominion government. The negotiations were conducted with no concern for the actual inhabitants of the land, many of whom were Métis and First Nations. The Métis, angered that their rights were being ignored, organized to resist the acquisition of their lands. In 1869, under the leadership of Louis Riel, they seized control of Upper Fort Garry from the HBC and declared a provisional government (*see* Red River Rebellion). After a protracted standoff, the Canadian government relented. The *Manitoba Act of 1870*, which transferred the lands of the northwest to the Dominion of Canada and created the new province of Manitoba, guaranteed Métis title to their lands along the Red and Assiniboine rivers and another 1.4 million acres for their descendants. Despite this apparent victory, Riel and the leaders of the rebellion were forced to flee as fugitives to the United States. In 1885, Riel was executed for high treason. The Canadian government failed to uphold the promises made to the Métis, while the settlers arriving in droves from Ontario discriminated against them. Many disaffected Métis moved west to continue practicing their way of life, setting the stage for future conflict.

Numbered Treaties: 1871–1907

In 1871, the Canadian government also began negotiating with the Indigenous people in the Northwest with the aim of extinguishing Aboriginal title to the land to facilitate orderly westward expansion, free from the violence that beset the American West. The resulting series of treaties are collectively known as the "Numbered Treaties." Manitoba is comprised of parts of Treaties 1, 2, 3, 4, 5, 6 and 10 which were signed between 1871 and 1907. Much like with the Métis, the Canadian government has failed to uphold the promises and assurances made during the negotiation and signing of these treaties.

Expansion: Late 1800s – Early 1900s

In 1870, Manitoba was slightly larger than the Red River Valley; the remainder of what is now Manitoba was still the Northwest Territories at the time, administered directly by the Dominion government. Settlement of the new province followed the Dominion Lands Survey and the projected route of the national railway. The lands of the original province of Manitoba were granted to settlers in quarter-section parcels for homesteading purposes under the *Dominion Lands Act of 1872*. (*See also* Manitoba and Confederation.)

It was soon evident that the diminutive province needed to expand. Settlers were rapidly moving to the northwest and spilling over the established boundaries. Between 1876 and 1881, 40,000 immigrants, mainly British Ontarians, were drawn west by the prospect of profitable wheat farming enhanced by new machinery and milling processes. Mennonites and Icelandic immigrants also arrived in the 1870s, the former settling around Steinbach and Winkler, the latter near Gimli and Hecla. Immigration then slowed until the late 1890s and was mostly limited to small groups of Europeans.

In 1881, after years of political wrangling with the federal government, the boundaries were extended to their present western position, as well as being extended farther east, and to 53° N lat. It was not until 1912, however, that the current boundaries of the province were set.

Between 1897 and 1910, there was great prosperity and development, and settlers from Eastern Canada, Britain, the United States and Eastern Europe, especially Ukraine, inundated the province and the neighbouring lands. The latter group, previously considered undesirable, were now actively encouraged to immigrate by Minister of the Interior and MP from Brandon, Clifford Sifton. Sifton believed that Eastern European peasants were better suited to settling and farming in the often-harsh conditions of Canada's West than the traditionally preferred immigrants from Britain.

Development: Early 1900s – Second World War

From 1897 to 1910, Manitoba enjoyed unprecedented prosperity. Transportation rates fell and wheat prices rose. Grain farming still predominated, but mixed farms prospered and breeders of quality livestock and plants became famous.

Winnipeg swiftly rose to metropolitan stature, accounting for 50 per cent of the increase in the province's population. The city developed a vigorous business centre, radiating from the corner of Portage Avenue and Main Street. Department stores, real estate and insurance companies, legal firms and banks thrived. Abattoirs and flour mills directly serviced the agricultural economy while service industries, railway shops, foundries and food industries also expanded.

Both the Canadian Pacific Railway and the Canadian Northern Railway (later the Canadian National Railway) built marshalling yards in the city, which became the hub of a vast network of rail lines spreading east, west, north and south. In 1906, hydroelectricity was first generated at Pinawa on the Winnipeg River, and the establishment of Winnipeg Hydro on 28 June 1906 guaranteed the availability of cheap power for domestic and industrial use.

The general prosperity ended with the depression of 1913; freight rates rose, land and wheat prices plummeted and the supply of foreign capital dried up. The opening of the Panama Canal in 1914 ended Winnipeg's transportation supremacy, since goods could move more cheaply between east and west by sea than overland.

During the First World War, recruitment, war industry demands and the cessation of immigration sent wages and prices soaring. By 1918 inflation seemed unchecked and unemployment was prevalent. Real wages dropped, working conditions deteriorated and new radical movements grew among farmers and urban workers, culminating in the Winnipeg General Strike of May 1919. The discontent of the farmers found expression in the Progressive Party, which garnered 65 seats (12 from Manitoba) in the federal election of 1921 and won Manitoba's provincial election in 1922.

The First World War was a particularly difficult period for the Eastern European immigrants who had come to Manitoba in the previous two decades, particularly the Ukrainians whose homeland was part of the Austro-Hungarian Empire with which Canada was at war. Several were interned as enemy aliens while those who were not faced discrimination.

In the midst of the First World War, on 28 January 1916, Manitoba became the first province to grant women the right to vote and hold political office provincially (*see* Women's Suffrage). Prominent members of Manitoba's suffrage movement included Margret Benedictsson, Nellie McClung, Ella Cora Hind, Francis Marion Beynon, Lillian Beynon Thomas and Amelia Yeomans (*see also* Timeline: Women's Suffrage in the West).

An industrial boom followed postwar depression in the late 1920s. By 1928, the value of industrial production exceeded that of agricultural production. Agricultural depression continued and deepened in the

1930s, aggravated by drought, pests and low world wheat prices. As a result the movement of the province's population from farm to city and town accelerated. During the 1930s, however, industry flagged and unemployment was high in urban centres.

To eliminate the traditional boom/bust pattern, attempts were made to diversify the economy, as exemplified by the expansion of the mining industry. The demands of the Second World War reinforced Manitoba's dependency on agriculture and primary production, but the postwar boom gave the province the opportunity to capitalize on its established industries and to broaden its economic base.

https://thecanadianencyclopedia.ca/en/article/manitoba

Winnipeg, city, capital (1870) of Manitoba, Canada. It lies at the confluence of the Red and Assiniboine rivers, 40 miles (65 km) southwest of Lake Winnipeg and 60 miles (95 km) north of the U.S. state of Minnesota. Winnipeg is the economic and cultural centre of Manitoba and is at the heart of the most populous metropolitan area in central Canada.

Fort-Rouge was established on the site in 1738 by the French voyageur La Vérendrye. It was followed later by Fort Gibraltar (built by the North West Company in 1810) and Fort Garry (Hudson's Bay Company, 1821). These, together with the Red River Settlement (founded 1811–12) of Scottish colonists, formed the nucleus of the new city, the name of which was taken from that of Lake Winnipeg and derived from the Cree Indian words *win nipee* ("muddy water").

The arrival in 1885 of the Canadian Pacific, the first Canadian transcontinental railroad, led to Winnipeg's becoming the major grain market and warehousing and distributing point for the Prairie Provinces. It has remained the headquarters of the Canadian grain industry. The city also serves the mining districts of the north and is now one of Canada's largest industrial, communications, commercial, and financial centres. The economy is highly diversified; major activities include food processing, finance, telecommunications, printing, and the manufacture of apparel, transportation equipment, and aerospace products and technology. Winnipeg is also home to the Royal Canadian Mint, which produces all of the country's coinage. The city's industrial growth has been stimulated by the availability of cheap hydroelectric power (from plants on the Winnipeg River) and excellent transportation facilities. A major junction on two transcontinental rail lines and the Trans-Canada Highway, Winnipeg also has a busy international airport.

A cosmopolitan city of many ethnic groups (including sizable populations of French-speaking and native peoples), Winnipeg dominates Manitoba's cultural life. It is the home of a symphony orchestra, the Manitoba Opera, the Royal Winnipeg Ballet, and the Manitoba Theatre Centre. It is the seat of the University of Manitoba (1877), the University of Winnipeg (1871), and Red River College (1938). The provincial Legislative Building (1920) is a Neoclassical structure with the well-known *Golden Boy* (a bronze statue of a youth carrying a torch in his right hand and a sheaf of wheat over his left arm) on top of its dome. The city's Centennial Centre includes the Museum of Man and Nature and a planetarium, and the Winnipeg Art Gallery has an extensive collection of Inuit art.

The Forks National Historic Site, at the junction of the Red and Assiniboine rivers, commemorates the history of the Canadian West. Assiniboine Park includes a zoo and a conservatory. Also nearby are Bird's Hill (northeast) and Beaudry (west) provincial parks. Winnipeg's professional sports teams include the Jets (National Hockey League) and the Blue Bombers (Canadian Football League). The city plays host to an annual (August) international festival of folk arts. Inc. 1873. Pop. (2011) 663,617; metro. area, 730,018; (2016) 705,244; metro. area, 778,489.

www.britannica.com/place/Winnipeg

Appendix D – Timelines

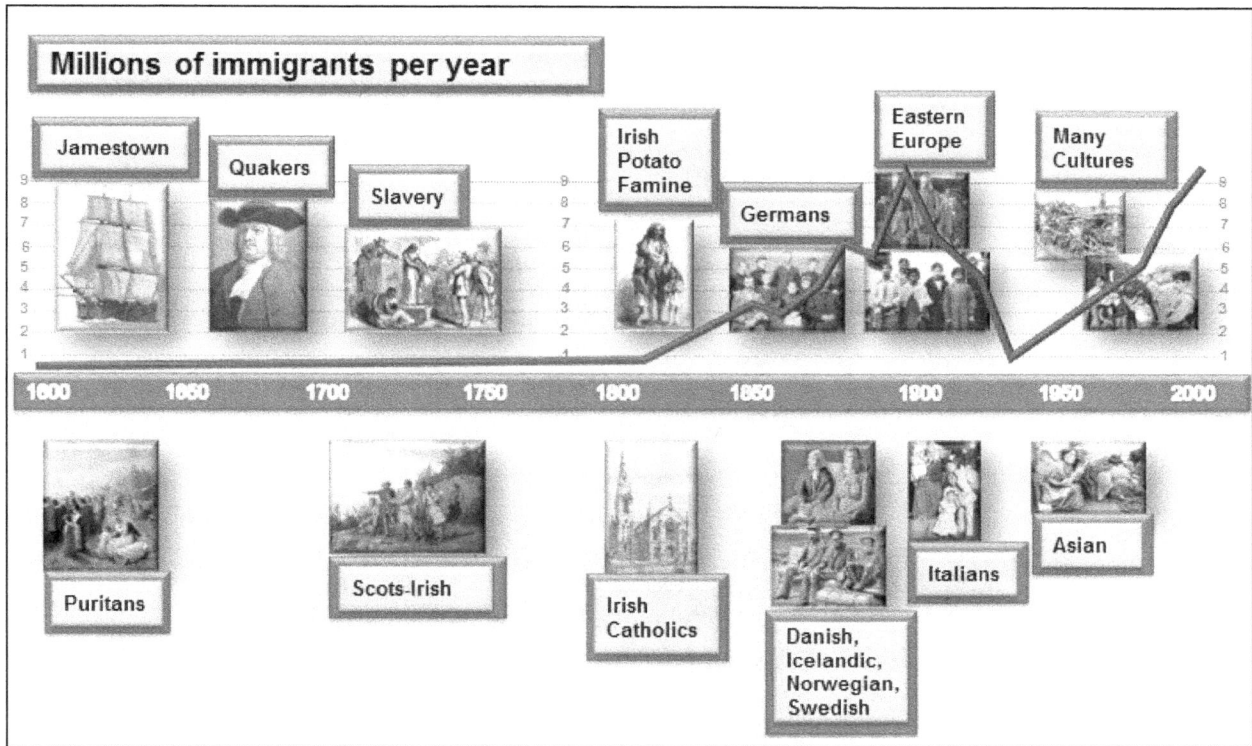

Millions of immigrants per year

Art History Timeline

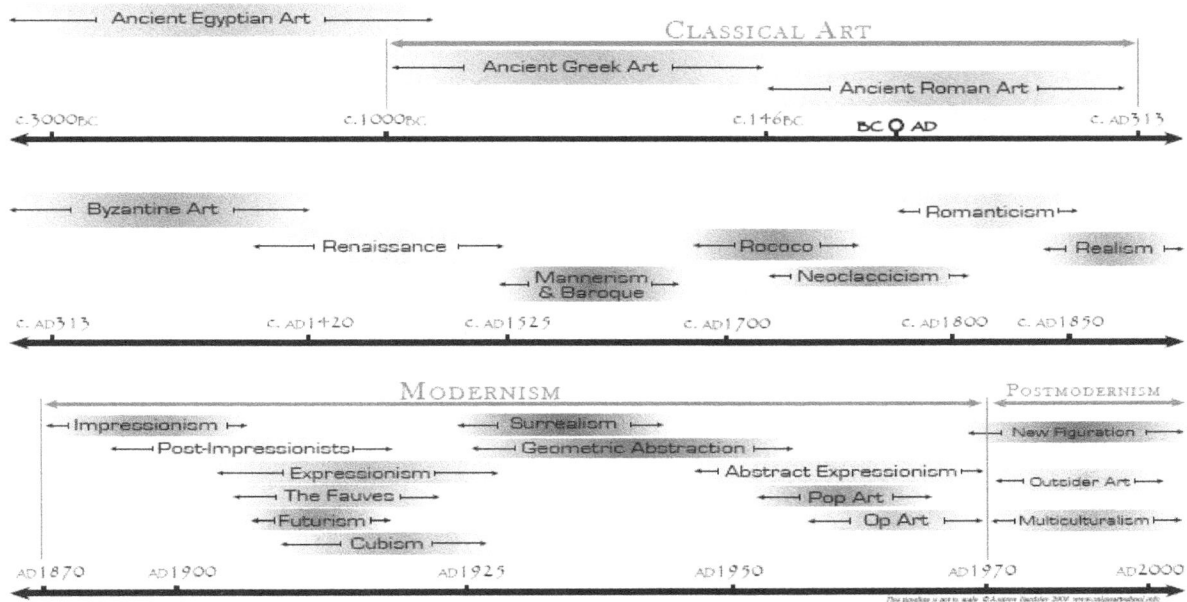

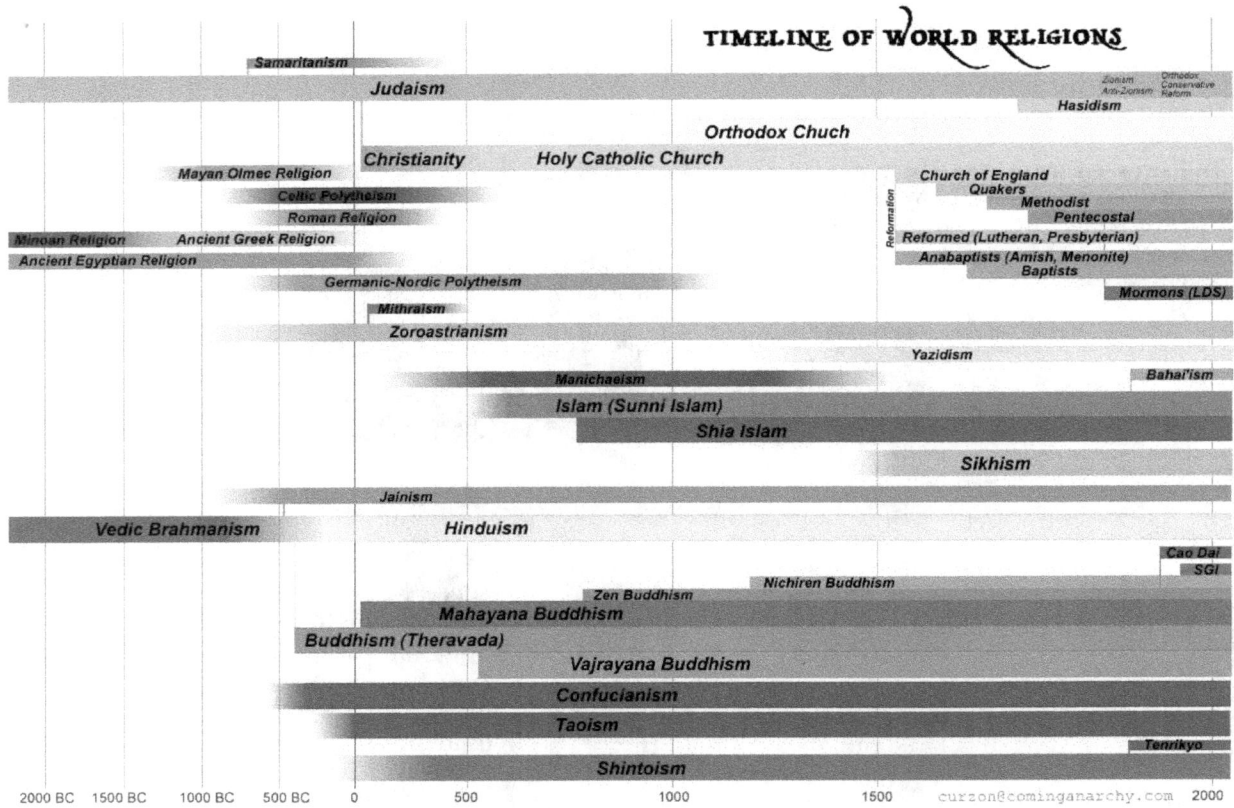

Appendix E – Clothes

England 17th Century Fashion

1600-1635   1635-1665

1700's

1600's

1770-1775

1800's

18th Century

4. US Farmers 1800

5. US Workers 1800

3. US Farmers 1900

2. US Workers 1900

Appendix F – DNA Nancy Marshall

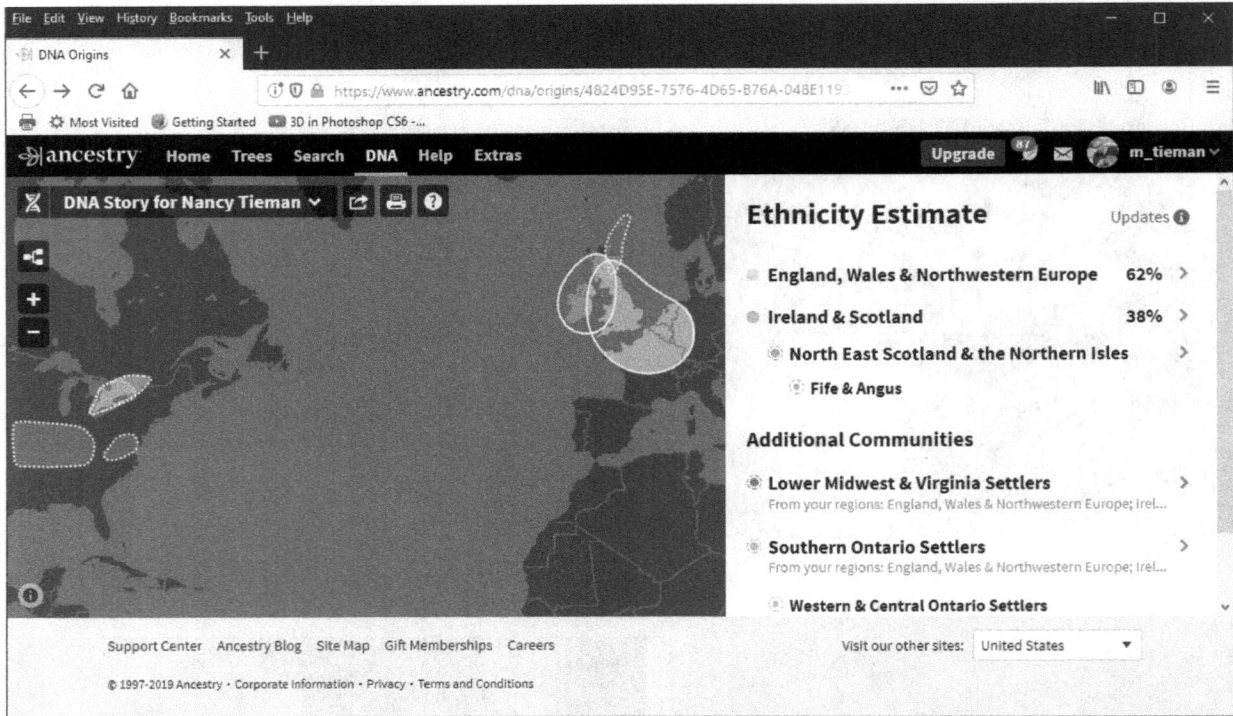

DNA results of AncestryDNA, June 19, 2019

www.ingramcontent.com/pod-product-compliance
Lightning Source LLC
Chambersburg PA
CBHW081357270326
41930CB00015B/3330